PERSPECTIVES IN AMERICAN CATHOLICISM

John Tracy Ellis

PERSPECTIVES IN AMERICAN CATHOLICISM

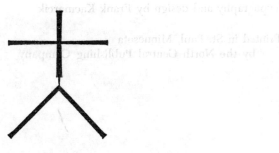

BENEDICTINE STUDIES

HELICON: BALTIMORE • DUBLIN

Nihil Obstat:
John F. Dede, S.S., J.C.D.
Censor Deputatus

Imprimatur:
✠ Lawrence J. Shehan, D.D.
Archbishop of Baltimore
April 17, 1963

This volume is the fifth in a series entitled *Benedictine Studies* sponsored by the American Benedictine Academy and published by Helicon Press, Inc., Baltimore 2, Maryland.

Library of Congress Catalog Card Number 63-12093

Typography and design by Frank Kacmarcik

Printed in St. Paul, Minnesota
by the North Central Publishing Company

TO

THE VERY REVEREND LOUIS A. ARAND, S.S.

PRESIDENT OF DIVINITY COLLEGE

OF

THE CATHOLIC UNIVERSITY OF AMERICA

IN GRATEFUL APPRECIATION FOR

THE WISDOM OF HIS COUNSEL,

THE INSPIRATION OF HIS EXAMPLE,

AND

THE LOYALTY OF HIS FRIENDSHIP

FOREWORD

The publication of twenty-three topical essays by Monsignor John Tracy Ellis in one volume is a provocation to think about the writing of history as well as about a particular writer. Surely this historian of American Catholicism has given our times an insight into the way a man goes about the task of reconstructing the past. A craft, it is often called, and such it may be, but history-writing is much more than that. The term "vocation" is not too lofty to designate the life-work of the real historian.

He who proposes to write history must handle the past. But, because he is a man as well as a writer, he can never treat it as disjointed from his own time. He is himself a creature of that past. Disadvantaged by the passage of years and the disappearance of data, the historian is greatly compensated by hindsight and the long view. To the watchful critic, it is true, he will never appear as cool and detached as the physicist. Yet just as much as the man in the laboratory, the writer of history must seek and strive for objective truth. The perspective he maintains will be the measure of his success. If it is pure and true and balanced, the past event will come alive. But exhaustive research and profound study are needed. So is honesty, and often, so is courage.

When the historian has proved, by repeated performance, that he can keep that pure and true focus on the past, he is honored by his contemporaries and presumably appreciated by those lucky and luckless departed spirits of whom he has written. Thucydides won the respect of the Greeks because he tried his honest best, by "the severest and minutest tests," to set down exactly "how things happened in the past." William Bradford, the narrator of the Puritans, observed the details carefully so that he might write "the simple trueth in all things at least as my slender judgmente can attaine the same."

In the field of Catholic history, many men have sat down to write about some figure, some institution, some episode of times gone by. Some have succeeded in writing history. Others have succeeded only in writing pious fiction. With possibly the best of intentions, the latter failed to help us understand what really happened — and so failed the truth. They wrote to edify, not to record. Now there is a facet of truth that fiction can light up — poetry is even better able to do it — but pious fiction, *posing as history*, does not reach any truth at all. Ironically, it fails even to edify. Somehow these writers lose viable contact with the best of the Catholic historical tradition. St. Luke wrote his *Gospel* and his *Acts* under divine inspiration, yet to give his "orderly account," he sought out "all things carefully from the very first." Nineteen centuries later, Pope Leo XIII refurbished and renewed that honorable Catholic heritage by his famous reference to Cicero's classic formula for good history. When the pontiff said that the historian must not dare to say anything false, nor dare to leave out anything of the truth, so that there could be "no suspicion of favor in writing, and no simulation," he was speaking in the authentic Christian tradition where truth must be the only goal and "managed history" an abomination.

John Gilmary Shea (1824–1892) was the patriarch of the historians of the American Catholic past. Author of the monumental *History of the Catholic Church in the United States* and many other sound and fruitful works, he added to his stature by an example of a long, dedicated life in which his poverty, physical pain and frustrations were balanced only by a tremendous expenditure of energy and zeal. For the early years of our century, Monsignor Peter Guilday (1884–1947) might be properly called Shea's successor. This assiduous priest taught history at the Catholic University of America for thirty-three years, established the American Catholic Historical Association, founded and edited the *Catholic Historical Review*, and produced fine studies of John Carroll, John England, the Councils of Baltimore, and many other subjects. His particular gift to this country was the succession of graduate students who caught up the spark of his inspiration, and carried it into the dim-lit corners of the nation's religious narrative.

Now many of these students, and dozens of others, are continuing this urgent work of illumination. Slowly but steadily, the dioceses and the decades are coming under proper scrutiny. Religious communities, educational and charitable institutions, episodes, movements and controversies are being studied. Celebrated and less celebrated churchmen and laymen are the subjects of careful biography. On the contemporary scene, no writer or teacher of history has greater stature than John Tracy Ellis. This volume, planned and carried out by the American Benedictine Academy, is a memorial to his continued inspiration. But it is a "memorial" only in the living sense. This scholarly priest, both as professor and writer, is very much alive, to the lessons of the past and the issues of the present.

Born in 1905, ordained a priest in 1938, he began teaching history while a student at the Catholic University of America. In 1941, he was appointed to take over the courses in American Catholic history from the ailing Monsignor Guilday. In characteristic fashion, he began by making a survey of existent works. Originally published in 1947, and revised as *A Guide to American Catholic History* in 1959, this small volume has been an indispensable compass to the beginner in a field otherwise quite uncharted. Ellis' doctoral dissertation, *Anti-Papal Legislation in Medieval England, 1066-1377*, had already appeared in 1930, and was followed by *Cardinal Consalvi and Anglo-Papal Relations, 1814-1824*, in 1942. *The Formative Years of the Catholic University of America*, thoroughly researched and gracefully written, was published in 1946, a welcome contribution to the relatively small number of works dealing with American educational institutions.

Six years later, *The Life of James Cardinal Gibbons, Archbishop of Baltimore, 1834-1921* (in two volumes), established Monsignor Ellis as the outstanding historian of Catholicism in the United States. Here was biography rich in context and broad in its relevance to the American as well as the Catholic scene of the decades from 1870 to 1920. The wise, kindly and thoroughly American prelate who "reigned in Baltimore like a king, but met every man like a comrade," came alive in these pages. The style left the reader grateful for the English language. Monsignor Ellis had won the tribute of being not only referred to, but gratefully read.

An excellent source-book, *Documents of American Catholic History*, was his next work, originally published in 1956 and revised in 1962. Since he interpreted "document" as "any written record that would illustrate an event from the contemporary point of view," the reader is delighted to find the poet, Abram J. Ryan, and the satirist, Finley Peter Dunne ("Mr. Dooley") rubbing shoulders with popes and presidents. A slender volume appeared the same year, *American Catholicism*, four lectures given at the University of Chicago under the auspices of the Charles R. Walgren Foundation. It is brief and concise, but not at all sketchy, as it proceeds to give the reader a passing review of the activities of the Catholic Church in this country. Then, *American Catholics and the Intellectual Life* appeared, also in 1956, but of that a little more later. At the request of several Catholic educators, Monsignor

Ellis expanded in book form, the Gabriel Richard Lecture of 1961, which was published as *John Lancaster Spalding, First Bishop of Peoria, American Educator, 1840–1916.*

In seeking authors for the series of which *American Catholicism* was a part, Professor Daniel J. Boorstin has written that he wanted scholars, "who both knew the raw material firsthand, and who would be bold enough to tell a meaningful story." The choice of John Tracy Ellis was excellent on both counts. No present Catholic writer has plied the historian's trade so patiently — the search of archives, the reading of dry newspaper columns and reels of dim microfilms, the personal interviews, and the day-by-day perusal of collateral history. His results have been in the best tradition of objective history, masterfully told.

Yet a word must be further said for the man "bold enough to tell a meaningful story." The lectures, articles and other "occasional" writing of Monsignor Ellis, as much as his books, have had much relevance for our times. Relevance can be disturbing. In May, 1955, he addressed the Catholic Commission on Intellectual and Cultural Affairs on the subject, "American Catholics and the Intellectual Life." It was frank, thorough, cogent and coherent. He argued that Catholics were not carrying their intellectual weight in the United States. Among the reasons for this, he claimed, were "the frequently self-imposed ghetto-mentality . . . their lack of industry and habits of work . . . their failure to measure up to their responsibilities to the incomparable tradition of Catholic learning of which they are the direct heirs. . . ." The resultant storm was loud and long. Some personal reactions to it are included in the essay, "No Complacency" (pp. 249–260 of this volume). In other situations, Monsignor Ellis has examined other present-day challenges. He is by nature urbane and kindly, but he sees no point in ever being innocuous.

The essays in this volume are chosen well. Generous appraisals of contemporary questions are followed by revealing vignettes of a series of great American churchmen. Catholic education is surveyed from several angles. The article on the First Vatican Council has special timeliness. The Benedictines come in for special inclusion, certainly not inappropriate in the light of their own intellectual tradition, not to mention the pleasant coincidence that they are publishing this book. My own favorites, among the essays, is "Church and State in the United States: a Critical Appraisal," a review of Anson Phelps Stokes' work. Stokes' three volumes were an overwhelming achievement, the gathering and presenting of thousands of facts from the three centuries in which the Church-State tension has moved through American life. When I first used the three volumes, I was disturbed by some of the unfortunate flaws, and friendly but slanted fissures, which mar this impressive mountain of scholarship. It is encouraging to find that Monsignor Ellis discusses the work with full appreciation of the "general fairness" of the editor, and "the opportunity which [the reader] will find here for enriching his knowledge of American religious history." But, with courtesy and patient detail he has pointed out Stokes' "ideological blind spots," and adds two pages of factual errors to be corrected in a later edition. This review is historical criticism at its best.

Two new volumes by Monsignor Ellis are promised in the very near future: *Catholics in Colonial America,* and a one-volume history of Catholicism in the United States. They will undoubtedly carry along the fine tradition of scholarship now so readily identified with his name. Meanwhile, readers will be grateful to Father Colman Barry, O.S.B., editor, and *Benedictine Studies* for bringing the public these occasional, but very significant, lectures and essays. These who love the Church, and who love the United States, will find here that Monsignor Ellis has written history in a manner for which readers can only be grateful.

✠ Paul J. Hallinan
Archbishop of Atlanta

PREFACE

It is at times a distinct advantage for a man to have a *causa agitans*, so to speak, who will spur him to undertake tasks that he would not otherwise do. I have enjoyed that advantage for over a decade now in the person of Father Colman J. Barry, O.S.B., of St. John's University in Collegeville. Father Colman possesses one of those alert and restless minds that are constantly bestirring themselves in behalf of some new project either for himself or for his friends. In all of these ideas he has been motivated by his desire to fill out and advance the story of the Catholic Church in the United States. Thus it was his idea that a selection of my lectures and sermons should be gathered together and combined with a number of reprints of articles that had previously appeared in various journals with a view to having them published as a book. For originating the idea, therefore, Father Colman must be given the credit, as well as for his generosity in including the book in the Benedictine Studies of which he is the editor.

But for the defects of the work, needless to say, I alone am responsible. Inevitably some spots of the volume will seem a bit dated. Yet it appeared better to leave them substantially as they were than to indulge the doubtful procedure of bringing the statistics and other factual data up to date, lest an anachronistic note be entered and an essay lose the character of the original. For that reason, therefore, with a very few exceptions these essays appear just as they did in their original published form, or as they were delivered in the case of the sermons and lectures.

To all who assisted in bringing about this work, I wish to express my sincere thanks. But a special debt of gratitude is owed to the Most Reverend Paul J. Hallinan, Archbishop of Atlanta, who found time to write the gracious foreword in the midst of a work schedule that would frighten most men. It was only one more of Father Colman's many good ideas to ask His Excellency to do this. And it was an idea with which I heartily concurred by reason of the honor it has done my book as well as the occasion it has afforded me to give public expression to the deep respect which I have long felt for Archbishop Hallinan both as a churchman and as an historian in his own right, to say nothing of the affection I bear him as a friend.

John Tracy Ellis

Washington, D.C., May 29, 1963

CONTENTS

PERSPECTIVES IN AMERICAN CATHOLICISM

1 CATHOLICS IN AMERICA

CHURCH AND STATE:
AN AMERICAN CATHOLIC TRADITION

Few subjects have aroused more interest among thoughtful Americans in recent years than that of the relations in this country between Church and State. Unfortunately the issue has not always been temperately discussed — with the result that much ill feeling has been engendered among the various religious bodies in the United States. And this bitterness has not only done a disservice to religion in general, but has also resulted in injury to the internal peace of the nation at a time when it was seriously threatened from outside its frontiers. One is reminded of the words of John Carroll, who in 1790 became the first Catholic bishop of the United States, when he reluctantly entered on a public controversy in defense of his religious faith while the Republic was still in its infancy.

Carroll deplored the necessity of replying to his antagonist lest he disturb the harmony then existing among men of differing religious beliefs, which, he said, "if we have the wisdom and temper to preserve, America may come to exhibit a proof to the world, that general and equal toleration, by giving a free circulation to fair argument, is the most effectual method to bring all denominations of Christians to a unity of faith."

In raising again the question of Church and State in this essay, I wish to make it clear at the outset that I have neither the intention nor the professional competence to discuss the theological aspects of the problem. The doctrinal teaching of the Catholic Church on Church and

1

State is accessible to all interested students of the subject. In the past several years American Catholic theologians have examined it in journals like the *American Ecclesiastical Review* and *Theological Studies*, where the divergent views of these theologians have been put forth in great detail. There the authoritative pronouncements of modern pontiffs, such as the encyclicals *Immortale Dei* of November 1, 1885, and *Libertas praestantissimum* of June 20, 1888, of Pope Leo XIII, have been analyzed in their application to the United States, where the Constitution forbids anything like a union of Church and State and where, too, the policy of religious toleration of all men is a recognized principle embodied in the fundamental law of the land.

What I intend, rather, is to set down some little known and seldom recalled statements on this question by the leading Catholic bishops of the United States over a century and a half. For I am convinced that, reflecting as they do the thinking of the most important members of the hierarchy in this country from the earliest years of the Republic to our own day, they reveal an authentic tradition.

First, let us go back to Father John Carroll. On February 27, 1785, he wrote a letter to an English friend about the constitutional power which had been granted the Maryland legislature to levy a general tax for the support of the Christian religion. This provision disturbed many Marylanders who belonged to religious bodies other than the recently formed Protestant Episcopal Church, which in its colonial counterpart had been accorded a favored status by the government. Father Carroll mentioned the misgivings which the provision had aroused among Presbyterians, Methodists, and Quakers; said that the Catholics would join these Protestant groups in opposing it with might and main; and added, "We have all smarted heretofore under the lash of an established church, and shall therefore be on our guard against every approach towards it." And three months after the Constitutional Convention had finished its work on the federal Constitution, Carroll made public his stand on religious toleration in the *Columbian Magazine* of December 1787:

Thanks to genuine spirit and Christianity, the United States have banished intolerance from their system of government, and many of them have done the justice to every denomination of Christians, which ought to be done to them all, of placing them on the same footing of citizenship, and conferring an equal right of participation in national privileges. Freedom and independence, acquired by the united efforts, and cemented with the mingled blood of Protestant and Catholic fellow citizens, should be equally enjoyed by all.

Thus did the founder of the American hierarchy accept wholeheartedly the separation of Church and State in the United States, with its accompanying principle of equal and universal religious toleration for men of all faiths.

Five years after the death of Archbishop Carroll there arrived in this country from Ireland in December 1820 the man who was destined to play a leading role in the development of American Catholicism during the next two decades. This was John England, first Bishop of Charleston, who assumed control of his vast Southern diocese at the age of thirty-four. He had been in the United States only a little over three years when he spoke his mind on the union of Church and State in no uncertain terms. In an address before the Hibernian Society of Savannah, Georgia, on March 17, 1824, the bishop struck out at the British government which at that time was trying to win the right of veto over the selection of Catholic bishops in Ireland.

Praising the resistance of the Irish clergy to this attempted concession, the bishop remarked, "May God long preserve the liberties of America from the union of any church with any state! In any country, with any religion, it is an unnatural increase of the power of the executive against the liberties of the people." And a year and a half after his Savannah speech he returned to the topic in a letter of September 17, 1825, to Daniel O'Connell, the Irish liberator:

I am convinced [wrote Bishop England] that a total separation from the temporal government is the most natural and safest state for the church in any place where it is not, as in the papal territory, a complete government of churchmen.

Meanwhile the Catholic Church in the United States had grown and expanded from an estimated 35,000 Catholics in 1790 to over 650,000 by 1840, two years before Bishop England died. By that time there had appeared on the American scene another Irish-born bishop who was to take the leading place left vacant by England and become the most prominent Catholic churchman of the mid-century: John Hughes, fourth Bishop of New York, and from 1850 to 1864 the first archbishop of that fastest-growing of American sees. Hughes' episcopacy began in 1838 at a time when the fury of the Nativist agitation against foreigners and Catholics was at its height. In the bitter controversies of those days the efforts of Bishop Hughes to win once more state funds for the education of Catholic children in New York, brought forth the charge that any renewal of financial assistance to the parochial schools would endanger the American principle of separation of Church and State. Hughes met the charge in a characteristically forthright manner, and said in a speech delivered at Washington Hall on June 1, 1841:

> The whole matter now stands in this position. At the commencement the great alarm raised was that the admission of our claim would be a step towards the union of Church and State. And if those who opposed us upon that ground were sincere in it, I respect them for their opposition; for there is nothing which every patriot should feel to be a more imperative duty than to resist to the uttermost any attempt to introduce measures tending to so disastrous a result.

That statement — and his reference, later on in the same speech, to the prevention of "the justly obnoxious union of Church and State" — made Bishop Hughes' position clear. And he expressed it even more positively two and a half years later in an address before a large audience in the Broadway Tabernacle in New York:

> I regard the Constitution of the United States as a monument of wisdom, an instrument of liberty and right, unequaled — unrivaled — in the annals of the human race. Every separate provision of that immortal document is stamped with the features of wisdom; and yet among its wise provisions, what I regard as the *wisest* of all is the brief, simple, but comprehensive declaration that "Congress shall make no law respecting the establishment of religion, or prohibiting the free exercise thereof."

The unhappy chapter of American history which was written by the strident anti-Catholicism of the Nativists and Know-Nothings during the eighteen-forties and fifties — and which has been so expertly described by the non-Catholic historian, Ray Allen Billington, in his volume *The Protestant Crusade* — found its denouement in the far more absorbing struggle which broke out over slavery and sectional conflict. And it was not until the late eighteen-eighties that another organized movement against the Catholic Church in the United States appeared, when the American Protective Association — the APA — was brought into being by Henry F. Bowers and his associates in March 1887. During the next ten years the country suffered the ignominy of a campaign of religious bigotry the like of which had not been seen since before

4

the Civil War. Once more the accusation of disloyalty to the nation was heard, and again the leaders of the Catholic Church were taxed with the charge that they represented a dangerous minority who, if they ever attained a majority of the population, would abolish the separation of Church and State.

In the same month that Bowers founded the APA the second American Catholic churchman to be honored with membership in the College of Cardinals received the insignia of his rank. This was James Gibbons, Archbishop of Baltimore. When as a newly created cardinal he took possession in Rome of his titular church of Santa Maria in Trastevere, he paid a glowing tribute to the political institutions of his native country and reflected his complete satisfaction with the relations of Church and State in the United States.

For myself [said Gibbons], as a citizen of the United States, without closing my eyes to our defects as a nation, I proclaim, with a deep sense of pride and gratitude, and in this great capital of Christendom, that I belong to a country where the civil government holds over us the aegis of protection without interfering in the legitimate exercise of our sublime mission as ministers of the Gospel of Jesus Christ.

The sentiments which Cardinal Gibbons expressed at Rome in 1887 deepened with the passing years, and nearly a quarter of a century later, in a memorable article in the *North American Review* in 1909, he made his position even more emphatic. He wrote:

American Catholics rejoice in our separation of Church and State; and I can conceive of no combination of circumstances likely to arise which would make a union desirable either to Church or State. We know the blessings of our present arrangement; it gives us liberty and binds together priests and people in a union better than that of Church and State. Other countries, other manners; we do not believe our system adapted to all conditions; we leave it to Church and State in other lands to solve their problems for their own best interests. For ourselves, we thank God we live in America, "in this happy country of ours," to quote Mr. [Theodore] Roosevelt, where "religion and liberty are natural allies."

In the long period from 1887 to his death in 1921 Cardinal Gibbons was dean of the American hierarchy, and no Catholic bishop of the United States ever made more manifest his perfect contentment with the relations of Church and State than he did. But in this attitude he had no monopoly, for among his contemporaries and friends were outstanding churchmen who shared entirely the Cardinal's point of view — such as, for example, John Lancaster Spalding, first Bishop of Peoria; John Ireland, first Archbishop of St. Paul; and John J. Keane, first Rector of the Catholic University of America and later Archbishop of Dubuque. Late in 1896 Bishop Keane went abroad to live for a time, and during his sojourn in Europe he found many strange notions among Catholics there concerning the relations of Church and State in the United States. These notions he described in an article which he published in the *Catholic World* for March 1898, under the title, "America as Seen from Abroad," describing the difficulties an American Catholic had in persuading Europeans of the truth about the position of the Church here.

But the *pons asinorum* is reached [wrote Bishop Keane] when they come to ask him about American relations between church and state. They have been used to either church establishment or church oppression, church patronized or church persecuted. A condition in which the church neither seeks patronage nor fears persecution seems to them almost inconceivable; and when our American assures them that such is the condition in his country, they think him more than ever a dreamer. . . . They cannot imagine a separation of church and state which means simply that each leaves, and is bound to leave, the other free and independent in the management of its own affairs; each, however, respecting the other, and giving the other moral encouragement and even substantial aid when circumstances require or permit. This, they recognize, while indeed a physical separation of church and state, would be in reality their moral union. Nay, they will acknowledge that a moral union of the kind would probably be more advantageous to both church and state than a union which would tend to blend and entangle their function, with a probable confusion of wholly distinct ends and methods, likely to prove pernicious to both sides. And among past and present Europeans they can find plenty of sad illustrations to bring the truth home to them. But, all the same, when our American assures them that such is really the relation of church and state in this country, and that, considering the circumstances of the times, it is the only practicable or even desirable one, then they are quite convinced that he is not only a dreamer, but even unsound in the faith.

If some of the Catholics of Europe at the turn of the century found it difficult to understand how the Church could function in a free and democratic society along American lines without imperiling the doctrinal integrity of the Catholic faith, this was not a phenomenon confined to Europe or to that day. The same sort of arguments have been heard frequently of late in this country. Critics of the Church have adduced the teaching of Catholic theologians on the ideal union of Church and State, in the abstract, as detrimental to American institutions, without noting the qualifications which Leo XIII and others have laid down about the concrete order and the position of those who are nationals of a country where the Catholic religion is not held by a majority of the population. These critics further adduce examples from the history of Spain and Italy, where the Catholic Church enjoys a favored position, to show what would happen were Catholics to become a majority in the United States. But they fail to examine the cases of Ireland and Portugal — two predominantly Catholic countries — where there is no union of Church and State; in the case of Portugal, a concordat was signed with the Vatican in May 1940 which demonstrated that the Holy See is quite willing to enter an arrangement other than that of union of Church and State.

Moreover, the tradition established by the American hierarchy on this question in the nineteenth century is still followed by their successors today. In October 1947, Archbishop Richard J. Cushing, in an address to the national convention of the Holy Name Society in his see city of Boston, spoke of recent attacks on Catholic loyalty and said:

Yes, our critics continue, but Church and State. Surely, there, Catholic principles are at variance with those of the American people. Well, first let it be said that Catholics are also among the American people. Catholics, we have already said, have gained as much from the American system as have their neighbors, and have given to the defense of that system the full share of brain and brawn and blood. Catholics grow weary of efforts to resurrect from the limbo of defunct controversies . . . the alleged danger from the Catholic side of union of Church and State in America.

At this point the Archbishop of Boston quoted the statement of Cardinal Gibbons in 1909 which I cited above and then added, "So spoke in his day Cardinal Gibbons. So do we speak in our day."

And three months later, the chairman of the Administrative Board of the National Catholic Welfare Conference, which is the most authoritative body in the Catholic Church of this country, issued a statement which was quite categorical in character. On January 25, 1948, Archbishop John T. McNicholas stated:

No group in America is seeking union of church and state; and least of all are Catholics. We deny absolutely and without any qualification that the Catholic bishops of the United States are seeking a union of church and state by any endeavors whatsoever, either proximate or remote. If tomorrow Catholics constitute a majority in our country, they would not seek a union of church

7

and state. They would then, as now, uphold the Constitution and all its Amendments, recognizing the moral obligations imposed on all Catholics to observe and defend the Constitution and its Amendments.

In a very thoughtful article which Will Herberg contributed to the November 1952 issue of *Commentary* on "The Sectarian Conflict over Church and State," he referred to the recent discussions of this question in responsible Catholic journals, and then remarked, "There *is* a new Catholic attitude, and it would be well if the public knew more about it." Yet most of what has been quoted here is very old, though it has not been cited by controversialists as have the pontifical statements which, in abstract and universal terms, call for a union of Church and State. The American hierarchy has always held, and still holds, that separation of Church and State in this country is the practical solution of this age-old problem; and nowhere will the student of American history find that the Holy See has ever rebuked them for their stand.

It is from the ideas and experiences that have been tested by age that a people's traditions evolve. More than a century and a half is sufficient time to test the quality of any tradition. When one considers, therefore, that the position which I have been outlining has been held from 1784, when the future Archbishop Carroll was first found publicizing his acceptance of the American pattern of Church-State relations, to 1948, when the late Archbishop McNicholas made unmistakably clear his whole-hearted avowal of the separation of Church and State in this country — and that no variation from this theme has been heard from an American Catholic bishop — this should constitute an argument entitled to respect.

CHURCH AND STATE IN THE UNITED STATES: A CRITICAL APPRAISAL

"A remarkable work, spacious, erudite, and magnanimous. . . . Nothing like it has been undertaken before; nothing like it will need to be done again. It is unique and definitive." Thus did Professor Henry Steele Commager of Columbia University characterize the monumental work of Dr. Anson Phelps Stokes in the New York *Herald Tribune* of July 9, 1950, two months after its publication on May 10 of that year.[1] It was a judgment with which most reviewers have been in substantial agreement, although a few others such as Thomas T. McAvoy, C.S.C., in the *Review of Politics* [XIII (April, 1951), 261–262] and William E. McManus in the *Commonweal* of April 18, 1952, found considerable fault with the work and were much more qualified in their evaluations, especially insofar as some of Canon Stokes' basic assumptions on separation of Church and State and personal theological predilections were concerned. In a publication of such magnitude and scope, embodying data and views on which men have differed radically since the dawn of American history, it was inevitable that varying reactions should be shown to a work embracing almost every conceivable phase of the often controversial relationship of the Church to the State.

At the outset some idea of the quantitative achievement of Canon Stokes may be conveyed to the reader by stating that he develops his theme in twenty-six chapters which comprise a total of more than 2,300 pages. His narrative opens with a brief introduction by Professor Ralph H. Gabriel of Yale University and a preface of twenty-four pages wherein the author sets forth his reasons for writing these volumes and the method he has pursued in the arrangement of material, footnotes, etc. The footnotes which are found at the end of the respective volumes total 128 pages, and Volume III closes with what is termed a "Critical and Classified Selected Bibliography," which runs to sixty-seven pages, a forty-five page table of dates, thirty-eight pages of appendices and addenda, and finally an index of 115 pages. The volumes are likewise embellished with 116 splendid illustrations that have been chosen with care and taste and, all things considered, the publisher has furnished Dr. Stokes with an attractive, dignified, and accurately printed medium which is worthy of his conscientious labors of so many years.

[1] *Church and State in the United States.* By Anson Phelps Stokes. Three volumes. (New York: Harper & Brothers. 1950. Pp. lxix, 936; 799; 1042. $25.00 per set.) A request for a review copy of this work was declined because of the high costs of production, and it was stated that in consequence the publisher was forced to consider "only those magazines of larger circulation or those which have a very special editorial interest in the book." (James S. Best to the author, New York, July 11, 1950). It would certainly appear that the *Catholic Historical Review* had a special editorial interest in the work. In fact, the editors considered the work so important that, in spite of limited space, it was suggested that the present review-article be written and published.

The arrangement is roughly along chronological lines, although that order is not strictly adhered to and the reader is not altogether spared the tedium of repetition which a work of this size and thoroughness frequently entails. Volume I traverses the colonial period and the early nineteenth century up to the time when Church-State problems relating to the Civil War began to appear. Volume II embraces all the leading questions as they touched upon the approach of civil conflict, its prosecution, and its aftermath. To this are added the post-war developments in Church and State over political and social issues, and the adjustments in the realm of racial and religious questions affecting groups like the Jews, the Irish, and the Mexicans in the Southwest. But by far the longest section of Volume II (270 pages) has to do with the Church and State in the field of public and church education, a subject on which Canon Stokes reveals a deeper feeling than on any other which he treats. Here he traces the problem down to August, 1949, where he ends with fourteen pages on the controversy between Cardinal Spellman and Mrs. Roosevelt which took place at that time. Volume III is confined principally to the twentieth century and deals with social problems such as legislation on divorce and birth control, social welfare programs, the attitude and conduct of the churches during the two world wars, and the public status of the churches and of religion as they have emerged in contemporary American society. The narrative of the final volume, furthermore, contains a summary and interpretation of Church-State relations in the United States from the respective viewpoints of the federal and state governments, the churches, and the public, as well as an exposition of the basic philosophical principles upon which these are thought to rest. In the last chapter Canon Stokes treats of religion in relation to a democratic society, of religious freedom to civil and political freedom, and of personal religious freedom to public responsibility on the part of the individual citizen.

It is manifestly impossible to consider here every phase of a work so tremendous in size and so rich and varied in content. For that reason the reviewer trusts he may be pardoned if he concentrates on points pertaining to the history of American Catholicism, in view of the special interests of readers of the *Catholic Historical Review*. This approach will at times entail real differences with the author, as well as fairly numerous citations of factual errors and slips, and it may, indeed, run the danger of producing a negative impression concerning the general merits of the work. This the reviewer would sincerely regret, for he would wish to make clear his admiration for the painstaking labors and over-all accomplishment of the author, and especially for the attempt to be fair to all concerned which characterizes his writing on this controversial theme. Canon Stokes' work is one which every educated American can read with profit and which every student of American religious history must regard as essential to his professional knowledge. With these points established it is to be hoped that the comments which follow will not leave readers under any false impression as to the solid value which the reviewer attaches to these volumes.

In Volume I and the first third of Volume II Canon Stokes has described what he terms the "Foundations and Historic Adjustments through the Civil War." After two chapters on the significance of the general subject of the relations of Church and State and the basic facts and considerations that govern a discussion of the subject insofar as the United States is concerned, there then follows a chapter wherein the old world background is laid by tracing the roots of ideas and historic events which have influenced American thinking and action on Church-State relations, democracy, and religious freedom. This section opens with the Old Testament prophets and continues through the Greek philosophers, the principal writers of the ancient and mediaeval Church, the Renaissance and the Religious Revolt of the sixteenth century, and the politico-religious changes which transpired in England during the seventeenth and eighteenth centuries (I, 65–151). The last topic afforded a natural transition to the English settlement of North America in the early seventeenth century, and from that point the author moves on through the colonial, revolutionary, and post-revolutionary periods in an exposition of ample proportions, comprising no less than 500 pages (I, 151–647). Thereafter the three major religious groups, Protestants, Catholics, and Jews, are treated in separate chapters from the viewpoint of their respective adjustments to American Church-State conditions up to the generation preceding the Civil War (I, 651–883).

Through all the myriad facets of the complicated theme of this first volume Canon Stokes preserves a benign air of objectivity, and the critical student of history will find little reason for serious fault-finding, even though at times he may differ with the author in his interpretation of ideas and evaluation of sources. The aim which Dr. Stokes stated in his preface, namely, "to state facts fairly" (I, xlviii) has in the main

11

been realized, and the reader's appreciation of the vast accumulation of factual data in Volume I will in no way be weakened by bias or prejudice that would detract from the profit and enlightenment to be derived from a close reading of the book. Nonetheless, there are some points on which the reviewer considers that Dr. Stokes is either in error or on which his interpretation is open to question. For example, it is incorrect to say that in the early days of the Republic the American minister to France, Benjamin Franklin, was approached by the representative of the Holy See with the proposal of a concordat with the United States (I, 32–33). Actually the nuncio in Paris, Archbishop Giuseppe Doria Pamphili, made no such proposal. He merely informed Franklin in a letter of July 28, 1783, that the Congregation de Propaganda Fide, in its desire to effect an organization for the infant American Church, had determined "to propose to the congress the installation of one of their Catholic subjects . . . with the powers of vicar-apostolic, and with the character of bishop. . . ."[2] Likewise, to speak of the many concordats with Latin American countries as "attempts on the part of the Roman Catholic Church to regulate the relation of the Church to the State" (I, 33) and to omit mention of the fact that in a number of instances the State was equally anxious for a concordat that would yield to it the appointment of bishops and other prerogatives in the ecclesiastical sphere, is to see and present only half of the picture. In reference to the charter granted to Sir Walter Raleigh in 1584 for settlement in North America, it was not "the first reference to religion in any charter or constitution in the regions which later became the United States . . ." (I, 38). Sixty-one years before the grant by the English crown to Raleigh, the Emperor Charles V, in his capacity as King of Spain, issued a patent to Lucas Vasquez de Ayllón on June 12, 1523, which stated that the principal intent of the discovery and settlement of new lands in Florida would be to bring the Indians "to understand the truths of our holy Catholic faith, that they may come to a knowledge thereof and become Christians and be saved, and this is the chief motive that you are to bear and hold in this affair. . . ."[3]

The treatment of the Catholic Church's role in the politico-religious

[2] Doria Pamphili to Franklin, Paris, July 28, 1783, in Jules A. Baisnée, *France and the Establishment of the American Catholic Hierarchy. The Myth of French Interference, 1783–1784* (Baltimore, 1934), p. 50.

[3] Charles V to Ayllón, June 12, 1523, in John Gilmary Shea, *History of the Catholic Church in the United States* (New York, 1886), I, 105.

questions of the Middle Ages (I, 84–99) is on the whole a balanced one, although this reviewer does not share the unqualified enthusiasm of Canon Stokes for the contribution of Marsiglio of Padua. To attribute to Marsiglio so much that is fine in modern thought, including "the beginnings of the notion of natural law and natural rights as principles of democratic government" (I, 87) prompts the regret that the brilliant analysis of the *Defensor pacis* and its influence on men like Thomas Cromwell in the field of Church-State relations to be found in Philip Hughes' *The Reformation in England* (New York, 1951) did not appear in time to be seen by the author. Father Hughes demonstrates how Marsiglio's conclusions, to the effect that religion should be wholly dependent upon the State and that in the Church the prince should be supreme, worked out in practice in the case of the English Church. That is a case study which might well give any churchman pause before he bestows upon Marsiglio praise of so high an order.[4] The author is generous in his tribute to the Catholic Church for its many works of social betterment during the Middle Ages, but his discussion does not gain in cogency by quoting with approval the statement from the *Encyclopaedia of the Social Sciences* to the effect that "the Franciscan movement stands as the first powerful assertion of the rights of the individual against church authoritarianism . . ." (I, 93). An examination of the constitutions of the Dominican Order, as well as those of its great contemporary, the Franciscan, should convince anyone that there existed within the Church of that age a genuine assertion of the rights of the individual which was not directed against "church authoritarianism," and which did not form any part in the "long series of explosions" which led to the Protestant Revolt. Canon Stokes likewise speaks here of the attempts of Gallicanism and Febroni anism as experiments of national Catholic churches in communion with Rome which, as he says, "may have their important bearings on the development of the Roman Catholic Church in this country" (I, 97; III, 454). There is no evidence in fact or tendency of which the re-

---

[4] Cf. Hughes, *op. cit.*, pp. 331–341. Hughes — no defender of absolutism in any form — characterizes Marsiglio's *Defensor pacis* as "perhaps the most mischievous book of the whole Middle Ages . . ." since, as he says, "its aim was the destruction not only of the papacy, or of the cleric's power to rule the layman, but of the whole position that religious ideas, which are independent of human authority, are the ultimate norms of man's conduct, in public affairs no less than in his private life" (*op. cit.*, pp. 331–332). His entire treatment of the influence of Marsiglio on Thomas Cromwell, Stephen Gardiner, Edward Foxe, *et al.*, is well worthy of close study.

viewer is aware to indicate such a possibility. Here the wish would seem to have been father to the author's thought.

Dr. Stokes has many precedents for his brave attempt to picture Oliver Cromwell as an example of relative religious toleration in the mid-seventeenth century, but to the mind of many readers he will have succeeded no better in this regard than his predecessors. For example, he quotes Cromwell's ban against the saying of Mass in Ireland and states that the Cromwellians were opposed to persecution or interfering with a man's religious belief, to which is added the comment, "But they could not recognize forms and ceremonies whose practice they thought inimical to civic liberty and security" (I, 122). This type of reasoning will hardly satisfy critical readers. To be told further that in an age of persecution Cromwell abstained from persecution "with a few tragic exceptions" (I, 123), is, to say the least, an understatement. In September, 1649, Cromwell personally led the attack on Drogheda where in a general massacre around 3,500 persons of both sexes were put to death out of vengeance for the earlier massacres in Ulster for which, as Professor Edmund Curtis, a non-Catholic historian, has said, "he quite mistakenly held all Irish papists responsible."[5] When one recalls the similar fate that befell Wexford, New Ross, and other Irish towns in that terrible year, one may be excused if he demurs from the canon's all too gentle handling of Cromwell in the story of religious toleration. One of the author's most winning qualities as a writer of history is his ability to treat unpleasant facts in a spirit of charity and benevolence. But in cases such as that of Cromwell — and there are too many in these volumes — the truth would have been better served by a little stronger mixture of the wisdom of the serpent with the innocence of the dove.

In the treatment of Church-State issues in colonial America Canon Stokes covers the ground with admirable thoroughness. But it is not accurate to speak of the Catholics as having "dominated" Maryland at any time in the colony's history since they were never in a position even numerically to do so (I, 166); and to say that Catholics did not "fare as well" after the Protestant conquest of Maryland as the Protestants had done under Catholic auspices (I, 194) is another one of those understatements which does not convey a true picture of the fate of the Catholics under the penal code. The praise which is given to Roger

[5] *A History of Ireland* (New York, 1937), p. 250.

Williams' *Bloudy Tenent* is understandable for the influence which it had on the doctrine of separation of Church and State, but that work — with its enlargement of the view that "God requireth not an uniformity of Religion" — also made its contribution to the gradual breaking down of religious dogma. In this connection it may be observed that Canon Stokes rarely fails to accord a welcome to any man or movement which dulled the edges of dogmatic differences. From the standpoint of lessening the potential friction spots between various religious denominations, this is well enough. But the problem is wider than that, and for that reason it is surprising to find the Episcopalian canon applauding a tendency in American Protestantism that for generations has been eating away at the dogmatic foundation of many American religious groups. It is a problem to which the author has given thought *en passant* in his volumes but in the opinion of this reviewer at least he has never faced it squarely.

Among the final factors considered before the American Revolution is that of Freemasonry (I, 244–253). The influence of Freemasonry in history is an admittedly difficult subject to trace and, on the whole, the author's handling of it may be regarded as adequate, although here again a too roseate coloring appears at times. To speak of European Masonry as undoubtedly opposed to "ecclesiasticism" and "all forms of priestcraft" (I, 251) is less accurate than to state candidly that it was opposed to the Catholic Church and its priests. One might ask if the Catholic schools of France in the days of Emile Combes and Aristide Briand and the Catholic parochial societies and associations of Italy during the ministries of Agostino Depretis and Francesco Crispi could justly be characterized as the off-shoots of "ecclesiasticism" and "priestcraft" which it was legitimate to persecute and to hound out of existence. And for Canon Stokes to say that in the United States there has never been anything in the laws of Freemasonry to bar a Catholic from joining the lodges if he cared to do so and his ecclesiastical superiors would permit, is not sufficient to explain the differences between the grimmer aims and methods practiced by the Masons against the Church in Europe and the milder opposition employed in this country.

When he reaches the American Revolution Dr. Stokes enters upon a period which was much more fruitful in religious liberty than had been true of colonial America. Emphasis is rightly given to the Quebec Act of 1774 as a cause of the Revolution, although the pointed insincerity of the letter of the Continental Congress of October 26, 1774, to the inhabitants of Quebec concerning their religion — when read against the petition to George III of the same day and the addresses to the inhabitants of the British colonies and the people of Great Britain five days before — robs it, in this reviewer's opinion, of much of the significance attributed to it by the author (I, 262, 459). One misses here, incidentally, any reference to the able monograph of Charles H. Metzger, S.J., *The Quebec Act. A Primary Cause of the American Revolution* (New York, 1936).[6] During the course of the war the churches in general supported the American cause, with the exception of many adherents of the Church of England who for obvious reasons sympathized with the mother country. General Washington showed a genuine awareness of the influence of religion, not only by abolishing celebration in the army of Guy Fawkes' Day on November 5, 1774, so offensive to Catholics, but in a more positive manner by directing the attention of his troops to the need for religious observance as, for example, in his order of May 2, 1778, wherein among other notable remarks he said, "To the distinguished character of a Patriot, it should be our highest glory to add the more distinguished character of a Christian" (I, 272).

Among the chief factors promoting the advance of freedom during the American Revolution the author enumerates thirteen leading citizens who, in his judgment, contributed greatly to that end. One of these was Thomas Paine to whom credit is rightly given for his leading and influential role as a propagandist for the cause. But the reviewer finds it a bit strange to note Canon Stokes' enthusiasm for a man whose indirect contribution to religious freedom stemmed, we are told, from his passionate desire to set men free from "the inherited tyrannies of orthodox views of political absolutism and ecclesiastical religion." The author admits that as a result of Paine's effort "the established churches were weakened and independence of thought encouraged" (I, 318), but it does not seem to strike him as too serious that religion itself was weakened by Paine's attacks. Immediately following the section on Paine there is an admirable sketch of Father John Carroll (I, 324–333)

[6] In treating Catholicism in the colonial period and the years of transition to a national state Stokes would have profited from a use of three able monographs not mentioned here, viz., Sister Mary Augustina Ray, B.V.M., *American Opinion of Roman Catholicism in the Eighteenth Century* (New York, 1936), Arthur J. Riley, *Catholicism in New England to 1788* (Washington, 1936), and Joseph F. Thorning, *Religious Liberty in Transition* (New York, 1931).

which succeeds in emphasizing all the sterling qualities of that remarkable churchman as they manifested themselves during this important period of American history. From the treatment of James Madison (I, 339–350) it is not difficult to see why his name has figured so prominently of late years in the constitutional aspects of Church-State problems, for of the early American statesmen he would seem to have been the most secular-minded on all matters touching the relations of Church and State. Madison had approved chaplaincies for Congress in 1789 and as president supported the system, but toward the end of his life he even changed his mind on this concession by government to religion and opposed its continuance (I, 456). The attitude of Madison was clearly revealed in 1822 in a letter to Edward Livingston in which he said, "I have no doubt that every new example will succeed, as every past one has done, in showing that religion and Government will both exist in greater purity the less they are mixed together" (I, 491).

During the Revolution and the years that followed most of the original states took long strides forward in throwing off the shackles of religious intolerance which they had inherited from their colonial law. It is a congenial theme to Canon Stokes, as it would be to anyone who cherishes the religious liberty that has become so fortunate a part of the American tradition. The action of the various state conventions in writing new constitutions is detailed and it is made clear that a number of them were quite tardy in the full grant of religious freedom to Jews and Catholics. Yet it is not entirely true to say that Catholics had enjoyed anything like adequate religious and civil liberty in colonial Rhode Island (I, 463).[7] Moreover, when North Carolina came much closer to that ideal in its convention of 1835, it was as a result of the personal triumph of William Gaston, the distinguished Catholic associate justice of the state supreme court, that the word "Christian" was substituted for "Protestant" as a qualification for office holders, a fact that is not mentioned here (I, 403). The struggle to remove the legal restrictions against Catholics encountered even greater resistance in other states. It was only in 1844 that New Jersey made them eligible for office, while the voters of New Hampshire as late as 1922 defeated a proposal of their state constitutional convention to remove the word "Protestant" from a phrase of their bill of rights which authorized public

[7] Cf. Evarts B. Greene, *Religion and the State* (New York, 1941), p. 51, for colonial Rhode Island's restriction of citizenship to Protestants.

17

support for "teachers of piety, religion and morality." In that critical period there were few men of prominence who had more personal reasons to rejoice over the dawn of real religious liberty for the infant Republic than Charles Carroll of Carrollton. Near the end of his long and eventful life he told a Baptist minister of New York in a letter of October 9, 1827:

To obtain religious, as well as civil liberty, I entered zealously into the Revolution, and observing the Christian religion divided into many sects, I founded the hope that no one would be so predominant as to become the religion of the State. . . . God grant that this religious liberty may be preserved in these States, to the end of time, and that all believing in the religion of Christ may practice the leading principle of charity, the basis of every virtue (I, 464).

If Carroll had been living 120 years later he would have welcomed the Freedom Train of 1947, but he would have noted with regret the absence of the Toleration Act of 1649 of his native Maryland from its exhibits, an item which would in truth seem to have been much more significant in the story of American religious freedom than the *Bay Psalm Book* of 1640 (I, 473).

Canon Stokes' next section is devoted to the provisions of the federal Constitution on religious freedom and separation of Church and State. Here, too, there is an ample record, and the opinions of the founding fathers on the first amendment are fully set forth, including that of Daniel Carroll who is quoted from the *Annals of Congress* as having thought "it would tend more towards conciliating the minds of the people to the Government than almost any other amendment he had heard proposed" (I, 542). In this section the author first makes clear — a viewpoint which he emphasizes at greater length in Volume II — his strong approval of the recent and more extreme interpretations of the Supreme Court on the separation of Church and State. To the canon, the Everson and McCollum decisions have shown that the first amendment "must be broadly interpreted in the interest of maintaining the separation of the two institutions" (I, 540). In support of his position he shows a commendable caution in his reliance on the views of James Bryant's *James Madison* (Indianapolis, 1941, 1948); nonetheless, he is obviously gratified with those decisions. For him the Supreme Court's application of the fourteenth amendment to the religious freedom guarantee of the first amendment is "the new substantive theory of law" (I, 577). Throughout his discussion (I, 580–599) he is in the main on the side of the Everson and McCollum decisions, although in the case of the former the author seriously questions in another connection the phrase which rules out laws to "aid all religions" (II, 705). But on the subject of financial aid to private schools his personal views show through to so marked a degree that as he approaches the end of his treatment one feels that he lays aside the garb of the historian and dons that of the advocate (I, 592–593).

From here to the end of Volume I the course of American religious freedom and its practical application during the early nineteenth century is detailed. Among the factors considered is the development of higher education and the break that followed in some of the older institutions, as well as in the new state universities, with orthodox religious doctrines of the colonial era. Dr. Stokes mentions the founding of Catholic colleges as one sign of an expanding freedom, which it was, but to say that it was "doubtful" if a Catholic college could have been established in colonial Maryland in view of its existing laws is scarcely realistic (I, 636). It was not doubtful; it was impossible, as the Carrolls and other Catholic families learned to their sorrow in having to send their sons abroad to gain a Catholic education. In speaking of the Great Awakening and the education fostered by the churches on the western frontier, it is stated that the church, "both Protestant and Catholic, had done some previous work in educating the Indian . . ." (I, 669). Actually what the Protestant churches had done before 1815 — the period under discussion — was relatively insignificant in comparison to the efforts which had been expended for over two centuries by the missionaries of the Catholic Church among the red men. Dr. Stokes laments the divisive results which ensued for American Protestantism in the bumptious new Republic, and he rightly assigns as reasons for them such factors as the spirit of freedom that pervaded the land in those years, the isolation of frontier life, and the controversy over slavery (I, 779). But he does not say anything of the basic and most important cause, namely, the Protestant doctrine of private interpretation and the lack of a source of religious authority which Protestants would respect and obey. Here, surely, was the principal cause of multiple denominationalism, for the Catholic Church on the frontier had to meet the same perils as its Protestant neighbors and yet no serious schisms broke its ranks. In relation to the frequent charge of divided loyalty which was hurled against the Catholics in the early years of the nineteenth century, Canon Stokes states that today the devotion of Catholics to the United States has been proved, but when he adds, "the old bugbear of divided loyalty seldom arises to afflict us . . ." (I, 806) one wonders if he has forgotten Paul Blanshard whose charges against Catholic loyalty in recent years have brought real afflictions upon the unity of the American body politic.

Volume II opens with a chapter devoted to twelve national issues which had their origins shortly before the Civil War and in which the churches figured. They included the anti-duelling campaign, Sunday mail controversy, anti-Masonic and anti-lottery campaigns, religious journalism, temperance, the Mormons, non-sectarian public education, the annexation of Texas, the Mexican War and annexation of California, diplomatic representation at the Vatican, and finally the communistic and what are called "other new religious communities" in the United States. In the author's remarks on religious journalism he names the *Shamrock* of the New York Irish colony as having really begun Catholic journalism in the United States in 1810 (II, 31). Actually the first professedly Catholic paper was started the previous year in Detroit by Father Gabriel Richard, S.S., in his *Michigan Essay*. Moreover, the nine Catholic daily papers mentioned for 1940 (II, 38) were almost entirely foreign language journals and only the *Catholic Daily Tribune* of Dubuque which had been founded in 1920 and lasted down to 1942 was in the language of the vast majority of American Catholics.

But it is the section devoted to non-sectarian public education in this chapter which will, in all likelihood, elicit the most disagreement, for in these pages (II, 47–72) the author's strong personal views appear as on no other topic. Canon Stokes views sympathetically the movement for secularizing the public schools which set in with Horace Mann in the 1830's and 1840's, and no one who has an acquaintance with religion as it was taught in the schools of that period can gainsay the fact that it endangered the religious convictions of some pupils while it strengthened those of others. Yet the dilemma which Mann himself adumbrated as early as January, 1838, when he said — as quoted from his first report to the Massachusetts Board of Education — the "entire exclusion of religious teaching, though justifiable under the circumstances, enhances and magnifies a thousand fold, the indispensableness of moral instruction and training" (II, 55), has not been solved in any satisfactory way.

The moral instruction and training called for by Mann, and whole-heartedly urged by Dr. Stokes, a sincerely religious man, have not kept pace with the speed of secularization which has overtaken American society since Mann's time, with the result that today the nation is confronted with the menace of a generation of youth that is in good measure religiously illiterate. Dr. Stokes' treatment of the New York school controversy of the 1840's fails to mention one of the prime arguments of Bishop John Hughes in asking for financial aid for Catholic schools, namely, that the so-called non-sectarian schools were actually sectarian by reason of their use of the King James Bible, as well as of textbooks which were seriously biased against the Catholic faith and which reflected the Protestant control of these schools (II, 65). More-over, to attribute a consistently liberal stand to the Catholic Church on immigration and to speak of its opposition to birth control in any sense as motivated by its desire that it might one day be "the dominant element in the American scene" (II, 71) will strike most American Catholics as rather ridiculous.

In the section devoted to American-Vatican relations (II, 85–112) the author tells the story from the time President Polk suggested American diplomatic representation at Rome in his message to Congress of December, 1847, through the Myron Taylor episode of the 1940's with its attendant furor. One meets here some interesting quotations, among which is one of Secretary of State William H. Seward on September 27, 1862, to the American minister at Rome, Richard M. Blatchford, which is significant for its appraisal of the role of the Catholic immigrant as an American citizen and for the attitude of the pope toward American institutions. Seward adverted to the increase in recent years of Catholic immigrants to this country and he then stated:

Our country has not been slow to learn that while religion is with these masses, as it is with others, a matter of conscience, and while the spiritual authority of the head of their church is a cardinal article of their faith, which must be tolerated on the soundest principles of civil liberty, yet that this faith in no degree necessarily interferes with the equal rights of the citizens, or affects unfavorably his loyalty to the republic. It is believed that ever since the tide of emigration set in upon this continent the head of the Roman Church and States has freely recognized and favored the development of the principle of political freedom on the part of the Catho-lics in this country, while he has never lost an opportunity to express his satisfaction with the growth, prosperity and progress of the American peoples . . . (II, 89).

The remark that Pius IX gave "virtual recognition" to the Confederacy during the Civil War (II, 90) is not borne out by the evidence when closely examined.[8] Canon Stokes handles the delicate matter of American-Vatican relations on the whole very judiciously. Yet it is hardly proper to quote the *Christian Century* (II, 100) and the *Federal Council Bulletin* (II, 108) on the "insistent demands" and "pressure" of the American hierarchy for appointment of an ambassador to the Vatican when no proof is offered. If the two authors whose words are cited above possessed evidence for their charges it was incumbent upon 'them to state it; if not, it was manifestly unfair for them to impute actions to the American bishops which they could not prove. Canon Stokes would seem to share to some degree in these suspicions, for among the causes which he enumerates for a revival of anti-Catholicism since World War II "has undoubtedly been the determination of the American hierarchy to secure full diplomatic representation from this country at the Vatican . . ." (II, 412). But here, too, no proof of this "determination" is adduced.

The very lengthy chapter entitled, "The Church and Slavery" (II, 121–249), carries the reader through the Civil War. The only episode of note which the reviewer missed is one that would have interested Canon Stokes, namely, the expulsion in July, 1864, of William Henry Elder, Bishop of Natchez, from his see city by the commander of the Union forces for not reading the prayer for the President of the United States. Elder was under practical arrest by the federal troops at Vidalia for a brief period, and this resistance to a command which the bishop thought went beyond the power of the military and his different appeals for redress to President Lincoln offer a good case study in wartime relations of the Church to the State.[9]

In the period after Appomattox there arose in the United States what has been called social Christianity, a movement wherein the churches began to sense more keenly their obligation to the cause of social reform and the betterment of the lot of the industrial masses. In the discussion

[8] Cf. Leo F. Stock, "Catholic Participation in the Diplomacy of the Southern Confederacy," *Catholic Historical Review*, XVI (April, 1930), 1–17.

[9] The correspondence between Elder and the federal officials is given *in extenso* in Richard O. Gerow, *Cradle Days of St. Mary's at Natchez* (Natchez, 1941), pp. 145–184.

of this question passing mention is made of the Catholic Church, but one finds no treatment of the very real way in which the Church entered into this movement as the author might have ascertained from a work like that of Henry J. Browne, *The Catholic Church and the Knights of Labor* (Washington, 1949). In fact, one gets the impression in more than one place in these volumes that the narrative was written quite a long time before its publication and was not brought up to date. An example is the reference to "the new and authoritative life of Archbishop Hughes" (II, 405) to be published by Monsignor Guilday, although the monsignor died as long ago as July 31, 1947. Moreover, there is little by way of assessment of the contribution made to social welfare by the numerous charitable institutions conducted under Catholic auspices. For example, in 1880 there were 373 such institutions maintained by private means and ten years later the number of these refuges for the poor, the sick, the aged and orphans had risen to 553.[10] In the action taken against the Louisiana lottery of the 1890's and public gambling in general (II, 297–304) no mention is made of the influential role played by Cardinal Gibbons against the Louisiana lottery in 1892, although Cardinal O'Connell is credited with helping to prevent legalization of lotteries in Massachusetts in 1941. The problems created for the churches by the Spanish-American War and the occupation of the Philippines receive due consideration (II, 311–322). Yet here the strenuous efforts made for peace before April 21, 1898, by Cardinal Gibbons and Archbishop Ireland, and the leading part they played in counseling the McKinley administration on post-war problems in the Catholic Philippines, would have added to the favorable aspects of Church-State relations during that brief conflict.[11]

Among the national issues discussed by the author as arising after the Civil War was that of what he terms "The Roman Catholic Adjustments to American Democracy." The subject is handled with the same

[10] *Sadliers' Catholic Directory . . . 1880* (New York, 1880), p. xxii, and *Sadliers' Catholic Directory . . . 1890* (New York, 1890), p. 408. For a recent and fuller development of the Catholic contribution made to American charitable enterprises cf. Aaron I. Abell, "The Catholic Factor in Urban Relief: The Early Period, 1850–1880," *Review of Politics*, XIV (July, 1952), 289–324.

[11] For the role of Ireland cf. John T. Farrell, "Archbishop Ireland and Manifest Destiny," *Catholic Historical Review*, XXXIII (October, 1947), 269–301; "Background of the Taft Mission to Rome," *Catholic Historical Review*, XXXVI (April, 1950), 1–32; XXXVII (April, 1951), 1–22. On Gibbons, cf. John Tracy Ellis, *The Life of James Cardinal Gibbons, Archbishop of Baltimore, 1834–1921* (Milwaukee, 1952), II, 86–110.

general spirit of fairness which characterizes other sections of the work relating to American Catholicism. However, several minor points may be worthy of mention. It is not true to say that Archbishop Carroll was not very popular with Rome because, among other reasons, of "his friendly attitude toward Protestants" (II, 357). The first Archbishop of Baltimore, to be sure, had his differences on administrative matters with the Congregation de Propaganda Fide, but the reviewer knows of no evidence that would indicate any dissatisfaction on the part of the Roman officials with Carroll by reason of his friendliness toward his non-Catholic fellow countrymen. Canon Stokes has included here a very sympathetic account of the work of Cardinal Gibbons in his career as a leading American citizen (II, 363–369). The reviewer could well imagine that Gibbons might, indeed, have been an "inopportunist" on the question of defining the pope's infallibility in 1870, but in all the material examined in preparation for the cardinal's biography he saw nothing that would warrant the statement that "he did doubt the wisdom of declaring it at that time" (II, 364). Major credit was, it is true, due to Gibbons for preventing the ban against the Knights of Labor from being applied to the United States in 1887, but he did not, as is said here, secure "the lifting of the ban against them in Canada" (II, 365). The author quite rightly emphasizes the love which the cardinal had for the United States as the land of his birth, but Gibbons would have considered that circumstance "the greatest good fortune of his life" (II, 369) only after the grace of his faith in the Catholic Church and his vocation to its priesthood.

The next chapter treats of the problems of church adjustment in the fields of racial and religious restrictions (II, 373–487). The prejudices that have operated in almost all walks of American life against minorities like the Jews, Negroes, and Catholics are all thoroughly canvassed, and the pages devoted to the movement of anti-Catholicism in the years after the Civil War are excellent. In that regard one or two observations may not be out of place. Dr. Stokes quotes one of the decrees of the Vatican Council defining the universal jurisdiction of the pope in the government of the Church, to which he adds, "As long as this constitution stands the Roman Catholic Church in the United States cannot be a strictly self-governing body" (II, 396). The author's statement is certainly not incorrect, but it should be remarked that it was never intended that the Church in this country should be self-governing in the sense spoken of here. If it were to become strictly self-governing it would no longer be a part of the Catholic Church. Seven pages are given to the problem of the freedom of Ireland in American politics and the part which the Catholic Church played in that question (II, 414-421). The assignment of equal guilt to England and Ireland for the latter's miserable state in the nineteenth century (II, 414) is surely not fair to the Irish, and when Canon Stokes speaks of the Irish immigrant group of 1840-1870 coming to the United States "smarting under what it believed to be 'oppression' in Ireland as a result of Protestant English rule . . ." (II, 415), he reveals little understanding of the abuse of English rule in Ireland in those terrible years of the potato famine and its aftermath. For that matter, many of the Irish were well aware that Catholic landlords were as oppressive as their Protestant counterparts. It is true that many of the American bishops of Irish birth or ancestry were enthusiastic for Irish home rule in 1918, but the leader of the American hierarchy at that time — Cardinal Gibbons — was one bishop who did not give himself "definitely and wholeheartedly" (II, 418) for the cause of Irish freedom. In fact, Gibbons was sufficiently reserved to bring criticism upon himself from some of the more extreme Irish enthusiasts.

When the author turns to the protection of coreligionists in other countries and speaks of Franco Spain, no one will dispute him when he says, "The case of Spain has caused special difficulties" (II, 446). But it is very doubtful if those difficulties are brought any nearer to solution by Canon Stokes. To the lonely position attributed to the *Commonweal* among American Catholic journals in advocating caution toward Franco there should be added the name of James M. Gillis, C.S.P., former editor of the *Catholic World*, who always took the Franco regime — as he had that of Mussolini — with great reserve. To speak of the following of the Spanish loyalists as "strong supporters of constitutional and administrative reform, popular rights, and religious liberty," — while acknowledging the presence among them of antireligious communists — and then, in turn, to characterize the supporters of Franco as "in general extremely conservative and 'respectable' Spaniards" who were out of sympathy with fundamental reforms and definitely anti-democratic (II, 446), is not to give an accurate and satisfactory alignment of the two sides. The present reviewer is no admirer of many features of the Franco government, nor does he sub-

25

scribe in any way to the use of violence against Protestants in Spain or elsewhere in recent years. But he believes he is doing no injustice to the author of this work in stating that his single lengthy paragraph on the subject sheds little real light on the Spanish situation.

Under another aspect of the problems of racial and religious minorities and their relation to national unity there are listed six organizations which, in the author's opinion, have been of assistance. Among them one finds, of course, the National Conference of Christians and Jews, which has made a serious effort since 1928 to lessen religious and racial tension. But when one notes the Protestants and Other Americans United for Separation of Church and State as the next name in the list he may be pardoned if he inquires how that organization has earned a place among those groups which have been devoting their effort to protecting minorities and attaining national unity (II, 456). The solid accomplishments of various Protestant groups in behalf of interracial justice are described in this section, but no mention is made of the similar work of the Catholic Interracial Council. Even more important, the 455 Catholic churches in predominantly Negro communities of the United States served by 637 priests with 329 schools enrolling 72,554 pupils, taught by hundreds of devoted religious, are a silent yet tremendous contribution which is being made by the Catholic Church to the welfare of the American Negro that should not be ignored.[12] The discussion on minority needs and the adjustment of the American churches to them closes with political Zionism as a national issue (II, 471–487). Dr. Stokes treats the case from the time of the Balfour Declaration for a Jewish national homeland in November, 1917, through the ensuing divisions of American Jewry over an independent home for its people down to and beyond the recognition of the new State of Israel. Incidentally, the warm reception given by President Wilson in August, 1918, to the Balfour Declaration that the British government would use its good offices to bring about a homeland in Palestine for the Jews (II, 477), was in striking contrast to the attitude the president took about six months later in regard to another British responsibility, namely, Ireland. In the latter case he was distinctly unfriendly to the

[12] *Our Negro and Indian Missions. Annual Report of the Secretary of the Commission for the Catholic Missions among the Colored People and the Indians* (Washington, 1952), p. 23. The Catholic Church also maintained in 1952 406 churches served by 222 priests and sixty-one schools for 8,107 children among the 100,722 Indian Catholics in the United States (*ibid.*, p. 33).

26

cause of Irish home rule and in a declaration before the members of the peace commission at Paris in March, 1919, he made that quite clear.[18]

The balance of Volume II is devoted to two very lengthy chapters on the problems of Church-State adjustment in the field of public and private education (II, 488–758). Insofar as the American public school is concerned the viewpoint of the author may best be summarized in his own words:

> It is realized that the public school in a democracy is almost necessarily a secular institution, being intended for pupils of all religious groups. This however does not and should not imply that it is irreligious, and a people with our background should not permit it to become antireligious. Indeed, every such school should show its sympathy with a spiritual outlook that involves recognition of the existence of God as the Creator of the world and of men, and the Judaeo-Christian teaching of our duty to Him and to our neighbor (II, 493–494).

The vast accumulation of data that follows attempts to show from history and from the interpretations of recent court cases involving religion in the public schools the way in which Canon Stokes believes his aims may be accomplished. But at the very outset he is involved in a dilemma which he is not able to resolve. If one is to take the McCollum decision of 1948 as the final word on the subject, as Dr. Stokes seems to wish (II, 515–523), then his hope that the public school will show its sympathy with a spiritual outlook involving the "recognition of the existence of God" will not stand, for Mrs. McCollum, a professed atheist, will not tolerate such recognition in the public school attended by her son. Moreover, to plead as the author does, for a recognition in public education of the value of religion and then to advance in its behalf "the collective value of culture" of John Dewey (II, 497) is of no help to the argument. There was no American educationist of the twentieth century who did more to accomplish the annihilation of the supernatural element in education than Dewey, and to cite one of the prime pragmatists of our age in this connection is, to say the least, incongruous. On this subject the author makes good use of many reliable sources of information, but the reader who has more than a passing acquaintance with Conrad Henry Moehlman's *School and Church: The American Way* (New York, 1944) is not going to have his confidence in Canon Stokes' critical acumen strengthened by

[18] Stephen Bonsal, *Unfinished Business* (London, 1944), p. 138.

27

his use of a book which is vitiated by so strong an anti-Catholic bias.

Canon Stokes welcomes the McCollum decision as one that, he says, "represented a step forward in supporting the Church-State separation and religious freedom clauses of the Constitution, though interpreting separation somewhat too rigorously" (II, 522). He quotes a report of the National Education Association made in 1949 as to what happened to the religious education programs in 2,639 public school systems as a result of this decision, and it was found that 11.8 per cent of those replying had given up their programs and of these 52.3 per cent did so by reason of the McCollum decision (II, 529). The author is aware of the implications of this action upon the future religious education of American youth, but the alternatives which he offers are not very promising in the light of past experience, and it is to be feared that little consolation will be derived from the statement that some more efficient method must be adopted by the churches to reach the great majority of youth in the public schools (II, 534). Dr. Stokes has apparently no serious misgivings about the contradictions in which the Supreme Court involved itself in the various cases relating to the Jehovah's Witnesses (II, 600–616), and he is seemingly unimpressed by the applicability to the McCollum case of March 8, 1948, of the language of Justice Felix Frankfurter and his colleagues in the Gobitis case of June, 1940. In the latter it was stated, "Judicial nullification of legislation cannot be justified by attributing to the framers of the Bill of Rights views for which there is no historic warrant" (II, 610). If Canon Stokes believes the Supreme Court's decision in June, 1943, in reversing its own decision of three years before on the salute to the flag of the Jehovah's Witnesses to be "an important milestone in the history of religious liberty" (II, 614), one might ask why he feels the McCollum decision should be regarded as so irrevocable.

In this connection a recent contribution to the official journal of the American Bar Association has some pertinence. There it was stated that on January 15, 1951, the Supreme Court unanimously held in *Niemotko vs. Maryland* that religious ministers had the right by reason of the first and fourteenth amendments to equal protection of the law to preach religion on consecutive Sundays in a tax-supported recreational park without the customary permit from the city. On the same day the Supreme Court in an eight to one decision in the case of *Kunz*

vs. *New York* stated that a religious minister could preach in Columbus Circle in New York City, which is tax-supported property,
without the ordinance required by the city, and this again on the
strength of his rights under the first and fourteenth amendments. Moreover, the minister would be in no way impeded from using insulting
language of other religious groups, for example, in declaring that "the
Pope is the Anti-Christ, etc."[14] In the latter case Justice Robert H.
Jackson, the sole dissenter, asked if the court had so quickly forgotten
one of the chief reasons for prohibiting release time for religious instruction was that the Constitution would not allow tax-supported
properties to be used to propagate religion. "How can the Court now
order use of tax-supported property for the purpose?" Jackson asked,
and he further inquired, "In other words, can the First Amendment
today mean a city cannot stop what yesterday it meant no city could
allow?"[15] In the light of these precedents and of the questionable interpretation used in the McCollum case — which Dr. Stokes himself
admits in another connection (III, 564) — it is not at all certain that
the Supreme Court will adhere to its own extreme position of 1948 on
the separation of Church and State. The six to three decision of March
3, 1952, by which the Supreme Court declined to assume jurisdiction
in the case of Bible reading in the public schools of New Jersey, and
the favorable decision by the same alignment handed down on April 28,
1952, in the released time of the New York public schools would both
point in the direction of a more moderate interpretation than that of
1948. In fact, one is justified in concluding from *Doremus vs. Board of
Education* that today the court is less eager to entertain "wall of
separation" controversies than it was in 1947–1948. When one reads the
demands of the American Association for the Advancement of Atheism
as formulated by the author (III, 594) and realizes that the McCollum
decision was a victory for this group more than any other, he is saddened
to find a man of Canon Stokes' undoubted religious faith giving comfort
to an association which would destroy the finest traditions upon which
the American Republic is founded.

As regards parochial schools, Canon Stokes has many generous
things to say concerning their contribution to the moral and spiritual

[14] T. Raber Taylor, "Equal Protection of Religion: Today's Public School Problem," *American Bar Association Journal*, XXXVIII (April, 1952), 277.
[15] *Ibid.*, p. 278.

betterment of their students, and through them to American society in general. He summarizes the pros and cons of parochial schools in the form of nine assertions made in their behalf by their supporters as against nine assertions made against them by their opponents (II, 659–660). This is surely a fair enough method to use, but a difficulty arises from the fact that with a single exception no authorities are cited for either group, and it is impossible, therefore, to tell whether or not the unnamed supporters and opponents of parochial schools are qualified to pass judgment on them. There are certain propositions set forth as arguments against the parochial schools which, in the opinion of this reviewer, are not justified. For example, it is said that the teaching in such schools is apt to be dominated by theological and ecclesiastical authoritarianism, that they devote so much time to matters theological, ecclesiastical, and religious as to crowd out modern studies, that their superiors object so much to state inspection and standardization that state laws are likely to go by default, and that they tend to present American history inaccurately by reason of over-emphasizing Catholic contributions and minimizing the contributions of non-Catholics in the national story. When an American Catholic reads these strictures he is fully warranted in asking: who is talking and how well qualified is he to speak on this subject? Any person well informed on the American Catholic parochial system will regard a number of these criticisms as hardly more than caricatures. And when the sole authority cited for the manner in which Catholic schools teach American history is found to be a letter from Professor William Warren Sweet of Southern Methodist University to the author and articles by the same professor in the *Christian Advocate* of June, 1922, his confidence in the accuracy of the judgments is not going to be strengthened. Professor Sweet has little real knowledge of what goes on in Catholic classrooms, and in many of the things he has written about American Catholicism he has proved himself to be a quite unsafe guide. An instance of the approach of Professor Sweet to matters affecting American Catholicism may be cited from a book he published some years ago. He commented on the growing strength and assertiveness of the Church in the United States and he noted that since 1918 there had been produced at the Catholic University of America over fifty doctoral dissertations in American Catholic history. Most of these he characterized as "histori-cally sound," to which there was appended the qualification that "practically all have been censored by the church. This fact in the eyes of outside historians renders them somewhat suspect. For censored history must be classed as propaganda, even though it may display much sound scholarship."[16] A man who has so badly misunderstood the true meaning of the ecclesiastical *imprimatur* which appears on many Catholic books — although information on the *imprimatur* is readily available to him — is scarcely the proper person to judge the quality of American Catholic historiography. If in his own field of history such a blindness in matters Catholic is evident, Professor Sweet certainly eliminates himself as an authority on the procedures and methods used in the Catholic parochial schools. Dr. Stokes' assertion that enrollment in Catholic elementary schools has "remained about the same during the past two decades" (II, 655) is a gross error in fact in the light of the statistics in the annual volumes of the *Catholic Directory* for the past twenty years and the even more enlightening survey of Benjamin Fine published in the New York *Times* of March 30, 1952. It is likewise untrue that Catholics have used the term "godless" of the public schools in the sense that the majority of the teachers in those schools do not believe in God (I, 661). It has been due to the lack of religious instruction that such a term has at times been employed by some of the more extreme exponents of religious education in Catholic ranks.

Throughout the entire section on the schools the canon insists again and again upon the necessity of strict adherence to a rigid separation of the public schools from any church connection in the spirit of the McCollum decision and, although acknowledging the contribution which parochial schools have made to American life, he is equally insistent that they be given no financial support from the State. After remarking that these schools have been almost entirely supported from private sources, the author concludes with this judgment: "If this continues to be policy and the few cases of state aid are eliminated, there will be more general appreciation by non-Catholics of the contributions which the Catholics are making to general education" (II, 733). In other words, it would seem the appreciation of the contribution of the Church's schools will not be based upon their intrinsic worth in promoting the national welfare, but will be measured by their remoteness from public financial assistance!

[16] William Warren Sweet, *The American Churches. An Interpretation* (New York, 1947), pp. 94–95.

This review article has already gone beyond a reasonable length and, therefore, no more can be done than to indicate in a very general way the rich content of Volume III and to give a few examples of further judgments which, in the opinion of the reviewer, are open to question. Under the heading of adjustments in social-legislative questions marriage problems are discussed, and here it might be stated that the regulations governing the celebration of mixed marriages in rectories or private homes no longer hold in many American dioceses and such marriages are now being performed in the churches (III, 54). It is disappointing to find a man of Canon Stokes' breadth and general fairness repeating the old and misleading statement that Catholics who win annulments of marriage "are frequently people of important position who are able to exert much influence in Rome" (III, 65) when annually the Catholic press carries a summary of the cases decided by the Rota which often shows half or more have been decided without even a fee for the court expenses. No one will deny that the question of birth control is, as the author says, difficult and complicated (III, 78), but to those who hold to the tradition of the natural law on the sanctity of human life there are eternal principles involved in this question which they try to defend objectively in the face of the emotional agitation of Margaret Sanger and her followers. In regard to chaplains in hospitals and other public institutions, nothing is said of the bitter struggle fought throughout a good part of the nineteenth century in many parts of the United States to keep Catholic priests out, or of the fact that they only won entry by long and persistent efforts to reach their spiritual charges in those institutions. Canon Stokes finds it "questionable" that the Waco, Texas, chapter of the National Council of Catholic Women should have sponsored the move by the Mayor of Waco in 1941 to issue a special proclamation giving official recognition to Good Friday on the grounds that such "might cause pain to many thoughtful Jewish citizens" (III, 199). Catholic observance of Good Friday is motivated solely by reverence for the day of Christ's death on the cross and has no relation whatever to the fact that it was the Jews who had condemned Him to death. If such an interpretation is put on the observance, then President Truman must have used equally questionable methods in issuing his suggestion that government clerks in Washington, D.C., be free from twelve to three o'clock on Good Friday, April 11, 1952. In this section the Legion of Decency receives high appreciation from the author for its work in censoring films (III, 236–239).

To the subject of World War I and the peace movement Dr. Stokes devotes a lengthy chapter (III, 252–365). In outlining the attitude pursued by the American churches toward the League of Nations, World Court, and other post-war international institutions no mention is made of Cardinal Gibbons' strong support of a league and of universal military training, two subjects on which he earned the gratitude of government officials along with the criticisms of other citizens who were opposed to these measures. When he comes to World War II and American participation therein the author is quite correct in saying that many American Catholics were "somewhat embarrassed" by the fact that the Russian communists were our allies, but it is a trifle absurd to suggest that they experienced any embarrassment from the official neutrality of the Holy See and of Ireland (III, 288). The reviewer has never met an American Catholic who was in the least embarrassed in the support he gave to World War II by reason of these factors. Catholics responded with the customary patriotism that has always marked their answer to the call of duty in the wars of their country and, in fact, among the 1,488 conscientious objectors tabulated here (III, 300) only twenty-nine, the smallest number for any single denomination, were Catholics. If the Catholic Church of the United States revealed deep uneasiness over the problem of Soviet Russia and the advance of communism during and after World War II, time has proved that it had ample warrant, and the attitudes of some of the American Protestant churches as revealed here have been shown to have been pitifully unrealistic (III, 356–364).

There are three chapters which deal respectively with the legal basis of church property, clergy rights, and Church-State relations, with the status in this country of religion in general, and with that of Christianity in particular (III, 369–626). These carry Canon Stokes up to the final section of his monumental work where he draws some over-all conclusions. In these three chapters the decisions of the courts are examined in all cases relating to important Church-State matters, and the attitudes of the various churches toward the State, social reform, and religious freedom are once more canvassed. In analyzing the present attitude of the Catholic Church toward the State and religious freedom, Dr. Stokes finds much to encourage him in his laudable desire for harmony and understanding between the two institutions. But he likewise believes that recent years have shown some "disquieting signs" in the form of the general support by the American hierarchy of General Franco and the opposition to the recognition of what he calls "the Republican Loyalists in Spain" (III, 466). Yet nothing is said of the fact that the hierarchy's opposition to the latter was due mainly to the fact that they were inspired and led by communists who had determined upon the complete destruction of all forms of supernatural religion and of Catholicism in particular. In any case, these matters relating to the hierarchy's policies give no reasonable basis for the fear of some unnamed Protestant leaders that the United States may witness "the development here of a counter-Reformation" (III, 466).

While Canon Stokes may approve the statement of Benedetto Croce on Church and State, it is incorrectly characterized as that of "a liberal European Catholic point of view" (III, 662) since the works of Croce are on the *Index of Prohibited Books* and may not, therefore, pass for Catholic in any true sense. The excellent suggestion of courses in American colleges and universities on the subject of American Church-State relations as a means to a better understanding of the complexities involved has been met in part in several institutions since Canon Stokes' correspondence with Wilfrid Parsons, S.J. (III, 687–688), for in the academic year 1950-1951 Francis J. Powers, C.S.V., of the Department of Politics offered a course in the Catholic University of America which was entitled "Church and State in the United States," and in 1951–1952 the School of Law of Columbia University also offered a seminar in the legal and religious aspects of American Church-State relations. Speaking of the influence of American religious freedom on other nations, Canon Stokes cites the adoption by France in September, 1791, of religious freedom as a principle (III, 689). But it should have been added that France failed to follow the example of the United States in practice when it drew up and put into force in August, 1790, the Civil Constitution of the Clergy which allowed little freedom to the Church to conduct its own affairs. In enumerating some of the areas of the world where limits to religious freedom still exist it is odd, to say the least, to find Spain and Peru included because of compulsory Mass in the army and the schools, and no mention made of the restrictions imposed by Soviet Russia and its satellites (III, 696). And if the Catholics of Scandinavia were to read that not many decades have passed since a dominant Protestantism made it difficult for them to practice their religion "with full freedom" (III, 697), they would remind the author that such is still the case, even though some concessions have been recently granted.

34

Apart from questions of content something should be said concerning Canon Stokes' methods of research. He deserves the highest praise for the thoroughness with which he has gone through a mountain of printed literature on the subject of Church-State relations. It was a formidable undertaking and only a man with the greatest perseverance and industry could have seen it to the end. Moreover, readers will always be grateful to the canon for assembling in one place the results of his extensive reading and the hundreds of pertinent quotations with which his volumes are filled. There were, however, a number of times when this reviewer felt that material might well have been omitted as, e.g., on the Swiss Confederation (I, 127–129), on duelling (II, 5–12), but more especially the largely repetitious Chapter XXVI (II, 645–697) which goes over again ground that had already been covered. The exceedingly lengthy quotations at times slow down reading interest and produce a certain tedium, although they do enhance the value of the work as a source book. On another point of method, the reviewer cannot agree that the reader would be "embarrassed by notes in the text" (I, xl), since these volumes were intended in the main for serious students and not for the popular reading public. For the former the presence of footnotes at the bottom of the pages is never an embarrassment.

It would be unreasonable, to be sure, to expect that the author of a work of this kind should in all cases seek out manuscript sources for his information, but the way in which certain printed sources are handled leaves much to be desired. For example, it is not good practice to take statements such as that from the *Civiltà Cattolica* of 1948 by way of the *Christian Century* of June 23 of that year (I, 18, 885). Nor is it very helpful to be told that a recent unnamed writer has stated that "all political problems are at bottom theological" (I, 701), and then find that the footnote reads: "Cf. his *The Theology of Politics*, and Quick, O.C., *Christianity and Justice, passim*" (I, 926). In like manner critical readers will not be reassured to find a quotation from the readily available *American Ecclesiastical Review* (II, 464) on Catholic participation in the National Conference of Christians and Jews resting on a reference to Paul Blanshard and a statement of "some bishops in *Commonweal*, July 14, 1944" (II, 783). In the same category is the use of a letter on chaplaincies in the *Commonweal* of April 16, 1943 (III, 732) relating to the service of Abbé François Louis de Latbinière as a chaplain with the American forces of Benedict Arnold in Canada (III, 111). Here a work like Aidan H. Germain, O.S.B., *Catholic Military and Naval Chaplains, 1776–1917* (Washington, 1939) would have served much better. The quotation of the statement on Church and State of one who is identified only as "a well-known Jesuit" (III, 451) from the *Christian Century* of December 31, 1947 (III, 750) is a further instance of this unsatisfactory method of documentation. To discuss a case like that of the sisters teaching in the public school of Dixon, New Mexico, and the controversy that ensued over them in 1947 is entirely pertinent in a work of this character (II, 668–671). But to draw one's sources altogether from the *Christian Herald*, the *Christian Century*, and the *Churchman*, three Protestant journals, is to hear only one side in the dispute.

But far more serious in revealing the author's lack of critical appraisal of his sources is his characterization of Blanshard's *American Freedom and Catholic Power* (Boston, 1949), as "an able but somewhat extreme presentation" (III, 480) of the position of Catholics in relation to Church and State. Dr. Stokes would not have needed to await the appearance of James M. O'Neill's *Catholicism and American Freedom* (New York, 1952) with its detailed exposure of Blanshard's shoddy scholarship to discover the crippling bias under which that author writes on any subject pertaining to American Catholicism. Although we are told that Blanshard's one-sided selection of evidence and unsympathetic interpretations produce an over-all effect that "is not wholly fair," yet Canon Stokes maintains that Blanshard's facts on the history of the Church, its canon law, and traditions are "basically sound" (III, 778). Just how a man's facts can be "basically sound" if they are selected to sustain his prejudice and to which, in turn, he gives an "unsympathetic interpretation" is a mystery that is best left for Canon Stokes to solve! Then, too, the canon was not happy in his choice of Albert Houtin, *l'Américanisme* (Paris, 1904) as the basis for his treatment of the American Catholic school controversy of the 1890's (III, 473–474). This book by an apostate French priest was no source for a topic of this kind, especially when the author had at his command two able monographs done from original sources, namely, Daniel F. Reilly, O.P., *The School Controversy, 1891–1893* (Washington, 1943), and Patrick H. Ahern, *The Catholic University of America. The Rectorship of John J. Keane, 1887–1896* (Washingington, 1949). In fairness to Canon Stokes due allowance must be made for the fact that he was beset by tremendous problems in making his way through hundreds of books and periodicals and in keeping in order his thousands of footnotes. That some awkward spots should fail to be ironed out and some bibliographical errors turn up was inevitable. But the uncritical use made of a number of items in his bibliography is more serious, and it is this which in the final analysis will tell more heavily against the enduring value of the work.

The reviewer trusts that he has made clear the appreciation which he feels for the general fairness — even if not unmottled by his own ideological blind spots — which has informed the impressive accomplishment of Canon Stokes in these three volumes. He would sincerely regret if the strictures which he has felt compelled to pass upon certain phases of the work should cause any reader to neglect the opportunity which he will find here for enriching his knowledge of American religious history. In this sense the reviewer cannot do better by way of conclusion than to express the hope that his criticisms may be interpreted in the spirit which has marked the tone of the pages he has criticized, and that nothing he has said will be out of harmony with the concluding judgment on *Church and State in the United States* as expressed in the *Times Literary Supplement* on November 9, 1951, where it was stated:

In a field of learning soaked in all uncharitableness, even to-day, it is a great achievement to have written so long and so learned a book, of which every page seeks to see and show the best in men and sects and whose author always remembers that the great need in all religious discussion is charity.

Dr. Stokes has expressed the hope that he may publish a brief condensation of these three volumes for popular consumption, and since he states that he will welcome corrections (I, lxix) the following slips on Catholic items are offered with a view to being of help in that regard.

Volume I: Don Sturzo was born in 1871, not 1870 (p. 28); it is the Republic of Ireland, not the "Irish Free State" (p. 58); read "1755" for "1775" (p. 214); provincial "council" of 1840, not "councils" (p. 251); the address of the Continental Congress to the people of Great Britain was October 26, 1774, not October 24 (p. 262); read "Citizen" for "Citizens" for the French document of 1789 (p. 265); Archbishop Carroll died in 1815, not 1813 (p. 293); John England was never an "archbishop" (p. 324); Carroll was made an archbishop in 1808, not 1811 (p. 326); Bishop England was born in 1786, not 1788 (p. 502); moreover, he preached at Christmas, 1825, in St. Patrick's Church, Washington, not St. Matthew's, as the latter was opened only in 1840

(p. 503); John Hughes was a bishop, not an archbishop in 1847 (p. 505); Pennsylvania is said to have ratified the Constitution in December, 1787, by a vote forty-six to twenty-three (p. 601) and by a majority of fifteen (p. 606); there was no "Bishop of Louisiana and the Floridas" at New Orleans in 1815; it was William Dubourg, administrator of the see (p. 687); James II came to the English throne in 1685, not 1684 (p. 785); one speaks of "a" congregation of cardinals, not "the" congregation (p. 790); Bedini was an archbishop, not a cardinal, on his visit to the United States in 1853 (p. 817); Hughes was a priest and not an archbishop in 1833 at the time of the debate with Breckenridge (p. 819), and he was made an archbishop in 1850, not 1847 (p. 825); read "J." M. O'Neill, not "I." M. (p. 910, n. 24).

Volume II: The lottery cited from Guilday's *Carroll* was for Holy Trinity School, Philadelphia, and not "a Roman Catholic parochial school in Baltimore" (p. 26); the *Freeman's Journal* of New York was begun in 1840, not 1839 (p. 32); Bedini was nuncio to Brazil in 1853, not to the United States (p. 90); Brownson was converted in 1844, not 1842 (p. 188); James Gibbons was nineteen, not eighteen, when he returned to the United States (p. 363), and on the same page the Second Plenary Council was held in 1866, not 1868, and Gibbons was thirty-four and not thirty-two when he was made a bishop; Gibbons was named coadjutor of Baltimore in 1877, not 1875, and his *Faith of Our Fathers* was published in 1876, not 1875 (p. 364). On page 365 the cardinal's Milwaukee sermon was delivered in 1891, not 1899, and the petition to Rome concerning German grievances was made by Father Peter Abbelen of Milwaukee and not by Missouri Catholic Germans, although Abbelen's case related in part to conditions in Missouri. The celebration in Baltimore in June, 1911, was in honor of Cardinal Gibbons' golden jubilee as a priest and silver jubilee as a cardinal (p. 368); read National Catholic Welfare Conference, and not "Council" (p. 381; III, 470, 472), and National Conference of Christians and Jews, not "Jews and Christians" (p. 391); Pius IX's reign was from 1846 to 1878, not 1848–1871 (p. 393). Great Britain has no "diplomatic interchange" with the Vatican (p. 412) since the representative of the Holy See in London is an apostolic delegate, not a nuncio; there is no such thing as the "Catholic Social Welfare Council" (pp. 414, 378–379); what is meant is likely the Social Action Department of the National Catholic Welfare Conference. The Confraternity of Christian Doctrine's edition of the Old Testament cannot be spoken of as having "been issued since" (p. 566) as its first books were scheduled for publication only in 1952. Francesco Satolli was an archbishop, not a cardinal on his visit to the United States in 1892 (p. 652); Dr. Edward McGlynn died in 1900, not 1899 (p. 653). The Archdiocese of Washington was erected on July 29, 1939, and not in 1948; an Archbishop of Washington was named on November 27, 1947, not 1948, and he is "chancellor" and not "rector" of the Catholic University of America (p. 662 n.). The convent inspection bill in Massachusetts came in 1855, not "shortly before 1850" (p. 737); Cardinal Spellman was born in 1889, not 1887 (p. 744); and the date of the letter of King to Seward was 1867, not 1887 (p. 764, n. 310).

Volume III: Benedict XV's letter to the American hierarchy was dated April 10, 1919, not April 19 (p. 11); for "Amieto" read "Amleto" in the first name of the Apostolic Delegate to the United States (p. 12); *Rerum novarum* was published in 1891, not 1899; Elizabeth Seton died in 1821, not 1810, and it is not so clear that it was she who established "the first completely free parochial school" in the United States (p. 33); mention is made of four Catholic chaplains as having served in the Mexican War at the top of page 112 and the number is given as three at the bottom of the same page; the Second Plenary Council was held in 1866, not 1870 (p. 411); Thomas Bouquillon's work on education was a pamphlet, not a book, and John J. Keane was then a bishop, not a monsignor (p. 473); the expression in regard to the papal letter on the Fairbault-Stillwater schools was "tolerari posse," not "tolerari possi" (p. 474); it was forty-one years from Dr. Stokes' publication date for Cardinal Gibbons' article in the *North American Review* of March, 1909, not "a quarter of a century ago" (p. 646); the New York Catholic paper was the *Freeman's Journal*, not the *Freedman's Journal* (p. 752, n. 97).

SAINT PATRICK IN AMERICA

Permit me at the outset to make clear certain limitations that have been set to this paper. I confess that when Archbishop John C. McQuaid of Dublin first suggested to me the title 'Saint Patrick in North America,' I felt a trifle dismayed at the thought of being held responsible either for

Canada or for our Latin brothers south of the American border. But His Grace quickly relieved my embarrassment by stating that it was understood I should devote most of the time at my disposal to the role played by the Irish and their descendants in the development and shaping of American Catholicism as we know it today. I was relieved for several reasons, the principal one being my lack of acquaintance with the Irish in Mexico and Canada. That certain Irishmen appeared at a very early date in Latin America, I was, indeed, aware; for example, Father Achilles Holden,[1] who was a teacher in the cathedral school of Santo Domingo in 1525, only fourteen years after Pope Julius II had erected the first dioceses in the new world, and twelve years before Henry VIII was declared by act of parliament head of the Church of Ireland. Moreover, during the succeeding 300 years Holden's fellow countrymen who followed after him in Latin America formed a numerous company whose labors constitute a chapter in its own right in the history of Irish missionary endeavor.

In regard to Canada I feel that I must be even more discreet since Uncle Sam is under rather heavy fire these days from his northern neighbors for what is described as the American tendency to take Canada for granted, or for what is worse, namely, submerging that fair land beneath an incessant flood of propaganda, salesmanship, and other less happy by-products of the American way of life. Consequently, I do not wish to add to my Canadian brothers' sense of grievance by presuming either to speak in their name or to slight the significant contribution which those of Irish blood have made to the rise and spread of Catholicism in English-speaking Canada. From the very earliest English settlements the Irish figured prominently in what came to be called British North America. Thus it was Edmund Burke, born in County Kildare in 1753, who became Canada's first English-speaking bishop as Vicar Apostolic of Nova Scotia. Nor has the influence of the Irish and their descendants slackened since that early time, as was evident in Toronto on May 31 of 1961 when James Cardinal McGuigan consecrated Father George B. Flahiff, Superior General of the Basilian Fathers, as the new Archbishop of Winnipeg.

In the 175 years that have elapsed, therefore, since John Carpenter,

---

[1] Archives of the Indies, Contaduria, #1050. The writer wishes to thank his friend, the Reverend Antonine Tibesar, O.F.M., of the Academy of American Franciscan History, for his kindness in supplying this reference.

Archbishop of Dublin, counseled Father Burke to direct his priestly labors toward the English missions in Canada, the Irish have written there — as they have in every land where the English language is spoken — a story which scarcely finds a parallel among the smaller nations of Catholic Christendom. And if in the course of the nineteenth century they went in greater numbers to the United States than they did to Canada, it was due in no small measure to the fact — as James Doyle, the famous Bishop of Kildare, perceived — that the letters written back to loved ones here in Ireland offered a brighter promise from the former than from the latter country. "The feeling of comfort," Doyle told a parliamentary commission of inquiry in 1830, "and the conviction that the family on removing to America would be happy, has been more strongly expressed in those coming from the United States than in those from our colonies."[2] Now may I add a final limitation? It is about the Catholic Irish and their descendants that I wish to speak, and not about the so-called Scotch Irish who, to be sure, often played a leading part in American affairs, but who came of a religious tradition other than the one that has brought us to Dublin for this Patrician Congress.

Precisely when the first Irishman set foot on the soil of what was to become the United States, will probably never be known. Many years ago a careful scholar concluded that though proof was lacking for the assertion that Saint Brendan had reached America, his story "was one of the moving causes that led Columbus to the discovery of the New World."[3] In any case, more than a thousand years lay between the holy Abbot of Clonfert and the first recorded presence of an Irish missionary in the future United States. At a time when the Catholic cause in Ireland had become closely linked to Spain, with Spanish troops fighting on the side of Hugh O'Neill in the Tyrone War against the forces of Elizabeth I, many Irish found their way to Spain in one guise or another. Among them was Richard Artur, who joined the Spanish army and fought in Italy and Flanders before he decided to become a priest. Following his ordination he served for a time as a military chaplain,

---

[2] *Parliamentary Papers, 1830 Reports from the Committees on the State of the Poor in Ireland* (London, 1830), VII, 396. Bishop Doyle gave testimony on June 3, 4, 5, 1830, and his answers to the questions put to him will be found in this volume at pp. 390–434 and 445–64.

[3] Joseph Dunn, "The Brendan Problem," *Catholic Historical Review*, VI (January, 1921), 470.

and when King Philip II was seeking a priest to accompany Gonzalo Méndez de Canzo, the newly appointed Governor of Florida, it was Father Artur who was chosen. Arriving in June, 1597, he was installed as pastor of St. Augustine, first of the more than 17,000 parishes that to-day make up the American Church, a post that he filled along with that of vicar general for the Bishop of Santiago de Cuba, to whose diocese Florida then belonged.[4]

That there is relatively little extant evidence of Catholic Irishmen in England's colonies up to the time of the American Revolution will occasion no surprise. Few had either the wish or the courage to risk their fortune, however small it may have been, in so unfriendly an atmosphere. Two brief examples of the kind of fleeting reference to the Irish Catholics that one meets in colonial America will illustrate the point. When Saint Isaac Jogues spent some time in what is today New York before he sailed back to France in November, 1643, he found there only two Catholics, one a Portuguese woman and the other a man who was described as an Irish Catholic from Virginia who made his confession to the future martyr.[5] Even in Maryland life was not long happy for the Catholics, among whom was a small number of Irish families such as that of Charles Carroll, the attorney general, who had left his ancestral home in King's County, Ireland, in 1685, studied law in London, and migrated to America three years later. Carroll was a man who was not easily daunted, and consequently, in spite of all the hardships imposed on the Catholics after the so-called 'glorious revolution,' he held on and raised a family from whom there issued a grandson who signed the Declaration of Inde-

---

[4] Maynard Geiger, O.F.M., *The Franciscan Conquests of Florida, 1573–1618* (Washington, 1937), pp. 71–75. The only Irish-born Jesuit whose name is found in the lists of those who came to the English missions in North America and the neighboring islands was Christopher Bathe, who was born in 1621, entered the Society of Jesus in 1643, was at Liège with his studies finished in 1652, and was sent thereafter to St. Christopher Island [St. Kitts]. Cf. Henry Foley, S.J., *Records of the English Province of the Society of Jesus* (London, 1878), VII, Part 4, 44, where the appendix of Irish-born Jesuits compiled by Edmund Hogan, S.J., speaks of Bathe as '*ingenium valde bonum.*' The next Irish-born Jesuit in the United States to appear in the list was Peter James Kenny (1779–1841) who came first in 1819 as visitor for the general of the Society, and who returned on a similar mission in 1830 and remained until 1835; he died in Rome. Cf. Foley, *op. cit.,* VII, Part 4, 85–86.

[5] Reuben Gold Thwaites (Ed.), *The Jesuit Relations and Allied Documents* (Cleveland, 1898), XXXI, 99. This relation of 1647 by Jerome Lalemant, S.J., includes Jogues' own account of his experiences with the Mohawks and the Dutch.

pendence in 1776 as well as a distant cousin who became the first Archbishop of Baltimore.

Few Irish, however, had either the prestige or the wealth of Carroll, the attorney general, and thus when the penal age descended upon Maryland at the same time that it began in Ireland, there was every reason for them to remain away. The spirit of Maryland's rulers at the time may be gauged in the law of October 3, 1704, which levied a fine of twenty shillings for every Irish servant brought into the colony, an action that was necessary, it was said, "to prevent the importing of too great a number of Irish Papists into this province."[6] Even this measure did not still the fears of the majority; and two years later John Seymour, Governor of Maryland, was still fretting over the Irish threat to the colony when he observed that most of the white servants being brought into Maryland were, as he described them, "generally Irish Papists who are induced to come hither by the false tho' specious Pretences, of the free Exercise of their Superstitious Worship. . . ."[7] Under this type of regime the Catholics continued to live up to 1776, with the result that the eighteenth century was about as dismal a time for the few Irish in the American colonies as it was for their coreligionists here at home.

But the rebellion of the colonists broke more than the chains that had bound them to the mother country; it was likewise the signal for the ultimate collapse of a judicial system that had denied to Catholics both their political and religious freedom. The story of Irish participation in the American Revolution is too well known to bear repetition here. Suffice it to say, when the struggle had been won and the government of the infant republic had been launched, the Catholics, like other religious groups, addressed a formal message of congratulation to the first president. In Washington's reply of March 12, 1790, he not only thanked the four gentlemen — two of whom had been born in Ireland — who had signed the address in the name of their coreligionists, but he stated that he presumed their fellow citizens "will not forget the patriotic part which you took in the accomplishment of their Revolution, and the establish-

[6] William Hand Browne (Ed.), *Archives of Maryland. Proceedings and Acts of the General Assembly of Maryland. September, 1704–April, 1706* (Baltimore, 1906), XXVI, 349.

[7] *Ibid.*, XXVI, 568–69.

[8] "The Catholics' Congratulations to President Washington, 1789, and His Reply, March 12, 1790," John Tracy Ellis (Ed.), *Documents of American Catholic History* (Milwaukee, 1956), p. 176.

ment of their government. . . ."[8] It was the affirmation, so to speak, of the era of genuine liberty that was dawning for Catholics in the new nation; and among the first to avail themselves of the opportunity to pass through the gates now opened wide upon the oppressed of every land, were the Irish.

When I first undertook this assignment I confess that I had a temptation to try a quick survey of all the contributions made by those of Irish birth and descent to American public life, as well as to recount the dominant role they assumed in the development of the Catholic Church soon after the beginning of heavy immigration in the 1830's. But a second thought was wiser than the first, for I soon realized that the subject was much too vast to be treated in a general way; and I have confined myself, therefore, to three aspects of American Catholic life which, I hope, may convey some idea of what the Irish element has meant to the Church in the United States. It is a hazardous undertaking to be sure, since so much must remain unsaid; and I fully agree with the judgment of a specialist in American-Irish history who, in speaking of the Irish influence on American institutions, once remarked, "There is no scale delicate enough to weigh such subtle and complex phenomena. . . ."[9] Yet limitation there must be, and thus, for whatever they may be worth, here are the three points to which I shall adhere in what follows: 1) relations of Church and State; 2) relationship between clergy and laity; and 3) attitude toward vocations to the priesthood and to the religious life.

It would be a grave misreading of the conditions that governed the relationship of Church and State in the early days of the United States were one to imply that their legal separation came about as the result of Irish influence. Actually, separation of the two was embodied in the first article of the Bill of Rights which was declared in force in 1791, in order to avoid anything like the established church that some of the founding fathers had known in Virginia and other colonies. It was likewise an outgrowth of the presence at the time of the Constitution's adoption of numerous churches and religious bodies among whom the framers of the new nation's fundamental law did not wish to show any choice or preference. In that sense separation of Church and State was a necessity springing from the pluralist character of the society of which the new republic was composed.

During the first seventy years of organized national life, that is, from

[9] William Forbes Adams, *Ireland and Irish Emigration to the New World from 1815 to the Famine* (New Haven, 1932), p. 351.

the adoption of the Bill of Rights (1791) to the outbreak of the Civil War (1861), the largest single increase made to the American Catholic community was that of Irish immigrants, the sheer force of whose numbers gave them as early as 1840 a decisive voice in ecclesiastical affairs. Had the Irish been hostile to the separation of Church and State, it would have meant no substantial change in that system; but it would certainly have made it much more difficult for the Church to adjust itself to an environment that was altogether strange to anything that the Holy See had ever before experienced. But that the Irish did, indeed, take readily to the general lines of the politico-religious framework in which their lives were cast, is well known. The reasons for this quick acceptance are not difficult to determine; and the statements of two Irish-born bishops in the year 1835, the one living in the United States, the other in Ireland, will help to explain why this was so.

In February of that year John England, Bishop of Charleston, whose forceful personality during fifteen years residence in the country had made him the most authoritative voice to those of Irish blood, told his fellow Corkonian, Michael O'Connor, Vice Rector of the Irish College in Rome:

The Irish are easily amalgamated with the Americans. Their principles, their dispositions, their politics, their notions of government, their language and their appearance become American very quickly, and they praise and prefer America to their oppressors at home.[10]

But if this happy transition to the customs and institutions of the Irishmen's adopted country was a genuine fact, it was due in no small measure to the tradition that had long been a part of their lives in the land of their birth. How that tradition was fixed in the Irish mind was well illustrated some months after Bishop England's affirmation concerning Irish assimilation in the United States. In July, 1835, Edward Nolan, Bishop of Kildare, had as his guest at Carlow a young man destined to win lasting fame in both the old and the new world for his acute observations on political and social institutions, namely, Alexis de Tocqueville. During their discussion of conditions in Ireland at that time, the curious Frenchman asked many questions, among which was this one: "Would you like a grant of money from the State?" His host answered, "No, certainly

[10] England to O'Connor, Charleston, February 25, 1835, Peter Guilday, *The Life and Times of John England, First Bishop of Charleston, 1786–1824* (New York, 1927), I, 481.

not. In general we are opposed to any link between Church and State."[11] In that brief but unhesitating reply there was embodied not only the view of most Irishmen of Bishop Nolan's generation, but that of their parents and grandparents as well.

It was that kind of background, therefore, that accompanied men like Bishop England to the United States, and during the succeeding decades they helped to fix the pattern of Catholic acceptance of separation between the Church and the State. In fact, before England had been more than a few years in his new home, he told Daniel O'Connell, ". . . I am convinced that a total separation from the temporal government, is the most natural and safest for the church in any place where it is not, as in the papal territory, a complete government of churchmen."[12] Such, too, was the view of the prelate who became the acknowledged leader of the Irish in the American Church after England's death. John Hughes, born in County Tyrone, and named by Pope Pius IX as the first Archbishop of New York, made his position clear in a public address in 1841, at a time when the Catholics of the United States were under fire for their alleged intrigues to bring about a union of Church and State. Hughes urged all American religious groups to alert themselves to the mutual protection of their rights. "No matter what sect is assailed," he said, "extend to it, in common with all your fellow citizens, a protecting hand. If the Jew is oppressed, then stand by the Jew. Thus will all be secured alike in the common enjoyment of the blessings of civil and religious liberty, and the justly obnoxious union of Church and State be most effectively prevented."[13]

In this manner, then, was there gradually imprinted on the American Catholic mind and heart — and that, it should be emphasized, with the full co-operation and assistance of the other national groups that composed the Catholic community — a preference for the relationship of Church and State as they experienced it in the Republic of the West. It was a view that received, according to most American Catholics, its classic expression, so to speak, at Rome in March, 1887, in a sermon

[11] J. P. Mayer (Ed.), *Alexis de Tocqueville. Journeys to England and Ireland.* Translated by George Lawrence and K. P. Mayer (New Haven, 1958), p. 133.

[12] England to O'Connell, Charleston, September 17, 1825, Sebastian G. Messner (Ed.), *The Works of the Right Reverend John England, First Bishop of Charleston* (Cleveland, 1908), VI, 77.

[13] Speech in Washington Hall, New York, June 1, 1841, Lawrence Kehoe (Ed.), *Complete Works of the Most Rev. John Hughes, Archbishop of New York* (New York, 1865), I, 269.

heard in the Basilica of Santa Maria in Trastevere. James Gibbons, American-born churchman of immigrant parents from County Mayo, in taking possession on that day of his titular church, declared:

For myself, as a citizen of the United States without closing my eyes to our defects as a nation, I proclaim, with a deep sense of pride and gratitude, and in this great capital of Christendom, that I belong to a country where the civil government holds over us the aegis of its protection without interfering in the legitimate exercise of our sublime mission as ministers of the Gospel of Jesus Christ.[14]

And such has remained the mind of Gibbons' fellow Catholics throughout the three-quarters of a century since the Cardinal of Baltimore spoke those memorable words. Unquestionably this influence has been noteworthy, even if it may not in the end prove to have altogether the far-reaching effects envisioned by a writer in the *Times Literary Supplement* who stated, ". . . it was in the Irish form that Catholicism was to be carried to the new world — to Australia as well as to America — and this is almost beyond doubt destined profoundly to influence the whole future history of the world."[15]

The second point in which, it seems to me, the Irish have made a conspicuous contribution to the fashioning of the Catholicism of my country, is the relationship that obtains between the clerical and lay members of the Church. Here again the problem had deep historical roots. This audience needs no reminder of the role played by the clergy in the darkest hours of Irish laymen's lives, whether that be the deadly calm to which they were reduced amid the degradation of the eighteenth century, or the series of sharp crises through which they passed in the years leading up to and during the great famine of the 1840's. Even a decade before the famine struck, the closely knit clerical-lay ties were already a matter of common observation and — one may add — of frequent and vain attempts on the part of politicians to sever the link that bound them to each other. Thus when de Tocqueville asked his host at Carlow in 1835 if he thought the clergy should receive an allowance from the English government, the Bishop of Kildare was quick to reply:

No. The Catholic clergy would then lose their influence over the people. I do not know what is suitable for other countries, but I do not doubt that in

[14] *Catholic Mirror* (Baltimore), April 2, 1887.

[15] Unsigned review of Kenneth Scott Latourette, *Christianity in a Revolutionary Age*, Volume III (London, 1961), *Times Literary Supplement* (May 26, 1961), 327.

Ireland the clergy would lose a great deal by the change, and that religion itself might suffer. Clergy and people in this country are unbelievably united.[16]

Among characteristics that marked the conduct of the Irish who crossed the sea was this same unity of priest and people that defied the stratagems of hostile elements to destroy. Indeed, it provided one of the most constant objects of grievance for those intent to bar the Catholic alien from citizenship in the new land. I do not mean to suggest, of course, that this relationship was never marred by tension or at times even by bitter strife. But it would be a mistake to regard those laymen who rose against their bishops and priests in the stormy days of what is known in the history of the American Church as lay trusteeism, as anything but a noisy minority. Far more typical of the laity's attitude of that period of more than a century ago was the alacrity with which those of Irish birth and descent rallied to the call of John Hughes and saved the ecclesiastical properties of New York which were threatened with destruction by the same mob violence that had brought disaster to Philadelphia's Catholics in the spring of 1844.

In the United States, as in Ireland, the priest was the impoverished immigrants' best friend; and during the trying years before the Civil War when the Catholic laity were still far removed from the position of strength they were destined to achieve by the end of the century, there was forged between them and their priests a union that has endured to our own time. Aside from the few involved in the angry episodes of lay trusteeism, it would be unthinkable, therefore, that the pastor of an American church whose parishioners were predominantly of Irish blood should find it necessary to inform his bishop, as did a pastor in Paterson, New Jersey, in the closing decade of the century, that his people were, as he expressed it, "full of mistrust" toward their priest by reason of the evil influence of the secret societies in their land of origin. "The mistrust towards the Priest of these poor people is something horrible," said this pastor of a predominantly Latin flock, "there must be something horribly wrong where they come from."[17]

There was much, indeed, that was wrong where the Irish had come from, but it was not the kind of thing that the worried pastor in Pater-

[16] Mayer, *op. cit.*, p. 132.

[17] Archives of the Archdiocese of Newark, Letter File, 1894–1898, John B. Kayser to Winand M. Wigger, Paterson, January 15, 1894, Carl D. Hinrichsen, "The Diocese of Newark, 1872–1901," p. 288, an unpublished doctoral dissertation, the Catholic University of America (1963).

son, New Jersey, was experiencing in 1894. While it would be easy to exaggerate the harmony that marked the relations of the clergy and laity of Irish descent in the United States, it has, nonetheless, been very real, and acute observers of American Catholicism who are neither American nor Irish have detected it and have sensed the source from which it sprang. The distinguished English philosopher of history, Christopher Dawson, for example, speaks of the influence of the Irish immigrants on the American Church. He says, "they brought with them from their native land that tradition of solidarity between priest and people which has been the common characteristic of American and Irish Catholicism."[18]

I need hardly say that American Catholics are grateful to Ireland for this contribution, and for that reason we are extremely anxious that this tradition should be able to withstand the pressures, changing circumstances, and ideas of a new day when the laity are very much better educated than they were a century, or even a generation, ago. This single circumstance — together with the Holy See's extraordinary emphasis in recent years on the role of the laity in the life of the Church — has already occasioned signs of strain here and there. They have raised a question in the minds of some as to whether the clerical-lay relationship of the nineteenth century is sufficiently flexible and resilient to make the adjustments that must inevitably ensue if we of this second half of the twentieth century are to meet the demands of our time. Whether or not this will take place, we do not know. One can only express the prayerful wish that the wonderfully fruitful union of these two divisions of the army of the Church Militant may be preserved, and that they may march side by side, as they have done for a century or more, through the dangerous days that lie ahead for all who cherish the Catholic heritage and name.

That brings us to the third and final point, namely, the attitude of the Irish toward vocations to the priesthood and to the religious life. Few factors are of more importance in the cultivation of a 'vocation,' as that term is understood in the Catholic sense, than the attitude of the parents

[18] Christopher Dawson, *The Crisis of Western Education* (New York, 1961), pp. 91–92. Dawson attributes the democratic tone of Catholicism in the United States to this same cause. He says, "Thus the democratic character of American Catholicism, which is the first thing that strikes the foreign observer, is not entirely a product of American conditions, but owes its basic character to its Irish inheritance" (p. 92).

and guardians of the young. And the pride and joy felt by Irish parents, grandparents, and other relatives of a boy or girl who elects to become a priest or a religious, are proverbial and held to account in part for the altogether unusual number of Irish youths who dedicate their lives to the service of religion. It was not always so among their ancestors, for one of the many piquant insights given by Saint Patrick in his 'Confession' was in connection with his mention of the young girls who came to him for the purpose of enlisting as virgins in the army of Christ. "Not that their fathers agree with them," said Patrick, "no — they often even suffer persecution and undeserved reproaches from their parents; and yet their number is ever increasing."[19] But in the course of the great missionary's apostolate that attitude changed, for Patrick would seem to have possessed a special grace for transforming the elders' reluctance on this score into an attitude of joy that still endures. It is doubtful if any people in the Catholic Church have given a higher proportion of their sons and daughters to religion than the Irish, and certainly no people has felt so much joy in doing so.

I hasten to say that the abundant vocations of the American Church are not unique with those of Irish descent, for the Germans, Poles, Italians, and other national groups have likewise contributed their share. But that it should have been thought a peculiarly Irish characteristic by many was due, I suppose, to their prominence, if not their preponderance, in the Catholic community for so long a time. In the estimated total net Catholic immigration of 9,318,494 who entered the United States during the century from 1820 to 1920, 2,248,435 or approximately twenty-five percent were from Ireland.[20] Moreover, by the mid-century the Irish had begun their steady climb toward high positions in both public and ecclesiastical life; and in 1853 James Campbell of Pennsylvania, son of immigrant parents, became the first Irish Catholic to be named to the president's cabinet when Franklin Pierce appointed him Postmaster General of the United States. In less than a generation William R. Grace, born in County Cork, became in 1880 the first Irishman to be elected Mayor of New York. Four years later Hugh O'Brien won the same office in Boston, to be followed there two decades later by John F. Fitzgerald, grandfather of President Kennedy. Moreover, of

[19] Ludwig Bieler (Trans. and Ed.), "Confession," *The Works of St. Patrick* (Westminster, Maryland, 1953), p. 34.

[20] For Catholic population figures cf. Gerald Shaughnessy, S.M., *Has the Immigrant Kept the Faith?* (New York, 1925), *passim.*

the 532 bishops who ruled the American Church in the 150 years between the nomination of John Carroll as first Bishop of Baltimore in 1789 and the hierarchy's sesquicentennial in 1939, those of Irish birth numbered 100 and slightly over 200 other bishops bore distinctly Irish names.[21] Is it any wonder, then, with so many of their countrymen doing remarkably well in both Church and State, that the former should at times have been spoken of as the 'Irish' Church, and that wide circulation should have been given to an Irish bull to the effect that "The only place in Ireland where a man can make a fortune is in America."[22]

America was, indeed, the land of Irish fortune in more ways than one, and not the least of these was the personal freedom with which it endowed many who had never known it before. How many thousands there must have been who echoed the sentiment of the farm laborer who in 1854 described for his friend in County Kildare how well he had prospered in Illinois, so well, in fact, that by the following spring he expected to purchase his own farm. "Come to this country," he wrote, "and I know you will do well — one thing is certain you can be your own master a good deal sooner."[23] And what man is there — be he Greek or Chinese or Irish — who does not long to be his own master? Nonconformists the Irish were when American customs and beliefs cut across allegiance to their religious faith, or when such national institutions as the Puritan sabbath struck them as unnecessarily lugubrious in the pall it cast over their weekly day of rest. But no group of immigrants conformed more wholeheartedly than the sons of Erin to the basic institutions of democratic government that they found in the new world. As a convert priest of New England background remarked about the Irish immigrants in 1855, at heart they had never accepted the constitution of England; but the American Constitution they had themselves chosen. And he continued:

They have resolved to live under it, and to die under it. They have sworn fealty to it. They revere it, and will stand by it. They will defend it against all enemies, and if need be, will die for it.[24]

[21] For data on the bishops of the United States cf. Joseph B. Code (Ed.), *Dictionary of the American Hierarchy* (New York, 1940), although this work has to be used with caution because of numerous errors.

[22] Quoted in Arnold Schrier, *Ireland and the American Emigration, 1850–1900* (Minneapolis, 1958), p. 20.

[23] Bartholomew Colgan to friend, Elmwood, Illinois, December 20, 1854, *ibid.*, p. 24.

[24] George Foxcroft Haskins, *Travels in England, France, Italy, and Ireland* (Boston, 1856), p. 287.

As a matter of fact, the Irish in the United States responded with tremendous zest to the kind of democracy which D. W. Brogan has described as "the maximizing of the area of uncoerced choice. . . ."[25] By the hundreds of thousands they flocked to the polls on election days, and by their special genius for political organization they helped to direct the course of the Democratic Party which had shown them a far more friendly countenance than was true of its traditional rival. Anti-English they certainly were, and in this respect they probably influenced American policy more than most men realize. But they never wavered in their loyalty to the fundamental tenets of the American political creed; and in the words of a non-Catholic historian who attempted an assessment of their place in his county's life, "Their services to the cause of democracy are unquestionable."[26]

Like the rest of the English-speaking world, the United States has been the beneficiary of Ireland's extraordinary outpouring of priestly and religious vocations, and only the recording angel knows exactly how many have gone from this island to the American mission field. Virtually every institution and religious community of the Irish Church has sent its quota as, for example, All Hallows College in Dublin which has educated fourteen bishops and 1,076 priests for the missions of the United States. Yet at the present time the more than 55,000 priests, the nearly 11,000 brothers, and the more than 170,000 sisters who staff the Church's works are far from sufficient for its expanding needs. In spite of that fact, however, these numbers constitute an impressive proof of the viability of Catholicism in its American setting. As I said before, the abundance of vocations must not be attributed exclusively to those of Irish blood, since the sons and daughters of the multiple national strains that make up the American Catholic community have likewise furnished their proportion of the whole. Up to recent years, however, those of Irish background have, perhaps, supplied the largest single contingent of vocations, although there are certain signs that indicate that this pre-eminence is now passing.

Of the more than 235,000 American priests and religious of today slightly over 7,000 are in the foreign missions, a relatively small figure, to be sure, in comparison to Ireland's notable contribution to that sacred cause. But as in so many other ways, so in this, we Americans are still

[25] D. W. Brogan, *America in the Modern World* (New Brunswick, 1960), p. 24.
[26] Adams, *op. cit.*, p. 376.

young and must be given time. In that connection, it is worthy of mention that in June, 1961, the first native American society for the foreign missions marked its golden jubilee at Maryknoll, New York. Maryknoll now constitutes, with its nearly 900 priests, 160 or more brothers, over 1,200 sisters — together with their novices and postulants — a religious family of over 3,500 Americans dedicated to the foreign mission ideal. I trust that this mention of a particular group will not be taken amiss by the numerous other congregations and societies of the Church of the United States who are serving so devotedly in the missions of the universal Church. My reasons for singling out Maryknoll are, first, its pioneer status as a native American missionary group; secondly, its jubilee which gladdens all American Catholics; and finally, the fact that it seems fitting to mention here a society whose two founders blended so happily the apostolic efforts of one of the finest products of Irish immigrant stock with one of the best types of native Protestant lineage, for the parents of Father James A. Walsh were both born in County Cork, while those of Father Thomas F. Price were converts from the Protestant Episcopal and Methodist faiths.

In Maryknoll, and in all its sister American missionary groups, then, there is found a living demonstration of the fact that Saint Patrick's message brought to Ireland over 1,500 years ago has also had a faithful transplantation in the United States. Just as Columban, Gall, and their contemporaries enriched the continent with the precious heritage that Parick had willed to them when Christendom was young, so in a far more remote time and place his bequest is still a living force among the descendants of his spiritual children who crossed the sea. It is found in the souls of many of the more than 130,000 converts who entered the Church in the United States in 1960 through the ministration and example of priests, religious, and laity of Irish ancestry; it is felt in the lives of numerous American-Irish who staff foreign mission stations around the world; and it is cherished as well by thousands of those who man the parishes and ecclesiastical institutions at home. Thus in the United States — as in other lands far distant from Ireland — men and women of apostolic vision in the second half of the twentieth century are still motivated by something of the holy compulsion of which Saint Patrick wrote in the fifth century, and in paraphrase of his moving 'Confession' we may say of them that

regardless of danger. . . . [they] make known the gift of God and everlasting consolation, without fear and frankly [they] spread everywhere the
name of God so that after [their] decease [they] may leave a bequest to
their brethren and sons whom they have baptized in the Lord. . . .[27]

AMERICAN CATHOLICISM IN 1960:
AN HISTORICAL PERSPECTIVE

Within the last few decades American Catholics have so frequently been
told that both their Church and their country have entered the age of
maturity that they are no longer disposed to question it. On December
18, 1959, when Pope John XXIII presided at the ceremony that proclaimed Elizabeth Seton, the native-born convert from Protestant Epis-
copalianism, a "venerable servant of God," who had practiced virtue to
an heroic degree, the pontiff, too, alluded to our changed status in speaking of this nation as having "passed its time of development," and having
approached what he termed "full maturity in national and international
service." About the fact, then, there is no serious dispute; but as to its
implications, there is less accord.

What is the present position of the American Catholic community
from the viewpoint of an historical perspective? The words "historical
perspective" open such immense vistas and embrace so vast an area of
subject matter, that I shall have to restrict myself severely to tracing a
few general features of the past that have helped to make us American
Catholics what we are today, and then dwell in more detail on one or
two matters which, in my judgment, have particular relevance for the
present hour.

As Americans we are accustomed, and rightly so, to think of our country as having launched something new in the world of government and
political institutions at the end of the eighteenth century. But as Catholics we may not, perhaps be as aware as we should be that the Church
likewise inaugurated something altogether new to its own experience
when at the same time it erected here the first diocese in 1789 and chose

[27] Bieler, *op. cit.*, p. 25.

54

a native-born American to govern it as the first bishop. Never before in its nearly 1800 years of history had the Church of Rome been confronted with the task of establishing itself in a democratic republic over 3,000 miles away, the overwhelming majority of whose nearly 4,000,000 inhabitants were committed to the Protestant faith, and whose government was based on a constitution and bill of rights that, while providing for a separation of Church and State, at the same time gave complete freedom of worship and liberty of action to the roughly 30,000 adherents of Rome's ancient Catholic faith.

And if the political and social structure of the new republic of the West was curious and strange to the Holy See, so, too, was the intellectual milieu in which the tiny Catholic minority began their corporate existence. It must be kept in mind that they were then only emerging for the first time as freemen from the fetters of the penal legislation that had held them outlaws through most of America's colonial past. They were in need of guidance, and yet they could find no precedents by which to chart their course among their coreligionists abroad. For at the very time that the lines of Catholic development in this country were beginning to form, the Catholics of Ireland, France, and the German world, and, in fact, of most of western Europe, were experiencing — along with their countrymen of other faiths — the strong currents of the romantic movement. We are all conscious of the varied connotations that have attached to the word "romanticism," but I am not here concerned with its conflicting meanings. I merely wish to suggest that in the age when Burke gave forceful expression to the best in the aristocratic way of life and the lyrics of Thomas Moore sang of the glories of the Irish race, when Chateaubriand awakened in French hearts a vision of their past, when Friedrich and August von Schlegel laid the foundation for a new school of thought among the Germans, when the novels of Scott made the Middle Ages come alive again for the English-speaking public; when, in other words, Europe's intellectual climate was conducive to a nostalgia for the departed ways of a Catholic society, or of a social order informed by Catholic principles, there was no parallel movement on this side of the Altantic. That is not to say that there were then no literary traditions, no artistic taste, no cultivated élite in the United States to foster the movements of the mind. For who does not remember Van Wyck Brooks' charming evocation of the Bostonians at whose tables, as he said, there met

. . . from week to week, members of the German and Russian legations, Spanish grandees and Danish princes, Chancellor Kent from New York and Lafayette, scientists and historians from England.[1]

But though the Catholics of that time had, indeed, a highly cultivated leader in the French-born Jean Cheverus, Boston's first bishop, neither in Boston nor in Baltimore did Catholics — save for an exceptional Cheverus or Carroll — have admittance to the circles where, both in politics and in letters, the American mind was being shaped.

Yet if there was no "romantic age" for Catholicism in this country, there was an heroic one in the struggle and ordeal of bishops, priests, and laymen who, striving amid an unfriendly environment to achieve the well nigh impossible goal of providing a Catholic setting for the millions of immigrants who landed on these shores, knew substantial success. And if they sometimes stumbled as they went forward along their uncharted course, they attained their principal goal in preserving for the majority of their impoverished charges the essentials of their religious faith. It must ever remain, therefore, one of our prime duties as Catholics of this age of affluence to enshrine the names and achievements of the relatively few leaders who reached a measure of fame, and of their countless and nameless followers, in our grateful memory. Without them, many of us would not so much as own the faith today, and for that alone they are entitled to an enduring remembrance.

But the "heroic age" for Catholicism in the United States is now, too, a matter of history, and we stand on the threshold of another act in the ceaselessly unfolding drama of the Church's life in this land. The period that is now closed, call it "heroic," or term it the age of the immigrant, as you will, took its heaviest toll in physical energy, sacrificial generosity, and raw courage. We are not beyond the time — nor, please God, shall we ever be — when to some degree, energy, sacrifice, and courage shall be expected of us. But no Catholic of the 1960's who has acquaintance with the history of the American Church will gainsay the fact that the demands made upon us in physical energy, financial sacrifice, and bold courage can in any way match those of our forebears in the faith. Primarily, these are not the qualities that are demanded of us in this new time; and it is rather with the sacrifices of our spiritual and intellectual faculties now called for if the Church of our generation is to fulfill its sacred mission, that we wish to concern ourselves in what follows.

[1] *The Flowering of New England, 1815–1865* (New York, 1936), p. 90.

Today's world and today's America have a right to expect from the third most numerous body of Catholics in the universal Church, who are at the same time incomparably the richest and most heavily endowed, a positive contribution to a remedy for the ills that beset them in the atomic age. And lest it be thought that I lack appreciation for what the Catholics of this country have done in a material way to lessen the world's grief and misery, let it be recorded here that the total value of over $800,000,000 in food, clothing, medicines, and other supplies that have been sent since 1943 throughout the world by the Catholic Relief Services, the agency of the American hierarchy, stands unparalleled in the history of man's charity to man. But it is another realm that I have in mind, less tangible, indeed, but, nonetheless, real. I can illustrate what I mean, perhaps, by an incident related to me by a young American priest recently returned from a period of training at the Catholic University of Louvain. He stated that when he called to bid good-by to the rector of the university, the latter was at pains to express the gratitude that the Catholics of the world feel for what we have done for them since World War II, and to say how much they look to us for leadership, and then he added, "You have not disappointed us, save in one respect, in the realm of thought."

If then, we are to make the contribution that is expected of us, it means that we must adjust ourselves to the changed circumstances and alter the kind of thinking that carried us through a less complicated and dangerous time. It is now asked of us that we learn to look beyond the narrow interests of our Catholic body to the interests of those around us, to show a greater sensitivity to relations with our separated brethren of other religious faiths; in a word, what is demanded is a broader understanding of the society of which we form a part, and of the world in which we live. And let it be said that one of the first requirements for a realistic and constructive approach to the innumerable contemporary problems that press more and more insistently for solution, is to have at the outset the humility to confess that often we have no ready-made answers, but that we do possess the will to exert whatever intellectual talent and energy we may have in searching out the answers, in company with our fellow citizens, wherever they may lie.

For the changed role that we are now asked to play, the historical formation we have known in this land of freedom has furnished Catholics with more resources than many of us may realize. Aside from the knowledge and training in a supernatural faith which gives its own unique advantages, we have gleaned from the America in which we have grown up a number of aids that can help to fit us for the tasks ahead. First, as to our political experiences in this country. Needless to say, none of us is unaware that on four or five occasions in the nation's history Catholics have known periods of insult and discrimination at the hands of fellow citizens under one or other of the banners of American nativism. But these have been temporary phenomena, and what is of far greater significance is the fact that we have been spared entirely the type of prolonged exclusion and humiliation endured by Catholics in other lands, in that never has there taken root in this republic an anti-Catholic political party of major proportions and lasting power which was either Protestant, liberal, radical, or revolutionary. Once the colonial penal legislation had been repealed in the original states, the Church had opened before it a free and untrammeled path through the nineteenth century for its schools, its press, and the other manifold expressions of Catholic life that found here a friendly soil in which to grow.

Thus the Catholic, like the Jew, has been able to associate himself with the total American experience in a way that would have been unthinkable for many of his European and Latin American brothers. Washington, Lincoln, and Theodore Roosevelt, for example, are his heroes in a way that Bismarck, Cavour, and Clemenceau could never be for the Catholic of Germany, Italy, or France. Moreover, this freedom — both to think and to act — opened wide to Catholics the doors of political parties, trade unions, fraternal orders, sporting groups, and social and service clubs wherein they mixed with fellow citizens of all religious faiths and of none, in a way that again would have been impossible to many Catholics elsewhere through a great part of the nineteenth century. And by reason of the basically sound philosophy that motivated these various national organizations, and the freedom the Catholic had to associate himself with them, there has never arisen here, as has so often been true abroad, the occasion or the necessity for Catholic political parties or Catholic trade unions. In the spring of 1901, John Ireland was asked by the Bishop of Trenton for his reaction to the latter's proposal for a federation of the Catholic societies of the United States. In his reply to Bishop McFaul, the Archbishop of St. Paul voiced the sentiments of the vast majority of American Catholics then — and now — when he said:

Whatever may be said of a union of Catholic Societies for purely religious, moral and social purposes, a Federation of such Societies for anything bordering in the most remote manner on politics, is to be deprecated. . . . We must admit that there is, alas, among too many of our fellow citizens a hidden dread and hatred of the Catholic Church. . . . A pretext only is needed to bring at any moment into a concrete form this dread and hatred. . . . A Federation with a tinge of politics would give the pretext.[2]

Fourteen years before, at the time of the crisis over Catholic membership in the Knights of Labor, the suggestion was made by certain officials of the Roman Curia that the American Catholic workmen be organized into separate labor groups. Cardinal Gibbons was quick to answer that he did not believe such to be "either possible or necessary" in the United States. Expressing his admiration for efforts of that sort made in lands where the workers had been victimized by the enemies of religion, he added:

. . . but thanks be to God, that is not our condition. We find that in our country the presence and explicit influence of the clergy would not be advisable where our citizens, without distinction of religious belief, come together in regard to their industrial interests alone.

The cardinal frankly confessed the danger in Catholics associating with laborers who might be atheists, communists, and anarchists. But, said Gibbons, "it is one of the trials of faith which our brave American Catholics are accustomed to meet almost daily, and which they know how to disregard with good sense and firmness."[3]

Thanks, therefore, to the favorable circumstances in which they were placed, and to the enlightened leadership which they received at the

[2] Archives of the Archdiocese of St. Paul, Ireland Papers, Ireland to James A. McFaul, St. Paul, March 26, 1901, copy. The author wishes to express his gratitude to the Reverend Patrick H. Ahern of the St. Paul Seminary for his kindness in furnishing copies of the Ireland-McFaul correspondence. Six years before this exchange, in a notable address at Chicago on February 22, 1895, Ireland stated in relation to forming political parties along racial lines: "No encouragement must be given to social and political organizations or methods which perpetuate in this country foreign ideas and customs. An Irish-American, a German-American, or a French-American vote is an intolerable anomaly." John Ireland, "American Citizenship," *The Church and Modern Society. Lectures and Addresses* (St. Paul, 1905), I, 206–07.

[3] The text of Gibbons' memorial to Giovanni Cardinal Simeoni on the Knights of Labor, Rome, February 20, 1887, is in the appendix to Henry J. Browne, *The Catholic Church and the Knights of Labor* (Washington, 1949), p. 365 ff.

outset from prelates such as Archbishop Carroll and later from men like the Cardinal of Baltimore and the Archbishop of St. Paul, by the early years of this century Catholics were not only actively participating in the life of the country's political and industrial institutions, but they had made their presence felt, as a labor historian of the Jewish faith has recently reminded us when he wrote: "The weakness of socialism in the American Federation of Labor at the close of World War I was, in part, a testimonial to the success of the Catholic Church's opposition to this doctrine."[4] Unfortunately, at times Catholic influence in the realm of politics was not on a similarly healthy plane. In still other segments of national affairs, up to this time they had either been denied entry or were not yet ready to play their full role. Meanwhile the Church went quietly on its way engrossed in the gigantic task of making good Americans out of the more than 9,000,000 immigrants who entered its fold before 1920, a task that strained every nerve and resource at its command. But in the end its mission was accomplished so well that an outside observer like Henry Steele Commager remarked that it might, indeed, be maintained that during these years the Catholic Church had been "one of the most effective of all agencies for democracy and Americanization."[5]

In spite of the fact, however, that Catholics' participation in political and industrial activities had in the main stood them in good stead, like Americans in general, their past had not adequately prepared them for the confrontation with the complex problems of World War I, and even less so with those that arose during and after World War II. As one writer has said, it was the first world conflict that brought the "end of American innocence,"[6] and the far more shattering experience that followed twenty years later unsettled our national equilibrium as nothing in the previous century and a half had ever done. While it would be profitable to pursue that theme on the national level, the limitations of this essay leave time to examine only a few of the principal features of Catholic life in these years.

Why, may we ask, did the two world wars find the Catholics of the United States unprepared by training and background for the hectic period into which, along with their countrymen of all faiths, they were

[4] Marc Karson, *American Labor Unions and Politics 1900–1918* (Carbondale, Illinois, 1958), p. 283.

[5] *The American Mind* (New Haven, 1950), p. 193.

[6] Henry F. May, *The End of American Innocence* (New York, 1959), p. 393.

so suddenly thrust? First, the all-absorbing interests of the Church throughout the previous century and down to the 1920's had been largely internal. Catholics' energies had been concentrated on the frantic race to keep abreast of the immigrant flood; to cite only one instance, to establish a school system such as no other Catholic national community had ever attempted. Thus, Catholic leaders, both clerical and lay, manifested relatively little concern for the broad moral and ethical issues that were then beginning to engage the attention of older American groups. In a certain sense, Catholics were, to use Riesman's word, inner-directed, and such their orientation remained until the exigencies of national involvement in the world crisis forced them to look beyond their own horizons.

Secondly, despite the periodic exposé of defects and scandals here and there, the moral and social order seemed substantially sound and stable, and to no appreciable extent did Americans question the principles and postulates on which the nation's churches were sustained, even if many well known public figures failed to live by them. But such a thing as an atheistic, radical, or socialist movement was practically non-existent, and in the reckoning of most Americans up to forty years ago even the threat of it seemed comfortably remote.

A third factor had to do with something that has often been described as peculiarly American. On the eve of an age that was to witness the greatest proliferation of organizational genius that this nation has yet known, Catholics had as yet done nothing to match it. True, the American Federation of Catholic Societies came into being in 1901, but its lack of cohesion and of a unified command made it a relatively ineffective instrument for action on a national scale, and the annual meetings of the metropolitan archbishops that had been taking place since 1890 were but a feeble reflection of ecclesiastical organization as we know it today in the National Catholic Welfare Conference.

Fourthly, the Catholic colleges from which one might naturally expect a trained leadership of superior quality to come, were rising like Topsy all over the land with no planning on even a diocesan scale, to say nothing of heed to national needs, and, it might be added, with little evidence that there was any true comprehension of what the growing commitment to higher education in itself implied. Finally, up to World War II one could not speak of a middle class in terms of significant numbers and strength among Catholic professional men, business executives, technicians, journalists, and educators. As a consequence, the nineteenth century and the first decades of the present century produced an essentially mute laity that made little real contribution on their own, beyond their marvelously generous response in material support to Catholic causes proposed to them by the clergy.

But how different is the picture of American Catholicism today to what it was when the century was young! And for that we must recognize the fact that although Catholics of the preceding age were wanting in many respects, we owe to them the inheritance of a courageous struggle that brought through the basic elements of our present strength. Now an immense and growing Catholic community of near to 45,000,000 Americans no longer answers to what, in the strict sense, is meant by a minority. At every turn one encounters the Church's numerous and impressive institutions, which all Americans know are maintained by the free will offerings of a laity that, allowing for admitted losses, has in the aggregate continued loyal to the faith of their fathers. In recent years the Catholic middle class has shown an almost startling increase, and today that paragon of American success, the millionaire, is no longer a curiosity in their ranks. The change is mirrored in a hundred different ways that could be illustrated from both within and without Catholic ranks. When, for example, in the 1890's there was a question of placing a statue of Jacques Marquette in Statuary Hall of the national capitol, the possessiveness of the Protestant America of those days saw nothing particularly amusing in the following rhyme that appeared in a newspaper of the Middle West:

> O, Nation first rocked on the bosom of God!
> O, Nation whose father the martyr-path trod!
> Preserve the Good Book which the Protestants learn,
> The foundation of wisdom, which priests love to burn,
> We always confess that we owe it a debt,
> And room for a Luther, but not for Marquette.[7]

The spirit that inspired that kind of possessive sense disappeared almost a generation ago. In 1960 the presidential address of Robert T. Handy of Union Theological Seminary, delivered before the American Society of Church History in Chicago, stated that Protestantism had

[7] Quoted from the *Wisconsin Patriot*, 6 June 1896, by K. Gerald Marsden, "Father Marquette and the A.P.A.: An Incident in American Nativism," *Catholic Historical Review*, XLVI (April, 1960), 8, n. 19.

entered the depression of the late 1920's "as the dominant American religious tradition, closely identified with the culture." But as Professor Handy went on to say, "Protestantism emerged from depression no longer in such a position."[8] And one of the most significant and gratifying signs of change to the Catholic American is the altered image of his Church in the minds of Americans of other faiths. The immigrant cast of the Catholic community was likewise shed a generation ago, and with it faded out the perennial cry of "foreignism" which from the birth of the nation was, perhaps, the most meaningful, as it was the most distasteful, charge that Catholics had to bear. But so far, indeed, has this religious community now come that a historian of Congregational background writing in the Yale Review, could say: "Catholicism has at last become a part of American culture."[9]

These things being true, it follows that the Catholic Church now commands a more respectful hearing in this country than it ever did before. But by the same token, it means that this increased respect and prestige carry a corresponding responsibility on the part of Catholic spokesmen. When, for example, leaders of Catholic thought have a message to impart that touches a vital and sacred matter in Catholic dogma or morals, it should be couched in terms that make it clear he appreciates the mixed character of our society and that his directives are addressed to his own coreligionists. In this way basic questions of Catholic belief, such as birth control and censorship of films, will be safeguarded for the Church's faithful, and at the same time their full and candid enunciation will furnish no basis for justifiable irritation on the part of residents of the community who do not share the beliefs of their Catholic neighbors. As several of the writers of the essays in American Catholics: A Protestant-Jewish View, the thoughtful volume edited by Philip Scharper of Sheed and Ward, were at pains to state, no reasonable American will ask that Catholics be silent on the things that pertain to the depositum fidei. The only obligation in that regard that we incur by reason of the pluralistic society of which we form a part, is to state clearly that in matters of this kind we speak to our own, and to others who do not share our Catholic faith but only to the extent in which these are willing to listen but not to be dictated to.

[8] "The American Religious Depression, 1925–1935," Church History, XXIX (March, 1960), 12.

[9] Robert D. Cross, "The Changing Image of Catholicism in America," Yale Review, XLVIII (Summer, 1959), 575.

Far, indeed, from wishing to silence Catholic spokesmen, a growing number of Americans wish very much to know what we have to say about such burning questions as nuclear warfare, the expanding world population, racial relations, the rights of Protestants in so-called Catholic countries, and unethical practices in government, labor unions, and the communication industries. These and a host of other issues now engage the attention of our fellow citizens *vis-à-vis* the Church in a way that was never previously true. That fact represents both a recognition and a challenge. In the nineteenth century Catholicism was respected by many leading Americans largely because it kept the Catholic masses in order as, for example, by Charles Eliot Norton, who was grateful to the Church in Massachusetts for seeing to it that the Irish maids and handymen who labored amid the spacious and scholarly elegance of "Shady Hill," the Norton estate, did not thieve at their employer's expense. Now, however, the Church is seen as something more than the policeman of an immigrant flock. In a word, since Catholics are today accepted as part of the national scene, it is anticipated that they will show evidence of mature knowledge and objective judgment on the problems of contemporary society such as were reflected in the resolutions adopted at the close of the fifty-seventh annual convention of the National Catholic Educational Association on April 22, 1960. Among those resolutions, the following would indicate the kind of awareness I have in mind. Catholic schools were urged to continue their efforts "to find increasingly effective ways of developing within their students a deep sense of social responsibility, and particularly of their responsibilities as Catholics within a pluralistic society."[10]

And this brings me to the "dialogue," an inevitable word which one cannot, I suppose, long escape today if he essays to speak of human relations in any form. While it is true that during the nineteenth century American Catholics were in a sense less separated from those outside the Church than were their European coreligionists, the basis for the political, economic, and social relationships with their separated brethren seemed to rest in good measure on a tacit agreement not to discuss religion. As a consequence, there developed among Catholics in this country a tradition which left no room for seeing ourselves through the

---

[10] Typed copy of resolutions adopted by the National Catholic Educational Association, Chicago, April 22, 1960, furnished by the national office, 1785 Massachusetts Ave. N.W., Washington 5, D.C.

eyes of others, for the technique of self-criticism, and for trying to learn something about the religious beliefs and practices of others. It was a frame of mind that represented a curious blend of Catholic superiority, arising out of the belief that our religion was the only true one, and an inferiority bred in the social and cultural exclusion which for so long a time had marked the Catholic community in this land. But here, precisely, is where Catholics of the 1960's must guard against what, in another context, Barbara Ward has called "the temptation of the easy option."[11] Rather it is our present duty to face up to the far more difficult and exacting task of self-scrutiny, of analyzing and criticizing ourselves among ourselves, so that through the medium of the dialogue between ourselves we may be the better equipped to engage with mutual profit in the dialogue with those of other faiths. There must then follow frank and open willingness to hear the other side of things and to accept the good faith of others. And this will, to be sure, be difficult, for unlike the nineteenth century when American Protestants concerned themselves with the historical papacy and the acts of Pius IX, but were not at serious issue with Catholics on many moral issues, today we are asked to answer for everything and anything that Catholic churchmen or statesmen do all over the world. In that sense the problem is actually more difficult than it ever was. Moreover, there is another fact that Catholics should insist upon among themselves; and it is that the time has passed when an assumed uniformity within our ranks on contemporary affairs, unrelated to dogmatic and moral issues, dominates our thinking, a time, in other words, when we were led to present a united front out of reaction to a hostile society around us. The historical causes that called that attitude into being are no longer with us, and it has in the meantime itself become a part of our history.

I should like to single out one of the numerous and complicated problems that today occupy Americans of all religious persuasions and of none, namely, the relations of Church and State, or more particularly, the question of religious freedom within a pluralistic society. The Church does, indeed, urge its members to perform their civic obligations and it reminds them of their duty to vote; but their personal participation in political campaigns, and the choice of candidates for whom they shall cast their vote, are entirely their own affair. In this respect matters

[11] "The Challenge of the Sixties," *New York Times Magazine*, December 27, 1959, p. 5.

have not changed since the first Sunday of November, 1912, when Cardinal Gibbons mounted the pulpit of his cathedral to exhort his flock to go to the polls on the following Tuesday in performance of the conscientious duty they owed their country; but on the question of the choice that they were to make between Taft, Roosevelt, and Wilson, he said:

Whatever may be my private and personal preference and predilection, it is not for me in this sacred pulpit or anywhere else publicly to dictate or even suggest to you the candidate of my choice.[12]

It was the statement of a tradition that had taken its rise over a century before with Archbishop Carroll, a policy that with a few exceptions that but prove the rule, the American hierarchy and their clergy have honored ever since.

It is not the alleged dictation that Catholics suffer from their hierarchy, however, that gives the really serious trouble to thoughtful Americans of other faiths. It is rather their knowledge of what has been termed the "traditional" teaching of theologians concerning the superior rights enjoyed by those who possess the Catholic faith over those who are outside the fold and, therefore, in religious error. And what strengthens their anxiety more than anything else, perhaps, is the history of religious minorities in some so-called Catholic countries where the rights of public worship and religious freedom have often been denied. I am here reminded of a letter that I received in 1958 from a distinguished Protestant professor of religious history in which the writer stated that he believed he was as sympathetic to different religious points of view as anyone in his field. But he said, "I find myself a bit uneasy some times as I see the growth of the power of the Catholic Church in America." "Why?" he asked, and he then proceeded to answer his own question in the following way:

Well I suppose that it stems in part from my background, and in part is emotional rather than rational. But I think it is more than that. Partly it is because I lived for ten years of my life in countries in South America where Roman Catholicism was not a minority group but the majority. I observed that they did not behave in the way the highminded leaders of American Catholicism, whom you rightly quoted, say majorities ought to behave toward

[12] "Will the American Republic Endure?", sermon preached in the Cathedral of the Assumption, Baltimore, November 3, 1912, *A Retrospect of Fifty Years* (Baltimore, 1916), II, 214.

minorities. What assurance is there that if Catholicism were a majority group here it would act differently than in other countries? Are there countries in the world where Catholicism is the majority faith where minority groups are freely granted complete religious freedom? I do not ask this captiously. I would really like to know.[13]

That paragraph, I am convinced, represents the heart of the matter in all that pertains to the present troubled relations of Catholics with other Americans. And I am further convinced that if a clear and cogent answer to that problem were forthcoming from an authoritative source it would serve to remove from the arena of public debate more quickly than any other remedy I know, discussion of the so-called "Catholic question" that bedeviled the 1960 presidential campaign.

I mentioned above Archbishop Carroll's inauguration of the policy of non-interference on the part of the American Catholic clergy in political affairs. I sometimes wonder if we Catholics realize what a tremendous debt we owe to that blessed man for having fixed so many wholesome traditions in the American Church. Six years before he became a bishop, while he was as yet only the superior of the scattered missions of an obscure little flock, Carroll was confronted in 1784 by a serious attack on Catholic doctrine by an apostate priest. In the lengthy reply which he prepared that summer he spoke of how distasteful the controversy was to him, and he stated that he would never have answered had he not felt that the faith of the Catholic people needed vindication against Wharton's charges. Carroll then added a statement which every student in the Catholic schools of the United States might well be urged to make his own. He said:

But even this prospect should not have induced me to engage in the controversy, if I could fear that it would disturb the harmony now subsisting amongst all Christians in this country, so blessed with civil and religious liberty; which, if we have the wisdom and temper to preserve, America may come to exhibit a proof to the world, that general and equal toleration, by giving a free circulation to fair argument, is the most effectual method to bring all denominations of Christians to a unity of faith.[14]

The founder of the American hierarchy thus made evident his under-

[13] Letter to the writer from Dallas, Texas, January 10, 1958.

[14] *An Address to the Roman Catholics of the United States of America by a Catholic Clergyman* [John Carroll], p. 116, contained in Charles H. Wharton, *A Concise View of the Principal Points of Controversy between the Protestants and Roman Churches* (New York, 1817).

standing and acceptance of the premises upon which the new republic was based, nor did he have any hesitancy in publicly proclaiming them. And in the years since he wrote those lines there has never been anyone who has overcast the honored name of Carroll by a suggestion of heresy or unsound doctrine. So well, indeed, did the first Archbishop of Baltimore fix the tradition on this point that, as I had reason to learn some years ago when I made a special study of the question,[15] every statement of a like nature that has since emanated from an American bishop has held fast to the policy of Carroll.

If this be true, then where, one may ask, is the justification for the misgivings of those outside the Catholic fold? Their anxiety arises from an acquaintance with the so-called traditional teaching that holds that error has no rights, that if Catholics came into a majority in the United States it would be expected that the rights of others to practice publicly their religious beliefs, would be curtailed. If to many American Catholics that doctrine sounds strange and, perhaps, harsh, it may be due to a defect or omission in their training, for many Catholic theologians have long taught the doctrine, often summarized in the phrase "thesis and hypothesis." Moreover, the history of certain countries of Europe and Latin America is replete with instances where that principle was invoked to the detriment of the personal rights of religious minorities. To say this is to indulge in no disparagement of our coreligionists of other lands; it is simply to recognize historical facts.

But what most outsiders do not know, and, I am afraid, too few Catholics as well, is that there is, and has been, another school of thought in Catholic theology that has espoused a belief in universal religious freedom, without in any way succumbing to the principles of philosophical relativism or opportunism. It finds its theological basis in the necessary freedom that there must be for the act of faith, in other words, in the sanctity of the individual conscience. For in Catholic teaching there is nothing that supersedes a man's conscience in the acceptance or non-acceptance of the truths of faith, nor is he ever compelled to recognize an allegiance or authority higher than his conscience. At a bitter moment in the Nazis' war of annihilation of the Church in Germany, Clemens von Galen, the great Bishop of Münster, reminded his flock of that fact when he recalled the command of King Frederick the Great of Prussia to Ernest von Münchausen, his Minister of Justice,

[15] "Church and State: An American Catholic Tradition," *Harper's Magazine*, CCVII (November, 1953), 63–67.

to alter a lawful sentence, to which the minister replied: "My head indeed is at the disposal of your Majesty, but not my conscience."[16] And we owe one of the most glorious chapters in Catholic history to the story of the heads of SS. Thomas More, John Fisher, and countless other saints and martyrs that have answered for a similar fidelity to conscience.

One of the most thoughtful and measured statements on the subject of religious tolerance and freedom in the tradition of the Church appeared in 1958 in Europe, and at the opening of 1960 became available in English translation in our own country.[17] In calling attention to this stimulating article by Giacomo Cardinal Lercaro, Archbishop of Bologna, the editors of America spoke of it as an indication that "a clarification of ideas on civil liberties is well under way in Europe."[18] I wonder if it might not be truer to say that this clarification has been in progress for nearly half a century, since the late Father Arthur Vermeersch, S.J., published his notable work entitled La Tolérance at Louvain in 1912. In any case, in the intervening time the literature emanating from Catholic sources on this topic has grown to the point where a writer for the World Council of Churches was able to compile a fairly large brochure, and that largely of quotations, from authentic Catholic sources carrying the ecclesiastical imprimatur, which showed the extent to which this type of thinking had reached within the Church.[19]

One of the most notable instances of this interpretation was that of the late Pope Pius XII who less than ten years ago treated the question in a discourse to the Union of Italian Catholic Jurists. In this memorable pronouncement the pontiff described the complex character of the international community as it now exists, composed of nations of the most widely varying religious beliefs, and he then raised the question as to whether in these circumstances God could choose toleration without contradicting His infinite perfection. By way of a reply to his own question Pius XII stated:

Could it be that in certain circumstances He would not give men any mandate, would not impose any duty, and would not even communicate the right

[16] English Catholic Newsletter, #105, November 15, 1941.

[17] Giacomo Cardinal Lercaro, "Religious Tolerance in Catholic Tradition," Catholic Mind, LXIII (January-February, 1960), 12–24.

[18] "Lercaro on Liberty," America, CII (January 23, 1960), 487.

[19] A. F. Carillo de Albornoz, Roman Catholicism and Religious Liberty (Geneva, 1959).

to impede or to repress what is erroneous and false? A look at things as they are gives an affirmative answer.[20]

He then went on to say that the belief that toleration is in itself immoral and, therefore, religious and moral error must always be impeded, is not valid in an absolute and unconditional sense. Such repression, said Pius XII, cannot be the ultimate norm of conduct since it must remain subordinate to what he termed "higher and more general norms," which in some circumstances permit, and may even dictate, toleration of error as the better policy in order to promote a greater good.[21]

No well informed Catholic will, of course, be so foolish as to think that the increasing number of writers who have followed in the wake of Vermeersch have pre-empted the field for themselves, and that the disciples of the opposing school have now been entirely vanquished. On the contrary, the issue is very much alive, and real differences still divide the theologians. But as Hubert Jedin, the historian of the Council of Trent, has said in explanation of the oftentimes furious controversies that marked the ecumenical councils of the Church, "Truth is reached by any community by means of an exchange of opinions, by arguments for and against, that is, by means of intellectual struggle."[22] There should be no surprise or scandal, therefore, in finding difference among theologians on the subject of religious freedom. But neither should it be thought that the position of the so-called traditional school is the only acceptable one in Catholic circles; in other words, that American Catholics — should the quite unlikely eventuality occur where they would find themselves a clear and powerful majority in this country — would then be compelled by their theological commitment to bring about union of Church and State or proceed to curtail or suppress the religious freedom of those outside the Church. To contend in this fashion is to call in question the orthodoxy of a number of reputable Catholic writers, and to question the soundness of doctrine of distinguished living prelates like Cardinal Lercaro of Bologna, Cardinal Cushing of Boston, and François Charrière, Bishop of Lausanne, Fribourg, and Geneva.[23] What would be a much more likely sequel to so unlikely a turn in American affairs, would be the complete and unqualified accept-

[20] Pope Pius XII, *The World Community. A Discourse to the Fifth Annual Congress of the Union of Italian Catholic Jurists, Rome, December 6, 1953* (New York, 1954) pp. 11–12.

[21] *Ibid.*, p. 12.

[22] *Ecumenical Councils of the Catholic Church. An Historical Outline* (New York, 1960), p. 234.

ance of a course like that outlined by the late Yves de la Brière, S.J., in an essay written in commemoration of the golden jubilee of Father Vermeersch. The essence of Father de la Brière's position was contained in two paragraphs which, I think, are worth quoting in full. He said:

In the medieval world and in ancient Europe, the consideration of the common good has often militated against the legal liberty of dissident sects. In the contemporary world, on the contrary, the consideration of the common temporal good militates in its behalf. In spite of the objective non-existence of a right of error, and even of the right of an erroneous conscience to the public profession of error, the psychological and moral condition of society demands, in the name of public tranquillity and the public interest, that the legal freedom of all cults be recognized everywhere as a universal rule of civilization, with the sole reservations of public morale and public order. This is, for all peoples, the subject of a universal duty and a universal contract of probity.

Such is the concept of which we are able to avail ourselves in all frankness and honesty, without disowning in any way the condemnations of the Popes against liberalism, either without being embarrassed by these condemnations or without employing deceit by resorting to overly clever ruses in regard to them.[24]

Permit me to make but one more point in conclusion. The general mood of responsible leaders both outside the Catholic Church and within, both throughout the United States and abroad, is as favorably disposed toward a calm and reasoned exchange of views on terms of mutual respect and charity as is known to the memory of living men. In that respect this is, indeed, as St. Paul said, the acceptable time, for signs of the improved climate of opinion are on every hand. Of the dozens of illustrations that come to mind, may I cite three? At St. John's University in Minnesota the annual summer institutes on mental health have since 1954 been drawing an increasing number of Protestant leaders who have joined with Catholic churchmen in week-long discussions on how pastoral psychology may improve the effectiveness of their ministry. In the summer of 1959 the institute drew, besides a Catholic bishop, four abbots, and nearly forty superiors and administrators of religious orders, a bishop of the Protestant Episcopal Church, a superior of an Episcopalian religious order for men, as well as executives from

---

[23] Richard Cardinal Cushing, *Pastoral Letter: The Christian and the Community* (Boston, 1960); François Charrière, "The Catholic Church and Religious Tolerance," *Catholic Mind*, LVI (July-August, 1958), 293–304.

[24] Yves de la Brière, S.J., "A Propos de la Tolérance Civile," *Miscellanea Vermeersch. Scritti Pubblicati in onore del R. P. Arturo Vermeersch, S.J.*, (Rome, 1935) II, 182–83.

the Lutheran, Presbyterian, and Congregational Churches. And at the close of their conferences they passed a resolution of thanks to the monks of St. John's for having provided them with what they termed "new insights for understanding ourselves and our fellow men [and] a better appreciation of the Christian faith we hold together and the fellowship and friendship made possible by Christ."[25]

Moreover, this spirit of friendly intercourse between men of differing faiths has, perhaps, reached even further in other countries than in our own. For example, in Switzerland in the summer of 1959 when the University of Geneva celebrated the 400th anniversary of its founding by John Calvin, the Catholic Church was invited to join in token of the 700 Catholics now numbered among the university's more than 3,000 students. Instead of that friendly gesture being spurned, as at many times in the past it would have been, the local Catholic bishop graciously accepted it. At a Mass celebrated in Geneva's Church of Notre Dame, Bishop Charrière preached an extraordinary sermon wherein he courteously, but candidly, chronicled the theological differences that divided the Catholics from the Calvinist tradition, and he then remarked:

We rejoice to see the University of Geneva imploring the blessing of God on its fourth centenary. We do so separately — Catholics, Protestants, and Old Catholics — for we cannot ignore our differences; but we do it at the same moment because we wish publicly to recognize our dependence on the Lord. Furthermore, publicly also, we wish to affirm before the whole country our will to seek that which unites us, to deepen it in order the better to understand it, and to persuade ourselves of it.[26]

Finally, the third example that I have chosen represents not only the changed temper of our time among men of varying religious beliefs, but also the new role of responsibility which the Holy See is now assigning to the Catholic laity. In Manila on January 2-8, 1960, there took place an international gathering where the delegates of Pax Romana, having concluded their own sessions three days before, were received at this congress held under the official sponsorship of UNESCO on the subject of the cultural values of the Occident and Orient. When we have come to witness an interdenominational conference under the purely secular auspices of a world organization like UNESCO having the Catholic Church represented with the full blessing of the Holy See, by an entirely

[25] *The Record* (St. John's University, Collegeville), August 28, 1959.
[26] "Calvin's University. Better News from Geneva," *The Tablet* (London), CCXIII (August 8, 1959), 670.

lay organization such as Pax Romana, one is included to say that this is progress, indeed!

Ours is a moment in time, therefore, when American Catholics owe it to themselves to become alert to the extraordinary mood of the hour, lest it should pass without their being heard. In spite of what some ill-informed Americans may have thought, we Catholics do not seek to occupy this or that national important office for the purpose of advancing the Church's power, for most of these positions, in any case, have inherent in them the manner in which their duties must be executed. Our goal, on the contrary, is to seek the transformation of public opinion toward the Church, and in so doing, to take our share in the ultimate liquidation of the accumulated animosity of more than four centuries, so that our fellow citizens may be given an enlightened concept of Catholicism and be thus enabled to dissipate the mistaken notions that may have been their inheritance from childhood. In brief, the attitude that should inform our relations with Americans of other religious faiths is that expressed by John Henry Newman in the summer of 1851 when the air of England was filled with a noisy clamor and bitter outcry against the Catholic name. Defining the duty which he conceived that Catholics had toward those outside the Church, the future cardinal spoke words that we can with profit make our own in reflecting upon the task that lies before us, when he said:

They must be made to know us as we are; they must be made to know our religion as it is, not as they fancy it; they must be made to look at us, and they are overcome.[27]

THE AMERICAN CATHOLIC LAITY—1962

The Brothers of the Christian Schools have left a deep impression upon their educational world during the two and a half centuries that have passed since their foundation. Although I never attended a brother's school, my study of the history of the Church both here and

[27] *Lectures on the Present Position of Catholics in England* (London, 1893), p. 378. The author wishes to express his appreciation to two kind friends and colleagues at The Catholic University of America who generously shared their ideas and their time in the preparation of this essay: the Very Reverend Louis A. Arand, S.S., associate professor of dogmatic theology, and Dr. John K. Zeender, associate professor of modern history.

73

abroad has been more than sufficient to deepen my respect and appreciation for the members of this vast religious family and for the lay professors who assist them in their apostolate of learning. At the present time approximately 2,500 Americans are enrolled in the Institute of Saint John Baptist de la Salle, men whose dedicated labors reach into six provinces of the United States and provide teaching staffs for 105 elementary and secondary schools, seven colleges, and four schools of a special character. In itself this is a notable contemporary fact.

Nor are the Christian Brothers a late arrival on the American scene. Almost 117 years have passed since that autumn day when their first permanent American establishment was opened at Calvert Hall in Baltimore. And if one were to judge by the first report of the brother in charge to the superior general's assistant, he would say that conditions have not radically changed, for in that letter of October, 1845, Brother Aidant remarked, "I had to refuse a good number in order not to overcrowd the classes."[1] Only twenty-three years after the beginning in Baltimore the brothers arrived on this distant Pacific Coast. Joseph S. Alemany, O.P., first Archbishop of San Francisco, had been acquainted with their work in his native Spain and he was eager for their services in his frontier diocese. Six years after his advent to San Francisco, therefore, the archbishop made his first appeal for Christian Brothers, but he failed in the request of 1857. Yet he did not lose heart; rather he went ahead with the purchase of property for a boys' school near the present College Avenue and Mission Street in San Francisco, and on that site on August 3, 1862, Archbishop Alemany laid the cornerstone of a building that would house Saint Mary's College which opened the following year with a faculty of two diocesan priests, four laymen, and two student-teachers.

Meanwhile the archbishop had not forgotten the brothers, and even a second failure in 1864 to enlist their aid did not discourage him. In fact, it may have challenged the prelate's ingenuity, for three years later he struck a happier approach by an appeal to Alessandro Cardinal Barnabò, Prefect of the Congregation de Propaganda Fide at Rome, who, in turn, used his powerful influence in July, 1867, to win the

---

[1] Brother Aidant to Brother Nicholas, Baltimore, October 6, 1845, Brother Angelus Gabriel, F.S.C., *The Christian Brothers in the United States, 1848–1948* (New York, 1948), p. 79.

brothers' superior general to a reopening of the case. This time the Archbishop of San Francisco's efforts ended in success and the visitor of the American province received instructions to assign eight brothers for Alemany's school with Brother Justin McMahon as superior, a religious who had already acquired a reputation in New York as an able educational administrator. The pioneer band left New York in July, 1868, aboard the *Ocean Queen*, sailed south to Panama, crossed the isthmus in a wagon, and then proceeded up the Pacific Coast by boat to San Francisco where they arrived on August 10.

No time was lost in formalities and three days later they took charge of Saint Mary's and opened the new school year with an enrollment of thirty-seven students which by the end of the first year had climbed to 157. One of the eight pioneers having withdrawn at Los Angeles, the seven remaining brothers offered a faithful reflection of the immigrant character of the American Catholics of that time in that five had been born in Ireland, one in Germany, and one in Switzerland. For the first twenty-one years Saint Mary's remained in San Francisco, but in 1889 the college was moved to Oakland, and then in 1928 it came to this charming valley where — like the Catholic community of which it forms a part — it has known expansion from the less than 600 students of 1928 to the more than 900 enrolled today.

Yet numbers are a poor criterion by which to judge the quality of any enterprise. I like rather to think of the academic accomplishments won by Saint Mary's graduates, and those of other American schools of the Christian Brothers, as offering a more meaningful norm of judgment. In that connection, as a professor of the Catholic University of America I have had in my own classes firsthand evidence of the superior type of student attracted to the Institute of La Salle. And since 1941 I have likewise been an annual witness to the extraordinary number of undergraduate members of this religious congregation whose excellent records have won them the coveted key of Phi Beta Kappa. The current year has been no exception, for among the seniors announced in mid-April as those upon whom this distinction was to be conferred one-third were Christian Brothers.

But neither the Christian Brothers, the lay professors, or the friends of this college would, I believe, wish me to rehearse here the academic honors of Saint Mary's or of other brothers' schools, however impressive

75

these may have been. I shall devote myself, therefore, to a topic which will not, I hope, be thought irrelevant to the graduates of 1962 or to those who have assembled to do them honor. Briefly stated, it is the present status of the laity in the Catholic Church of the United States, and the position to which they must be advanced if the Holy See's directives are to find serious application in this country, and if the laity are themselves to render the contribution which their rapidly strengthening status merits and deserves.

Some years have now passed since there was touched off a lively debate concerning the fortunes of the intellectual life in Catholic circles. I have no desire to reopen that debate here today. I should merely like to observe that the circumstance that finds thousands of young American Catholics completing their higher education either in one of the Catholic colleges or in one of the secular institutions of the land, or preparing to enter a graduate or professional school, in itself suggests how much stronger, intellectually speaking, the American Church is today than it was a generation ago, and it suggests, too, that this tremendous reservoir of trained lay talent should be recognized lest it be alienated and lost to the lay apostolate of our time.

It would be easy to conceive the recent emphasis on the lay apostolate as a new thing in the life of the Church. Such an impression, however, would be mistaken, for though the present stress is in part caused by startling increases in world population that have left growth in the priesthood and religious life far behind, it must never be lost to view that from the beginning the layman has played a necessary and vital role in the Church. How otherwise is one to account for Tertullian whose powerful mind did so much in the third century to shape the Christian thought of his own and succeeding ages? By what other norm than that of the lay apostle may one measure the careers of medieval rulers like Henry II of Germany, Stephen of Hungary, Ferdinand of Castile, and Louis IX of France, in their relation to the Church that numbers them all among its saints? If not as a layman, how is one to assess the place of Saint Thomas More in sixteenth-century Christendom, or that of Frederic Ozanam and Contardo Ferrini in the nineteenth century?

As has been mentioned, what lends a sharpness to the focus on the laity that it did not previously possess is the shortage of priests and religious, and the constant refrain of the Vicar of Christ that laymen should prepare themselves to replace the over-extended clergy in every way they can. It was with this in mind that the late Pope Pius XII, in addressing the second world congress of the lay apostolate in 1957, called this goal the *consecratio mundi*, the consecration of the world, which to use his own words, "is essentially the work of the laymen themselves. . . ."[2] And lest the laity should be impeded in the attainment of their objective by a clergy reluctant to see them brought actively to the fore, the pontiff declared on the same occasion:

They [ecclesiastical authorities] should entrust the layman with tasks that he can perform as well or even better than the priest, and allow him to act freely and exercise personal responsibility within the limits set for his work or demanded by the common welfare of the Church.[3]

In all of this evolving pattern, to be sure, the bishops remain the constant element of the *Ecclesia docens*, the teaching Church, for to them alone has been entrusted the divine mandate to teach and to exercise authority in such matters as pronouncing final judgment on the validity of the activity performed within their dioceses in the Church's name by both priests and laymen. And under the hierarchy are the priests to whom it is given primarily to execute the bishops' will. But once that principle has been understood, once there has been assured in any functioning group of the lay apostolate the respect for that priestly dignity which Pius XII described in terms of having "always been one of the most characteristic traits of the Christian community," it then becomes the duty of churchmen of every rank to heed the final point made by the pope in this section of his address when he declared, "laymen also have rights, and the priest should recognize them."[4]

Fortunately, the American Church does not suffer from the handicap of having to overcome a deep and ancient tradition of distrust between its clerical and lay members. True, in the early years of the last century a movement known as lay trusteeism got out of hand and the gravest tension resulted between the two orders in some sections of the country. But serious as it was, the evil of lay trusteeism proved a passing phenomenon and by the time of the Civil War it had all but expired. Far more typical of the Catholic community were the close and friendly

[2] "The Lay Apostolate. An Address of Pope Pius XII to the Second World Congress for the Lay Apostolate, October 5, 1957," *The Pope Speaks*, IV (Autumn, 1957), 123.

[3] *Ibid.*, p. 123.

[4] *Ibid.*, p. 122.

harmony and co-operation that obtained between churchmen and laymen as, for example, between John England, first Bishop of Charleston, and the leading layman of his diocese, William Gaston, Associate Justice of the Supreme Court of North Carolina. England sought Gaston's advice in every major undertaking, and when in June, 1822, he founded the first Catholic newspaper in this country he turned again to the learned jurist. "I should be greatly obliged," he said, "by your candid opinion upon the manner in which the paper is conducted, and of what improvements it is susceptible. I think you know me sufficiently well to write as you think."[5] Seven years later in a similar vein the bishops of the United States assembled in Baltimore for their first provincial council in October, 1829, invited in three prominent lawyers to counsel them on legal questions among whom was Roger Brooke Taney, future Chief Justice of the United States.

But if the layman is to fulfill his role to the greatest advantage of the Church and of himself, he must be treated with dignity and assigned to positions of trust that befit his talents and skill. In other words, he must be treated as the Most Reverend Lawrence J. Shehan, Archbishop of Baltimore, has treated the laity of the premier see in naming two of Baltimore's most prominent laymen as members of the Archdiocesan Commission on Christian Unity, and in announcing his intention that among the commissions that will be set up for the forthcoming archdiocesan synod there will be one especially designed to serve as a channel through which the laity may make known their opinions on subjects to be treated in the synod. This is the sort of action that will inspire the laymen's confidence in clerical leadership, the kind of recognition the laymen receive, for example, in the Archdiocese of Montreal where Paul-Emile Cardinal Leger has converted the entire archdiocesan school board from clerical to lay membership and has turned over to the laity Saint Paul's College, an institution previously directed and staffed by diocesan priests.

And what seems to give special promise in the cases just cited is the fact that both Cardinal Leger and Archbishop Shehan show their awareness that the true potentialities of this lay action will be fully realized only if the laymen are given freedom with which to plan, to speak, and

[5] John England to William Gaston, Charleston, September 21, 1822, "Letters from the Right Reverend John England to the Honorable William Gaston," *Records of the American Catholic Historical Society of Philadelphia*, XVIII (1907), 383.

to act. In this way, and in this way only, can there be created within the Church the enlightened public opinion that is so necessary to assist the bishops in their direction of ecclesiastical affairs. Twelve years ago Pius XII, the pontiff to whom so much is owed by way of the guiding principles that have shaped the Catholic life of our generation, emphasized that point when he addressed the international convention of the Catholic press. "Public opinion," he said, "is the mark of every normal society composed of men who, conscious of their personal and social conduct, are intimately concerned with the community to which they belong."[6] Noting that subjects such as doctrine were not open to free discussion, Pius XII, nonetheless, made it plain that public opinion should be fostered within the Church as well as in the secular world, because, as he said, since the Church is a living organism

something would be wanting in her life if public opinion were lacking — and the blame for this deficiency would fall back upon the pastors and the faithful.[7]

This being the case, I can conceive no more appropriate task for the Catholic layman who has enjoyed the superior advantages of a college education than that he should think of himself as one whose duty it is to articulate his thought concerning the crucial issues of our time; that he employ his intellectual training in weighing, measuring, and refining these issues, first in his own mind, and then in the public forum. In this way he will not only shed light upon the issues themselves, but he will also illumine for his bishop and for the priests with whom he is associated what one may call the "lay Catholic mind" on these problems. Churchmen definitely need to know the minds of the laity in order that they may be helped in insuring the future security and welfare of the Church itself. The distinguished Austrian theologian, Father Karl Rahner, S.J., expressed the idea several years ago in these words:

They need to know how people are thinking and feeling, what they have set their hearts and wishes on, what their problems are, what they find difficult, in what respects their feelings have changed, where they find the traditional answers or rulings insufficient, what they would like to see changed. . . . The greater the number of people involved, the more complex their

[6] "Catholic Press and Public Opinion. Allocution of Pius XII to the International Convention of the Catholic Press, Rome, February 18, 1950," *Catholic Mind*, XLVIII (December, 1950), 749.
[7] *Ibid.*, p. 753.

relationships, the more diverse their mentalities, the more difficult it is to obtain this knowledge of the situation, and, therefore, the greater the need for a public opinion.[8]

But it is an elementary truth that the human spirit does not accomplish its finest efforts or produce its most enduring results if it is constantly fettered by restrictions and admonitions and warnings, to say nothing of its being intimidated by the occasional bad tempered outburst that leaves a stain upon the memory of harshness and abuse. And in pleading for this freedom I have here in mind no aspect of the Church's life that touches upon the sacred terrain of dogma, but rather freedom in the numerous and varied avenues of contemporary Catholic life and action where the prudent layman can and should be allowed to travel with as much warrant and right as the priest and bishop. Here, then, in these areas the laity must be free if the Church in the United States is to escape the curse of anti-clericalism, a condition that the Cardinal of Montreal frankly stated exists in his diocese. In acknowledging that there was severe criticism of bishops and priests among the intellectuals and professional people, he did not see a remedy in the tactics of repression and the heavy handed wielding of the disciplinary rod that are reminiscent of an earlier time when an unlettered laity were easily cowed by a show of ecclesiastical authority. On the contrary, Cardinal Leger said:

I call upon our laity for a solution to this problem. If we have enough profoundly Christian laymen who are aware of their responsibilities, we shall convince the people that they are the Church and they have a vital role to play.[9]

It would be less than honest to pretend that all the high churchmen of our day share the views of Cardinals Leger, Koenig of Vienna, Montini of Milan, Alfrink of Utrecht, Cushing of Boston, Döpfner of Munich, Lercaro of Bologna, and Bea of the Roman Curia. As in every other age of the Church's history, the members of the household do not see eye to eye on matters of this kind. Ecclesiastics of a conservative turn of mind find it difficult to reconcile themselves to the enhanced position of the laity as outlined in the discourses of Pius XII. Yet in spite of that fact, and at the risk of incurring mistakes and errors here and there, the lay-

[8] Karl Rahner, S.J., *Free Speech in the Church* (New York, 1959), p. 22.

[9] Paul-Emile Cardinal Leger, "The Bishop and the Laity," *America*, CVII (May 12, 1962), 229.

men must be freed to speak and to act without hindrance on the vital problems that press for solution outside the realm of doctrine. If they are not given such freedom the superior training and education of which they are now the recipients in rapidly mounting numbers will have been — insofar as the Church is concerned — largely wasted, and the Church itself will be exposed to the very real threat of having the laymen's repressed zeal and frustrated ambitions for the Mystical Body turned into a disillusionment and embitterment that will breed in our land the kind of spirit that has poisoned the relations of clergy and laity in so much of western Europe and in Latin America.

Americans are by constitutional government and by national tradition free men, and in this Catholic Americans are no exception. More than 170 years of organized Catholicism in this land bear witness to the fact that the adherents of both the authoritarian Church of Rome and of the democratic Republic of the United States find no basic conflict in the loyalty they owe to each. By the same token these 170 years that have passed since the consecration of John Carroll, first Archbishop of Baltimore, offer striking testimony to the extraordinary fidelity and deep sense of obedience that American Catholics have paid to the Bishop of Rome in whom they have ever seen the Vicar of Christ. Yet the absence from the history of American Catholicism of anything that bears a real resemblance to heresy or a genuine departure from orthodoxy of doctrine does not mean that the Catholics of the United States have been passive or indifferent to the way in which their relationships to their Church are governed or directed. They have an instinctive distrust of one who is heedless of their traditions as free men, and they are deeply pained and hurt when the open and heartfelt reception they have given to their obligations as Catholics are met with the tactics of needless repression and harsh anathemas. For as Pius XII told the Catholic journalists of the world in 1950, the Catholics of this country are, too, "intimately concerned with the community to which they belong," and in the negative measures to which reference has been made Americans do not recognize the normal way in which their Church has brought about obedience to its will. Numbering forty-three million or more souls and thus constituting the third largest group of Catholics anywhere in the world, by the gift of divine Providence and their own dedicated labors, the richest body of the faithful within the universal Church, and steeped in more than three centuries of practice in the veneration

81

and love they have manifested for their clergy and for the Church, the Catholic laity of the United States constitute a vibrant and moving force in the realm of the spirit that has not been excelled in modern times.

It is to this noble and inspiring company, then, that you Saint Mary's men are now summoned and welcomed. If you and your counterparts throughout the land will, therefore, each conceive himself as a Catholic layman whose duty dictates that he know his faith and that he study his Church and its needs, and that he then articulate freely, yet prudently, his reactions for the benefit of his contemporaries — both clerical and lay and both within and without the Catholic fold — you will have made a lasting contribution to the advancement and maturity of Catholicism in the twentieth century. You will also have performed an enormously important service in helping to prevent the growth among your fellow laymen of anything resembling the unhappy relations between clergy and laity of which mention has been made. And you will likewise have rendered incarnate, so to speak, the centennial theme of your college which is "The liberal arts — the language of free men." For in characterizing a liberal education Cardinal Newman spoke of it as forming "a habit of mind that lasts through life, of which the attributes" — and it is noteworthy what he placed first — "are freedom, equitableness, calmness, moderation, and wisdom."[10] Finally, you will thus have fulfilled in your earthly pilgrimage — against the hour of ultimate judgment that inevitably lies ahead for each of us — the words which Saint Peter wrote to his converts nearly 2,000 years ago when he told them:

Such is the will of God, that by doing good you should put to silence the ignorance of foolish men. Live as freemen, yet not using your freedom as a cloak for malice but as servants of God.[11]

THE CULT OF QUALITY

This is a memorable year in the life of this College, rounding out in 1958, as it does, the fiftieth year of collegiate instruction on this campus.

[10] John Henry Newman, *The Idea of A University* (New York, 1898), p. 101.
[11] 1 Pet 2:15–16.

Fifty years is a brief span of time in the life of any educational institution, but in the case of the College of Saint Teresa it has been sufficient to establish it as one of the ranking Catholic colleges for women in this country. This is neither the place nor the time to review the history of the institution from which you, the largest graduating class yet to complete its curriculum, are about to receive your degrees. And yet it is, I think, an appropriate occasion to recall briefly a few facts which, although some of them happened as long as eighty years ago, have a bearing upon the lives of you young ladies of which you may, indeed, be only dimly aware.

It was in the autumn of 1877 that a small but valiant band of religious of Saint Francis came to southern Minnesota from Illinois at a time when here in Minnesota the frontier was still a living memory and the state had not yet completed twenty years within the American Union. Out of the little academies at Owatonna and Rochester which opened in that fall of 1877 there has grown an educational system, sponsored and informed by the Franciscan ideal, which in these eighty years has produced a college that enjoys a national reputation for the inculcation of Christian womanhood and superior scholarship, and a hospital whose fame is worldwide by reason of the thousands who have benefited from the combination of supernatural charity and professional efficiency that have characterized its management. And this is to say nothing of the twenty-one high schools, the more than forty elementary schools, the nurses' training schools, and the other institutions for the aged and the infirm staffed by nearly 800 dedicated religious and spread through four archdioceses and four dioceses of the United States. Here, indeed, in this Franciscan Congregation of Our Lady of Lourdes is a key regiment, so to speak, in the mighty army of American men and women whose devoted labors have helped to rear the impressive structure that the Catholic Church of the United States presents in the month of June, 1958, when it celebrates the fiftieth anniversary of its removal by St. Pius X from the status of missionary territory under the jurisdiction of the Congregation de Propaganda Fide and its auguration as a mature branch of the Universal Church.

To you young women of the Class of 1958 the early hardships and trials of the Franciscan Sisters of the years that have gone naturally seem very remote. And yet, would you not be missing something of the meaning and reality of the tradition in which you have been bred were you to be unmindful of their story? You are but the most recent among the nearly 2,700 American women who have earned a degree from this College, each of whom is heir to the ideals that were first translated into action on Minnesota soil in the then frontier towns of Owatonna and Rochester over eighty years ago; heirs of the brave Mother Alfred Moes and her original associates; heirs as well of the traditions of Saint Mary's Hospital which received its first patients at Rochester in September, 1889, almost two months to the day before the erection of the Diocese of Winona by the Holy See. You may never have heard of the struggle of that distant time in Rochester when, for example, in order to circumvent the hostility of a bigoted minority — then known as the A.P.A. — who had vowed that the sisters' hospital should never strike root in the community, the shrewd old Dr. William Mayo engaged a leading Presbyterian of the town as nominal superintendent of the hospital in order to throw the enemy off his guard and thus permit the sisters to continue their works of mercy for the sick. Many of you may likewise be unaware of the stark simplicity of the circumstances in which this educational institution first opened its doors in September, 1894, as the Winona Seminary, and that the two sisters who had been sent from Rochester in the previous March to launch the undertaking were provided with the sum of $4.28 as they left the motherhouse. These are, it is true, obscure and homely facts. But they are representative of the pattern of trial and self-denial that accompanied the birth pains of the two splendid institutions of which for the past four years you have been the beneficiaries; they are part, in other words, of Minnesota's Franciscan history, and in the felicitous phrase of Robert Speaight, it is history that "breeds a respect for tradition and for the graces which are the gift of time."

We Americans are not, generally speaking, given to an abiding respect for history. But that is our loss, for it is only through a knowledge of a people's past that one can fully appreciate their present culture and can truly understand the factors that have made them what they are. You young women are justly proud of the College of Saint Teresa. But it is well for you to remind yourselves that its present imposing buildings, its well equipped library and laboratories, its tasteful dormitories and social rooms, and its splendid chapel have not been achieved save at a price. And the price paid in personal sacrifice and self-effacing labor has at times been very high for these daughters of Saint Francis, and the fact that they have paid it generously has produced for you what you cherish today as a vital part of your heritage.

It is not, however, in buildings, be they ever so impressive, that the true greatness of an educational institution lies. It is rather in the spirit or ideal that informs its life. Here from the very outset the ideal was a lofty one. In the statement of aims embodied in the first catalog of the Winona Seminary in 1895 one reads:

It is the conviction of the founders of this school that woman's influence is best exerted not at the polls or on the rostrum, but in the sacred precincts of the Christian home. There, by her mental attainments . . . she may obtain and exercise a limitless power for good . . . she should have the broadest, the deepest, the highest culture of heart and mind. To afford its patrons such an education, is the aim of the Ladies Seminary.

We of the mid-twentieth century may be inclined to smile at this implied restriction of women's role to the home as expressed in the aim of 1895. But it is rather in the emphasis on "the broadest, the deepest, the highest culture of heart and mind," that there is to be found the central idea of this institution's original definition of purpose, and this, I think you will agree, the College of Saint Teresa has done its utmost to sustain and realize.

What, then, may your alma mater ask of you in return for what it has expended to fit you for the varied walks of life into which you pass today? As I mentioned a moment ago, the American Church reached its canonical maturity a half century ago, and in the intervening years it has perfected that maturity and is today — with its more than forty million members — the wealthiest, in many ways the strongest, and in numbers the third largest of any branch of the Universal Church. More may be expected of the American Church, then, in this second half of the present century than in its earlier years. And by the same token more may be expected of you, mature daughters of that Church, than has been asked of you during the twenty-some years of your lives up to this time of your college graduation.

As Americans we have frequently been criticized for placing too much value on mere size and numbers with consequent neglect of the quality that lies behind these impressive displays of quantity. It is in many ways a just criticism, and insofar as it is true, it is a manifestation of a somewhat adolescent approach to life. But the time of adolescence for America has passed, for the problems it now faces are too grave for the

85

trifling pastimes of a child. We have entered upon an age when it is imperative that quality be permitted to reassert its claims. I need not remind this audience of the deep and widespread discontent that has overtaken the American public within recent years regarding the education of its youth. That awakening is, in my judgment, one of the most heartening signs upon the national scene. If, then, you graduates are to be part of what we may call a "new awakening," it is incumbent upon you to respond to the demand for quality in your personal lives and in the lives of all who may be touched by your influence.

Over four centuries ago one of the most attractive saints in the history of the modern Church — who was at the same time one of the most learned men of his day — expressed the thought I have in mind in so simple and clear a way that I cannot improve upon it. In his famous little book, *Utopia,* Saint Thomas More remarked:

What part soever you have taken upon you, play that as well as you can and make the best of it.

I can think of few mottoes that are more appropriate to young American Catholic women about to embark on the high venture of their adult years than this. To "play it as well as you can," means to set your sights high for the goal of your earthly years; to be stout of heart in the face of difficulty and discouragement; to be resolute in purpose, and to be outdone by no rival in industry and in the dedication of your effort; to steel yourself to a spirit of sacrifice of the allurements of the world with their manifold distractions, knowing that their uncontrolled indulgence will paralyze every possibility of superior achievement in whatever line of endeavor you may espouse; to be determined that "what part soever you have taken upon you," will be pursued with the unflagging energy that will bring you out at the top of your capacity, for only there will your highest quality show forth and only there can you discover the finest expression of your talents in the pursuit of life's ultimate purpose.

In all of this effort and striving to attain quality, to reach the top in the walk of life you elect to follow, you will need, like all of us who have gone before you, a principle to guide your steps, to light your way, and to steady your progress as the years move on. And this principle of action is not lacking, for the proper motivation in this matter is found — as is an unfailing guidance in all the problems of life — in the greatest of all guide books, the New Testament. In two widely separated discourses our blessed Lord gave the mandate, the motivation, and the warning concerning the way in which you and I should employ whatever abilities He may have given to us. At the opening of His public life in the Sermon on the Mount He told His followers:

You are the light of the world. A city set on a mountain cannot be hidden. Neither do men light a lamp and put it under the measure, but upon the lamp-stand, so as to give light to all in the house. Even so let your light shine before men, in order that they may see your good works and give glory to your Father in heaven.

There is the mandate concerning the quality of your performance, concerning the light — no matter how faint it may be — that shines from your intellect into the lives of those in the society in which you will move. There, too, is the motivation for the exercise of your spiritual and intellectual faculties, namely, that whatever results they may yield in the making of a home as wife or mother; in the pursuit of science as a nurse or medical technician; in the advancement of the mind as a teacher or creative artist; in the promotion of scholarship as a writer or research worker; in the progress of the marts of trade as a clerk or secretary; and last — but in reality first — in your response to the call to the life of a religious — in whatever you do, let men see and recognize in your "good works," as our Lord expressed it, deeds that have emanated from sterling characters, from noble minds, from intellects prompted and inspired by the love of truth. And seeing them as such, your contemporaries will give the glory where it belongs, to the Father from Whom this light of yours has come and to Whom its products will one day return to be weighed in the scales of divine justice.

In similar fashion at the end of His life Christ returned to the subject of the use men should make of the gifts that they had been given. Shortly before He went up to Jerusalem to begin His passion He addressed His disciples in a series of parables on the meaning of the kingdom of heaven. In one of these He related the story of the man who, before setting out on a distant journey, called his servants and to one he gave five talents, to another two, and to another one. Upon his return the master found that the first two had doubled the sums that he had left with them, and to them he said, "well done, good and faithful servant." But the third, who had hidden his single talent and had put forth no effort to multiply it, he upbraided as "wicked" and "slothful," and ended by ordering this man, whom he characterized as an "unprofitable serv-ant," to be cast into the darkness without.

It is not, I think, putting too fanciful an interpretation upon the sacred text to say that the parable of the talents applies to you and to me with special force by reason of the superior advantages of higher education that we have enjoyed. It is easy to do nothing — or very little — with whatever talents we may have; it is, in fact, the more comfortable — and some would say the "safe" — thing to apply oneself in only a routine way, that is, to follow the crowd. Yet as John Ireland, Archbishop of St. Paul, once remarked, "The timid move in crowds, the brave in single file." And it is only the brave who move toward distinguished achieve-ment in life and to the ultimate fulfillment of the hope that other less gifted men place in their leadership.

Within the last few years we have heard much concerning the failure of American Catholics to attain posts of national influence, to furnish their proportionate share of the top-ranking positions in scholarship, the professions, and in those areas where there are taken the truly significant decisions of a nation's life. That there is still much to be desired among the American Catholic community in this respect, I am convinced. And I wonder how much of our failure to measure up may be accounted for by the absence among many of us of a sense of dedication to our in-dividual commitments, to the presence of a certain contentment with something less than the best that is in us, of our shying away from the personal sacrifices entailed in the process of reaching the top? It was not in this fashion that the Franciscan Sisters of the Diocese of Winona brought the College of Saint Teresa and Saint Mary's Hospital to the rank and reputation they enjoy today in the realm of instruction in the liberal arts and in the science of nursing and medical care. In any case, this much, I think, is certain: you and I as adult members of the American Church can anticipate little by way of improvement in the position occupied by our coreligionists in this country unless the coming generation of Catholics are ready to dedicate themselves to the pursuit of their varied walks of life in the sense meant in the parable of the talents and in the Saviour's discourse on the light that each one of us bears within us from His Father's gift.

The history of the Church is rich in examples of women who have conceived their life work in the exalted terms laid down by Christ in the two passages of the New Testament to which I have referred. From

88

His blessed Mother, fulfilling perfectly her assigned role at Bethlehem, at Nazareth, and in Jerusalem in that final awful week of Christ's life, there extends on through the centuries of Christian history an unbroken line of women, imperishable figures like Saint Teresa of Avila, your heavenly patron, who amid the greatest difficulties made over, as it were, the face of contemplative life in her native Spain in the sixteenth century; of women like Mother Elizabeth Seton, convert widow and the mother of five children, whose determination that everything she did should bear the stamp of the highest spiritual quality within her power resulted in her founding the first native religious community for women in the United States, and through these daughters laid the foundation of the teaching sisterhoods of our country before her death in 1821; of women nearer to our own day like Sister Aloysius Molloy of this College, and of Sister Joseph Dempsey, if I may be pardoned for singling out for mention only two among the many Sisters of Saint Francis whose memory deserves to be kept fresh for the inspiration of posterity. Following her death in 1939 the world famed Dr. William J. Mayo spoke of Sister Joseph in terms that offer a striking illustration of what I have in mind. He called her, "A woman of heroic stature in her life as a humble religious . . . and above all, in her endeavor to stimulate co-workers and subordinates to the highest possible achievement."

Nor does one need to reach back into the history of the Church of Europe or America for examples of women who have followed the cult of quality in their lives, a cult enlightened and inspired by the lofty concept of their role in American life and of their membership in the Church of Christ. Let me mention but two names that are familiar to you all. Such a one is Helen C. White, professor of English in the University of Wisconsin, distinguished author of numerous books among which are several charming historical novels, a lady accepted without question in the highest circles of literary scholarship, as well as one who has been chosen for two of the ranking posts within the gift of women who follow the academic life, first as President of the American Association of University Women, and more recently, as President of the American Association of University Professors. A second, Irene Dunne, the lovely and charming lady, whose artistic talents and noble bearing have graced the stage and screen of the world of American entertainment for more than a generation and have won for her as well the distinction of being chosen by the President of the United States as alternate representative of our country's delegation to the United Nations. In Miss White and Miss Dunne, and more could be enumerated, the American public has witnessed that happy combination of the fullest expression of the superb talents with which God has endowed them, the deepest devotion to their Catholic faith, and the qualities that characterize them as ladies whose refined and cultivated manners have endeared them to every American of our generation who gives serious thought to the values of life that ennoble and endure.

And before I take leave of these personal examples, I cannot refrain, by reason of the circumstances of this particular place, from citing to you one final instance of singular achievement, in this case outside the fold of the Church. It would, indeed, be carrying coals to Newcastle for one like myself who comes to you from a distant place to endeavor to picture for this audience the accomplishments of the famous Drs. Mayo of Rochester. May I simply quote for you the answer of Dr. Will Mayo to a visitor who had been deeply impressed by his visit to the Mayo Clinic where he had seen the display of honors that had come to the Mayos in token of the world's appreciation of their tremendous contributions to medical science. To this visitor, who exclaimed over what he had seen in that collection, Dr. Will replied in words that have a close bearing on the principal theme of this address on what I like to call the "cult of quality." He said:

Yes, we have them from all over the world. To be frank about it, we have accomplished much, my brother and I. But we *should* have done great things; we were given the opportunity. We were born at the right time and to the right parents. Perhaps no one will ever again have the opportunity to accomplish as much. That day is gone, unless for some genius. We were not geniuses. We were only hard workers. We were reared in medicine as a farmer boy is reared in farming. We learned from our father.

If, then, there would be a final word that I might leave with you, it would be this: that you seek, each in her own personal and individual way, to exercise to the utmost the talents with which God has endowed you; that you think of yourself in this wise as accomplishing in the best way known to you — in whatsoever vocation you may choose — your role as a witness to the faith, to the Church of which you are a privileged daughter, and to this great Republic of which you are a grateful citizen. Of the period since World War II many untoward things will be recorded by the future historian; but one of the more encouraging signs that he will note will be the certain vague longing for religion and religious values that has overtaken the American people during these years. You are going forth, therefore, at an opportune moment when Americans in general are more receptive than they formerly were to the appeal of religion, to the inspiration that may be drawn from their observation of the life of an exemplary Catholic woman lived out before their eyes. Here, then, lies your opportunity; here is your chance to enable your finest qualities as women of deep religious faith and cultivated mind to share in overcoming prejudice against the Church, in opening minds hitherto closed to the truth and reality of Catholic doctrine, in revealing to those who are strangers to the faith something of its depth, its consolations, and the beauty of its central dogma of brotherly love. And they will be touched and influenced the more quickly and effectively if they see these highest qualities of your educated and disciplined minds shine forth from the persons of women whose dedication has raised them to the pinnacle of their respective professions by fidelity to the cult of quality in their lives.

There may well be those among you graduates who through a sense of modesty may think that there is little that has been said here today about superior achievement in life that applies to you. If that should be the case, may I remind you that when the final reckoning comes for you and me we will be judged, not by the world's estimate of what has — or has not — impressed it in our doing. That eternal judgment will rest rather on whether or not we have employed to the utmost our God-given talents, few and meager though these may have been. Those of you, therefore, whose sense of inadequacy might prompt you to shrink from striving for the highest quality in all that you do should be heartened, as many of us have before you been heartened, by the perceptive vision of John Henry Newman. When the Irish bishops sought out the great English Oratorian to begin the work of founding a Catholic university in Ireland, he sensed that what he might accomplish toward that end would be small by comparison with what was required for so ambitious an undertaking. Yet in contemplating that prospect he gave expression to a view, expressed in his famous *Idea of a University*, that reaches out over a century of time to faint hearts in accents of encouragement, words that may form a fitting close to what has been said here today. On that occasion Cardinal Newman said:

It is enough for one man to lay only one stone of so noble and grand an edifice; it is enough, more than enough for me, if I do so much as merely begin, what others may more hopefully continue. One only among the sons of men has carried out a perfect work, and satisfied and exhausted the mission on which He came. One alone has with His last breath said "Consummatum est." But all who set about their duties in faith and hope and love, with a resolute heart and a devoted will, are able, weak though they be, to do what, though incomplete, is imperishable. Even their failures become successes, as being necessary steps in a course, and as terms (so to speak) in a long series, which will at length fulfill the object which they propose. And they will unite themselves in spirit, in their humble degree, with those real heroes of Holy Writ and ecclesiastical history, [with] Moses, Elias, and David, Basil, Athanasius, and Chrysostom, Gregory the Seventh, St. Thomas of Canterbury, and many others, who did most when they fancied themselves least prosperous, and [who] died without being permitted to see the fruit of their labours.

UNITED STATES
CATHOLIC CHURCH HISTORY

JOHN CARROLL, FOUNDER OF THE
AMERICAN HIERARCHY (1735–1815)

"We cannot afford wantonly to lose sight of great men and memorable lives . . ." Nearly sixty years ago Lord Acton, the nineteenth century's most distinguished English Catholic historian, spoke those words in his inaugural lecture at the University of Cambridge. And what age, one may ask, needs the inspiration to be derived from the memorable deeds of men of the past more than our own? It is with the counsel of Lord Acton in mind that we present these brief sketches of the careers of five outstanding American bishops, in the belief that through a closer understanding of their lives we may better appreciate the contributions which they made to American Catholicism and to the United States, for these bishops served both Church and State with high distinction and singular devotion.

More than two centuries have passed since that January day of 1735 when there was born at Upper Marlboro in the colony of Maryland the man who was destined to become the father of the Catholic Church in the United States. The American Revolution was then forty years in the future; yet the family of this child had been Americans for generations. John Carroll could say with full justification — in the words of a great prelate of our own day — "I belong here." Belong, indeed, he did, for there was no more patriotic family in colonial Maryland than the Carrolls, who were to give in the person of the future bishop's distant

93

kinsman, Charles Carroll of Carrollton, the sole Catholic signer of the immortal Declaration of Independence. But unfortunately for this loyal family and their Catholic friends, the religious toleration in which the later Bishop of Baltimore was so strong a believer, had not yet dawned in the colony of his birth. At the time John Carroll was born Maryland was held tightly in the grip of severe penal laws against Catholics which forbade the followers of that faith to educate their children in Catholic schools. The best that young Carroll could do, therefore, by way of fulfilling his desire for a religious education, was to spend a brief time at the furtive little academy of Bohemia Manor and then to embark for Europe where he could be educated without restraint in the Jesuit colleges at Liège and St. Omer. Thus he left his home and family in America at the age of thirteen, and not until he had entered upon his fortieth year was John Carroll again united to those whom he loved most in life. Time does not permit us to say more of those years of separation other than that he found his vocation to the priesthood among the English Jesuits teaching in the colleges of Belgium, and when he returned home in the summer of 1774 it was as a priest seasoned by over five years of rich experience in the ministry.

What a vast change had come over his homeland during his absence! The fires of resentment against the mother country had enkindled the spirit of revolution in American hearts and by early September of 1774 the first Continental Congress had assembled in Philadelphia to unite the efforts of all the colonies in the coming struggle against British rule. Father Carroll took no part in any of the political agitation of his day, but went quietly to the home of his mother at Rock Creek near the present city of Washington where he spent his time in spiritual min- istrations to the Catholic families of the surrounding settlements.

Meanwhile the revolutionary cause gained momentum and in February, 1776, the Continental Congress — seeking to win Canada to their side — sent a commission headed by Dr. Benjamin Franklin to per- suade the Canadians of the justice of the American cause. To this dis- tinguished delegation of Franklin, Samuel Chase, and Charles Carroll of Carrollton the congress added the name of Father Carroll as one who, they hoped, might have a special appeal in the approach to the Catholic French of Quebec and Montreal. It was not an assignment to the liking of the young priest, who put so high a value on the spiritual character of his calling, for as he stated at the time, "I have observed that when the ministers of religion leave the duties of their profession to take a busy part in political matters, they generally fall into contempt . . ." But his country called and, therefore, he laid aside his scruples in favor of its overruling interests. Try as they did, the American commissioners made no headway against the loyal adherence of the French Canadians to the British crown. The end of the mission was not attained, true, but it brought Father Carroll into close acquaintance with some of the leading personalities of American public life, and old Dr. Franklin, enfeebled by the long and arduous journey, was accompanied home by Father Carroll whose help to him was acknowledged after they had reached New York when Franklin told a friend. "I could hardly have got so far but for his friendly assistance and tender care of me."

The years that lay ahead were not easy for those who had raised the standard of revolt against a powerful foe. Nor were they tranquil ones for the Catholic priests and their scarce and scattered flocks. War is never kind to a populace and the American Revolution was no exception. But at last victory was in sight and September, 1783, brought peace once more to the distracted people of America.

All through the war Father Carroll had carried on as best he could in giving a helping hand to his harassed countrymen of every creed and class, and as the new Republic emerged it was evident to all who knew anything of the infant Church of the United States that John Carroll was the man to give it life and form. Word of his noble character, his resourceful mind, and his firm will had long before reached the Holy See. After a period during which he served with singular success as superior of the American missions this admirable priest was nominated in November, 1789, at the age of fifty-four to become the first Bishop of Baltimore and the first Catholic prelate to exercise episcopal powers within the United States. George Washington had been inaugurated as first president the previous April; the Church and the Republic were, then, in a sense born the same year.

Seldom has the Holy See made a wiser choice of one to lay the foundations of the Church in a new land. John Carroll knew intimately the American attitude of his day concerning the Church he was now called upon to lead. He understood the bias that had colored so many American minds on the Church of Rome, for he had more than once felt its unkindly sting. But he knew, too, the spirit of fair play that characterized his fellow countrymen and the steadfast loyalty of American Catholics to their political allegiance. His life was dedicated to the elimination of misunderstandings between Americans of all creeds, and as he told an archbishop in France, "To dissipate this prejudice time will be our best aid, as also will Divine Providence, and the experience of our fellow-citizens in our devotion to our country and to its independence."

No American ever had occasion fairly to charge Bishop Carroll with deviation from that devotion, and the tributes paid to him at his death by Americans of other faiths remain as an enduring record of the success with which he carried out his solemn obligations as a leading citizen of the new Republic of the West.

Imagine, if you can, the staggering burden which rested upon the shoulders of the new bishop as he returned in December, 1790, from his consecration in England! The entire United States was his diocese; he had not more than thirty priests to carry on the work of the ministry, and the roughly 30,000 Catholics were scattered in small communities from Maine to Georgia and beyond the western mountains whence they clamored for the bread of life to nourish their souls. One of the elements of true greatness in any leader is moral courage, and in the face of his gravest trials the first Catholic bishop of our country never faltered. Hardly had he settled himself in Baltimore before disturbing rumors reached him of discord and strife that had broken out in several Catholic communities, torn as they were by the rivalries of clashing nationalities. Here, indeed was a peril to the Church and here, too, was a peril to the State. Bishop Carroll acted quickly and vigorously in recalling men to a sense of their duty and to the obligations they had incurred as Americans and no longer citizens of Ireland, Germany, or France. The United States in its formative years as a nation had no more ardent defender of its character as an American state before the thousands from abroad who were even then landing on these shores, than the Maryland-born bishop whose special pride it was to make loyal Americans out of the Catholics of multiple national strains who had been entrusted to his spiritual care.

In this Bishop Carroll not only served his Church, but he rendered a service to Americans of every faith and class in dedicating his high authority to the inculcation of patriotism and civic virtue.

This Bishop Carroll could do with perfect sincerity, for he believed with all his heart in the principles upon which the United States had been established as a nation. The Constitution had not been signed more than three months when he took up his pen in defense of his religious beliefs, and in the course of that defense he said, "Freedom and independence, acquired by the united efforts, and cemented with the mingled blood of Protestant and Catholic fellow-citizens, should be equally enjoyed by all." Nor was this a new argument in the bishop's armor, for three years before he had expressed his reluctance to engage in public controversy lest, as he remarked, "it would disturb the harmony now subsisting amongst all Christianity in this country, so blessed with civil and religious liberty; which, if we have the wisdom and temper to preserve, America may come to exhibit a proof to the world, that general and equal toleration by giving a free circulation to fair argument, is the most effectual method to bring all denominations of Christians to a unity of faith." Could any American ask for a more forthright and wholehearted endorsement of equal religious liberty for all?

Shortly after the inauguration of the new president, among the first to greet him in formal address were the Bishop of Baltimore and four leading Catholic laymen when they pledged their loyalty to George Washington and to the nation which he now led. It was a glowing tribute which drew from the president in the early days of 1790 a letter of thanks, in which he recalled the patriotic part which the Catholics had played in the Revolution and the assistance rendered to that cause by Catholic France.

Even when engaged in strictly ecclesiastical affairs, the Bishop of Baltimore was not unmindful of the welfare of the nation. It was during the first synod of his clergy in November 1791, that John Carroll submitted for their use in the Catholic churches and chapels of the land the beautiful prayer which he had composed for the welfare of the Republic, a prayer wherein he pleaded for the divine spirit of counsel and fortitude for the President of the United States, for the Congress, and for all who were in any way charged with government and rule. Nor did he forget American citizens of other faiths, for Carroll's prayer included this plea to God:

"We recommend likewise, to Thy unbounded mercy, all our brethren and fellow-citizens throughout the United States, that they may be blessed in the knowledge and sanctified in the observance of Thy most holy law; that they may be preserved in union, and in that peace which the world cannot give; and admitted to those which are eternal."

97

And when the day came that General Washington, that peerless leader of young America, was taken in death there was no citizen of the United States who was more articulate in his grief than Bishop Carroll. He led the Catholics of the country in the observance of the day of national mourning decreed by Congress for February 22, 1800, and on that day he preached a eulogy of the departed Washington in his pro-cathedral, a panegyric that breathed in its every line a noble testimony to greatness. The bishop closed his long discourse with these words:

"May these United States flourish in pure and undefiled religion, in morality, peace, union, liberty and the enjoyment of their excellent Constitution, as long as respect, honour, and veneration shall gather round the name of Washington that is, whilst there shall be any surviving record of human events."

John Carroll found the Catholic Church of the United States in 1790 a poor, despised, and widely dispersed aggregation; he left it a quarter century later a strong and vibrant band of priests and people who had grown and prospered so that by 1808 four new dioceses were established in the young Republic and the venerable Carroll himself was raised to the dignity of first Archbishop of Baltimore. It was the unfailing wisdom, good sense, and administrative genius of Carroll that had guided both the Holy See and the infant Church; it was this same man's deep conviction of the inestimable value attaching to an educated and enlightened people that prompted him to found, out of his slender resources, Georgetown College, the first Catholic college for boys in the United States, to further the action of the Sulpician Fathers in their establishment of the mother seminary of St. Mary's in Baltimore, and to serve as the constant source of authoritative support to Mother Elizabeth Seton in founding her Sisters of Charity and in opening her first school for Catholic girls. It was likewise Carroll who consecrated the first four bishops of the American Church. In fact, there was scarcely a major enterprise of the Catholic Church in this land at which he had not stood sponsor. Carroll's was a genius endowed with breadth and understanding; an intelligence that was quick and penetrating; a heart that was consecrated to the moral uplift of men of every shade of belief. That is why Cardinal Gibbons could characterize his selection almost a century after his death as "a most providential event for the welfare of the American Church." Truly, as the great cardinal stated, if a bishop "of narrow views, a man out of sympathy and harmony with the genius of the new Republic had been chosen, the progress of the Catholic religion would have been seriously impeded."

But Carroll's sympathy and understanding were among his most striking characteristics, and he proved that in every problem that came before him, whether it was the project for a public library for the city of Baltimore on whose board he ultimately served for many years, or in rallying his people to the support of Madison's administration during the War of 1812 and the flock of his own see city when it was attacked by bombardment of the British fleet.

By the time that the United States concluded its second war with Britain in 1815 Archbishop Carroll had entered upon his eighty-first year. His erstwhile strength had ebbed and enfeeblement had overtaken his once healthy frame. When he was invited to deliver the principal oration at the laying of the cornerstone of the Washington Monument in the capital on July 4 of that year, he begged to be excused for, as he pleaded, his "half extinguished" voice could not be heard. The aged prelate lingered on for a few more months and finally on December 3, surrounded by the members of his family and the priests of his household, this noble churchman passed to his eternal reward. His funeral two days later was the largest that Baltimore had ever seen, and one of the city's newspapers related after the event: "We have never witnessed a funeral procession where so many of eminent respectability and standing among us, followed the train of mourners. Distinctions of ranks, of wealth, or religious opinion, were laid aside in the great testimony of respect to the memory of the man." The reporter caught in part the reason for this universal grief at the passing of Archbishop Carroll when he added, "The liberality of his character, and his Christian charity, endeared him to his Protestant brethren, with whom he dwelt in brotherly love."

Nor had Carroll's distinguished service to his country escaped remembrance, for the newspaper of that distant day remarked, "He was a patriot and loved his native land, nor should Americans forget that his exertions and benedictions as a man, and as a christian prelate, were given to the cause and independence of his country."

In Archbishop John Carroll one finds, indeed, the father of the Catholic Church of the United States, and the founder of its hierarchy. To this great man there may fittingly be applied the words which the ancient writer in *Ecclesiasticus* spoke of Moses centuries ago, "He was beloved of God and men: whose memory is in benediction." (14:1).

JOHN HUGHES, LEADER OF THE CHURCH AT MID-CENTURY (1797–1864)

Archbishop Carroll, the first Catholic bishop of the United States, was a man whose extraordinary gifts of moral leadership, organizing genius, and sterling patriotism had earned for him at his death in 1815 the unstinted praise of Americans of every shade of religious and political belief. In the interval of years between the passing of Carroll and the emergence into national fame of John Hughes, the first Archbishop of New York, the Catholic Church of this country had grown from a small band of less than 200,000 to an immense flock of over 1,600,000 souls. By 1850 Carroll's original Diocese of Baltimore had expanded to six archdioceses and twenty-five dioceses, and by this time the great city of New York — wherein Hughes' episcopacy was to be exercised — had far outdistanced all its rivals in size and future prospect.

Who, then, was this man John Hughes who twelve years before had been called upon to serve as coadjutor to the aging Bishop John Dubois, and who in the summer of 1850 was raised by the Holy See to the dignity of first archbishop of the American metropolis? Born in County Tyrone, Ireland, in 1797, Hughes had emigrated with his family to the United States as a lad still in his teens. Possessed of a superior mind and a firm will, he had augmented as best he could the meager income of his family by the performance of varied tasks until he found entry into Mount Saint Mary's College at Emmitsburg, Maryland, where he earned his way through school as a gardener and a tutor to younger boys.

For in this immigrant youth there was more than a strong mind and will; from early age there had been as well a desire in his heart to be a priest. Hampered by poverty through all his formative years Hughes,

100

nonetheless, succeeded in reaching his goal, and on October 15, 1826, Bishop Henry Conwell ordained him as a priest of the Diocese of Philadelphia.

It was a turbulent time in the United States, a period when the rising nativist hatred of foreigners and Catholics was first showing its ugly head. Father Hughes plunged into the work of the ministry with fiery zeal, and amid his pressing parochial duties he found time for repeated defences of his Church on both the public platform and in the press. The Nativists, who would deny to immigrants their right as new citizens of the United States, and to Catholics the freedom granted to them by the Constitution, found in this young priest one of the stoutest opponents in all their long and unpleasant history. Not only did Father Hughes meet them fearlessly in public debate, but seeing the evil effects that ensued from the lack of a friendly press, he founded in January 1833, the *Catholic Herald* as a weekly newspaper wherein the Catholics of Philadelphia and surrounding areas might find a defense from calumny and abuse. The valiant struggle which John Hughes carried on in these early years of his priesthood in behalf of those whose rights were threatened continued through the balance of his life. When, for example, in 1844 Philadelphia became the scene of bloody riots and the burning of the homes and churches of the immigrant poor, Hughes — by that time Bishop of New York — stood astride the path of nativist rioters in his own see city, and by his bold determination to protect the properties of the Church and the homes of innocent folk, his forthright conduct earned for him the admiration of all citizens who cherished the maintenance of law and order.

Nearly a century later Ray Allen Billington, a distinguished non-Catholic historian, in commenting on these events, said of him, "Bishop Hughes deserves credit for saving New York from a period of mob rule such as that which had racked Philadelphia."

It is not surprising, therefore, that this forceful character should have so soon recommended himself to the bishops of the United States and to the Holy See as one who was equal to rule the diocese of America's largest city. It was in January 1838, that Father Hughes was consecrated a bishop, and from the moment he entered upon his duties New York's leaders in both Church and State realized they had now at the helm a captain who was worthy of his ship. Hughes had risen in defense of the foreign-born, it is true, but he was not content merely to guard in

101

a negative way this motley crowd of newcomers against attack. On the contrary, he displayed the qualities of constructive leadership when he undertook to direct the immigrant's course into the channels of a sound and enduring American sentiment. He gave every assistance within his power to the establishment of immigrant aid societies, to programs of education in the schools which he built for the children of the immigrant, and fostering in their hearts a love for their adopted land.

So successful had he been after the first five years that when he was about to set out for a visit to Europe in 1843, William H. Seward, twice Governor of New York, sent regrets at the bishop's impending departure, and he remarked, "You have begun a great work in the elevation of the rejected emigrant, a work auspicious to the destiny of that class and still more beneficial to our common country."

The tireless efforts of John Hughes in lifting the immigrant to a respected status in American society were, indeed, a benefit to the country. But that was only one service that the first Archbishop of New York performed for his adopted land. It was Hughes who exposed the injustice practiced against the children of Catholic citizens in the common schools by the use of textbooks inimical to their religious beliefs; it was he who interrupted his conferences with his fellow bishops at the Sixth Provincial Council of Baltimore in May, 1846, when summoned to Washington by James Buchanan, Secretary of State, to advise President Polk on the delicate question of the appointment of chaplains for the armies advancing into Mexico under General Winfield Scott; and it was Hughes who arranged for the appointment — at the request of the president — of Fathers John McElroy and Anthony Rey so that these priests might help to offset the fears aroused in the Catholics of Mexico by nativist agitators that the American armies were coming to suppress their religious faith.

Every period of history is a victim to misunderstanding and misrepresentation in the realm of controversy, and the lifetime of Archbishop Hughes was no exception to the rule. Fantastic falsehoods were abroad in Hughes' day about the danger to American liberties from the Catholic doctrine on Church and State. Hughes met this misrepresentation in a typically bold way. In a meeting in New York in June, 1841, he made his position clear. He told his Catholic audience:

I would again say to you, not to mind the clamors which may be raised about a union of the Church and State. There is no danger that any one sect will ever attempt to marry itself to the State. Such an apprehension would be absurd. If ever the spirit or the letter of the Constitution of the country shall be violated in this particular, it will happen, not from any one sect rising above and lording it over all others, but from the coalition of all the others to suppress, first the weakest or most unpopular, and then next, and so on, until finally a few of the most powerful will arise and remain in the ascendant. It behoves you all, therefore, and every citizen, to see that all are protected alike — the weakest as well as the strongest, but the weakest especially. No matter what sect is assailed, extend to it, in common with all your fellow citizens, a protecting hand. If the Jew is oppressed, then stand by the Jew. Thus will all be secured alike in the common enjoyment of the blessings of civil and religious liberty. . . .

As an adopted son of the United States and as an alert and appreciative citizen Hughes knew how to value the blessings of democratic government under American constitutional rule. At a lecture in December, 1843, he again spoke on the relations of the Church to the State, and on this occasion he paid a memorable tribute to the fundamental law of the land which is worthy of record. He said:

I regard the Constitution of the United States as a monument of wisdom, — an instrument of liberty and right, unequaled — unrivaled — in the annals of the human race. Every separate provision of that immortal document is stamped with the features of wisdom; and yet among its wise provisions, what I regard as the *wisest* of all, is the brief, simple, but comprehensive declaration, that "Congress shall make no law respecting the establishment of religion, or prohibiting the free exercise thereof."

Splendid American that he was, John Hughes was no less a Catholic prelate. No voice was raised in more stirring tones than his in defense of the rights of Pope Pius IX when that pontiff was beleaguered by the radical and revolutionary movements which swept the Italian peninsula in the 1840's and forced him to flee from his own city to a refuge in the Kingdom of Naples.

To a man of the moral sensitivity of the Archbishop of New York this was wanton cruelty and theft, and he was at pains to let all his American fellow countrymen know where he stood. And yet the love which he had for the Holy Father and, too, for his ancestral home in Ireland, never tempted him to forget that he was an American. In fact, when Daniel O'Connell, the great Irish liberator, and Father Theobald Mathew, the Irish apostle of temperance, saw fit to call upon the Irish in the United States to blot out slavery, Hughes — no lover of that unhappy institution — was the first to sound his resentment of this interference in the affairs of his adopted country by two leaders of the land of his birth. So well did he balance his roles as a Catholic churchman and an American citizen that Thurlow Weed, the famous New York political leader and journalist, could say of him:

That he is a Catholic who will exert his utmost efforts to vindicate and extend his religious principles, is most true; but that he is also a Patriot and Philanthropist in the broadest and most enlightened sense of the terms; and that he will devote a clear head and a warm heart to the advocacy of rational Freedom, of universal Education, of pure Morals, and of those true Christian virtues, Charity and Peace, is equally true.

But among all the services which Archbishop Hughes rendered to his country the most famous instance came in the twilight of his life. Through the closing years of the 1850's he had watched — as had all thoughtful citizens — with increasing alarm as the dark clouds of civil strife rose more threateningly across the horizon of America's internal peace. He did all he could to counsel a preservation of peace and to prevent the outbreak of the Civil War, but in that — like the many others who had bent their efforts to a similar goal — he failed.

In the first months of the war things went badly for the Union cause and the government at Washington was gravely worried. The Confederate States had many sympathizers abroad and President Lincoln was uneasy lest this sympathy should extend itself to diplomatic recognition of the South. In his perplexity the harassed president turned to his able Secretary of State, William H. Seward, the man who years before had come to know and to respect so deeply the Archbishop of New York. Hughes had been in correspondence with Seward for many months on questions relating to the war. But he was not prepared for the sudden summons that reached him in October, 1861, when the Secretary of State asked him to come immediately to Washington to confer with the president and himself.

Briefly what Lincoln and Seward asked of Hughes was that he should go on a mission to France to persuade the government of Emperor Napoleon III to maintain its neutrality in the War between the States. The prelate answered the call of duty to his country and in less than three weeks he was on his way. The archbishop had several long and cordial interviews with Napoleon III and the Empress Eugenie in which he explained the issues at stake in the war to end slavery in the United States, and he then traveled on to Rome where he was able to offer Pope Pius IX and Cardinal Antonelli, the papal Secretary of State, similar enlightenment on the principles which motivated the Union government in the pursuit of its military aims.

Archbishop Hughes' mission proved a success, and when he died two years later that attainment was uppermost in the mind of Secretary Seward in the public tribute he paid to the archbishop in the name of President Lincoln.

Seward alluded to the service which Hughes had done the nation with, as he expressed it, "all the loyalty, fidelity, and practical wisdom which, as on many other occasions, illustrated his great ability for administration." American statesmen had fully understood the singular benefit that redounded to the Union cause from the effort of the Archbishop of New York, and Alexander W. Randall, American Minister to the Papal States, a man who had occasion to observe at close range the prelate's skillful accomplishment of his mission in the Eternal City, had told Secretary Seward a few days before Hughes left Rome, "It is a source of regret, to thousands of good men, that the Government of the United States cannot, in any appropriate way, testify its appreciation of such services."

By the time that Archbishop Hughes came home from Europe in August, 1862, his health was already showing severe strain. The war had taken its toll upon other leading churchmen, too, and on the night of July 7, 1863, while the great battle was still in progress at Gettysburg, Archbishop Francis P. Kenrick of Baltimore was taken in death. It required a supreme effort just then for John Hughes to undertake the journey south to pay his last respects to the memory of a fellow archbishop. Yet he made the trip, although he was unable to finish the Mass he had begun in the cathedral of Baltimore on the morning of the funeral.

Hughes returned to New York a very sick man, only to be drawn at once into fresh anxiety by the outbreak of the draft riots that highlighted the nation's growing weariness with war. The Governor of New York sent a hurried plea asking the archbishop if he would, as it was said, "exert your powerful influence to stop the disorders now reigning in this city."

105

The old churchman made his final effort in behalf of a public cause when he prepared an address, begged the rioters to come to him since he was physically unable to go to them, and then before a crowd of three to four thousand men gathered before his residence he pleaded in an enfeebled voice for them to lay aside the tactics of revolt and to obey the laws of their country. It was the last public appearance of this intrepid churchman. Through the next six months Archbishop Hughes continued to decline and on January 3, 1864, his life ended at the age of sixty-seven.

How inadequate is a sketch of this kind to convey the true significance of the eventful life of the first Archbishop of New York! How much remains unsaid of his mission to souls, his daily priestly concern for the spread of the faith over the far-flung expanse of his archdiocese, of his struggle to found what is today Fordham University, and of so much more. No one can hope to assess in full measure what the remarkable increase in priests, churches, and schools over the years since 1838 had cost the archbishop by way of money, energy, and anxious hours. The incoming crowds of Catholic immigrants swelled the population of the city and archdiocese so fast that never in all his years as a bishop had he been able to keep ahead of this tremendous growth. Yet through more than a quarter of a century he had given these milling thousands vigorous moral leadership, provided churches for their religious worship and schools for their children, and insistently taught them all both the principles of the gospel of Christ and those of the Constitution of the land.

Five and a half years before he died Archbishop Hughes on August 15, 1858, laid the corner-stone of a structure that had become for him a glorious and enduring dream, St. Patrick's Cathedral on Fifth Avenue. He was not destined to see the completion of this grandest of all the Catholic churches of the land, but it was due to him that its superb location was purchased and that the great edifice was conceived on so noble and impressive a scale. Beneath its magnificent vaulted roof the visitor of today who knows something of John Hughes' story may, in the words of the Machabees, "Call to remembrance the works of the fathers, which they have done in their generations" (1 Mac 2:51). It was fitting, therefore, that when the cathedral was finished fifteen years after Archbishop Hughes had left this world that his mortal remains should have been brought in January, 1883, from old St. Patrick's on Mott Street to rest in the crypt of the splendid church on Fifth Avenue, there to lie with those of his successors to await the judgment day when there will be for John Hughes — as for each of us — the final and true assessment of our lives.

JOHN LANCASTER SPALDING,
SCHOLAR BISHOP (1840–1916)

Just as the millions of Americans today represent the descendants of almost every nation on earth, so the Catholic hierarchy of our country has been drawn from the national strains of many lands. Whereas Archbishop Hughes of New York was born in Ireland, John Lancaster Spalding was the off-spring of an English ancestry which had its American origins among the earliest pioneers who crossed the Atlantic from their native Lincolnshire before the year 1650. In St. Mary's County, Maryland, this English family took root, and before the Bill of Rights had as yet become the law of the land in 1791 a branch of the family had passed over the mountains and settled on the frontier of Kentucky. There in the little village of Lebanon on June 2, 1840, was born the child who one day would rank as the most scholarly and learned American Catholic bishop of his age.

From his earliest years this lad showed an extraordinary interest in anything that would add to the cultivation of his mind; and his was the good fortune to belong to a family which had a deep appreciation for the ennobling dignity which education bestows upon the human person. Young Spalding was given, therefore, the best educational opportunities which his family could afford, and he was a youth who knew how to make the most of them. After his first schooling in Marion County, Kentucky, he spent his college days in Emmitsburg, Maryland, and in Cincinnati where at Mount Saint Mary's of the West he took his first degree in 1859.

Having decided to be a priest, he went abroad to the American College at Louvain where he enjoyed the special advantage of living in proximity to one of the greatest Catholic centers of learning in the world, the University of Louvain. Even after his ordination as a priest there in December, 1863, he still did not abandon his formal training, for he pursued further studies at the University of Freiburg in Germany before he passed on to the Eternal City and in 1865 registered at the University of Rome. This enforced absence of nearly six years from family and friends had not been spent without sacrifice of many of the pleasures which are dear to every American youth; but it enabled him to return to his native land as one of the best educated Catholic clergymen of his day.

Father Spalding was only twenty-five in that year 1865 which saw the close of the Civil War, but so unusual were his talents that his superior, Bishop Peter J. Lavialle of Louisville, did not hesitate to entrust to him the responsible office of his personal secretary. These were the years of Reconstruction when the country faced the gigantic task of healing the wounds that had been left by the War between the States. The Church no less than the State had suffered as a consequence of four long years of war, and with that in mind the Catholic bishops sought the benefit of mutual counsel in their grave concerns by convoking the Second Plenary Council of Baltimore in October, 1866. Normally it is only the older and wiser priests who are summoned to assist and advise bishops when they convene a council. But the striking qualifications of this remarkable young man of twenty-six recommended him for the post of theologian to Archbishop Francis Norbert Blanchet of Oregon, and too, to be one of only three priests chosen to preach a sermon during the council. Thus had Spalding entered upon the stage of national Catholic affairs, and he had made his mark!

Yet endowed as he was with splendid gifts which showed to such advantage in the pulpit of the cathedral of Baltimore and in the editorial offices of the *Catholic Advocate* of Louisville, the weekly newspaper for which he wrote with so much verve and taste, Father Spalding was not the kind of man to allow these signs of favor to cloud his vision with ambitious dreams of ecclesiastical preferment and honor. On the contrary, it was not long after his success in Baltimore that he asked to be relieved of his duties as secretary of the bishop so that he might devote all his energies to founding in Louisville the first parish for the colored Catholics of that city. It was due to Spalding's priestly zeal for the more neglected of God's flock that St. Augustine Church was opened, and before he was yet thirty years of age he had become the center around which there moved the thriving parochial life of Louisville's Catholic Negroes.

Father Spalding enjoyed immensely his life as a pastor of souls, and he showed every disposition to remain permanently where he was. But the death of his distinguished uncle, Archbishop Martin J. Spalding of Baltimore, in February, 1872, changed the course of his life. The archbishop's many admirers were anxious that his biography should be written before his memory had dimmed in the minds of those who had known him in life, and for this task Father Isaac Hecker, founder of the Paulists, to whom the prelate's papers had been entrusted, believed that the priest's nephew was the proper choice. Such were the circumstances in which Father Spalding relinquished his parish, moved east to undertake the new assignment, and settled down in New York for the next five years as an assistant at old St. Michael's Church.

But in New York, as in Louisville, his special gifts were soon found out and they brought him closer than before to the notice of the leaders of the Church. When, therefore, the Diocese of Peoria was established by the Holy See in 1876 it was this same young priest who was chosen to assume responsibility for its new-born life.

Consecrated by John Cardinal McCloskey in May of 1877, what were the prospects that lay before the new bishop as he turned his eyes to the west? Peoria, his see city, was then a town of 30,000 people and in the diocese which embraced nearly 17,000 square miles of north central Illinois, there were then seventy-five churches, fifty-one priests, twelve parochial schools, and a Catholic population of 45,000 souls. Bishop Spalding, consequently, had a foundation whereon to build; nonetheless, it was an immense undertaking for any man to mold and shape so many disparate elements over so large an area into a smooth and harmonious whole. But Spalding was equal to the task.

During the more than thirty years of active rule that lay ahead of him as Peoria's first bishop John Lancaster Spalding went about through the towns and villages of Illinois, inspiring the clergy and laity by his nobility of purpose, his self sacrifice in their behalf, and his ceaseless efforts for the progress of their spiritual life. How he found time for all he accomplished is a question that will always hover around his name. For in addition to inaugurating new parishes, building new schools, and providing a proper refuge for the sick, the orphan, and the aged, Bishop

109

Spalding never left off with what had been so deep an attachment of his early years, namely, his love of the things of the mind.

From year to year his fame as a preacher, his attraction as a writer, and his reputation as a thinker grew, and following the biography of his uncle in 1872 there issued from his pen a steady stream of books until by the time he was struck down by physical paralysis in 1905 he had written no less than twenty volumes which were highly prized by the reading public of his day and have an enduring value for our own.

Bishop Spalding possessed the kind of mind that was capable of conceiving truly great enterprises, and he had the force and drive to press his ideas upon his fellowmen with cogency of argument and a grace of style that could enkindle in others some of the sense of urgency that he felt so keenly in his own heart. It was such an idea about which he had begun to dream in the first years of his priesthood and of which he wrote and spoke insistently at every turn. Fresh from Europe with the intellectual ferment which had been engendered in him at the University of Louvain, Spalding felt that for the proper training of future Catholic leaders of the United States nothing less was needed than a university under the auspices of the Church. Time and again he returned to the subject in sermons, lectures, and letters to his fellow churchmen. So in earnest was he in his pursuit that in October, 1880, he told Cardinal McCloskey of New York, "I should be willing to devote my whole life to such a work, for I am persuaded that in no other way shall we be able to meet the demands which the near future will make upon us." As the preacher at the silver jubilee of St. Francis Seminary in Milwaukee in June, 1881, he rehearsed his case again, and when he learned that a plenary council of the bishops was called for 1884, he redoubled his efforts in behalf of a national university for the Church.

Spalding had not only urged his idea with force and eloquence; by the time the council met he confronted certain doubtful bishops with the handsome sum of $300,000 which he had secured from a generous Catholic laywoman to begin the work. The result was that a committee was appointed by the council, the project moved forward, and in November, 1889, Bishop Spalding had the supreme satisfaction of seeing the fulfillment of his dream when the Catholic University of America in Washington opened its doors.

Through all the awkward years of its infancy the university enjoyed the utmost in support and loyalty from the learned Bishop of Peoria. Nearly a quarter century after the inauguration of the university Spalding celebrated the golden jubilee of his priesthood. Many deserving tributes were paid to him on that November day of 1913, but none came with greater grace than that of Monsignor Thomas J. Shahan, fourth rector of the university, when he rose at the dinner in the jubilarian's honor to review the present prosperous state of the institution over which he ruled. The words of Shahan are worthy of record. He said:

No one who knows the beginnings of this work will gainsay me when I say that all this is owing to John Lancaster Spalding, that it originated in his heart and mind, and that its first measure of realization was owing to his faith in such an enterprise, his readiness to lead with voice and deed, his power of inspiring the first generous and noble gift that made it possible to pass from velleities to action, and his wisdom and courage in its earliest years, when the new institution that he had called into being walked, so to speak, through the Valley of Dispute . . .

The Catholic University of America is the most striking and enduring monument to Spalding's noble life; and as long as there are students to ascend the central staircase of its handsome library they will there look upon the features chiseled in marble of the man to whom they owe — more than to any single person — the university of which they are a part.

John Lancaster Spalding was a man whose constant preoccupation with the advancement of education in every field won many admirers and friends outside the circles of his own Church. When he appeared in Washington for a lecture in 1899 he was introduced by William T. Harris, one of the most famous men to hold the office of United States Commissioner of Education, and on that occasion Harris said:

All serious and earnest minded thinkers engaged in solving the problems of education . . . have received help from the personal counsels or from the educational writings of the Bishop of Peoria. He is the most beloved of American educational leaders.

Spalding was loved because — like Cardinal Newman's gentleman — he had his eyes on all his educational company, and the lofty spiritual principles which he so tirelessly enunciated in the graceful diction of his numerous lectures and essays carried an application for thoughtful educators, no matter to what religious affiliation they belonged.

Long before the turn of the century the Bishop of Peoria had attained national fame, and when in 1902 President Theodore Roosevelt, perplexed as to how to settle the long and bitter dispute of the operators and miners of the anthracite coal fields, decided to name a commission for a searching study of the differences that divided them, he chose Bishop Spalding as a member, a member whom the president characterized in his own words, as "one of the very best men to be found in the entire country." Spalding served with distinction in this difficult role, and to the commission's exacting duties there was given with complete generosity all the sound sense and penetrating wisdom of his superior mind in restoring peace to the prostrate industry and its suffering employees. It was Spalding, too, who lent his time and talent to the Irish Catholic Colonization Association, of whose board he was chairman for many years, that through this means the new immigrants might be directed to the farms of the West and thus be spared the hardships of so many of their brothers in the slums and factories of the industrialized areas of the East.

Bishop Spalding was personally incapable of practicing persecution and abuse; yet like his fellow Catholics he was often the victim of such unpleasantness in the days when the notorious A. P. A. was rampant throughout the land. At the height of that ugly agitation he wrote in defense of his Church in the *North American Review*, but he scorned to offer proof of Catholic's loyalty to the nation, for he said, "To protest is half to confess . . . and to urge American Catholics to love their country, which is as dear to them as their heart's blood, is to imply that they fail in this high duty. Our record for patriotism," he continued, "is without blot or stain, and it is not necessary for us to hold the flag in our hands when we walk the streets (or) to wave it when we speak . . ." Nor were love and loyalty to his native land themes which Spalding reserved for the polemics of public debate at home. He spoke the same sentiments in the center of Christendom when in a famous sermon of March, 1900, he preached in the Church of the Gesù at Rome, where he set before his Roman listeners the splendid prospect of freedom in the English-speaking world. He said in part:

In the ever-widening domain of the British Empire, in the ever-growing territory of the American Republic, democracy is triumphant; and in all these vast regions, with the exception of the Anglican Establishment, which is . . . confined to England, there is a separation of Church and State; a separation which those who are competent to judge recognize as permanent. There is everywhere freedom to write, to publish, to discuss, to organize; and there is no subject of thought, no sphere of action, no interest which it is possible to fence about and shut in from the all-searching breath of liberty . . .

112

Spalding was a man who by reason of his love of country, his appreciation of its greatness, and his awareness of its frailties could merit from Archbishop John J. Glennon of St. Louis on the day of his golden jubilee these words:

In the long roll of great men, priests and prelates of our country from Bishop Carroll's day to our own, I have no fear in placing Archbishop Spalding . . . as the one Catholic who has best understood the American mind."

This noble churchman, who was overtaken by a crippling paralysis that forced him to resign his diocese in 1908, had long before earned the admiration of all thoughtful minds. On June 11, 1902, Columbia University in New York bestowed upon him the honorary degree of doctor of letters in a citation which read:

Descendant of a house honored among two peoples; Christian, priest and prelate, man of letters, orator, educator and patriotic citizen.

Two years later a similar honor was conferred upon the learned bishop by Western Reserve University in Cleveland. When physical incapacity had rendered his active service as a minister God no longer possible, a grateful Church raised him to the rank of a titular archbishop. Archbishop Spalding lingered on in his retirement for eight years and died on August 25, 1916. To this scholar bishop there may appropriately be applied the words of the writer of the Old Testament:

Many shall praise his wisdom; and it shall never be forgotten. The memory of him shall not depart away, and his name shall be in request from generation to generation. — (Sir 39:12–14)

JOHN IRELAND, DEFENDER OF DEMOCRACY (1838–1918)

The annals of the nineteenth century record few events of a more pathetic character than the terrible famine which struck Ireland in 1845. As a consequence of this disaster the island was for years a scene of desolation, and thousands fled before the dreadful scourge to a happier home beyond the seas. Among that impoverished throng was Richard

Ireland who came to the United States in 1849 with his wife and family, among whom was an eleven-year old son John. After temporary residence in Boston and Chicago this thrifty carpenter and his little flock sought a permanent haven in the rising pioneer town of St. Paul. Here young John served as an altar boy to Joseph Cretin, the first Bishop of St. Paul, whose spiritual insight told him that in this Irish lad he had found a future priest; and it was through the initiative of this good bishop that he was sent to a seminary in Cretin's native France. The eight years he spent in France offered to the agile mind of the youth from the American frontier an opportunity to master French in such a way that for the balance of his life it remained for him a second mother tongue. Returning to the United States at the age of twenty-three, Ireland was ordained a priest in December, 1861, and in the following spring the deep love of country which was so characteristic of him had its first open manifestation when he enlisted as a chaplain of the Fifth Minnesota Volunteers. During the second year of the Civil War, Father Ireland gained the admiration of all his men in the role of their spiritual counselor and friend, and only a severe attack of yellow fever which overtook him at Vicksburg forced the intrepid priest to resign his post just as General Grant was opening his historic siege of that Mississippi town.

The former chaplain went home to rest, but not for long. As soon as he had regained his strength his extraordinary energies were again geared for priestly work, and so successful was he in its pursuit that his bishop made him rector of the cathedral and his principal adviser in the expanding responsibilities of the Diocese of St. Paul. From the outset of his priesthood Father Ireland actively identified himself with every worthy public cause. Using to the utmost the oratorical gifts, of which he was such a master, the towns of the Northwest rang with his denunciations of political corruption and with his forthright championing of a movement which he made the crusade of a lifetime, the temperate use of drink. John Ireland had seen ample evidence of the havoc wrought in men's lives through excessive drink, and when Minnesota's legislature in 1887 passed a high license law to curb the abuse, the state owed that enactment to no single man more than it did to him.

From the time that Bishop Thomas Grace had ordained this outstanding priest he had realized what a force for good he could be in the Diocese of St. Paul. Personally unable to attend the Vatican Council in

1870, the bishop sent young Father Ireland to Rome to represent him, and five years later Grace — by now a somewhat weary man — consecrated his favorite at the age of thirty-seven as coadjutor bishop with right of succession to the See. Bishop Ireland responded with zest to the challenge of a larger field of action. Fulfilling with fidelity the routine assignments of his office as a shepherd of souls, he had time besides for enterprises beyond the strict call of duty, when he sensed that they would lift the moral and material well being of his people.

During his first years in the United States he had known something of the dangers that surround life in the slums of large industrial towns; his bold imagination was fired, then, by the chance to relieve these city dwellers' plight on the vast and rolling farm lands of the West. In 1879 Ireland bought up huge tracts of land in his native state and parceled them out to colonizers on easy payment, for which he made himself responsible. Thus did he render practical the aims of the Irish Catholic Colonization Association he had helped to found, and which now enabled so many needy immigrants from Ireland, as well as families from the crowded cities of the East, to start life anew on the healthful open prairies of Minnesota.

But it was in the field of education that John Ireland made even a greater contribution to his Church and to his country. The Catholic University of America owes much to the memory of this man, for it was he who joined with Bishop Spalding in insisting on its location in the nation's capital; it was he who gave it its name; and it was he who battled valiantly with the forces arrayed against it when the university was still in the discussion stage. Nor did the Archbishop of St. Paul content himself with playing a leading role in the establishment of a national university for the Church. He deserves as well to rank in the forefront of those who advanced the growth of religious elementary schools, and it was he who became the special champion of those who sought justice for these schools. John Ireland's contribution to American education has likewise left its enduring mark upon higher learning in the Northwest, for in the city of St. Paul today there stand as monuments to his resourceful mind the College of St. Thomas for boys, the St. Paul Seminary for priestly studies, and the College of St. Catherine, in which the Sisters of St. Joseph before its opening in 1905, had no more powerful and courageous friend than the archbishop.

Just as Archbishop Ireland had in earlier years extended a helping hand to those who earned their living from the soil, so as the industrialization of his country quickened its pace, he gave greater time and thought to the vexing problems which beset the world of labor. From 1887, when he stood beside Cardinal Gibbons and nobly seconded the latter's efforts to win the Church's blessing for the Knights of Labor, the Archbishop of St. Paul never allowed his interest in labor's cause to wane. Yet his support of the working man against the evils of the industrial order was always given with discrimination. A half century ago the archbishop foresaw the dangers of socialism and warned the laborers of the peril which it concealed. In a famous address to the unions of St. Paul on Labor Day of 1903, he gave them hearty backing for their rights, but he urged them, too, to keep in mind their duties and to be as sparing as they could in the use of strikes to gain their ends. In conclusion to that stirring talk of 1903 he said:

Because I love the cause of labor, and give to it the deepest sympathies of my heart, I pray that it be ever honorable and honored, ever worthy of itself and of the high interest of humanity entrusted to its keeping.

Long before John Ireland was raised in 1888 to the dignity of first Archbishop of St. Paul, he had earned a reputation as one of the great orators of his time. Small wonder, then, that for the principal speaker of so many prime events the choice should have fallen on him. And how he delighted to direct these discourses to the harmony subsisting between Church and State in the United States! Intensely American as he was, he never tired of dwelling upon this harmony, upon the blessings which the Catholic Church conferred on the nation and the wonderful results which the Church had reaped from the freedom and liberty granted to it by the great Republic of the West! His fellow bishops heard this theme when he preached before them in the Third Plenary Council of 1884, and five years later in the same cathedral of Baltimore, and before an even more distinguished audience, he hailed the centennial of the country's hierarchy in a masterly sermon on "The Mission of Catholics in America."

Nor was the majestic eloquence of this man limited to the solemn celebrations of his Church. Time and again leaders in the world of politics and business chose him for their spokesman. For example, in October, 1899, Chicago played host to William McKinley, President of the United States, and Archbishop Ireland was among those who were asked to speak. He entitled his address, "The American Republic: The

Ideal Embodiment of Democracy," and after reviewing the unparalleled record of the United States for personal freedom through its century of constitutional rule, the archbishop asked "Have I fear for America?" to which he gave his own resounding answer when he said:

I have no fear. I know America and her people; I see her in the history of a century; I see her in her aspirations and her resolves. It matters little to me what the difficulties are that may confront us, be they political, social, or industrial. I have trust in the good sense of the people, I have trust in the power of public opinion. I have trust in the freedom of the Republic and in the healthful discussion which it allows. I have trust in American justice. I have trust in American democracy and in the civic virtues that are begotten of its life and inspirations. Perils have arisen and perils will arise; America has overcome those of the past; she will overcome those of the future. I have no fear.

No Catholic churchmen of the United States in these years — with the single exception of Cardinal Gibbons — enjoyed more widespread fame in Europe than the Archbishop of St. Paul; and there, too, he was heard as the featured speaker at many memorable events. In May, 1899, Ireland preached the panegyric in the cathedral of Orleans, France, in honor of Joan of Arc. He emphasized the lessons to be learned from the life of the maid, for Joan of Arc enabled him to inculcate a sentiment that was ever near to his heart, namely, the love that men should have for their native land. There at Orleans the archbishop uttered words which we of this generation may ponder to our profit. He said:

Today, with the lowering of exalted ideals, which are the springs of disinterested and generous enthusiasm, love of country is in peril of losing its fervor and power of sacrifice: cold, calculating selfishness, masking itself under a vague humanitarianism, is striving to take its place. To-day, love of country needs a solemn consecration.

A year later when President McKinley sought an American who would best voice the sentiments felt by the United States for France at the presentation of a statue of Lafayette that would stand in Paris as a symbol of our friendship, it was to John Ireland that he turned. On July 4, 1900, the Archbishop of St. Paul stood before the immense throng in the Place du Carrousel as the spokesman of his fellow countrymen to the populace of France, and he seized the chance to pronounce again his deep conviction in the superior merits of democratic

rule. "The age of the people has come," he said, (and) "It will remain
. . .

The people never abandon rights which they have once possessed, or
powers which they have once wielded in defense of those rights. To seek
arguments against democracy on account of its perils to society, is to waste
time. These perils are to be studied, but only in order to be averted. The
progress of democracy cannot be stayed.

One would not wish to over-emphasize the oratory of John Ireland,
lest, perhaps, the impression be created that he was but a man of words.
Few men of his time would less deserve such imputation. Not only did
he serve his Church and country by dedicating his superb gifts of public address to their advance; but his life was itself a practical fulfillment
of the ideals of religious truth and moral rectitude which he preached
so strikingly by word of mouth. In the emergency of 1898 with Spain he
put forth strenuous efforts as the personal emissary of Pope Leo XIII
at Washington to find a peaceful solution to that conflict. In that he
failed, but when the war was over no citizen of our country gave more
unselfishly of his time and talents in assisting Presidents McKinley and
Roosevelt in solving the tangled problems inherited with our new island
empire than did the Archbishop of St. Paul. Moreover, at a time when
communism was already on the march and radical movements were
coloring the thought of the working classes, Ireland was among the foremost promoters in Americanizing the immigrant and in repelling with
all the force at his command any threat — whether real or imagined —
that might harm the body politic from abroad. Archbishop Ireland loved
the United States, with a devotion so intense as sometimes to arouse an-
noyance within less patriotic hearts. But he never allowed this love of
country to dim his sense of what was owing to his Church. In a famous
sermon preached at Washington in 1896 when the A.P.A. had again enkindled the fires of anti-Catholic bigotry, he made that clear. He proclaimed:

I am a Catholic; I am a priest and bishop; but I am an American citizen,
and I must be debarred from no rights or privileges accorded to other citizens
because I am a Catholic, or because I carry upon me the insignia of my priesthood. Separation of Church and State? Most assuredly. The State must not
aid in the propagation of the faith of a church, but she must not impede and
hamper the Church in her work and close her out from the necessary opportunities to do it. Separation of Church and State? Most assuredly again.

But let there not be in the working out of this separation, wild and extreme measures, which would tend to make society Godless and destroy in it all moral life and supernatural hopes.

John Ireland was a big man, and he did everything in a big way. In 1907 he laid the cornerstone of the magnificent Cathedral of St. Paul, and in the following year there followed a similar ceremony for Minneapolis' handsome Basilica of St. Mary. Henceforth the Twin Cities would have noble churches worthy of the strength and grandeur, into which Archbishop Ireland through the labors of nearly a quarter of a century had elevated Catholicism in the Northwest. It was typical of the size and breadth of this man's thought and action that in May, 1910, he should further highlight this growth when he consecrated six of his priests on a single morning as bishops of his suffragan sees, the largest episcopal consecration ever to be held within the United States.

No one in the American Church of these years appreciated Archbishop Ireland more highly and loved him more dearly than Cardinal Gibbons of Baltimore. For over forty years these two cherished friends had struggled side by side through one of the stormiest periods of the Church's history, and as they grew old the bonds of affection were more tightly knit between Baltimore and St. Paul. Each Christmas season Ireland despatched his greetings to his friend, and in Christmas week of 1917 — Ireland's last upon earth — he remarked that the approaching new year gave him one more opportunity, as he expressed it,

of telling you of my gratitude for all your kind acts and affectionate tenor of soul in my regard during the many years of our ministerial labors for Church and country, and of wishing you the most precious blessings in the keeping of the Divine Hand.

He marveled at the old cardinal's constant health, and adverting to the trying ordeal of the first world war through which they were then passing, he said, "It is delightful to notice how you are holding the Church in the fore-ground in these meaningful days of war."

As Cardinal Gibbons approached the golden jubilee of his episcopacy in 1918 he invited Ireland to preach again, as he had done at the silver jubilee twenty-five years before. But by now the archbishop was in his eightieth year and his end was near at hand. On October 20, 1918, the friends of the cardinal gathered about him in Baltimore to commemorate his anniversary, but by that time Archbishop Ireland had been dead a month. Yet he was not forgotten, for as Gibbons reminisced about his own very long and eventful life, he recalled at the dinner in his honor how most of his friends of other days were gone, and he then paid to the memory of the Archbishop of St. Paul a touching tribute which so well summarized the accomplishments of his departed friend that it may serve, we hope, as a fitting close to what we have wished to say here. The cardinal stated:

> The last Prelate who has descended below the horizon of the tomb was the Venerable Patriarch of the West, the great Apostle of temperance, the sturdy Patriot who had endeared himself to the American people, without distinction of race or religion, the man who had contributed perhaps more than any other to demonstrate the harmony that exists between the Constitution of the Church and the Constitution of the United States. Needless to say, I am speaking of John Ireland, the Lion of the fold of Juda.

JAMES GIBBONS, FRIEND OF POPES AND PRESIDENTS (1834–1921)

It is appropriate that these five biographical sketches should conclude with an account of one of the seventeen American churchmen who since 1875 have been honored with membership in the College of Cardinals, in this case a man who, in the judgment of many thoughtful observers, was the greatest single figure in the history of American Catholicism.

James Gibbons was born in Baltimore on July 23, 1834, of Irish immigrant parents. His childhood was spent in Baltimore and in Ballinrobe, Ireland, and the education that was begun in that little village of County Mayo was taken up again in 1855 when he enrolled at St. Charles College in Maryland to begin his studies for the priesthood. It ended at old St. Mary's Seminary, Baltimore, just two months after the outbreak of the Civil War, for Gibbons' ordination occurred less than a month before the battle of Bull Run. Thus was he launched upon his life's career at a time when his country was entering the long and cruel ordeal of the War between the States. Throughout the war Father Gibbons not only served the people of his two parishes with complete fidelity, but he found time as well to minister to the sick and wounded soldiers who filled to overflowing the military hospitals of his native city. It was a foreshadowing of this young priest's life-long devotion to his country that he should have been one of three Catholic clergymen to follow the body of Abraham Lincoln on that sad day of April, 1865, when the remains of the martyred president were escorted through the streets of Baltimore on the way to their last resting place in Springfield.

The course of men's lives is often changed by circumstances of which they had never even dreamed. Father Gibbons had been supremely happy in his work as a parish priest, and in that role he would have gladly spent his days. But that prospect was radically changed with the advent to Baltimore in 1864 of a new archbishop, Martin J. Spalding, whose discerning eye at once detected in the winning ways, the quick mind, and the priestly bearing of this man one who combined uncommon qualities for the advancement of the Church's interests. And from the day that Gibbons was summoned from his pastorate to act as secretary to Archbishop Spalding his rise was rapid. In less than three years he found himself, at the age of thirty-four, the first Vicar Apostolic of North Carolina and the youngest bishop in the United States. Four years of notable service in the Tar Heel State recommended him for further honors, and in 1872 he was nominated as Bishop of Richmond. In less than five years thereafter, upon the death of Archbishop James Roosevelt Bayley, Bishop Gibbons, still only forty-three, became the eighth successor to John Carroll as Archbishop of Baltimore and the occupant of America's premier see.

Surely something more than the friendly favor of a powerful archbishop was necessary to account for such a rise as this! The full explanation is to be found in the man himself. James Gibbons was a person whose code of personal conduct was so obviously based upon the law of love that all who came in contact with him felt instinctively that they had met a man of God. High intelligence, exquisite tact, profound wisdom, and interests that were well nigh universal supplemented a noble bearing and a lofty moral tone that bespoke the Christian gentleman and called forth from high and low, from rich and poor, from Catholic, Protestant, and Jew a respect seldom accorded to any living man.

In brief, these were the reasons for his speedy advancement in the ecclesiastical state, and these were the reasons, too, why he had attained at the end of his life a position in American society which enabled a non-Catholic journalist to say of him shortly after his death, "He was, more than any other man, in and out of official life, the mentor of the nation."

Americans of every class and creed were joyful, therefore, when Pope Leo XIII chose the Archbishop of Baltimore as the second son of their country to wear the cardinal's hat. And they were confirmed in their high opinion of the pontiff's choice when Cardinal Gibbons took possession of his titular church in Rome in March, 1887, and preached a sermon that will never be forgotten. He first spoke of the ordeals which the Church had suffered wherever despotism had cast its dark shadow over the government of men. But, as he added, "in the genial atmosphere of liberty she blossoms like a rose." It was the new cardinal's way of introducing to his distinguished Roman audience the principal point of his address. He then said:

For myself, as a citizen of the United States, and without closing my eyes to our shortcomings as a nation, I say, with a deep sense of pride and gratitude, that I belong to a country where the civil government holds over us the aegis of its protection, without interfering with us in the legitimate exercise of our sublime mission as ministers of the Gospel of Christ. Our country has liberty without license, and authority without despotism.

It was little wonder that an enthusiastic newspaper editor should write some days later:

No such words have ever been uttered to the world by an American bishop since Archbishop Carroll founded the See of Baltimore, nor ones to make every true American citizen thank God he has such a representative at the Eternal City.

Yet the cardinal's famous sermon on Church and State at Rome was only the first of many such pronouncements which he made over the years. Nearly a quarter century later in a memorable article which he contributed to the *North American Review* he remarked:

American Catholics rejoice in our separation of Church and State; and I can conceive no combination of circumstances likely to arise which should make a union desirable to Church or State. . . . Other countries, other manners; we do not believe our system adapted to all conditions; we leave it to Church and State in other lands to solve their problems for their own best interests. For ourselves, we thank God we live in America, in this happy country of ours, to quote President Theodore Roosevelt, where "religion and liberty are natural allies."

122

This normally mild and gentle churchman could, in circumstances which he felt demanded it, reveal hidden depths of courage and boldness that almost startled men. In 1887 when the suspicion of many highly placed in both Church and State overshadowed the Knights of Labor as a secret and evil society, Cardinal Gibbons rose to the defense of this early organization of working men in a way that was long remembered. In a remarkable document which he submitted to the Holy See to save the knights from condemnation, he marshaled in cogent fashion every argument he could advance, for, as he told the Roman cardinals, "To lose the heart of the people would be a misfortune for which the friendship of the few rich and powerful would be no compensation." In the sequel the American knights were not condemned. That same forthrightness came to light a few years later when there arose within American Catholic ranks a danger to both Church and State from clashing national rivalries. In a sermon delivered in August, 1891, at Milwaukee the cardinal struck out at these ultranationalists when he declared:

Woe to him who would sow tares of discord in the fair fields of the Church in America! Woe to him who would breed dissension among the leaders of Israel by introducing a spirit of nationalism into the camps of the Lord! Brothers we are, whatever may be our nationality, and brothers we shall remain.

All through his life Cardinal Gibbons was a keen student of history, and the more he read and pondered the history of the Church and the history of the United States the more was he convinced of the remarkable development which both owed to the instrument of government framed by the founding fathers of the Republic. When the nation celebrated the centennial of the Constitution in September, 1887, he was one of the principal figures at the side of President Grover Cleveland during those events, and no one who knew the cardinal doubted for a moment his sincerity when in accepting the invitation to participate he told the centennial commission, "The Constitution of the United States is worthy of being written in letters of gold." Ten years later he presided in his capacity as Chancellor of the Catholic University of America at the installation of its second rector. On that occasion he set before his university audience the twin ideal which he felt should motivate their academic lives, namely, service to God and to nation, and he then stated:

If I had the privilege of modifying the Constitution of the United States, I would not expunge or alter a single paragraph, a single line, or a single word of that important instrument. The Constitution is admirably adapted to the growth and expansion of the Catholic religion, and the Catholic religion is admirably adapted to the genius of the Constitution. They fit together like two links of the same chain.

The prestige which Cardinal Gibbons attained in American public life was such as probably few other private citizens have ever enjoyed. In the summer of 1898 the perplexing problems surrounding the conquered possessions of Spain were causing grave concern to President McKinley. He sent for the cardinal to ask his advice as to whether the United States should keep the Philippines, and he received an answer that in all likelihood came as a surprise. "Mr. President," said His Eminence, "it would be a good thing for the Catholic Church but, I fear, a bad one for the United States." Two years later President Theodore Roosevelt sought his counsel on the best manner of handling the tangled case of the Church's lands in the Philippines, and before William Howard Taft left the country at the head of the Philippine commission that bore his name he went to Baltimore to confer with this wise little man. Nearly twenty years thereafter at the end of World War I the covenant of the League of Nations was before the American Senate. It was made known to the cardinal by a high source in Washington that a statement from him would be appreciated, and when President Wilson had read the cardinal's favorable interview in the press he told him:

You have perceived, as is habitual with you, the really profound interests of humanity and of Christianity which are involved in the issue of the adoption of the League Covenant, and it is with profound pleasure that I find myself aligned alongside of you in this great cause, to which the anxious and prayerful thought of every Christian man, it seems to me, must turn with hope that will permit no denial.

In the same manner the sovereign pontiffs sought and won the support of Cardinal Gibbons in the many crises that beset them in their governance of the Universal Church. For twenty-five years the Cardinal of Baltimore was the prime interpreter to America of the policies of Leo XIII.

For example, in the days when an anti-clerical government in Italy was threatening the independence of the Holy Father's rule, Gibbons spoke out in clear and ringing tones that carried the story of that injustice to the citizens of the United States. When Pius X was harassed by the cruel persecution of the Church in France, it was an interview to the press from the cardinal that won international attention and served to clarify the issue and to remove from men's minds the misunderstanding of what had so aggrieved the old pontiff. During World War I the neutral position of Benedict XV was fiercely assailed by both the warring camps and every imaginable falsehood was spread abroad concerning his secret aid to the enemy of each. In this intolerable position the pope found a strong defender in a far off land, and in 1918 Cardinal Gibbons published an article which was thought so able an exposition of the neutrality of the Holy See that Pope Benedict XV ordered it translated for use abroad.

Throughout all the years of his exceedingly busy life the cardinal always found time for prayer, reflection, and the careful preparation of all that he spoke and wrote. It is difficult to understand how a man in his position could have written five books, as well as numberless articles and sermons. Yet he did, and there was on all he wrote the stamp of meticulous care. If he had written *The Faith of Our Fathers* and nothing else, he would have earned a title to lasting fame, for that book — published over ninety years ago — is still an active item in religious bookstores, and its sale of more than two million copies entitles it to rank as the most successful work of Catholic apologetics in the English tongue. Hundreds found their way into the Catholic Church through a perusal of the cardinal's famous volume, and over the years he received countless testimonies of its beneficent effect upon men's lives.

There were many who in substance told the cardinal what the daughter of Nathaniel Hawthorne wrote him in 1906 when she said of *The Faith of Our Fathers*, "It has kept me observant of the beautiful influence of your holy power during many years." The same enduring memory followed his sermons, and he frequently had evidence of their helpful effects. For example, on one occasion an atheist doctor wandered accidentally into the cathedral of Baltimore on a day that the cardinal preached. Years later the doctor wrote him and he said, "The little seed of hope which you planted in my heart that Sunday, began to grow, and in the course of time I made a public profession of my allegiance to God."

How many little seeds of hope had this blessed man not dropped into the souls of men through his richly abundant life of nearly eighty-seven years! In attempting to sketch the elements of his greatness within this narrow a compass, one feels how inadequate it is to convey the secret of his fame. By 1911 when he had reached the golden jubilee of his priesthood Cardinal Gibbons had long since won international repute. And yet, famous as he was, the civic demonstration held in Baltimore on June 6 of that year surprised in size and magnificence even his closest friends. President William Howard Taft, former President Roosevelt, members of the cabinet, the Congress, the Supreme Court, and the diplomatic corps appeared on that June day before the great throng of 20,000 people who had gathered to do honor to the aged churchman. And those who witnessed the event and heard the laudation of him from the highest men of state, agreed with the Washington *Post* when it remarked on the following day, "Such a demonstration was never before seen on this hemisphere." The old cardinal lived on for ten more years, and during World War I men turned more and more to him for his treasured counsel. It was during these anxious days of war that Theodore Roosevelt told him in a letter, "Taking your life as a whole, I think you now occupy the position of being the most respected, and venerated, and useful citizen of our country."

Death took the noble cardinal on March 24, 1921. The funeral was held in his beloved cathedral, crowded by the great of Church and State, and Archbishop John J. Glennon preached the eulogy. As we now take leave of Cardinal Gibbons there returns to mind the prayer of the Archbishop of St. Louis uttered on that solemn occasion over forty years ago, a prayer in which every man who has ever known anything of the genius of Cardinal Gibbons will gladly join. It was Easter week, and in allusion to that holy season the archbishop said:

Let us hope that in the white light of that Resurrection we are still commemorating, the Saviour triumphant, meeting His servant in the garden there, may greet him with the words of eternal life: "I am the resurrection and the life, he that believeth in me, though he be dead, shall live," and crown him with blissful immortality.

ARCHBISHOP CARROLL AND THE LITURGY IN THE VERNACULAR

The trend toward a more generous use of the vernacular in the liturgy has gained considerable headway of recent years in certain countries of Europe. It is a movement which has been attracting increasing attention in the United States, and in view of that fact it may be of interest to students of the liturgy to know the views once held by the father of the American hierarchy on this subject of current interest.

John Carroll himself came of old American stock, having been born at Upper Marlboro, Maryland, on January 8, 1735. By reason of the penal legislation against Catholics in colonial Maryland the only formal education he could receive in his native land was a short period of schooling in the furtive little academy at Bohemia Manor which was located in Cecil County near the Pennsylvania-Maryland border. Fortunately, the family was one of means and they were able, therefore, to send young Carroll abroad where he secured a finished education at the Jesuit schools of St. Omer and Liège, entered the Society of Jesus, was ordained a priest, and spent several years on the continent and in England as a teacher and missionary. He was thirty-nine years of age when he returned home in 1774 after an absence from his family and friends of more than a quarter of a century.[1]

The young American priest arrived in the land of his birth on the eve of the revolution that would win for his country its independence. Cut off as they then were from contact with ecclesiastical superiors in England, it became necessary for the few and scattered Catholics to seek some kind of organization. After prolonged negotiations the Holy See finally named Carroll as superior of the missions of the United States. This important step in the history of the Church in America occurred on June 9, 1784.

Besieged as he was from the very outset by a multitude of problems in his efforts to bring the little Catholic flock through these critical pioneer days for both Church and State, Carroll was confronted — even before he knew of his appointment from Rome — with the very un-

[1] For full biographical details cf. the two-volume work of Peter Guilday, *The Life and Times of John Carroll, Archbishop of Baltimore, 1735–1815* (New York, 1922).

pleasant duty of answering a serious attack upon Catholicism that had been made by a priest who had recently apostatized from the Church, the Maryland-born ex-Jesuit, Charles Henry Wharton. Wharton's pamphlet of nearly forty pages was published at Philadelphia in the early summer of 1784 and was entitled *A Letter to the Roman Catholics of the City of Worcester* (England) where he had been stationed for some years before his return to the United States in 1783.

The appearance of the Wharton work, polished and urbane as it was in both style and tone, made it imperative that a Catholic answer should be furnished to his attack upon the Church's doctrines, and for this task it was decided that Father Carroll was the best equipped of all the American priests of the time to provide an adequate reply. It was in no sense a congenial assignment and yet Carroll sensed the importance of the issue at stake and was at pains to outline the dangers to the integrity of faith for American Catholics if an answer were not forthcoming to Wharton. John Carroll expressed the high evaluation which he revealed all through his life on American Catholics maintaining kindly and charitable relations with their fellow citizens of other religious faiths when he said:

But even this prospect should not have induced me to engage in the controversy, if I could fear that it would disturb the harmony now subsisting amongst all christians in this country, so blessed with civil and religious liberty; which if we have the wisdom and temper to preserve, America may come to exhibit a proof to the world, that general and equal toleration, by giving a free circulation to fair argument, is the most effectual method to bring all denominations of christians to an unity of faith.[2]

Carroll worked hard at the job during the summer of 1784 and in the autumn of that year Frederick Green, a printer at Annapolis, brought out his brochure which was almost three times the length of Wharton's and which bore the title, *An Address to the Roman Catholics of the United States of America*. Library facilities were severely limited at that early date and among the meager sources at his command Carroll had found much helpful material in the work of the English priest, Joseph Berington, called *State and Behaviour of English Catholics from the Reformation to the Year 1780* (London, 1780). Both sides of the Wharton-Carroll controversy were widely read among interested Angli-

[2] A Catholic Clergyman [John Carroll], *An Address to the Roman Catholics of the United States of America* (Annapolis, 1784), p. 114.

cans and Catholics in England during the next few years. The English Catholics were at that time still under the heavy pressure of the penal laws of earlier years to which the Catholic relief act of June, 1778, had only opened a faint prospect of future remedy.

Several years after the appearance of his answer to Wharton the American superior expressed to Berington the admiration he had for the latter's book and suggested further subjects for the pen of the gifted English priest who by this time had attained considerable fame by his able, if at times unconventional, writings.

It was in the course of this letter — undated but from internal evidence known to have been written in 1787 — that there occurred a strong plea for the liturgy in the vernacular. Carroll stated that in his judgment the two principal obstacles to a proper understanding of Catholicism by Protestants were the character and extent of the spiritual jurisdiction of the Holy See and the use of the Latin language in the liturgy. He then told Berington:

With respect to the latter point, I cannot help thinking that the alteration of the Church discipline ought not only to be solicited, but insisted on as essential to the service of God and benefit of mankind. Can there be anything more preposterous than for a small district containing in extent no more than Mount Libanus and a trifling territory at the foot of it, to say nothing of the Greeks, Armenians, Coptics, etc., to have a "liturgy" in their proper idiom and on the other hand for an immense extent of Countries containing G.B., Ireland, also N. Am., the W. Indies etc. to be obliged to perform divine service in an unknown tongue; and in this country either for want of books or inability to read, the great part of our congregations must be utterly ignorant of the meaning and sense of the publick offices of the Church. It may have been prudent, for aught I know, to refuse a compliance in this instance with the insulting and reproachful demands of the first reformers; but to continue the practice of the Latin liturgy in the present state of things must be owing either to chimerical fears of innovation or to indolence and inattention in the first pastors of the national Churches in not joining to solicit or indeed ordain this necessary alteration.[3]

This striking statement was so much in sympathy with Berington's own views on the question that he took the liberty of publicizing it in the controversy in which he was then engaged with his superior, John

[3] Archives of the Archdiocese of Baltimore, Special C, C–1, Carroll to Berington Baltimore [1787], copy. The version of this letter in Guilday, *op. cit.*, I, 130, differs in a number of particulars from the original copy.

Douglass, Vicar Apostolic of the London District. As a consequence Carroll received letters of protest against the stand he had taken from several quarters in the British Isles where there then existed rather grave tension between conflicting groups within the Catholic body.[4] Among those who deprecated his opinions on the liturgy in the vernacular were John Thomas Troy, O.P., Archbishop of Dublin, who informed Carroll that he had written a pastoral letter of some sixty pages against the proposal, and Arthur O'Leary, O.F.M., chaplain to the Spanish Embassy in London and a famous controversialist of the period.

But John Carroll was not a man to be easily frightened or dissuaded from his views. He replied to O'Leary's strictures on his criticism of Pope Clement XIV for having suppressed the Jesuits and for his opinions on the liturgy, and in acknowledging that he had used Berington's book in preparing his reply to Wharton, Carroll then informed the Franciscan:

> In a letter to him [Berington] and before I had a thought of ever being in my present station, I expressed a wish that the pastors of the Church would see cause to grant to this extensive continent jointly with England and Ireland, etc. the same privilege as is enjoyed by many churches of infinitely less extent; that of having their liturgy in their own language; for I do indeed conceive that one of the most popular prejudices against us is that our public prayers are unintelligible to our hearers. Many of the poor people, and the negroes generally, not being able to read, have no technical help to confine their attention.

But being the true realist that he was Carroll made it plain to O'Leary that Berington had attributed to him projects in the United States which far exceeded his powers, projects in which, as he candidly added, "I should find no co-operation from my clerical brethren in America, were I rash enough to attempt their introduction upon my own authority."[5]

Meanwhile, of course, Father Berington was delighted with Carroll's broad approach to the question of the liturgy and other matters discussed in their correspondence, and in a letter of March, 1788, he remarked that for some time they had been hearing in England that he was designed for what he called "the American Mitre," although a recent report had it that the rumor was premature. He was sorry if it

[4] For the internal strife among the Catholics of Great Britain and Ireland during the 1780's cf. Bernard Ward, *The Dawn of the Catholic Revival in England, 1781–1803*, 2 volumes (London, 1909), *passim*, and the briefer account in David Mathew, *Catholicism in England, 1535–1935* (London, 1936), pp. 136–158.

[5] Carroll to O'Leary, Baltimore, undated, cited in Guilday, *op. cit.*, I, 131.

should turn out that Carroll was not to be the first American bishop, for, as he said, "With your liberality of mind, we had every reason to know, that the Catholic Church of the United States would have been raised on proper foundations."[6] But the report that had circulated among the English Catholics about Carroll was at length verified and on November 6, 1789, Pope Pius VI erected the Diocese of Baltimore and named John Carroll as its first ordinary. He was consecrated by Bishop Charles Walmesley, O.S.B., at Lulworth Castle, one of the estates of the wealthy English Catholic, Thomas Weld, on August 15, 1790, and after some weeks spent among his English friends the new bishop returned to his immense charge at the close of that year.

After he had attended to the most pressing problems demanding his attention Carroll sent out a call to the priests to assemble at Baltimore on November 7, 1791, for the first synod of the infant diocese. He was in session with his twenty-two priests for four days and on November 10 they drew up the regulations which should govern the carrying out of the ceremonies and offices of the Church for Sundays and the principal feast days of the ecclesiastical year.

In the synod of November, 1791, the advanced position assumed by Carroll in his correspondence of 1787–1788 with Berington and O'Leary on the subject of a vernacular liturgy was greatly modified. Whether or not he made any attempt during the synod to implement his ideas of earlier years, we have no way of knowing. In all likelihood the realization of his lack of power to decide such matters without reference to the Holy See, plus the fine balance and common sense which never seemed to fail Carroll during his long and eventful life, prompted him to pass over the question until a more propitious time.

At any rate, among the synodal rules it was specified that at Masses on Sundays and feast days the gospel of the day should be read in the vernacular, but that was the only mention made of it here. At afternoon vespers benediction of the Blessed Sacrament was ordered with a catechetical instruction to follow, and in this connection it was added, "*Optandum est ut inter officia hymni aliqui aut preces lingua vernacula cantentur* — It is desirable that some hymns or prayers be sung in the mother tongue during the services."[7] In cases where there was but a

---

[6] Berington to Carroll, Oscot near Birmingham, March 27, 1788, quoted in Guilday, *op. cit.*, I, 132.

[7] *Concilia provincialia Baltimori habita ab anno 1829 usque ad annum 1849* (Baltimore, 1851), p. 20.

single priest to carry out all the ceremonies it was prescribed that after he had heard confessions and completed preparations for Mass there should be recited either the litany of the Holy Name or of Loretto — unless the choir should wish to sing in the *"lingua vernacula."* After Mass the whole congregation was to recite, once more in the vernacular, the Lord's prayer, the Hail Mary, the Apostles' Creed, and the acts of faith, hope, and charity.[8] These were the only references to the liturgical use of English in the synodal decrees.

Seventeen years after this first diocesan synod of the United States, on April 8, 1808, Rome raised the premier see to the status of the Archdiocese of Baltimore with suffragan sees at New York, Philadelphia, Boston, and Bardstown. The interval had witnessed grave disturbances and dangers to the unity and integrity of faith among the American Catholics by reason of the abuses of lay trusteeism and the clash of rival national groups within the Church. Therefore, when the consecration ceremonies of the new bishops were held at Baltimore in late October and early November, 1810, Archbishop Carroll took the occasion of the prelates' presence in his see city for a series of conferences with his coadjutor bishop, Leonard Neale, and the three suffragans, John Cheverus of Boston, Michael Egan, O.F.M., of Philadelphia, and Benedict J. Flaget, S.S., of Bardstown, in order that they might offer some remedy to the situation.

That there had arisen differences in practice, insofar as the use of the vernacular in the liturgy was concerned, was evident by the regulations enacted by the bishops at this time, for among them there was found the following:

It is being made known to the Archbishop and Bishops that there exists a difference of opinion and practice among some of the clergy of the United States concerning the use of the vernacular language in any part of the public service, and in the administration of the Sacraments. It is hereby enjoined on all Priests not only to celebrate the whole Mass in the Latin language, but likewise when they administer Baptism, the Holy Eucharist, Penance and Extreme Unction, to express the necessary and essential form of those Sacraments in the same tongue according to the Roman ritual; but it does not appear contrary to the injunctions of the Church to say in the vernacular language the prayers previous and subsequent to those Sacred forms, provided however, that no translation of those prayers shall be made use of except one authorized by the concurrent approbation of the Bishops of this ecclesi-

8 *Ibid.*

132

astical Province, which translation will be printed as soon as it can be prepared under their inspection. In the meantime the translation of the late venerable Bishop Challoner may be made use of.[9]

The various manifestations of the mind of John Carroll on the subject of the liturgy in the vernacular between 1787 and 1810 provide an interesting insight into a minor aspect of the life of the first Archbishop of Baltimore. The liberal attitude which he displayed in his letters to clerical correspondents in England as superior of the American missions during the late 1780's gave way before the practical difficulties which he encountered after he had assumed the episcopal character. We find, therefore, that the regulations of the synod of 1791, over which he presided as bishop, permitted only a very limited use of the vernacular. And by 1810 the harassed Archbishop of Baltimore was so plagued by administrative problems of all kinds arising within his ecclesiastical province that he joined with his fellow bishops in November of that year in discountenancing the abuses that had appeared in the form of unwarranted use of the vernacular by priests in some parts of the country, even in the celebration of the Mass.[10]

No American churchman of that age could be found who would more quickly frown upon practices of this kind without the proper permission of the Holy See than John Carroll. Yet had he lived in a more disciplined age, when he might have moved forward on this question without the danger of giving further rein to unruly trustees, rebellious priests, and quarreling nationalist groups within the American Church, it is safe to say that Archbishop Carroll would have been in the vanguard of any movement to bring the sublime offices of the Church closer to the faithful and to those outside the fold by having as much as possible of the liturgical services performed in a language which they fully understood.

[9] The volume cited above contains the synodal regulations of 1791, but only "*quidam ex articulis*" from the disciplinary rules of the hierarchy's meeting in 1810 (pp. 25-28), and that on the vernacular is not among them. The passage quoted in the text has been taken from Guilday, *op. cit.*, II, 592.

[10] But these modifications should not cause one to lose sight of the important fact that the regulations issued in 1810 by Carroll and his suffragans imply permission for priests to employ a maximum of English in administering the sacraments. In fact, the bishops seemingly took for granted in 1810 something for which many students of the liturgy have been pleading for a long time, namely, the use of the vernacular in all aspects of sacramental administration except the words embodying the essential forms of the sacrament.

THE CENTENNIAL OF THE FIRST PLENARY COUNCIL OF BALTIMORE

On Sunday, May 9, 1852, there took place in the Cathedral of the Assumption in Baltimore the formal opening of the First Plenary Council of the Catholic Church in the United States. Over twenty-six years had elapsed since that day in October, 1829, when Archbishop James Whitfield and five of his suffragans had assembled in the same cathedral for the First Provincial Council of the American bishops. In the interval six other provincial councils had been held in Baltimore and at the last one, in May, 1849, the prelates had petitioned the Holy See for the erection of three new ecclesiastical provinces, namely, Cincinnati, New Orleans, and New York.[1] On July 19, 1850, Rome had responded favorably to this petition by erecting the three provinces so that, with Oregon City and St. Louis having been created metropolitan sees several years before, it became necessary to broaden the base of the next conciliar gathering of the American hierarchy to that of a plenary character.

Before the council of 1849 disbanded the prelates had decided to seek the permission of Rome to hold a plenary council and the subject, therefore, had been on their minds during the intervening period. Archbishop John Hughes of New York had discussed the question of a national council on his visit to the Holy See early in 1851, and the day before he sailed from Liverpool for home in June of that year he urged Bernard Smith, O.S.B., professor of theology in the Urban College of the Propaganda Fide and Vice Rector of the Irish College in Rome, to do what he could to hasten the Holy See's appointment of a prelate to take charge of the necessary preparations. As Hughes reminded his Benedictine friend, the American bishops lived at great distances from each other and a good deal of time would be needed for proper consultation on a project of such vast scope.[2] But it was Francis Patrick Ken-

[1] Peter Guilday, A History of the Councils of Baltimore (1791–1834) (New York, 1932), pp. 156–57. This work is the only general account of the conciliar activities of the American hierarchy.

[2] Department of Archives and Manuscripts of The Catholic University of America, Smith Papers, Hughes to "Revd. dear Friend," Liverpool, June 9, 1851, microfilm. Hereafter this depository will be designated as CUA. The need for mutual consultation was expressed by Bishop John J. Chanche, S.S., of Natchez to Archbishop John B. Purcell of Cincinnati three weeks before the council opened. He

rick, the Archbishop of Baltimore, who would have to assume the principal burden of preparations on this side of the Atlantic after Pope Pius IX had appointed him as apostolic delegate for the council on August 29, 1851, and it was Kenrick, too, upon whom there would devolve the duty of acting as host to the American hierarchy and their theologians in his see city.[3]

Archbishop Kenrick began his preliminary plans months in advance and on November 21 he issued the formal letter of convocation to his fellow bishops and set May 9 of the following year as the opening date of the council.[4] On the same day he issued a pastoral letter to the priests and people of the Archdiocese of Baltimore in which he informed them of the coming event, asked their prayers for its success, and told them:

The object for which this Council is summoned, is by wise enactments and measures to promote discipline, and enforce the sacred Canons, or to submit such modifications of them as local circumstances may require, to the mature and enlightened judgment of the chief bishop, who is divinely charged with the solicitude of all the churches.[5]

was anticipating a visit to Cincinnati before the council and he remarked, "I do feel the necessity of talking to you so much about matters & things — The Archb. of New Orleans, too, feels the same cravings." (Archives of the Diocese of Natchez, Chanche to Purcell, Natchez, April 14, 1852, photostat of original from the Cincinnati Papers in the Archives of the University of Notre Dame.) The writer is indebted to the kindness of the Most Reverend Richard O. Gerow, Bishop of Natchez, for typed copies made from these photostats in the archives at Natchez. Hereafter this archives will be referred to as ADN.

[3] Some weeks before the council Kenrick told his brother, the Archbishop of St. Louis, "Up to the present time I have not determined where to lodge the priests; but perhaps the faithful may offer them lodging." Kenrick to Kenrick, Baltimore, March 20, 1852, in [Frances E. Tourscher, O.S.A., (Ed.)], *The Kenrick-Frenaye Correspondence . . . 1830–1862* (Philadelphia, 1920), p. 331. The papal brief appointing Kenrick as apostolic delegate is printed in Donald C. Shearer, O.F.M. Cap., *Pontificia Americana* (Washington, 1933), pp. 270–72. There is a discrepancy in the sources on the date of this document. In *Concilium plenarium totius Americae Septentrionalis Foederatae Baltimori habitum anno 1852* (Baltimore, 1853), p. 4, it is given as August 19, and so also in Guilday, *op. cit.*, p. 172. However, Shearer, *op. cit.*, p. 272, gives August 29 which he took from Raphaëlis de Martinis (Ed.), *Juris pontificii de Propaganda Fide*, (Rome, 1894), VI (Pars prima), 122.

[4] Archives of the Archdiocese of Baltimore, 32B-Z-1, "Acta episcopalia," p. 53. The writer wishes to express his gratitude to the Reverend Paul L. Love, Archivist of the Archdiocese of Baltimore, for his generous assistance in helping to locate items for this essay. Hereafter this archives will be designated as AAB.

[5] CUA, Guilday Collection, a printed copy of Kenrick's pastoral letter of November 21, 1851.

All through the winter and early spring of 1852 Kenrick continued to keep in close touch with his colleagues in the hierarchy, and his correspondence was especially heavy during these months with his brother, Archbishop Peter Richard Kenrick of St. Louis,[6] and with close friends like Bishops Martin J. Spalding of Louisville and John Timon, C.M., of Buffalo. After Bishop John B. Fitzpatrick of Boston had declined to preach the sermon at the customary requiem for the bishops who had died since the council of 1849, Kenrick turned to Spalding. He remarked that Fitzpatrick had begged off for the reason that he had not known the deceased prelates enough, and especially, added Kenrick, "the venerable Flaget who ought to be the main subject of the panegyric." Benedict J. Flaget, S.S., the pioneer bishop of the Middle West who had ruled the See of Bardstown (Louisville) from 1811 to his death in February, 1850, would, indeed, be the principal figure to be treated in any sermon dealing with the prelates who had died since they had last assembled. Referring to the explanation given for Fitzpatrick's refusal, Kenrick stated, "You cannot put in that plea; so waiving all excuse, please prepare for that grand occasion." He went on to say that in the coming council they must consider the necessity for new dioceses and it was his belief that Boston and Philadelphia should be made metropolitan sees, while he quoted the Bishop of Boston as having indicated his desire that new dioceses be established at Burlington, Vermont, and Portland, Maine.[7]

As the weeks passed Kenrick gradually completed his choices for the various conciliar offices and functions. In the councils of 1843, 1846, and 1849 the Sulpician Bishop of Natchez, John J. Chanche, had acted, along with Bishop Michael Portier of Mobile, as the promoters. But when Kenrick asked Chanche to serve once again in that capacity the latter remembered an objection that had been raised by Peter Kenrick of St. Louis at an earlier council to the promoterships being held by two bishops. Therefore, before he replied he consulted his own metropolitan, Archbishop Antoine Blanc of New Orleans.[8] Only after having received assurances that Portier no longer wished to fill the office and that Kenrick would explain the arrangement he had in mind to the Bishop of

[6] For an English translation of the Latin letters of Francis to Peter Kenrick on council business from December 24, 1851, to December 30, 1853, cf. Tourscher, *op. cit.*, pp. 320–362.

[7] AAB, 34-J-14, Kenrick to Spalding, Baltimore, Jan. 21, 1852, copy.

[8] ADN, Chanche to Blanc, Natchez, January 24 and February 7, 1852, copies.

Mobile, did Chanche give his consent. As he told Blanc, "I think now, I can say no more. If any objection is raised, it must be the Prelates at the Council. I have acted with all the delicacy which the circumstances require."[9]

In the course of his correspondence with Kenrick on the subject of the promotership Chanche took occasion to say that he believed that the council ought to last more than a week and he emphasized, too, that the bishops should agree on a unified mode of action in dealing with secret societies. He then added, "Would it be proper that the national council should repeat the request of the last Provincial Council with regard to the Immaculate Conception of the Blessed Virgin?"[10] In 1849 the bishops had petitioned the Holy See to make a doctrinal pronouncement on the Immaculate Conception, and it was this action to which the Bishop of Natchez was referring.[11] A copy of the Archbishop of Baltimore's reply could not be found, but a few weeks later Chanche expressed himself to Kenrick as satisfied to leave the subject of the Immaculate Conception off the agenda.[12] In a letter of the same day to Archbishop John B. Purcell of Cincinnati, Chanche revealed something of what lay behind his decision not to press the matter. He said:

I think with you, it is better to say nothing more on the subject of the Immaculate Conception. We have expressed our opinions & our wishes to the Holy See with sufficient clearness. Besides any further action on the subject might wound the feelings of those who dissented.[13]

[9] *Ibid.*, same to same, Natchez, March 13, 1852, copy: AAB, 28-G-4, Chanche to Kenrick, Natchez, Feb. 3, 1852; 28-G-5, same to same, Natchez, March 15, 1852; Chanche summarized the negotiations over the promotership to the Archbishop of Cincinnati and he remarked, "I shall have this office by prescription if the Prelates don't take care" (ADN, Chanche to Purcell, Natchez, March 15, 1852, copy).

[10] AAB, 28-G-4, Chanche to Kenrick, Natchez, February 3, 1852.

[11] According to the official record of the first public congregation of May 7, 1849, Archbishop Samuel Eccleston, S.S., sought the opinions of the theologians as to the desirability of petitioning the Holy See for a definition of the doctrine. *Concilia provincialia Baltimori habita ab anno 1829 usque ad annum 1849* (Baltimore, 1851), p. 270. Later in the council there were enacted two decrees relating to this subject. The first was in response to a request of Pius IX of Feb. 2, 1849, asking for information concerning the attitude of their people toward the Immaculate Conception, in which the bishops declared that there was a strong devotion among American Catholics to the Virgin Mary under this title; in the second decree it was stated that the bishops would be very gratified if the pontiff were to define the doctrine if in his judgment it were thought opportune (*Ibid.*, pp. 277–78).

[12] AAB, 28-G-5, Chanche to Kenrick, Natchez, March 15, 1852.

[13] ADN, Chanche to Purcell, Natchez, March 15, 1852, copy.

Apparently there had been opposition from some of the bishops when the petition was voted upon three years before.

It was natural that the apostolic delegate should be particularly anxious to have the opening sermon at the first solemn session of the council set the tone for their deliberations, and for this important task he first turned to Bishop John McCloskey of Albany. McCloskey's reply could not be found but in all likelihood he declined out of deference to his own metropolitan, the Archbishop of New York.[14] Not only was it fitting that the great See of New York should thus be honored, but John Hughes enjoyed at that time the best reputation in the hierarchy for pulpit eloquence. Upon receipt of Kenrick's invitation Hughes remarked that he had seen nothing to be added to the topics proposed in the preliminary schema for the council which he had recently received and, as for the sermon, he would be willing to undertake the assignment. "I understand it, however," he said, "as an awful responsibility — and I shall arrange my thoughts in regard to it in such a manner, that it will be impossible to refer *hereafter* to any thing said at the first National Council, except as going to strengthen the bonds of the Catholic Unity, as tested by eternal devotion to the See of Peter." The Archbishop of New York then gave the apostolic delegate the benefit of some comments that he had picked up in Rome the previous year. He had found the officials at the Congregation of the Propaganda annoyed at the American bishops over the increasing flow of requests for dispensations of one kind or another that had been reaching them of recent years from the United States. They had likewise complained that in former American councils the "censuerunt Patres" had been presented in too naked a form and had not carried a brief outline of the reasons and motives of the bishops for the views they had advanced on many questions. These were reflections that might be considered with profit, although the lack of cordiality that for some years had marked the relations between the two archbishops probably deprived them of some of the cogency they might have enjoyed had they emanated from another source.[15]

[14] Archives of the Archdiocese of New York, Kenrick to Hughes, Baltimore, March 1, 1852. Hereafter this archives will be designated as AANY. Over three months before Kenrick communicated with Hughes he had told his brother in St. Louis, "I have invited the Bishop of Albany to give the opening address in the Council. . . ." (Kenrick to Kenrick, Baltimore, November 24, 1851, in Tourscher, *op. cit.*, p. 329). No reply of McCloskey to Kenrick could be found in the AAB.

[15] AAB, 29-I-1, Hughes to Kenrick, New York, March 15, 1852. Apparently Hughes' suggestion on the last point was not heeded, for nearly a year later Kenrick

Knowledge of the forthcoming council at Baltimore had reached Ireland by the early spring and Paul Cullen, Archbiship of Armagh, sent his greetings to the American hierarchy through Kenrick and wished the latter to assure them that the Irish Catholics would be forever grateful for the assistance the Americans had given to the Catholic University of Ireland. Cullen felt they would be glad to learn that the plan for a university in Dublin was making headway. Those were dark days in Ireland when the devastating effects of the potato famine of the late 1840's were still keenly felt. The Archbishop of Armagh and his colleagues of the Irish hierarchy were deeply concerned, as he said, over the wholesale emigration that was taking place among their people and the frightful condition in which so many of these unfortunates were leaving their homeland. With the approaching council at Baltimore in mind he told the apostolic delegate:

Should you or the other Prelates think it well to propose any measures to us regarding the innumerable emigrants now flying from this unhappy land, it would afford us great pleasure to receive and act on your suggestions. Direct and frequent communication upon this and other important matters between the Prelates of the two countries where their interests are common, might be the means of impeding many of the evils, to which our poor exiles are subjected whilst flying from their native land.[16]

---

informed his brother that he had been told by Giacomo Cardinal Fransoni, Prefect of Propaganda, and Bishop John McGill of Richmond that the Roman congregation wished, as he expressed it, "to have more detailed information on the reasons which move us to ask for the erection of new sees, and the merits of the men named" (Kenrick to Kenrick, Baltimore, Jan. 18, 1853, in Tourscher, *op. cit.*, p. 347). For the earlier differences between Kenrick and Hughes cf. Hugh J. Nolan, *The Most Reverend Francis Patrick Kenrick, Third Bishop of Philadelphia, 1830–1851* (Washington, 1948), pp. 202 ff. and John R. G. Hassard, *Life of the Most Reverend John Hughes, First Archbishop of New York* (New York, 1866), pp. 144 ff.

[16] AAB, 28-T-3, Cullen to Kenrick, Drogheda, April 19, 1852. There are no copies of Kenrick's replies to Cullen in the AAB. Cullen was transferred from Armagh to Dublin less than two weeks after this letter was written. At this time John Henry Newman was getting ready to cross to Ireland to deliver his famous series of lectures on university education. On the very day of Cullen's letter Newman, writing from the Oratory in Birmingham, told his friend, Thomas W. Allies, "I am going to Ireland every day. . . ." Cf. Fergal McGrath, S.J., *Newman's University. Idea and Reality* (New York, 1951), p. 151. Newman crossed on May 7 and delivered his first lecture in the Rotunda at Dublin on May 10, the day after the council opened in Baltimore (*Ibid.*, pp. 152–53).

Cullen had given attention to the subject of Irish immigration to the United States soon after his consecration at Rome in February, 1850. He had been commissioned by the Holy See to convene a plenary council in Ireland, the first since

But by the time this letter reached him Kenrick's hands were more than full and neither the meager records of the sessions nor the decrees of the council gave any indication that the subject of the Irish immigrants was discussed in May, 1852.

By the last days of April the final schema for the council was in the hands of the bishops, as John N. Neumann, C.SS.R., newly consecrated a month before by Kenrick himself as fourth Bishop of Philadelphia, informed the latter.[17] Only a few important matters concerning the organization of the gathering remained to be settled, and one of these was the place to be given to the superiors of the religious orders and congregations. It was a question that worried Bishop Michael O'Connor of Pittsburgh and, although he made it clear that he was willing to abide by whatever the Holy See might direct, he set forth his views at some length. He said:

I think we should guard carefully against our feeble hierarchy being swamped by the number and influence of the religious orders which are not of natural growth in the country. They are rather organizations encouraged and blown into life by influences from abroad who did not wish to work through the regular authorities, than the material growth and expression of the piety of the country.[18]

O'Connor was inclined to believe that abbots and provincials had a right to sit in the council, but of this he was not certain. In the sequel the single abbot in the United States at the time was accorded only a consultative vote in the morning private congregations at which he sat with the bishops, and the eleven other religious superiors of various ranks were permitted to cast a consultative vote on proposed legislation at the afternoon public congregations.[19]

1642. It opened at Thurles on August 22, lasting until September 9, 1850. About six weeks in advance of the Irish national council the Archbishop of Armagh acknowledged Kenrick's congratulations on his promotion and he stated, "I would be particularly obliged if you would give me any hints regarding our synod. You see so many of our poor people in America, that you must know what their wants are, better than we do. It would be most useful for me to know what your experience in America is regarding mixed colleges and mixed education in general" (AAB, 28-T-2, Cullen to Kenrick, Drogheda, July 5, 1850). On the action taken by the Irish bishops at Thurles on the subject of education cf. McGrath, *op. cit.*, pp. 73–77.

[17] AAB, 30-U-6, Neumann to Kenrick, Philadelphia, April 29, 1852.

[18] *Ibid.*, 30-W-9, O'Connor to Kenrick, Pittsburgh, April 19, 1852. O'Connor was certainly no enemy of the religious, for he had wished in his younger years to become a Jesuit and in May, 1860, he made good that desire by resigning his see and entering the Society of Jesus.

[19] *Concilium plenarium* . . . , pp. 26–27.

A week before the date set for the formal opening the *Catholic Mirror* of Baltimore carried an editorial on May 1 in which it spoke of the signally favored position of the American Church which was free to hold councils at will, unlike the Church in some other countries. The progress of Catholicism in the United States during the first half of the nineteenth century was emphasized and the editorial writer then stated:

What a contrast between the meeting of Catholic prelates at Baltimore, in 1810, consisting of the venerable Carroll, with his coadjutor and three other bishops, and the council that is to assemble a few days hence. What an expansion of the Church, even since the first provincial council in 1829, at which only six prelates and fourteen priests assisted.

The following week the *Catholic Mirror* noted in its issue of May 8 the fact that Archbishop Francis N. Blanchet of Oregon City, the farthest removed from Baltimore, had been among the first to arrive. Bishop Maurice de Saint-Palais of Vincennes was in Europe and would not attend, but the *Catholic Mirror* reported it as probable that Archbishop William Walsh of Halifax and Bishop Armand F.-M. de Charbonnel, S.S., of Toronto, who were expected to be visitors in the city, would be there. But the chief interest of the writer in the council's personnel was reserved for Abbot Maria Euthropius Proust, O.C.S.O., of the Abbey of Our Lady of Gethsemani near New Haven, Kentucky, who had been blessed the previous October as the first mitred abbot in the United States and who was scheduled to appear. Apparently the *Mirror's* reporter found bishops in Baltimore a commonplace sight, but a mitred abbot in 1852 was still a curiosity to many American Catholic eyes.

At last all was in readiness and on Sunday morning, May 9, the solemn procession of the participating prelates and clergy moved from the archbishop's residence on Charles Street along Mulberry Street and into the cathedral. The procession was headed by students from St. Mary's Seminary who acted as acolytes, after whom came the theologians and the minor conciliar officers to the total of about sixty priests, followed by twenty-five bishops, the five archbishops, and finally Archbishop Kenrick, the apostolic delegate, and his chaplains. The music of the Mass, that of Mozart's Mass No. 12, was sung by the cathedral choir who were not only accompanied by the organ but by the Germania Band which added a further touch of pomp to the occasion. The Mass was celebrated by Kenrick and the sermon was preached by Hughes

141

who took for his text the discourse of our Lord to His disciples wherein He described Himself as the door to the sheepfold and the good shepherd (*Jn* 10:1–16). "If there was any thing," said the Archbishop of New York, "that seemed to press on the heart of the divine Redeemer more than another, it was the unity of the disciples." The preacher then went on to show how, in spite of the variety of races and tongues embraced within the Church, its children had remained through the centuries united in one faith. Near the end of his sermon the archbishop referred to the prelates gathered before him for the council about to open, and he remarked, "They meet here as the early Apostles met. They meet as brethren, to examine into the affairs of the Church; and when the proper time comes . . . in the joint name of the Holy Ghost and themselves, they promulgate the decisions."[20]

Following the Mass and sermon the list of the principal officials of the council was read and it included Bishop Chanche and François Lhomme, S.S., Vicar General of the Archdiocese of Baltimore, as promoters with Edward L. Damphoux, S.S., as notary, and the secretaries were to be Patrick N. Lynch, Vicar General of the Diocese of Charleston, and Thomas Foley, Chancellor of the Archdiocese of Baltimore, both destined to be future bishops. The man chosen for the office of master of ceremonies was Francis Burlando, C.M., and the cantors were announced as Louis de Goesbriand, Vicar General of the Diocese of Cleveland who within a year and a half was to be named first Bishop of Burlington, and Mr. John Dougherty, a student of St. Mary's Seminary, who was ordained the following year as a priest of the Archdiocese of Baltimore. Bishops John Martin Henni of Milwaukee and Joseph Cretin of St. Paul arrived several days after the formal opening of the council so that ultimately there were six archbishops, twenty-seven bishops, including de Charbonnel of Toronto, one abbot, and fifty-eight priests who participated in the sessions that occupied the next ten days.

What were the events that were highlighting the American scene in the period that the bishops chose for their first plenary council? At the time Millard Fillmore, a Whig, was President of the United States and the nation had reached a total population of 23,191,876 in the census of

---

[20] The full text of the sermon was published by Lawrence Kehoe in his edition of the *Complete Works of the Most Rev. John Hughes, Archbishop of New York* (New York, 1865). The quoted passages may be found in II, 193, 197. The *Catholic Mirror* of May 15, 1852, apologized for giving only excerpts since the reporter upon whom they were counting ran off to Washington before he had fully transcribed his notes.

1850. Only four years before the country had come through the excitement that had attended the discovery of gold in California and the acquisition of a new imperial domain wrested from Mexico after a brief war that had terminated in the Treaty of Guadalupe Hidalgo in February, 1848. The first women's rights convention had met the same year at Seneca Falls, New York, and American audiences were to hear much in the days ahead from female reformers like Lucretia Mott and Elizabeth Cady Stanton, while in another sector of the reform front Maine had passed its famous prohibition law in 1851. The expansion of the nation was mirrored in the accelerated pace of railroad construction after Congress had adopted the policy of liberal land grants for that purpose in 1850. The State of Illinois, for example, had been the recent recipient of a bountiful grant with which the Illinois Central Railroad was soon under construction, and by June, 1851, the Erie Railroad had reached Dunkirk, New York, to win the honor of being the first railway to make connections with the Great Lakes. But the bishops of the Far and Middle West were not served on their journey to the council by the pioneer Baltimore and Ohio since it did not reach Wheeling, Virginia (West Virginia), until Christmas of 1853.

The question that overshadowed all others, however, in the period immediately before the calling of the council was that of slavery. The startling growth of California that followed the discovery of gold, and the knotty problem of whether to organize the new domain wrung from Mexico as free or slave, threatened for a time to endanger the Union. It was only the series of compromises submitted to Congress by the aged Senator Henry Clay of Kentucky and which finally passed into law in September, 1850, that postponed for another decade the final adjudication of this tantalizing question by a resort to arms. Far-sighted men realized that the settlement of 1850 was only a compromise; nonetheless, they were grateful to Clay and to those who supported him for having offered a plan that had at least gained them more time. But the political compromises did not come promptly enough to preserve the unity of some of the principal Protestant churches, for as early as May, 1845, the southern Baptists and Methodists had broken with their northern brethren over the slavery issue and schism was to follow among the Presbyterians on the same question in 1857.[21] Yet differ as they did

[21] William Warren Sweet, The Story of Religion in America (New York, 1939), pp. 430–440.

143

over the burning question, the Catholic bishops of the North and the South did not allow it to divide their counsels, and when they convened at Baltimore in the spring of 1852 Archbishop Blanc of New Orleans and his suffragans from the deep South sat side by side with their northern episcopal colleagues during the debates on the measures that were to be taken to advance the spiritual welfare of their respective flocks.

The decade immediately preceding the holding of the plenary council had been one filled with unpleasantness for these bishops and their people by reason of the Nativists' campaigns of hate against Catholics and foreigners. True, the worst fury of the Nativists had been spent by 1852, but there were still painful reminders in all sections of the land of their ugly handiwork. Nor had the movement completely died out; it was only temporarily dormant. In the month before the council opened a secret society, calling itself the Order of the Star Spangled Banner and first organized in 1849, passed into the hands of more energetic management when James W. Barker took control. Under Barker who assumed charge in April, 1852, the order expanded rapidly and, as the historian of this movement stated, "within four months more than a thousand members were enrolled and its influence was felt in the municipal elections of 1852."[22] Secret though this rising Know-Nothing group then was, the Catholic bishops were quite aware of the opposition which previous councils of the American Church had aroused and they knew the same forces were still watchful of their every move. This fact was probably in the minds of a number of the prelates as they set out for Baltimore in May of that year.

The year of the plenary council was a presidential election year, and the publication on March 20 of Harriet Beecher Stowe's *Uncle Tom's Cabin* helped to heighten the political tension that filled the air until after the close of the campaign in November. As a recent authority on the period has said:

It was obvious as 1852 opened that personalities and party loyalty, not questions of public policy, would decide the coming contest. The country was enjoying a prosperous lull after the storm, and any mandate it gave would be for a continuance of the truce. Business interests had decreed that the recent

[22] Ray Allen Billington, *The Protestant Crusade, 1800–1860* (New York, 1938), p. 381.

compromise must stand, and with business was aligned the great mass of farmers, workmen, and professional folk.[23]

It was only ten days after the bishops had closed their meeting in Baltimore that the Democrats gathered in the same city and nominated Franklin Pierce, a small town lawyer from New Hampshire to be their candidate, after leaders like Lewis Cass, James Buchanan, and Stephen A. Douglas had failed to win the necessary votes. Two weeks later the Whigs followed their rivals into Baltimore and in this convention, too, the outstanding leaders killed one another off and General Winfield Scott of Virginia emerged the victor for the nomination of his party.

The city to which the American Catholic bishops came in the spring of 1852, to be followed so soon by the nominating conventions of the two leading political parties, offered in itself an example of the era of expansion through which the nation was passing. Baltimore then had a population of 170,000 people and it was growing steadily. Not only was it the metropolis of the State of Maryland and the largest city and seaport between Philadelphia and New Orleans, but for over sixty years now it had been the center of American Catholic activities with most of the leading events of the Church held in this premier see. In the three and a half decades since John Carroll's death the Church of the United States had shown a growth parallel to that of the nation, and in the year of the mid-century the Catholic population of the country was estimated to be 1,606,000.[24] The Catholic people were scattered over the entire United States and their religious life was then organized in six archdioceses, twenty-five dioceses, and three vicariates apostolic. Within the confines of these thirty-four ecclesiastical jurisdictions there were 1,411 churches and 681 so-called stations in which the Catholic people worshipped, with their spiritual needs cared for by a total of 1,421 priests of whom 1,242 were engaged in parochial work and the remaining 179 in teaching and other duties.[25]

If the Catholic increase since the meeting of Carroll's hierarchy in

[23] Allan Nevins, *Ordeal of the Union* (New York, 1947), II, 3. Nevins' is a very detailed account of these years.

[24] Gerald Shaughnessy, S.M., *Has the Immigrant Kept the Faith?* (New York, 1925), p. 134.

[25] *Metropolitan Catholic Almanac and Laity's Directory . . . 1852* (Baltimore, 1852), p. 257. There was one vacant see at the time of the council, Walla Walla, which was being administered by Bishop A. M. A. Blanchet and which was suppressed by Rome in July, 1853.

1810 drew the surprised comment of the writer in the *Catholic Mirror* in the week before the opening of the First Plenary Council, how much more surprised would he be by the comparative figures of a century ago and those of the present time! The 1952 *Catholic Directory* listed the Catholic people in the United States as numbering 27,766,141 who were governed by twenty-four archbishops, of whom three were cardinals, 102 bishops, one vicar apostolic, and one abbot nullius. Counting the two sees that were then vacant one gets a total of 130 ecclesiastical jurisdictions against the thirty-four of a hundred years before. Moreover, besides the 128 ordinaries there were likewise one coadjutor archbishop, seven coadjutor bishops, and forty-six auxiliary bishops to make a hierarchy of 182 prelates in contrast to the thirty-three bishops who ruled the Church of the United States in 1852. The 1,421 priests of a century ago had now increased to 43,889 and the 2,092 churches and stations of 1852 had multiplied during the century to a total of 28,488 churches, chapels, missions, and stations wherein religious services are held.

But to return to the council at Baltimore. There were some interesting personalities among the prelates and priests who participated in the sessions of May, 1852. Mention has already been made of Archbishop Kenrick, the apostolic delegate, who was easily the outstanding theologian of the American Church at the time, and of John Hughes, the colorful Archbishop of New York, who had already won national fame for his great fight over the question of religion in the public schools, but who yet had before him what was probably the most famous episode of his life, namely his mission to Europe in November, 1861, for President Lincoln and the Union government. Seated with them in the places reserved for the metropolitans were Blanchet of Oregon City, Kenrick of St. Louis, Blanc of New Orleans, and Purcell of Cincinnati. Of the twenty-four American bishops who took counsel in those days with their metropolitans one third were members of religious orders or congregations. They numbered one Redemptorist (Neumann of Philadelphia), one Sulpician (Chanche of Natchez), two Vincentians (John M. Odin of Galveston and Timon of Buffalo), two Dominicans (Richard P. Miles of Nashville and Joseph S. Alemany of Monterey), and two Jesuits (James Van de Velde of Chicago and John B. Miège of Indian Territory). The oldest bishop in the council by date of appointment was Portier of Mobile, consecrated on November 5, 1826. From far off New Mexico came its vicar apostolic, John Baptist Lamy, who with Kenrick of St. Louis and Alemany of California were the only ones to attend all three plenary councils of the American Church as bishops. Among the prelates at Baltimore in 1852 the two who were destined to play the most prominent roles in the years ahead, apart from several already mentioned, were Spalding of Louisville who as Archbishop of Baltimore (1864–1872) would convoke the Second Plenary Council in 1866, and McCloskey of Albany who in 1864 succeeded Hughes as second Archbishop of New York and eleven years later became the first cardinal of the United States. Eight countries figured among the birthplaces of the thirty-three American ordinaries of 1852 and these were ranked in the following order: the United States and France nine each, Ireland eight, Belgium and Canada two each, and Austria, Spain, and Switzerland one each. Only a fraction over one-fourth of the prelates, therefore, were native-born Americans in this year, and the leading role which France had played in American Catholicism in the early nineteenth century was still evident with the French-born bishops ranking equal in number to those of the United States. The national origins of the American hierarchy would change considerably in the ensuing decades and France would ultimately fall behind Germany as the birthplace of bishops who ruled American sees.

Of the twelve superiors of religious orders the man who attained the greatest fame before his death in 1887 was undoubtedly Boniface Wimmer, O.S.B., who three years after the council was named the first Benedictine abbot in the United States and who exercised a wide and beneficent influence on American Catholicism from the flourishing St. Vincent's Abbey at Latrobe, Pennsylvania, which he founded and over which he ruled for so many years. Among the priests who were designated as theologians and officials of the council there were nine future bishops: Augustine Vérot, S.S. (Savannah and St. Augustine), Anthony O'Regan (Chicago), Napoleon J. Perché (New Orleans), John Loughlin (Brooklyn), James Roosevelt Bayley (Newark and Baltimore), Josue M. Young (Erie), Thomas Foley (Chicago), Patrick N. Lynch (Charleston), and John J. Conroy (Albany).

Likewise numbered among the priests who were in Baltimore in the spring of 1852 were several who were to acquire outstanding reputations within their own dioceses and beyond. For example, two of the theologians to the apostolic delegate were Henry B. Coskery, who for so many years was the Vicar General of the Archdiocese of Baltimore, and Charles I. White, the first editor of the *Catholic Mirror* and the author of several books, among them the *Life of Mrs. Eliza A. Seton, Foundress and First Superior of the Sisters of Charity in the United States* which was announced in the *Catholic Mirror* of May 15, 1852, as having recently been put to press by Edward Dunigan & Brother of New York. There was also James Fitton of Boston who served as theologian to Bishop Chanche and who had already made a name for himself in his native New England, a man whose life proved to be one of the most fruitful missionary careers in the American Church before its close in 1881.[26] Another priest who had shown a missionary zeal in the Middle West almost equal to that of Fitton in New England was Peter Kindekens, Vicar General of the Diocese of Detroit, who served his ordinary, Peter P. Lefevere, as theologian in the council. Father Kindekens was the man who four years later was chosen to act as the agent of Bishops Spalding and Lefevere in founding an institution to train priests for the American missions at the Catholic University of Louvain, and it was Kindekens who in March, 1857, became the first Rector of the American College at Louvain, an office he held until December, 1859.[27] Ignatius Reynolds, the Bishop of Charleston, had as his theologians John Murray Forbes and Sylvester Malone, two well-known priests of the Archdiocese of New York. The former was a convert from the Protestant Episcopal Church in 1849 who, unfortunately, apostatized from the faith a decade later, and the latter was a friend of liberal causes and a defender of Dr. Edward McGlynn in the single tax controversy of the 1880's.[28] Also numbered among the theologians were the prominent Jesuit army chaplain of the Mexican War, John McElroy, who acted as theologian to Bishop Bernard O'Reilly of Hartford, and John McCaffrey, who for thirty-four years was President of Mount Saint Mary's College in Emmitsburg and who served as theologian for Bishop Francis X. Gartland of Savannah.[29]

[26] For Fitton cf. Robert H. Lord, John E. Sexton, and Edward T. Harrington, *History of the Archdiocese of Boston* (New York, 1944), II, *passim.*

[27] On Kindekens cf. George Paré, *The Catholic Church in Detroit, 1701–1888* (Detroit, 1951), pp. 450 ff., and J. Van der Heyden, *The Louvain American College, 1857–1907* (Louvain, 1909), pp. 12–67.

[28] For Forbes cf. John Cardinal Farley, *The Life of John Cardinal McCloskey* (New York, 1918), pp. 195–97, and on Malone, Sylvester L. Malone, (Ed.), *Memorial of the Golden Jubilee of the Rev. Sylvester Malone* (Brooklyn, 1895).

[29] On McElroy cf. the biographical sketch by Richard J. Purcell in the *Dictionary*

During the course of their deliberations the bishops held four solemn sessions in the cathedral and seven public and eleven private congregations in either the cathedral or the archbishop's residence. The agenda of the various meetings traversed a wide range of subjects. At the outset much time was devoted to a discussion of the need for new dioceses and of their delimitation. Matters such as the demand for Catholic elementary schools held the bishops' attention on May 11 and they agreed on a decree that might be thought to have put the question beyond debate for the future. On the following days the prelates discussed the problems pertaining to the legal incorporation of church properties and the best way of handling rebellious lay trustees, the attitude they should take toward secret societies, the responsibility they should assume toward Catholic children in public schools, and freedom of worship for Catholics in the armed services. In the fourth and fifth public congregations on May 13–14 the theologians debated before the bishops the expediency of extending canonical status to pastors in the United States. Other subjects that engaged the attention of the fathers were what dispensations from the lenten fast should be sought from the Holy See by bishops of the western dioceses, what steps should be taken to bring about a uniform catechism, the form of a petition to Rome for more ample faculties in marriage cases, the curriculum of studies in the seminaries. Early in the council five committees were appointed for the investigation of specific topics and other committees evolved as the debates progressed as, for example, when the apostolic delegate on May 14 named Bishops Reynolds, Timon, and Spalding to constitute a committee for drawing up recommendations on a uniform catechism. In the closing days of the council these committees reported back to their colleagues and in some cases their recommendations were accepted, in others they were voted down. A case in point occurred when the fathers declined to give approval to a new edition of the Roman Ritual which the committee on that subject suggested on May 18.[30]

At the outset of the council the apostolic delegate assigned the writing of the customary conciliar letters. Bishop O'Connor was chosen to compose the Latin letter of the hierarchy to Pius IX, Portier was assigned

---

of American Biography, XII, 36–37, and for McCaffrey, Mary M. Meline and Edward F. X. McSweeny, *The Story of the Mountain* (Emmitsburg, 1911), I, 378 ff; II, 1–90.

[30] The meager record of the council's various sessions is contained in *Concilium plenarium* . . . , pp. 7–43.

the French letter to the Society for the Propagation of the Faith, Neumann was asked to write a similar letter in German to the Leopoldinen-
Stiftung of Vienna and to the other German societies that had aided the
American missions, Archbishop Purcell was to compose a letter in
the name of all to Archbishop Cullen and the Irish hierarchy, and finally the pastoral letter to the priests and people of the United States was
to be the work of Archbishop Kenrick of St. Louis. During the last three
private congregations on May 19–20 the drafts of these letters were
read by their authors and received the consent of the bishops that they
should be sent in their names.[31]

During the course of the council a sermon was preached in the cathedral every evening with the preachers numbering Archbishops Purcell, Peter Kenrick, and Hughes, Bishops McCloskey and McGill, and
Fathers Lynch of Charleston and two Jesuits, William S. Murphy and
Charles H. Stonestreet, the latter the President of Georgetown College.
On May 13 the pontifical requiem for the prelates deceased since the
last council was sung by Bishop Chanche and Spalding preached the
eulogy which was centered around Samuel Eccleston, S.S., Archbishop
of Baltimore, Flaget of Louisville, and William Tyler, Bishop of Hartford, who had died since 1849. The third solemn session on May 16 had
Archbishop Blanchet as the celebrant of the Mass with the Bishop of
Pittsburgh as the preacher, and at the final solemn session four days
later, the feast of the Ascension, Archbishop Blanc pontificated and
Bishop Fitzpatrick preached the sermon. After the Mass and sermon
had been concluded on May 20 the secretaries read the twenty-five decrees that had been passed by the prelates during the twelve days they
had been in session and each bishop thereupon gave his public assent
to the legislation. The Archbishop of New York then voiced the thanks
of the participating bishops to the apostolic delegate for the tact and
wisdom with which he had presided and for the hospitality he had afforded to them during their stay in his see city. Following Hughes' brief
remarks Kenrick rose to reply but he said very little since he was so
deeply moved by the occasion that, as the minutes quaintly put it, "lacry-
mis sermonem abrumpere coactus est."[32]

At first sight it might seem strange that the final product of nearly two
weeks of discussion on the part of the hierarchy should have resulted in

[31] *Ibid.*, pp. 11–12, 37–39.
[32] *Ibid.*, p. 41.

only twenty-five decrees. But it should be remembered that a great deal of the prelates' time was consumed in hearing the arguments for and against various measures and in private consultations on the advisability of particular legislative proposals. The participants had been entirely free throughout the days of debate to register their disapproval of suggested laws, and that they availed themselves of their right there was no doubt. A case in point concerned the best means of providing for parochial schools. On May 11 the bishops had listened as the theologians debated at length the advisability of legislating on the necessity of such schools, and in the end the prelates passed a decree (XIII) that strongly urged that parochial schools be attached to every church in the American dioceses. But a week later when it was suggested that societies be instituted for the financial maintenance of parochial schools the views of the fifteen bishops who voted for such societies were overruled by the sixteen votes cast against the proposal.[33] In this way a number of measures fell by the wayside and thus the debates were at times prolonged over subjects which failed to find their way into the final decrees of the council. But the freedom of debate and the leisurely pace with which the council moved more than made up for any defect in the number of laws enacted and helped to assure solid legislation in the end.

Insofar as the decrees themselves were concerned, the historian of the Baltimore councils pronounced the legislation of 1852 "the most important step so far made by the hierarchy for complete uniformity of Church life in the United States."[34] What, in brief, were the enactments of the bishops of 1852 that became law for the American Church after they had received the approval of the Holy See? The first decree affirmed their loyal adherence to the sovereign pontiff as the successor of St. Peter and to the complete enactments of the ecumenical councils which the popes had promulgated for the Universal Church. This was followed by a proclamation that all the laws of the seven provincial councils that had been held in Baltimore between 1829 and 1849 were binding on the entire Church of the nation. The next decrees commanded that the Roman Ritual and the *Manual of Ceremonies*, previously ordered by the council of 1829 and approved by Pope Gregory XVI, should be used in all churches of the country. The fifth decree legislated that bishops

[33] *Ibid.*, pp. 27, 37.
[34] Guilday, *op. cit.*, p. 178.

should not be absent from their dioceses for more than three months without permission of the Holy See, the metropolitan, or the senior suffragan of the province.[35]

Decrees VI and VII dealt with the organization of diocesan administration and revealed how imperfect such administration had been up to that time. In the former the ordinaries were exhorted to appoint consultors who would meet at least once a month, while in the latter decree the establishment of a chancery office in every diocese was strongly urged. The next decree counseled the bishops to name one or more censors of books for the examination of prayer books and other publications pertaining to religion, and the practice of seeking the *imprimatur* from any other bishop than the one in whose diocese a book was published was discouraged. Mention was made in the following decree of the danger to souls involved in admitting to the active ministry unknown priests from Europe without first receiving credentials from their bishops and obtaining the consent of the ordinaries to whose dioceses they desired to transfer. It was further decreed that ecclesiastical districts (there were no parishes in the canonical sense at the time) were to be given clearly defined limits by the bishops as soon as possible and the jurisdiction and privileges of the priests within those districts were likewise to be laid down. Banns of marriage were to be proclaimed in all American churches after Easter of 1853, from which there was to be no dispensation except in cases of the gravest necessity. It was also decreed that priests were to institute catechetical instruction classes in their parishes and they were not to delegate this duty to others. Decree XIII, as has been mentioned, exhorted the bishops "per viscera misericordiae Dei" to provide a parochial school for every church in their dioceses, and declared that parish funds might be used to engage competent teachers for these schools. In the fourteenth decree the bishops who did not have a diocesan seminary were advised to consult with their fellow suffragans of the same province so that there might be established at least one seminary in every province.[36]

The fifteenth, sixteenth, and seventeenth decrees had to do with the administration of ecclesiastical properties and the safeguards that should be taken to avoid abuses from lay trustees, a system from which the

[35] *Concilium plenarium* . . . , pp. 43–45. Reference is made here to the official edition of the decrees as finally approved by the Holy See.

[36] *Ibid.*, pp. 45–47.

152

American Church had suffered so much since the days of Archbishop Carroll. The fathers likewise prescribed that the ritual was to be strictly observed throughout all their dioceses in giving benediction of the Blessed Sacrament. And at a time when the rights of conscience of Catholic men enrolled in the army and navy were not infrequently violated, it was not surprising to find the bishops in 1852 including a decree which urged that infractions of this kind be reported to the civil authorities in a tactful manner in order to win for the service men their full rights. Another decree exhorted the prelates to promote the establishment of the Society for the Propagation of the Faith in their dioceses, a society which, it was said, had done so much among the French to advance the cause of religion. The fathers, moreover, recommended that the American Catholic laity be encouraged to join a society devoted to prayers for the conversion of non-Catholics, and it was stated that they would petition the pope to favor such groups by granting indulgences for this pious work.[37] This was another canon wherein a current trend was reflected, for a considerable number of converts had been received into the Church of late years, and the bishops were doubtless hopeful that an American counterpart to the Oxford Movement — then showing such promise in England — might develop in the United States.[38] Two further decrees related to the sacrament of marriage and the need which the prelates felt for extraordinary faculties from the Holy See in certain marriage cases. After a statement on the necessity of petitioning Rome for use of the short form in administering the sacrament of baptism, the legislation of 1852 closed with Decree XXV which declared that the foregoing laws would be in force for the American Church as soon as they had received the approval of the Holy See and had been published by the authority of the Archbishop of Baltimore.[39]

At the close of every Baltimore council of the American bishops from 1829 to 1884 the prelates issued a pastoral letter to their priests and people, and to this rule the council of 1852 was no exception. The docu-

[37] The petition for indulgences was granted in Barnabò to Kenrick, Rome, September 5, 1852, *Concilium plenarium* . . . , pp. 59–60.

[38] There is no adequate history of the American convert movement of the mid and late nineteenth century. For a popular account of some of the American converts to Catholicism in these years cf. Edward J. Mannix, *The American Convert Movement* (New York, 1923), pp. 11–19; 107–110. For an earlier period cf. Sister Laurita Gibson, *Some Anglo-American Converts to Catholicism Prior to 1829* (Washington, 1943).

[39] *Concilium plenarium* . . . , pp. 47–50.

ment was written by Archbishop Peter R. Kenrick and in a day when anti-Catholic bigotry again stalked the land and when the ghost of lay trusteeism had not yet been entirely laid, it was natural to find the Archbishop of St. Louis devoting the first section of the pastoral to an analysis of the Catholic doctrine on episcopal authority and an explanation of the source from which it had taken its rise. From this topic there was an easy transition to an outline of the proper method of administering the properties of the Church and a summary of the discipline which the Church was divinely commissioned to enforce on its faithful.

Kenrick next passed to the needs that then confronted the Church of the United States, and while he was careful to pay tribute to the past generosity of the American Catholic people, he did not fail to appeal for their continued support so that more churches, seminaries, and schools might be built for the rapidly expanding population. The faithful were reminded of Pius IX's letter of November 21, 1851, which had called on the bishops of the entire Catholic world to provide for the religious education of youth. In this regard the archbishop remarked that the American bishops were following the example of the Irish hierarchy who had been so courageously opposing the introduction of a system of education in Ireland based on a principle which the prelates of both countries condemned, and who were at the moment attempting to unite religious with secular learning of the highest order by the establishment at Dublin of the Catholic University of Ireland. The Irish Catholic university, said Kenrick, was "an undertaking in the success of which we necessarily feel a deep interest, and which, as having been suggested by the Sovereign Pontiff, powerfully appeals to the sympathies of the whole Catholic world."[40] The pastoral letter had words of high commendation for the Society for the Propagation of the Faith and it contained special paragraphs for the priests, the sisters, and the laity. In an oblique manner Kenrick referred to the agitation of the Nativist enemies of Catholicism in the United States who had been so busy of recent years spreading calumnies against the Church. But his only suggestion to the faithful in the face of these attacks was the practice of restraint and a strict obedience to the laws of the Republic. On this subject he said:

Show your attachment to the institutions of our beloved country by prompt compliance with all their requirements, and by the cautious jealousy with

[40] Peter Guilday (Ed.), *The National Pastorals of the American Hierarchy* (*1792–1919*) (Washington, 1923), p. 191.

which you guard against the least deviation from the rules which they prescribe for the maintenance of public order and private rights. Thus will you refute the idle babbling of foolish men, and will best approve yourselves worthy of the privileges which you enjoy, and overcome, by the sure test of practical patriotism, all the prejudices which a misapprehension of your principles but too often produces.[41]

On May 20 the bishops began to take their departure for home and there to await the formal approval of their legislation from the Holy See. Ten days after the council closed Archbishop Hughes told his friend, Father Terence J. Donaghoe, "Our great National Council is over, and has been among the most agreeable I ever attended. The President was kind and impartial and at the close he gave evidence of more heart and feeling than I thought he possessed. He fairly shed tears."[42] Hughes' previous relations with Kenrick apparently had not led him to believe that the latter was capable of such a show of emotion. The conciliar decrees were entrusted to the care of Bishop Van de Velde of Chicago who left Baltimore on May 25 for Rome.[43] All through the late spring and summer the bishops were in correspondence on affairs of the council with Kenrick, and from time to time they revealed their uneasiness over the failure of their legislation to win a prompt approval in Rome. Bishop Timon for one had already experienced a severe trial with the rebellious trustees of St. Louis Church in Buffalo. At that time the Taber Bill was before the New York legislature and Archbishop Hughes was hopeful that this bill might make it possible for the bishops of the State of New York to hold church properties as corporations sole.[44] But the prospects of the measure being enacted into law were very slim and Timon was, therefore, all the more anxious that some assistance might result from the council's decrees on the holding of church property. In communi-

[41] *Ibid.*, p. 192. Kenrick may have been tempered by remembrance of the fact that the pastoral letters of the hierarchy following the provincial councils of 1829, 1837, and 1843 had all taken pains to refute in some detail the lies of the Nativists, but with little or no result other than to stir the latter to more vigorous outbursts against the Church. For the bishops' statements on the subject in the councils mentioned cf. Guilday, *National Pastorals* . . . , pp. 27–28; 80–95; 153–54.

[42] Hughes to Donaghoe, New York, May 30, 1852, in *In the Early Days. Pages from the Annals of the Sisters of Charity of the Blessed Virgin Mary*, 3rd ed. (Dubuque, 1943), p. 149.

[43] ADN, the rough draft of a letter in French from Bishop Chanche to Raffaele Fornari of Propaganda, Baltimore, May 26, 1852, copy.

[44] Robert F. McNamara, "Trusteeism in the Atlantic States, 1785–1863," *Catholic Historical Review*, XXX (July, 1944), 149–150.

cating some of his worries on this score to Kenrick, the Bishop of Buffalo alluded to a pet project of his friend in Baltimore which was of more than local interest. He said:

I would not now trouble you, it is not necessary, were it not that I feel myself pressed to express how much I rejoice that you again entertain the idea of a Bishopric at Washington. It seems to be certain that such a step will produce the greater glory of God and the salvation of souls; it will add a jewel to your crown; one only objection seemed to me to have weight, the danger of political intrigue; but if a man of ordinary good sense be there, should he even try such a thing, he would be so scorched in the first attempt, as to verify for his after conduct, the old proverb, a burnt child, etc. May God guide you in this, as He has done in so many things for his glory.[45]

In the days before the establishment of the American College at Rome in 1859 the bishops of the United States frequently employed the officials of one or other of the national English-speaking colleges in the Eternal City as their agents at the Holy See. It was to Tobias Kirby, Rector of the Irish College from the departure of Archbishop Cullen for Armagh in 1850 to the former's death in 1895, that Kenrick now turned to help American legislation through the Congregation de Propaganda Fide. Kirby was in fairly steady correspondence with Baltimore during the summer of 1852 and in a letter of late August he informed the archbishop that Bishop O'Connor of Pittsburgh had just arrived and that the latter could now assist the cause they all had at heart by giving verbal explanations of some of the decrees to the Propaganda officials. The Rector of the Irish College pronounced the pastoral letter of the Baltimore council "magnificent," and he added that everyone in Rome was likewise impressed by the conciliar letter to the Archbishop of Armagh on the Catholic University of Ireland. Cullen had sent a copy of the latter document on to Rome and it had received high commendation, not only from the men at Propaganda but, as Kirby expressed it, "even the *zucchetto bianco* itself was most gratified." He hoped, therefore, that the message from the Americans would help to bring some of the opposing Irish bishops around to support the university.

[45] AAB, 31-Q-8, Timon to Kenrick, Buffalo, July 16, 1852. Kenrick had not been in Baltimore three months when he told his brother, "I am thinking of having the city of Washington erected into an episcopal see." (Kenrick to Kenrick, Baltimore, December 24, 1851, in Tourscher, *op. cit.*, p. 321.) Almost a century was to pass before this idea was translated into action with the erection of the Archdiocese of Washington on July 22, 1939.

Meanwhile Kirby was doing what he could to hasten the approbation of the conciliar legislation. In a postscript added to his letter a week later he said he had hoped that he might tell Kenrick that confirmation of the decrees had been given; but Cardinal Fransoni, Prefect of Propaganda, had informed him that day that they had not been able to finish their work. Several of the cardinals had remarked that they thought the task of the secretaries of the council had been "rather clumsily executed," and this Kirby felt Kenrick should know.[46]

All through September Bishop O'Connor maintained his vigil at Propaganda. Early in the month he informed Kenrick that he had been unsuccessful in trying to find out what was causing the delay in the approval of the decrees. One thing he had learned, and that was the opposition that had developed to Father Edward Purcell of Cincinnati whose name had been submitted to the council by his brother, the archbishop, as a candidate for one of the projected new sees.[47] Three weeks later O'Connor explained to his metropolitan that he was still answering Propaganda's questions and handing in memoranda there for the officials, but he said he realized that his memoranda lacked any official authority. One matter that he had been told was holding up the confirmation of the decrees was the question of the financial support that was owing to the bishops from their priests and people.[48] But the end was nearer than the Bishop of Pittsburgh had supposed, and two days after his letter Cardinal Fransoni signed the document on September 26, 1852, which gave the official approbation of the Holy See to the conciliar decrees of the previous May.[49]

Yet the news of Propaganda's action took a long time in reaching the United States. In mid-November Kenrick was still in a somewhat fretful state of mind when he told Hughes that O'Connor had reported the

---

[46] *Ibid.*, 30-I-7, Kirby to Kenrick, Rome, August 22, 23 and 31, 1852 (one letter). Earlier that month Kenrick had told the Bishop of Richmond, "The Cardinal Prefect has acknowledged the receipt of the decrees, and Bp. Van de Velde reports a very gracious reception from His Holiness. He thinks that it will take a long time to obtain the confirmation" (Archives of the Diocese of Richmond, Kenrick to McGill, Baltimore, August 2, 1852, microfilm).

[47] *Ibid.*, 30-W-11, O'Connor to Kenrick, Rome, September 3, 1852. The opposition to Purcell's nomination for the episcopal office was expressed by Bishop Reynolds for one, although O'Connor of Pittsburgh was in favor of the brother of the Archbishop of Cincinnati. (Kenrick to Kenrick, Baltimore, August 10 and October 20, 1852, in Tourscher, *op. cit.*, pp. 334–35.)

[48] *Ibid.*, 30-W-12, O'Connor to Kenrick, Sept. 24, 1852.

[49] *Concilium plenarium* . . . , pp. 56–57.

Roman officials as disposed to restrict very much the American bishops' dispensing powers and to require recourse to the Holy See in individual cases. "They refuse to retrench feasts, or fasts," he said, "deeming uniformity not desirable, as it tends to give a national character to the Church of United States in matters discordant from general discipline." The Romans, he continued, were urging the observance of the feast of the Circumcision in all American dioceses and that of the Immaculate Conception as a national festival. On another matter in which Kenrick had more than a passing interest he remarked to Hughes, "They refuse recognising the primacy of Baltimore, but offer to give it some token of favor as mater ecclesiarum, 'honorificum aliquod privilegium' quod a caeteris illam distinguat."[50] On the same day that he wrote to the Archbishop of New York he was somewhat more explicit to his brother. He stated:

At last the Bishop of Pittsburgh has arrived here bringing the documents which refer to the decrees of the Council. Many of these have been recast. The Holy See refuses to recognize the Archbishop of Baltimore as Primate, also refuses to abrogate certain days of fast which are observed in some dioceses.

. . . The Catechisms it sends back with corrections suggested by certain theologians, but withholds approbation.[51]

Other prelates besides Kenrick were puzzled about how they should proceed in enforcing some of the recent legislation without Rome's confirmation. Archbishop Purcell was probably reflecting the divided opinions of the bishops on several subjects in council and the narrow margins by which they had been voted into decrees when he told Kenrick:

From the kind of approbation given to some of the Acts, I fear, we shall be at a loss, without a special instruction from yourself, to determine what

[50] AANY, Kenrick to Hughes, Baltimore, November 18, 1852. The unanimous request of the bishops of the Seventh Provincial Council in May, 1849, that Baltimore be raised to the dignity of a primatial see was deferred by Rome at that time without any reasons being given. (Guilday, *Councils*, p. 157.) However, in a decree of Propaganda signed by the prefect, Alessandro Cardinal Barnabò, on August 15, 1858, the Archbishop of Baltimore was granted "prerogative of place" in all gatherings of the American hierarchy. It meant that he would take precedence over all archbishops in the United States, regardless of seniority in date of consecration or ordination. The only exception to this rule was when an American archbishop was a cardinal and in this case, of course, he would outrank the Archbishop of Baltimore.

[51] Kenrick to Kenrick, Baltimore, November 18, 1852, in Tourscher, *op. cit.*, pp. 339–340.

arc of binding force & what *ad libitum*. For instance, must we observe the 8th of December as a Holiday of obligation? . . . And must we cease to use — suppress — our present diocesan catechism with which we may have no fault to find?[52]

These were questions which the formal approval and accompanying instructions from Propaganda would in good measure answer when they arrived in the United States. But even after the Roman confirmation was received in mid-November it was seen that time would be needed to bring the legislation into full force and to settle the doubtful points about some of the new regulations.

Although the subject of new ecclesiastical jurisdictions for the rapidly growing Church of the United States had been one of the first topics discussed in the preliminary meeting of the prelates at Baltimore on May 8, it was the last to receive a final settlement in Rome. Over six months after the official confirmation of the decrees the Holy See had not yet acted in erecting the new dioceses which the bishops had recommended.[53] Kenrick was plainly not happy with the way Van de Velde of Chicago had carried out his mission as the bearer of the decrees to Rome. Early in the new year he told his brother:

The man from Chicago has unsettled everything, stating that the Archbishops arranged things just as they chose: that they determined upon the erection of this new diocese [Quincy] without consulting him, and recommended priests [to head the new see] without his knowledge.[54]

Meanwhile Dr. Kirby was trying to push matters, but as he told Kenrick in early May the principal cause of delay had arisen in the United States, not in the Roman Curia. On the day of his letter he had conferred with Monsignor Filippo Vespasiani, one of the *minutanti* of Propaganda, on whom, said Kirby, "a great deal depends as far as the preparation of the Ponenza is concerned." Vespasiani had explained that they were receiving "a multitude of letters" from all parts of the United States and, although it was not likely that these communications would cause any substantial variation in the bishops' desires, Propaganda felt that the points of view which they expressed must be examined and con-

[52] AAB, 31-B-6, Purcell to Kenrick, Cincinnati, November 23, 1852.

[53] In early April Kenrick reported a letter of March 6 from Bishop Spalding in Florence who said that Propaganda would not finish with the affairs of the council until after Easter (Kenrick to Kenrick, Baltimore, April 5, 1853, in Tourscher, *op. cit.*, p. 354).

[54] Kenrick to Kenrick, Baltimore, January 18, 1853, in Tourscher, *op. cit.*, pp. 347–348.

sidered, and this, of course, took time.[55] A letter of July 21 from Fransoni to Kenrick on other business threw no light on the question of the delayed new sees, and in referring to the long wait and to this letter of the Prefect of Propaganda, Kenrick remarked a month later to Hughes, "Not the slightest reference is made to our Council, or the nominations."[56]

But things were not as bad as they seemed, and on July 29, 1853, the Congregation de Propaganda Fide acted in pursuance of most of the recommendations of the First Plenary Council in a series of decrees that brought about the greatest territorial changes in the American Church up to that time. On that date nine new dioceses were created, namely, Brooklyn, Burlington, Covington, Erie, Natchitoches (Alexandria), Newark, Portland in Maine, Quincy (Springfield in Illinois), and Santa Fe. Moreover, a new metropolitan see was established on the Pacific Coast with the Archdiocese of San Francisco, the Vicariate Apostolic of Upper Michigan (Marquette) came into existence, and the Diocese of Walla Walla was suppressed and its territory divided between the Archdiocese of Oregon City and the Diocese of Nesqually.[57] The delay of a year and two months had proved a bit irksome to some of the American bishops but the action when it came was on the whole in accordance with their wishes. Kirby believed, as he told Kenrick, that all the new bishops appointed were in every case "juxta votum Rmi. Praesulis." The news contained in the letter of the Rector of the Irish College in all likelihood made up to the Archbishop of Baltimore for much of the anxiety he had experienced over the final outcome. Kirby had appreciated his uneasiness over the delay and he told him:

At the winding up of all the S. Cgn. more clearly understood the wisdom of the decisions made by the council. So that as one of the Minutanti told me, the delay was useful in that respect, and turned out to be honorific to the council as the examination of every objection proved more validly the reasonableness & justice of the grounds on which it acted. Ringraziamo Iddio. I am happy to mention that the C. Prefect, Mgr. Barnabò and indeed all Propa-

[55] AAB, 30-I-8, Kirby to Kenrick, Rome, Feast of St. John of the Latin Gate [May 6], 1853.

[56] AANY, Kenrick to Hughes, Baltimore, August 21, 1853.

[57] For the texts of the documents covering these jurisdictional changes cf. Shearer, op. cit., pp. 274–92. The requests of the council for a diocese at Wilmington, North Carolina, a vicariate apostolic in Florida, and a metropolitan see for Boston were disallowed by Rome as either inexpedient or needing to be deferred for the present. Cf. Fransoni to Kenrick. Rome, August 12, 1853, in Concilium plenarium . . . , pp. 63–64.

ganda, fully understood the debt which religion owes to Y.G. for the vast services rendered toward the good cause on the present occasion.[58]

Fourteen and a half years were to pass before the American bishops would again assemble at Baltimore in October, 1866, for a national council. In the meantime the nation endured the long and cruel ordeal of the Civil War which put a number of the thirty-two American prelates who had shared each other's counsel so closely in 1852 completely out of touch with their brethren, and created for them vexing problems of which they had previously never even dreamed. Moreover, in the interval between the two meetings fifteen of the bishops of the First Plenary Council passed to their eternal reward and one, Michael O'Connor, resigned his see to enter the Society of Jesus. However, of the forty-four prelates who gathered under the leadership of Archbishop Spalding in the year after the Civil War ended fifteen had been there fourteen years before. The continuity of the conciliar tradition of the American Church was thus, in a sense, living in their persons and these veteran legislators enabled the bishops of 1866 to integrate more skillfully the legislation of May, 1852, with the new canons which were necessary to meet the altered circumstances of the country.[59]

By an interesting coincidence it was less than two months after the close of the American bishops' First Plenary Council that there assembled on July 6, 1852, at St. Mary's College, Oscott, under the presidency of Nicholas Cardinal Wiseman, the First Plenary Council of Westminster. Here the eleven bishops of England and Wales, newly restored as a hierarchy only two years before, gathered in an atmosphere still charged with tension and suspicion over the "papal aggression" which Pius IX had dared to perpetrate against Her Majesty's kingdom in September, 1850. The hierarchies at both Baltimore and Oscott knew from personal experience, therefore, what it meant to live through days of public insult and painful calumny. Yet both groups in this year 1852 went quietly about their spiritual business as bishops of the Church of God. The prelates in Baltimore had not been privileged, as were their brothers at Oscott, to hear so unforgettable a sermon as John Henry Newman preached before the latter on July 13 in "The Second Spring."

[58] AAB, 30-I-9, Kirby to Kenrick, Rome, July 29, 1853.

[59] Numbered among the forty-four prelates at the Second Plenary Council were Bishop de Saint-Palais of Vincennes who had been absent in Europe in 1852 and Bishop Modeste Demers of Vancouver who also participated in the sessions of 1866.

Nonetheless, as the Americans viewed their accomplishment in retrospect they might fittingly have applied to their own gathering the words which Newman addressed to his friend, Henry Wilberforce, on the day following the close of the council at Oscott when he said, "We ended the Synod yesterday in great triumph, joy, and charity."[60]

THE CHURCH FACES THE MODERN WORLD: THE VATICAN COUNCIL (1869–1870)

He would be a rash man, indeed, who would attempt to do justice to the manifold aspects of the First Vatican Council in a brief essay. One need but recall that it was the first ecumenical gathering in over 300 years, that it was more than five years in preparation, that it drew nearly 750 bishops from every corner of the globe, that its sessions lasted over nine months, that the official record of its proceedings fill five large volumes in the continuation of Mansi's famous conciliar collections,[1] and that the council has been universally regarded as having marked — both in doctrine and in the Church's relationship to the State — a significant and enduring milestone in modern ecclesiastical history. Even a momentary reflection on these purely external features makes it evident why limitation is a stern necessity.

In a certain sense the Vatican Council set its own limitations, for it was the only one of the twenty ecumenical assemblies to date that enacted no disciplinary decrees. True, there was extended discussion of disciplinary matters during the bishops' time in Rome, but their debates ended in no formal legislation on this head, as was the case, for example, with the two dogmatic constitutions which by mid-summer of 1870 had emerged in the *Dei Filius* on Catholic faith and the *Pastor Aeternus*[2] on

[60] Wilfrid Ward, *The Life of John Henry Cardinal Newman* (New York, 1912), I, 295.

[1] Mansi, *Collectio Conciliorum* . . . Volumes XLIX–LIII (Paris, 1923–1927).

[2] The apostolic constitutions, *Dei Filius* of April 24, 1870, and *Pastor Aeternus* of July 18, 1870, are contained in Latin and English texts on facing pages in an appendix to Cuthbert Butler, O.S.B., *The Vatican Council* (London, 1930), II, 247–295.

the primacy and infallibility of the pope. A second limiting factor came from without. On July 19, the day after the final vote on infallibility, France declared war on Prussia, and in the face of this grave danger most of the bishops quickly departed for home. Sessions continued to be held through August and September, but the effort to reassemble the bishops at Malines in Belgium, or elsewhere, failed, and on October 20 Pius IX prorogued the council, a status that technically obtained for the succeeding ninety years until Pope John XXIII's action in summoning a new council to bear the name of Vatican Council II may be said to have written an end to the 1870 gathering.

I shall confine myself to four main points. First, in the hope of conveying an impression of the intellectual climate in which the assembly met and carried out its work, I shall try to sketch in a few broad strokes the general *mise en scène* of these years of the mid-century. Secondly, certain features of the council's preparatory stages will be presented from the viewpoint of three highly interested groups: 1) the theologians, gathered in Rome at an early date to shape and refine the material for the conciliar agenda; 2) the bishops, as yet at home in their diocese reflecting Catholic reaction at a distance from the Eternal City; 3) the statesmen, representative of how the council appeared either to those outside the Church, or to Catholics prominent in the service of the State. Thus with the scene having been laid, the theologians having completed their task, with the bishops gradually converging on Rome by the early winter of 1869, and with the secular governments watching suspiciously from afar, we shall, I hope, be in a position to treat the third major point. And here I must forego any treatment of the theologically important debates that led to the constitution on Catholic faith, as well as any further mention of the lively exchange of views on disciplinary matters; in other words, in point three we shall proceed directly to the most controverted question, the definition of papal infallibility. Finally, with the bishops' decisive vote on that crucial issue having been taken on July 18, and the outbreak of the Franco-Prussian War twenty-four hours thereafter, which for all practical purposes brought the council to an end, an attempt will be made to interpret its significance in terms once more of three groups: 1) the Roman Curia or the central governing body of the Holy See; 2) the universal Church as represented by the bishops and priests; 3) the secular interests as heard through the cabinet ministers, diplomats, and parliamentarians of an age that prided itself on its scientific advance and on its success in having discovered what it believed to be the avenue to unlimited human progress.

In one respect the reaction of the mid-nineteenth century toward the Catholic Church resembled that of most generations that had preceded it. Few men of commanding station and influence had indulged themselves in the luxury of indifference toward the ebb and flow of Catholic life, regardless of the casualness with which they may have seemed to view it. And in this the ranking figures of the 1860's were no exception. Ecclesiastical developments were closely observed with the eye of either friend or foe, and the strength of these two opposing schools of thought *vis-à-vis* the papacy would be felt from Pio Nono's earliest intimation that it was his intention to issue the historic summons.

First, let us briefly recall what might be called the friendly factors conducing to the convening of a council. Here a prominent place should be assigned to the personality of the reigning pontiff. Warmhearted, impetuous, free of official hauteur, and easily approachable, Pius IX had endeared himself to great numbers of people since the opening of his reign in 1846. True, in later years he had lost heavily with men of liberal sympathies; yet Frédéric Ozanam's description of him in the early months of the pontificate retained sufficient validity two decades later to warrant being heard. In January, 1847, Ozanam wrote:

This pontiff whom one encounters on foot in the streets, who this week went one evening to visit a poor widow and to aid her without making himself known, who preaches each fortnight to the people assembled at San Andrea della Valle, this courageous reformer of abuse in the temporal government, seems truly sent by God to conclude the great affair of the nineteenth century, the alliance of religion and of liberty.[3]

Although it proved to be a sadly mistaken prophecy, the pontiff, nonetheless, held the affection of many to the end, and no small part of the attraction he had for others were his *bons mots* that went the round of certain circles the world over. Some weeks after the opening of the council, for example, in the midst of discussion on the advisability of introducing the controverted question of the pope's infallibility, Pius IX was quoted in one of his frequent plays on words when he remarked, "Non so se il Papa uscirà di questo Concilio fallibile od infallibile; ma questo è *certo* che sarà fallito."[4]

[3] Frédéric Ozanam to Prosper Guéranger, Rome, January 29, 1847, quoted in Roger Aubert, *Le Pontificat de Pie IX, 1846–1878* (Paris, 1952), p. 20.

[4] Butler, *op. cit.*, I, 170, n. 1.

Of deeper significance, however, than the personality of any single churchman was the rising tide of a new ultramontanist movement that had been gaining ground since the opening of the century, and that served to create an enthusiasm for the papacy in sharp contrast to the cold and aloof manner in which even many Catholics had regarded the See of Peter through most of the eighteenth century. In German-speaking lands one sensed its dawning manifestation with the succession of prominent converts to Catholicism which began with Friedrich Leopold Count von Stolberg in 1800 and which continued with the Schlegels and their literary associates, as well as the return to an ardent practice of the faith after years of estrangement of men like Josef Görres and Clemens Brentano. *Der Katholik* of Mainz and the *Stimmen aus Maria Laach* of the German Jesuits gave the conservatives a voice while the *Kölnische Blätter* after 1860 furnished the same to the German Catholics of liberal sympathies. A decided impetus had been provided in November, 1837, by the blunder of the Prussian government in arresting and imprisoning the Archbishops of Cologne and Gnesen-Posen in a dispute about jurisdiction over mixed marriages. The release of the two archbishops in 1840 by the new King Frederick William IV amounted to an admission of defeat on the part of the State and the consequent victory for the Church had a bracing effect on Catholics of all shades of opinion.

Meanwhile, the publication in 1802 of Chateaubriand's *Génie du Christianisme* foreshadowed a reviving religious trend in France, and seventeen years later neo-ultramontanism received a classic expression in *Du Pape*, the celebrated work of Comte Joseph de Maistre, the tone of which blended well with many of the dominant ideas of the romantic movement then in its heydoy. It was France, too, that was the scene in the generation that preceded the council of the series of apparitions of the Virgin, first to Catherine Laboure in 1831 and then at La Salette, a phenomenon which was crowned, as it were, in 1854 by Pius IX's definition of Mary's immaculate conception, so soon to be confirmed by our Lady herself when in March, 1858, at Lourdes she answered Bernadette Soubirous' question concerning her identity. It was in France likewise that there was founded in 1822 through the inspiration of Pauline Jaricot and her associates, the Society for the Propagation of the Faith that was destined not only to play a significant role in the spread of the faith in pagan lands, but to rekindle it in the hearts of many for whom it had all but disappeared. Here as well were witnessed the mounting pilgrimages to the saintly curé at Ars, at times so numerous as almost to suggest a mass movement. Running parallel, therefore, to the scientific and secularist spirit of French public life was this extraordinary revival in the nation's ancient faith. For if at this time France gave birth to the father of positivism in Comte, and to the parent of anarchism in Proudhon, it was simultaneously the home of Ozanam and his strikingly successful Society of St. Vincent de Paul, of a highly articulate group of liberal Catholics who in 1843 revived *Le Correspondant* in the form of a monthly journal, as well as of Louis Veuillot whose enthusiasm for the See of Peter knew no bounds and whose newspaper, *l'Univers*, became the stoutest ultramontanist organ to be read outside Rome.

The most original and challenging aspects of mid-century Catholicism arose, therefore, in Germany and France. Yet it would be a mistake to ignore the Oxford Movement which by 1840 had become identified as the *causa agitans* for the surprising number of distinguished English minds that made their submission to Rome during that decade. Among these men none was more articulate than William George Ward who took over the *Dublin Review* in 1863 and soon made it the most pronounced ultramontanist journal in the English-speaking world. And Ward's editorship opened at the very time that the *Home and Foreign Review* of Sir John Acton and Richard Simpson, another convert, bowed to ecclesiastical authority and ceased publication, thus leaving the English Catholics of liberal sympathies with no outlet for their views. Likewise among traditionally Catholic peoples like the Belgians, Poles, and Irish the old faith took on new meaning in these years as a support to the strong nationalist spirit that prompted them to rise against their Protestant and Orthodox overlords. Needless to say, most of this religious ferment north of the Alps was a source of joy — and of hope — to Rome, gravely threatened as it now was by the full tide of the *Risorgimento*. Yet Rome was not without its own resources, for at this time Italian ultramontanism had its most effective organ in the Eternal City in the bi-weekly journal of the Jesuits, the *Civiltà Cattolica*, which was rounding out the first decade of its existence.

These were the factors, then, that were conducive to the holding of a general council. But it was not the Catholics, whether of the liberal or ultramontanist persuasion, who set the prevailing patterns of thought for western Europe at the mid-century. And that brings us to the forces militating against the council's success. Among these were the rationalism and religious indifference that pervaded so large a part of the upper classes, for among them the toll taken by the philosophy of the Enlightenment had been exceedingly heavy. In fact, the Catholic revival of the years after 1800 had touched hardly more than a fraction of those in high places. Even more serious, perhaps, was the widespread religious illiteracy among the masses. The French Revolution and its aftermath had thinned the ranks of the clergy, and those who later pursued a religious vocation to completion experienced in their seminary training a lack of solid preparation and of intellectual stimulation that left them quite unfit to cope with the problems of their time. The intellectual and scientific elite, of course, were in good measure hostile to traditional religion, and at centers like Tübingen with its higher criticism of the Scriptures and Berlin with its school of scientific history of which Leopold von Ranke was the soul, the imagination of the learned world's future leaders was often captured and permanently alienated from religious values. What was equally unfortunate was the absence of a corresponding intellectual force and an atmosphere of freedom of inquiry in Catholic circles to offset the damage to souls and to win them back to the Church. When it is recalled that as late as 1820 a book that maintained that the earth went around the sun was refused the ecclesiastical *imprimatur* at Rome, although over two centuries had passed since Copernicus' famous treatise had won general acceptance, it is not difficult to understand why the achievements of solitary Catholic scientists like Gregor Johann Mendel and Louis Pasteur should have had relatively little effect in offsetting attacks by secular scientists and philosophical liberals upon the Catholic Church as the enemy of learning.

Obviously natural science was not the proper domain of churchmen who might, therefore, be excused for having done so little to promote it, even though they could scarcely be excused for refusing to accept its clearly demonstrated facts. Theology and philosophy were their domain, yet here Catholic achievement in the generation immediately preceding the council was anything but distinguished. The Catholic University of Louvain, reopened in 1834 after an interval of forty years, was for much of this time absorbed in the ontologist controversy centering around Professor Casimir Ubaghs whose teaching was censured by the Holy See in 1864. At Rome itself the higher schools of philosophy and theology, in which one might have anticipated a serious concern with the moral aspects of contemporary problems, were still intellectually stagnant, a condition that endured into the next pontificate until they were finally stirred by the Thomistic revival initiated by Pope Leo XIII. For example, a priest-historian of exemplary piety like Johannes Janssen was shocked on a visit to Rome in 1864 in seeing the neglect in exploiting the Eternal City's incomparable research resources and in being told by a young Italian scholar, "Here studies are dead, it is only the practical that counts."[5] In Germany alone could one then find in any numbers Catholic scholars who were a match for their secular counterparts. But even the celebrated Munich school could make little impression on a generation captivated after 1859 by Darwin's *Origin of Species* and by the more damaging *La Vie de Jésus* of Ernest Renan that appeared four years later, to mention only two works that enjoyed an immense vogue and that destroyed the belief of so many erstwhile Christians in the authenticity of the Scriptures and the divinity of Christ. Had the Church been able to marshal an array of first-class scholars, such as the French Benedictines of St. Maur and the Jesuit Bollandists of the Low Countries who had served Catholic scholarship so admirably in the seventeenth century, much of the damage might have been repaired. Instead the energies of too many writers who caught the fancy of the masses, and by the same token repelled the learned, were directed largely toward the production of popular and uncritical works that provided no defense of the Catholic position where it was under the heaviest fire. Wilfrid Ward described the situation in these words:

Incredible and unsupported stories in history and extravagances in dogma were the order of the day. . . . The disparagement of the individual intellect, which Bonald had so carefully limited, was extended by later writers, without his genius, to the disparagement of scientific research itself; and even after the condemnation by Rome of such exaggerations, the temper which prompted them — of distrust of modern science and civilization — remained.[6]

[5] Janssen to Maria von Sydow, Rome, March 13, 1864, Ludwig Freiherrn von Pastor (Ed.) *Johannes Janssens Briefe* (Freiburg im B., 1920), I, 285. A similar impression was created in the mind of Newman when he went to Rome to finish his studies for the priesthood in 1846. Not long after his arrival he told John D. Dalgairns, "Hope [James R. Hope-Scott] told me we should find very little theology here, and a talk we had yesterday with one of the Jesuit fathers here shows we shall find little philosophy." Newman to Dalgairns, Rome, November 22, 1846, Wilfrid Ward, *The Life of John Henry Cardinal Newman* (London, 1912), I, 167. Cf. also his later letters to Dalgairns (*Ibid.*, I, 169, 172–173). Hereafter this work will be cited as: Ward, *Newman.*

[6] Wilfrid Ward, *William George Ward and the Catholic Revival* (London, 1893), p. 120.

Equally formidable were the forces ranged against revealed religion in the marketplace and in government. To most men who accorded it any heed at all the *Communist Manifesto* of Marx and Engels in 1848 was but a bizarre pamphlet by two obscure German radicals. But by 1864 the force that lay behind that publication had gathered enough momentum for Marx to organize the First International and to earn a condemnation in Pius IX's encyclical *Quanta cura* published on December 8 of that year. In the economic and social order a powerful attack had thus been mounted upon all the traditional values which showed every sign of spreading. In government the moral power that the popes had once wielded had long since disappeared, and the episode of Ercole Cardinal Consalvi, Pius VII's Secretary of State, at the Congress of Vienna in 1814–1815, was only the exception that proved the rule of a virtual exclusion of papal influence from international affairs. Observers of the political order were afforded a rehearsal, as it were, for Otto von Bismarck's era of *Realpolitik* by Prussia's two brief wars, first against Denmark (1864) and then against Austria (1866), thus giving a quick foretaste of what was in store for Europe by way of the Prussian minister-president's declared policy of "blood and iron." And if Great Britain was not so nakedly provocative as Prussia, there was little by way of religious persuasion informing its official policies, and certainly no Catholic influence, as the national hysteria against the so-called 'papal aggression' demonstrated when Pio Nono restored the hierarchy to England in 1850. Nor was the public temper toward the Church more friendly across the Atlantic where three years later the Know-Nothing agitation in the United States created a series of riots in major American cities on the occasion of the visit of Pius IX's representative, Archbishop Gaetano Bedini. One would not be warranted in dismissing the Know-Nothing excesses as solely the doing of an ignorant rabble, and, therefore, in no sense typical of national sentiment, for one of the best educated Americans of that generation, George Bancroft, United States Minister to Prussia, was found a year and a half before the council characterizing for a friend the Catholic trends in Europe in these words:

In theology the most marked phenomenon in Europe is the concentrated unity and activity of the Roman clerical party. No band of conspirators was ever more closely welded together. The one will of the Pope rules the creed, the politics, the conduct of all.[7]

[7] Bancroft to Samuel Osgood, Berlin, February 21, 1868, M. A. DeWolfe Howe, *The Life and Letters of George Bancroft* (New York, 1908), II, 203.

If that could be believed in the green wood, what of the dry? True, during this period there were other states that were governed by Catholic rulers who in some instances regulated their ecclesiastical affairs by concordats with the Holy See, but in no instance was there any real sympathy and support for the objectives that Pius IX had in mind in summoning a general council.

Finally — and this was obviously not a professedly hostile element — there was the attitude of the pope and the Roman Curia toward the political realities of their time. The failure of the pontiffs from Pius VI to Pius IX to comprehend, much less to accept, the fact that the day of the absolute monarchs was over, that the era of parliamentary rule had come to stay, and that such was the type of government that was winning more and more of their spiritual subjects throughout the western world — this was a barrier that tended to separate the popes, not only from their contemporaries outside the Church but even from many Catholics. Having experienced harsh, at times brutal, treatment at the hands of men who, ironically enough, liked to style themselves disciples of the liberal creed, it was altogether understandable that the pontiffs should have fought to prevent what they regarded as an evil revolutionary inheritance from taking lodgement in their own domain. But where Rome's lack of political realism unwittingly inflicted injury on the Catholic name was its refusal to distinguish between the principles of philosophical liberalism which in many respects were, indeed, totally unacceptable to Catholics, and the perfectly legitimate aspirations with which many of the Holy See's spiritual subjects supported freedom of conscience, of assembly, of speech, and of the press. In that connection if only the Roman curial officials had been able to sense the worth and wisdom in warnings from so friendly a source as that of the devout Catholic laymen who edited *Le Correspondant*, much harm might have been undone. Two months before the council opened the Paris journal published a notable article in which the liberal-minded editors made an eloquent and touching appeal for the reconciliation of the Church with those aspects of modern society which were above suspicion. The day of the absolute monarchy, they said, was gone, and the regime of liberty that had succeeded it was both the providential law of the new age and the test to which it now pleased God to put the world and the Church. To these laymen liberty was the supreme test of both institutions and of character, and applying the point to the Church they said:

The Church is passing through it today. She has experienced others like it and each century brings its own. There was first of all the terrible test of persecution; then the test of schism full of turmoil and anguish; then the enervating and corrupting test of prosperity; and there is today the virile and militant test of liberty.[8]

But voices like those of Le Correspondant were not heeded at Rome, if they were heard, and as a consequence there was created an abyss between the mid-century papacy and the contemporary world which entailed a blurring, as it were, of the spiritual and temporal roles of the pope, and which a generation before even Giuseppi Cardinal Sala, a member of the Roman Curia, who has been described by a recent historian as "the most clear-sighted political thinker in the Sacred College," had not thought proper to try to rectify.[9] And once strong hands like those of Consalvi and Sala had been removed from the helm both the government of the Papal States and the prestige of the pontiffs steadily deteriorated. In the eyes of most observers the nadir was reached in Gregory XVI's fiery condemnations of the universal desire for freedom, and that not excepting the Catholic Poles who in their uprising of 1830 against the oppression of Czar Nicholas I had hoped for at least the Holy Father's sympathetic understanding. By 1850 Pius IX had fallen in with many of Gregory's policies, and it was thus understandable that some statesmen and diplomats should have reacted to his call for a council as having sounded an ominous note for the political order, and that at one point the great assembly's freedom should have momentarily seemed threatened in a way that was reminiscent of the Emperor Charles V at Trent over 300 years before.

Let that suffice for a description of the kind of world in which the Vatican Council was held; and let us now proceed to the preparatory stages of the gathering. It was on December 6, 1864, two days before his encyclical Quanta cura, with its accompanying Syllabus of Errors, was published, that Pio Nono first privately intimated to the cardinals of the Congregation of Rites what he had in mind. He stated that he had been thinking of a general council for a long time, and he now wished to have

[8] P. Douhaire pour le Conseil de redaction, "Le Concile," Le Correspondant LXXX (October 10, 1869), 40.

[9] E. E. Y. Hales, Revolution and Papacy, 1769–1846 (Garden City, New York, 1960), p. 257. The last two chapters of this work (pp. 261–295) give an excellent summary of the papacy vis-à-vis the political world from the restoration in 1815 to the loss of the temporal sovereignty in 1870.

171

the cardinals' reactions to the idea. Of the twenty-one replies all but eight were favorable.[10] There then followed in the spring of 1865 a confidential letter from Pius IX to thirty-four bishops of the Latin Church and to certain Oriental prelates asking for their opinions. Again a large majority pronounced in favor with a half dozen or more raising serious doubts and objections, and it is interesting to note that among the answers eight specifically stated that they thought the pope's infallibility should be defined. Having thus satisfied himself about the support of the episcopate, the pontiff chose to make the public announcement on June 26, 1867, to a gathering of approximately 500 bishops from all over the world who had come for the celebration of the eighteenth centennial of the martyrdom of SS. Peter and Paul. A congratulatory address to Pius IX was drawn up in the name of the assembled bishops in which the convening of a council was strongly favored, although this early the voice of the minority was heard when Jacques-Marie Ginoulhiac, Bishop of Grenoble, exclaimed in a fury to William Ullathorne of Birmingham against the tactics of the Archbishop of Westminster: "Ce n'est pas le temps de casser les vitraux." [11]

The issue having thus been determined formally, the preparations that had been shaping for two and a half years went forward under the auspices of the directing commission of eight cardinals who, in turn, gradually evolved five major commissions to deal with the council's business under the following headings: faith and dogma; ecclesiastical discipline; religious orders; Oriental churches and foreign missions; and, finally, politico-religious questions involving the relations of Church and State. The hierarchies of the principal countries were invited to send representative theologians to Rome to work on the agenda, and by November, 1868, these men had arrived and had been assigned to their respective duties. The Christmas issue of the *Civiltà Cattolica* listed their names to the total of ninety-seven, including the eight cardinals of the directing commission, and of this number about sixty were Italians with the others drawn from various national groups.[12] John Henry Newman had received a personal invitation from both Pius IX and Félix Dupanloup, Bishop of Orléans, but the great Oratorian asked to be excused, explaining to a friend:

[10] The best history of the council in English is that of Butler where an ample account of the preliminary stages may be read (I, 3–153).

[11] Butler, *op. cit.*, I, 86.

[12] Serie VII, V (December 26, 1868), 98–104.

172

I am more happy as I am, than in any other way. I can't bear the kind of trouble which I should have, if I were brought forward in any public way. Recollect, I could not be *in* the Council, unless I were a Bishop — and really and truly I am *not* a theologian. . . . Like St. Gregory Nazianzen, I like going on my own way, and having my time my own, living without pomp or state, or pressing engagements. Put me into official garb, and I am worth nothing; leave me to myself, and every now and then I shall do something.[13]

As for the United States, the choice fell upon the outstanding American theologian of the day, James A. Corcoran, a priest of the Diocese of Charleston who had already made a name for himself at the Baltimore plenary council in October, 1866, for his knowledge of theology and canon law as well as for his use of Latin.[14] Corcoran's letters to Martin J. Spalding, Archbishop of Baltimore, afford valuable insights into some of the problems before the theologians then assembled at the Holy See. For example, early in March of 1869 he expressed dissatisfaction with the *segreto pontificio* under which they were expected to operate. Since the theologians were supposed to represent their bishops, Corcoran could not see how this could be done unless they consulted them from time to time and acquainted them with what was going on. "I have decided for myself," he told Spalding, "and as I would not scruple to tell you my mind and my present situation, were I in your company, I shall not hesitate to tell it by letter." At this particular time, however, he had something more serious on his mind than methods of procedure; it was the subject matter of the proposed decrees and the spirit in which it was being approached that gave him cause for misgiving. "If it were left to these theologians," he said, "the nineteenth [*sic*] ecumenical council would issue more decrees, I mean *doctrinal definitions*, than all its predecessors from Nice [*sic*] to Trent." Adding to his discomfort were the twenty some canons already approved that touched on the Church's relations to the State, in some of which, he remarked, "I verily believe the fundamental principles of our (American & common sense) political doctrine are condemned . . ." In spite of the fact that he had stood alone, he had held out against certain decrees on which he felt

[13] Newman to Sister Maria Pia Giberne, February 10, 1869, in Ward, *op. cit.*, II, 281. In the end Dr. William Weathers, President of St. Edmund's College, Ware, represented the English hierarchy.

[14] For Corcoran cf. the unpublished doctoral dissertation of Sister Mary Marcian Lowman, O.S.U., "James Andrew Corcoran: Editor, Theologian, Scholar, 1820–1889," Saint Louis University (1958).

the Church had no right to pronounce. As for papal infallibility, Corcoran told the archbishop nine months before the opening of the council, "if I can judge aright, this definition is a foregone conclusion . . ." Not unnaturally he wished to know Spalding's mind and would be glad, as he put it, "to have your sentiments on this point for my instruction and guidance." [15]

In Archbishop Spalding's reply the United States bishops' attitude was summarized on several leading questions in about as satisfactory a way as one is likely to find anywhere. Spalding was grateful for Corcoran's clear expression of views and stated that in general he endorsed them and approved his course; moreover, he was confident that all the bishops "of this region," as he expressed it, would unite in these opinions. As for the three key points of papal infallibility, the proposal to define the condemnations of the *Syllabus of Errors*, and relations of Church and State, the titular head of the American hierarchy answered as follows.

1. We believe firmly the infallibility of the Pope ex Cathedra, but incline to think its formal definition unnecessary and perhaps inexpedient, not only for the reasons you allege, but also on account of the difficulty of fixing the precise limits of these doctrinal decisions. When they are formal — as is that of Im. Conception — there is no difficulty; but are all the declarations of Encyclicals, Allocutions, etc. to be received as doctrinal definitions? And what about the decisions of Congregations, confirmed by the Pontiff?

2. While we adhere ex corde to the principles enunciated in the Syllabus, we look upon them in *concreto* et in *subjecta materia*, not generalizing what is special, & not stretching their meanings beyond that inferrible from the circumstances to which they were applied. While freedom of worship is condemned when it implies a right not given by Christ, & is concerned . . . with introducing false worship into a Catholic country, it is not only not censurable but commendable & the only thing practicable in countries like ours, England, Russia, etc. And so of the liberty of the press, & progress in the American & Anglo-Saxon sense — not in the Liberal European. There is a wide distinction & any attempt to confound things so wide apart would be wrong & nugatory, putting us in a false position, in fact, untenable.

3. So, in regard to Church & State. The principle is all right; but the application to circumstances must vary with them. With us, & in half of Christendom, wholly impracticable; in countries once Catholic — as [France?]

[15] Archives of the Archdiocese of Baltimore, 33-M-12, Corcoran to Spalding, Rome, March 1, 1869. Hereafter these archives will be designated as AAB.

Austria, Spain, Italy, the tendency is to separation. It is an open question whether the Church does not lose more than she gains by the union; & it is not in the order of Providence that we are to come back to the type of primitive ages.[16]

More light could be derived from this exchange of letters if space permitted, especially in the revealing vignettes of some of the council's leading figures. For example, Corcoran came to know well Aloisio Cardinal Bilio, president of the dogmatic commission on which the Americans served, and he had the highest praise for Bilio's intelligence, kindliness, and candor. "But like too many of the rest," he said, "he has never looked boldly in the face the world in which we live and to which we are coming. The Syllabus is in his head and heart; it must be defined, every word and syllable of it." [17]

For nine months preceding the opening of the council strenuous attempts were made by the so-called majority and minority parties among the bishops to persuade the uncommitted on the validity of their respective positions on a number of questions, but especially on the definition of papal infallibility. In a sense the strife that followed was inevitable, for as Hubert Jedin, the historian of Trent, has said, "Truth is reached in any community by means of an exchange of opinions, by arguments for and against, that is, by means of an intellectual struggle." [18] And

[16] AAB, Letterbook of Archbishop Spalding, Spalding to Corcoran, Baltimore, March 27, 1869, p. 585. Spalding further developed his thought on these subjects in a letter of June 19, 1869, to Paul Cardinal Cullen, Archbishop of Dublin, when he said: "I fear from what little I can learn on the subject, that there will be a tendency to take very high church grounds in the approaching Council in regard not only to the infallibility of the Pope & the Syllabus in its *letter*, but also as to Union of Church & State, religious toleration, the brachium saeculare etc., etc. This last particularly would be unfortunate. We who live in a totally different state of things which is likely to be permanent & to be more & more extended, will be compelled to take a decided stand on the subject, especially the application in detail (*ibid.*, p. 776). If an unsigned article in the *Catholic World* of June, 1860, entitled "The Approaching Council of the Vatican" [IX, 356–366] was any indication of the state of American Catholic opinion, it was quite ill-informed and given to unwarranted expectations and predictions.

[17] AAB, 36A-E-11, Corcoran to Spalding, Rome, May 21, 1869. At the time Corcoran was reading with much admiration the recent work of the Bishop of Mainz, Wilhelm von Ketteler, *Deutschland nach dem Kriege von 1866* (Mainz, 1867), which had been written to give courage to the Austrian Catholics after their severe defeat by Prussia. "He treats fully and fearlessly of the present state of things," remarked Corcoran, "and gives indirectly some very good advice to the powers that be and to the future Council."

[18] Hubert Jedin, *Ecumenical Councils of the Catholic Church. An Historical Outline* (New York, 1960), p. 234.

the acute stage of the struggle in this instance opened on February 6, 1869, when the *Civiltà Cattolica* published under the heading of "Correspondence from France," a report alleged to represent French opinion on the forthcoming meeting. When the opponents of the new ultramontanism read that the majority of French Catholics felt that the council would be as brief as Chalcedon in 451 which lasted less than a month, that it was their wish that the propositions of the *Syllabus of Errors* should be defined, and that they were likewise calling for a definition of our Lady's assumption, it was evident that there was going to be trouble. But what caused the greatest sensation was the statement that insofar as papal infallibility was concerned, it was hoped "that the unanimous manifestation of the Holy Spirit through the mouth of the Fathers of the future ecumenical council will define it by acclamation."[19] It is little wonder that one historian of the council should have characterized the *Civiltà's* article as "the sign of battle."[20]

Through the ensuing spring and summer and into the autumn the party lines among the bishops were gradually taking shape. By August an anonymous tract highly critical of the tactics of the infallibilists was in wide circulation, and in the following month the twenty bishops of Germany met at Fulda and revealed their anxiety over developments such as that adumbrated by the article in the *Civiltà Cattolica*. So worried were they, in fact, that fourteen of them signed a letter to Pius IX expressing the conviction that a definition of infallibility would be inopportune. Among these was Wilhelm von Ketteler of Mainz who in his early years had been one of the strongest promoters of papal interests among the German Catholics. But von Ketteler's keen sense of the role of the bishops in the direction of the Church had taken a jolt in recent years. For example, Pius IX's definition of the Immaculate Conception in 1854 had prompted him to tell Dupanloup of Orleans:

assemblies of bishops uniquely held for the purpose of providing a brilliant aspect to certain major festivities or to give formal approval of decisions already made in advance without having shared in their formation — such assemblies displease me.[21]

[19] *Civiltà Cattolica*, V, 7th Series (February 6, 1869), 352.
[20] Butler, *op. cit.*, I, 108.
[21] Fritz Vigener, *Ketteler, Ein Deutsches Bischofsleben Des 19. Jahrhunderts* (Munchen und Berlin, 1924), p. 569, n. 1. The writer is indebted for this and the following reference to his friend and colleague, John K. Zeender, associate professor of modern history in the Catholic University of America.

As a result in the council von Ketteler was a stout inopportunist, the name given to those opposed to the definition of papal infallibility, as he came to realize more fully how far off the mark had been the works of the pastoral letter that he had published on the eve of his departure for Rome. In that document he had expressed his belief that all major definitions *de fide* must be made by what he called "the unity of the whole episcopal magisterium, not through an approximate majority," and that these decisions were made in council "either with the absolute unity of the assembled bishops or with a majority which is equivalent to unity . . ."[22]

Meanwhile as the German hierarchy had shown a division of opinion at Fulda in September, 1869, between men like von Ketteler on the one side as against Ignaz Senestréy, Bishop of Regensburg, on the other, so the hierarchies of other countries — with the exception of Hungary — showed hardly any more real unity either before the council's opening or thereafter. As von Ketteler had passed from the ultramontanist ranks to those of the inopportunists, so also did others change their ground, as, for example, Spalding, who left Baltimore an inopportunist, but who became so aroused after observing at Rome what he regarded as the unfair methods employed by the minority party that he ended an ardent infallibilist. Yet the switch of the titular leader of the American hierarchy in no way influenced the conduct of men like Augustin Verot, the Sulpician Bishop of Savannah (he was transferred to the new See of St. Augustine on March 11, 1870), whose candid criticisms on that and other matters earned him the name of *l'enfant terrible* of the council, of Michael Domenec, C.M., Bishop of Pittsburgh, whose adhesion to the infallibility decree after all was over was so long delayed that there was considerable relief in orthodox quarters when it arrived a year and a half after the council, and of Peter Richard Kenrick, Archbishop of St.

[22] Pastoral letter of November 12, 1869, John Michael Raich (Ed.) *Wilhelm Emmanuel Freiherrn von Ketteler, Bischof von Mainz. Hirtenbriefe* (Mainz, 1904), pp. 600–601. For the inopportunist views of another German prelate cf. the letters of Gustav Adolf Cardinal von Hohenlohe, brother of the Bavarian foreign minister, who felt isolated in the ultramontanist atmosphere of the Roman Curia. He was anxious to have either Ignaz Döllinger or Johannes Friedrich, two priest-professors of the University of Munich with strongly anti-infallibilist views, sent to him as theologians for the council. Cf. George W. Chrystal (Editor of English Edition), *Memoirs of Prince Chlodwig of Hohenlohe-Schillingsfuerst* edited by Friedrich Curtius (New York, 1906), I, 364–365; 369–374. Hereafter this work will be referred to as: Hohenlohe, *Memoirs*.

Louis, described by one historian as, "perhaps the stiffest opponent of the definition."[23]

An analysis of the positions taken by the bishops of other countries, both before and during the council, would in general produce a similar picture to that of the Americans. For example, while the infallibilist views of Paul Cardinal Cullen, Archbishop of Dublin, were shared by a majority of the Irish bishops, that did not move men like John Mac-Hale, Archbishop of Tuam, and David Moriarty, Bishop of Kerry, from the firmly inopportunist stand which they maintained to the end.[24] Nor did the sharp and forceful action of the titular leader of the English prelates, Henry Edward Manning, Archbishop of Westminster, in the least frighten William J. Clifford, Bishop of Clifton, who outdistanced all his countrymen in his opposition to papal infallibility. From the very first, of course, no one had been in any doubt about the man who did more than any other to shape the mind of France against the definition, and here Félix Dupanloup, Bishop of Orléans, had ranged on his side an impressive group of French prelates, including Georges Darboy, Archbishop of Paris, who less than a year after the final vote would lose his life at the hands of the Paris Commune (May 24, 1871). Moreover, in the case of the French there was likewise a fairly large middle group led by Henri-Marie Cardinal de Bonnechose, Archbishop of Rouen, who remained for some time uncommitted on the great question.

Meanwhile what was the state of opinion in the world outside the Church? In certain foreign offices the prospect of a council had aroused alarm, and the first to give expression to this state of mind was the Foreign Minister of Bavaria, Prince Chlodwig von Hohenlohe, whose

[23] Butler, *op. cit.*, II, 176. For the Americans cf. Raymond J. Clancy, C.S.C., "American Prelates in the Vatican Council," *Historical Records and Studies*, XXVIII (1937), 7–135. Ullathorne of Birmingham found the Americans in general "able and businesslike" and having "a great affection and respect" for Newman (Butler, *op. cit.*, I, 211). Ullathorne thought the Spanish-born Vincentian, Thaddeus Amat, Bishop of Monterey–Los Angeles "the shrewdest man in the Council . . . and he never speaks above a few minutes, but he hits the nail on the head invariably. He neither argues, nor talks, but simply proposes amendments on the text and comes down again." (*Ibid.*, II, 113).

[24] For a recent brief treatment cf. Peadar Mac Suibhne, "Ireland at the Vatican Council," *Irish Ecclesiastical Record*, 5th Series, XCIII (April, 1960), 209–222; (May, 1960), 295–307. In addition to the customary sources, this writer had access to the diary of James A. Goold, Bishop of Melbourne, and the papers of Nicholas Power, Coadjutor Bishop of Killaloe. It is amusing to find the bishop from Australia as late as 1870 referring to two American bishops as "from the colonies." (p. 303).

brother was a cardinal in curia. On April 9, Hohenlohe sent a note to the powers which had been prompted by the *Civiltà Cattolica's* article of the previous February, mention of which has already been made. Characterizing the Jesuit journal as "a semi-official organ" of the Holy See, he went on to say that it had recently declared it a duty for the council to transform what he termed "the damnatory judgments" of the *Syllabus of Errors* into "positive decisions." Since some of these propositions were directed against what the prince called "important axioms of State organization" that all civilized people had come to take for granted, he maintained that the governments were now confronted with a situation, which he described in these words:

whether and in what form they would have to advise either the Bishops subject to their authority, or, at a later stage, the Council itself of the perilous consequences to which such a deliberate and fundamental disturbance of the relations of Church and State must inevitably lead.[25]

That Hohenlohe's concern was shared by others, there was no doubt. His note was the subject of a tense cabinet meeting at Downing Street where Prime Minister Gladstone, his mind colored by the biased reports reaching him from Sir John Acton at Rome, moved for a demonstration by the powers. Fortunately, the foreign secretary, the Earl of Clarendon, in closer touch with the true state of affairs through the despatches of Odo Russell, unofficial British agent at Rome, felt that English policy would be best served by the government's remaining aloof. In the end Clarendon won, and the threat to the council's freedom that some had hoped might be initiated at London was removed. Gladstone's fears concerning the evil effect that the council might have on the civil allegiance of British Catholics, nonetheless, grew stronger with the passing months, but in a somewhat resigned air he confessed to Archbishop Manning, "the prevailing opinion is that it is better to let those influences take their course, and work out the damage which will naturally and surely entail upon the see of Rome and upon what is bound to it." [26]

[25] Hohenlohe, *Memoirs*, I, 327; the full text of the note is given here, pp. 326–328.
[26] Gladstone to Manning, April 16, 1870, John Morley, *The Life of William Ewart Gladstone* (New York, 1903), II, 511. Gladstone felt that the American bishops were in the best position to prevent the worst from happening in the council. He told Lord Acton: "Of all the prelates at Rome, none have a finer opportunity, to none is a more crucial test now applied, than to those of the United States. For if there, where there is nothing of covenant, of restraint, or of equivalent between the church and the state, the propositions of the Syllabus are still to have the countenance of

In Berlin, needless to say, no sympathy for the council and its promoters was entertained by Bismarck and his colleagues. Yet, as he told Hohenlohe when the latter visited him in early June, while in general he agreed with his views, he would propose that the German states take joint and secret action to deprecate at Rome what he called "too sweeping measures," rather than to make any official protest.[27] As for Austria-Hungary, the Protestant chancellor, Count Friedrich Ferdinand von Beust, had replied to Hohenlohe's original note, that since the Vienna government espoused the principle of religious freedom, it could hardly be said to have accepted its consequences were it to attempt any "preventive and restrictive measures," as he termed them, concerning so fundamental a part of the constitution of the Catholic Church as an ecumenical council. As for the fears for the State which Hohenlohe foresaw from the council, Beust remarked, "We can neither affirm nor deny the imminence of such a danger." [28] Nor did a visit from Hohenlohe to Vienna in late August bring Beust around. He shared entirely the Bavarian foreign minister's views about the evil being done by the ultramontanist churchmen; but he was resting his hope that something

the episcopate, it becomes really a little difficult to maintain in argument the civil rights of such persons to toleration, however conclusive be the argument of policy in favour of granting it." (*Ibid.*, II, 511, n.d., n.p.). For further details and correspondence touching the crucial London cabinet meeting of April, 1860, cf. Edmund Sheridan Purcell, *Life of Cardinal Manning, Archbishop of Westminster* (New York, 1896), II, 433 ff.

[27] Hohenlohe's diary, June 12, 1869, Hohenlohe, *Memoirs*, I, 346–347. In the following spring when, according to Bismarck, the press asked the government to support those German bishops who were in opposition to the Roman Curia's conciliar policies, he asked how this was to be done, discounted any such attempt, and then stated: "We cannot take preventive measures as they would be of no value, but it is open to us to adopt a repressive policy in case a decision is come to in opposition to our wishes." This statement is given under date of March 21, 1870, in Moritz Busch, *Bismarck, Some Secret Pages of His History* (London, 1898), I, 20. A few days later chagrin at the progress of the infallibilists prompted Bismarck to suggest a conference of the powers as being, perhaps, useful; even if it could no longer hope to influence the council, something might be gained by considering "how far the injurious effects of its decisions on the peace of Church and State could be minimised." (*Ibid.*, I, 22). Daru, however, turned down the idea and Beust would not act; with the Catholic powers thus declining to move Bismarck fell back on the policy of supporting the efforts made by the German bishops to prevent what were styled "illegal changes" in the Church's constitution and "to preserve both Church and State from a disturbance of the peace." (*Ibid.*, I, 24).

[28] Beust to Count Friedrich von Ingelheim, Austrian Minister to Bavaria, Vienna, May 15, 1869, Hohenlohe, *Memoirs*, I, 335. Actually, Hohenlohe had not proposed any 'preventive and restrictive measures,' but had only asked for Beust's views.

might be gained by a split in the Austrian hierarchy which, he said, "would not come to pass unless the Government maintained a completely passive attitude."[29]

Thus the first major attempt of outside intervention in the council came to nothing. Six months later the threat was revived by the liberal Catholic, Comte Napoleon Daru, Foreign Minister of France, whose independent action in sending a somewhat menacing note to Rome on February 20, 1870, not only startled the cabinet of Emile Ollivier, but touched off a chain of events that so frightened Giacomo Cardinal Antonelli, Secretary of State, that he called together his principal supporters among the cardinals and on March 25 they went in a body to Pius IX to beg him to withdraw the infallibility question from the council. But the pope would not yield, and in the end the second and final threat passed when its chief instigator, Daru, resigned from the cabinet on April 22 over a difference on domestic issues with the Emperor Napoleon III. At this juncture Ollivier, well disposed toward the Church and friendly toward Pio Nono, took over the foreign ministry, immediately reversed Daru's policy, and the episode was closed with the despatch of a telegram from Paris to Rome that read, "Daru se retire, Ollivier remplace, Concile libre."[30] Free, indeed, it was, and that curiously enough by the grace of a Protestant Premier of France who seven years later would publish a history of the Vatican Council about which the leading English historian of that gathering would remark that of all the books he had read, "this one comes perhaps the nearest to the ideal of historical objectivity and impartiality."[31]

That brings us to the great debate itself where in an abbreviated form we shall hope to see what the council had in the meantime done with its freedom. It is doubtful that any event in the history of the modern Church ever gave rise to a greater flow of misinformation than the Vati-

[29] Hohenlohe's diary, August 25, 1869, *ibid.*, I, 363. Beust was quoted as placing hope in Maximilian von Tarnoczy, Archbishop of Salzburg, "as a Liberal." In the end the Austrian bishops split over infallibility, even though it was not in a way to fulfill Beust's expectations, with Josef Rauscher and Friedrich Schwarzenberg, the Cardinal Archbishops of Vienna and Prague, respectively, among the strongest inopportunists; while Vincenz Gasser, Prince Bishop of Brixen, was an ultramontanist and Josef Fessler, Bishop of St. Polten, secretary of the council, a moderate infallibist.

[30] Butler, *op. cit.*, II, 25.

[31] *Ibid.*, I, 100. Butler called Ollivier's explanation and defense of the *Syllabus of Errors*, "the best — better than Dupanloup's, better than Newman's." (*Ibid.*, I, 101).

can Council. This misinformation, both accidental and deliberate, not only rendered accurate knowledge of what was transpiring almost impossible for those outside, but at times it seriously darkened the minds of those within the council chamber. This circumstance not only later made the historian's tasks of disentangling the web of error, misunderstanding, misinterpretation, and downright lies an exceedingly difficult one, but at the time it contributed mightily to the bitter spirit in which prelates of opposing opinions at times fought their battles. As usually happens when feeling runs high, on both sides men gave voice to absurdities, and that both in public and in private. In the earlier stages of the neo-ultramontanist enthusiasm, for example, Gaspard Mermillod, later to be Bishop of Lausanne and Geneva and a cardinal, preached a sermon which he entitled, "The Three Incarnations of the Son of God," wherein he described the divine action as having taken place "in the womb of a virgin, in the eucharist, and in the old man of the Vatican." [32] But this piece of theological nonsense was more than matched by the malice and virulence against the pontiff's person and official prerogatives that began to appear in the *Allgemeine Zeitung* of Augsburg in March, 1869, chiefly from the pen of the learned priest-scholar, Ignaz Döllinger, professor of church history in the University of Munich, writing under the name of "Janus." Bishop Ullathorne was amply justified, therefore, in warning his priests and people in a lenten pastoral letter against these falsehoods where, as he said:

designs are attributed to the Council of which the Council knows nothing; and bishops are invested with views and notions, and are described as taking this or that course of action, which are utterly unbefitting their characters, and are often in direct opposition to their real sentiments.[33]

Yet the situation continued unrelieved to the end, and years afterward fantastic stories about certain churchmen were still in circulation and being believed.[34]

[32] Aubert, *op. cit.*, p. 303.

[33] Pastoral letter of Ullathorne from Rome, February 10, 1870, Butler, *op. cit.*, I, 255. After the 'Janus' letters came out in book form as *The Pope and the Council* in July, 1869, Ullathorne stated on October 22, "It is the gravest and severest attack on the Holy See and the Jesuits, and especially on the policy of Rome for a thousand years, and will be a great storehouse for the adversaries of the Church." (*Ibid.*, I, 111).

[34] One of the most egregious examples of this bias was the article of Lord Acton, "The Vatican Council," in the *North British Review*, LIII (October, 1870), 183–

Although the formal opening of the Vatican Council had taken place on December 8, 1869, for many weeks little or no real progress was made. In fact, up to the following March 18 not a single decree had yet been enacted. Prolonged discussions continued week by week on a universal catechism, on reform of the breviary, on priests' retreats and other aspects of clerical life and discipline, while simultaneously extensive debates were conducted on the elements entering into the definition of Catholic faith. But the bishops were not to be hurried, nor were some of them easily to be pleased. Nearly two months after the sessions had begun Ullathorne gave Newman a vivid description of the pace of business when he stated that if the Oratorian could see, as he expressed it, "schemata brought in, only to be pulled to pieces and sent out again, bleeding in every limb," he would realize that in the end what he termed "party views and idiosyncracies" would be forced to yield before the consensus of the fathers.[35] Under these circumstances it was hardly to be wondered at that the *Dei Filius* on Catholic faith should not have been enacted until April 14; but when the final vote came that constitution's four chapters received the unanimous assent of the 667 bishops present. The catechism, the breviary, and like topics, however, were not so fortunate and in the sequel they were lost to view.

All the while the shadow of the infallibility issue hung over the assembly. Through December those intent upon its definition worked steadily, and in secret, to rally support, and by the first days of the new year this majority party, as it was called, felt sufficiently strong to move into the open as the petitions circulating among the bishops for the question's introduction into the council accumulated the necessary signatures. Through January and February frantic efforts to influence one way or another Pio Nono, the presiding cardinals, and the uncommitted bishops, filled the Roman air with the excitement of secret intrigues, tactical maneuvers, and sharp personal encounters. But the minority party was playing a losing game, for in opposition to the 380 names signed to the petition to bring on the question they could muster only

---

229. Acton's scholarly training might have been expected to preserve him from this sort of thing, but such was not the case. Moreover, it was Acton — and Döllinger — who were in no small measure responsible for agitating Gladstone against the Holy See and the council. Cf. his pamphlet, *The Vatican Decrees in Their Bearing on Civil Allegiance: A Political Expostulation,* which was published in London in November, 1874, and by the end of the year had sold 145,000 copies.

[35] Ullathorne to Newman, Rome, February 4, 1870, Butler, *op. cit.,* I, 217.

140. It was not enough to block the majority party's plans and on March 6, therefore, the public announcement was made that the infallibility question was coming before the council.

There followed a period that gave evidence on both sides of deep searching of souls and at times of notable displays of courage in response to the voice of conscience, as well as an occasional revelation of actions unworthy of so high a cause. Among the minority's outside sympathizers was Newman, who from the outset had opposed the definition. He was kept in close touch with events by the lengthy accounts of the proceedings that reached him regularly from the Bishop of Birmingham. It was in reply in late January to such a letter that Newman, in the deepest confidence, laid bare for Ullathorne his inmost thoughts on the subject. Referring to the fears then current from the exaggerated news stories coming out of Rome, he said:

I look with anxiety at the prospect of having to defend decisions which may not be difficult to my private judgment, but may be most difficult to defend logically in the face of historical facts. What have we done to be treated as the Faithful never were treated before? When has definition of doctrine *de fide* been a luxury of devotion and not a stern painful necessity? Why should an aggressive and insolent faction be allowed to make the hearts of the just to mourn whom the Lord hath not made sorrowful? Why can't we be let alone when we have pursued peace and thought no evil?[36]

Incredible as it may seem, this letter got out of Ullathorne's possession and was published in the newspapers. Differences of this kind naturally engendered critical comment about those in the opposite camp as, for example, Bishop Moriarty of Kerry who as a member of the minority, which he styled the Church militant, remarked of the majority:

It is composed of men who have not come into conflict with the unbelieving mind, or into contact with the intellectual mind of the time. When I read the school of theology in which they were trained I am not surprised that they treat every doubter as a heretic.[37]

Yet in spite of the participants' conflicting views, and of the depth of feeling that at times motivated their expression, on the whole the conciliar debates were conducted with dignity and moderation and those governing the procedure acted with objectivity and fairness. Only once,

[36] Newman to Ullathorne, Birmingham, January 28, 1870, Ward, *Newman*, II, 288.

[37] Moriarty to Newman, Rome, February 3, 1870, Butler, *op. cit.*, II, 29.

on March 22, was there a scene when Joseph Strossmayer, Bishop of Diakovár, was the principal in a disorderly exchange with Anniballe Cardinal Capalti over the decree then under discussion attributing errors to Protestants of which the Bosnian bishop felt they were not guilty. There was likewise one serious breach of fairness when no provision was made for a representative of the minority on the commission *de fide*, and once Pio Nono, whose heart was clearly set on the definition, resorted to unfair tactics when he administered a severe rebuke to the distinguished Dominican theologian, Filippo Cardinal Guidi, Archbishop of Bologna, for his speech on June 18 which sided with the minority party. In fact, there were even moments of high amusement, as on January 27 when Verot of Savannah, during a debate on the morals of the clergy, demanded that priests not only avoid theatres but also hunting with weapons, and with that in mind he asked to have a paragraph embodying his idea added to the proposed canon which would contain the following sentence: "The wretched spectacle of a man of God wandering through the fields and highways in search of birds and beasts should never be shown the faithful." [38] Some bishops spoke at very great length, a factor that caused acute distress to many of the more aged prelates, especially when the heat of the Roman summer began to set in. Even during the winter months a session could be trying as that on January 4 when Johann B. Greith, Bishop of St. Gall, made a speech that prompted Ullathorne to comment:

We have got home from a meeting of the Council where we were almost stunned by a Swiss bishop, who spoke for an hour, and roared as if he were talking from one mountain to another against wind and thunder. [39]

Yet the cardinal presidents rarely cut the speakers off. In that connection, years later Cardinal Gibbons, who was at the time the youngest bishop in the council, reminisced about the freedom of speech that prevailed, and he remarked:

I can safely say that neither in the British House of Commons, nor in the French Chambers, nor in the German Reichstag, nor in our American Congress would a wider liberty of debate be tolerated than was granted in the Vatican Council. [40]

[38] Mansi, *op. cit.*, L, 539.
[39] Quoted in Butler, *op. cit.*, I, 194.
[40] James Cardinal Gibbons, "Personal Reminiscences of the Vatican Council," *North American Review*, CCCCXLIX (April, 1894), 393.

The point made by the Cardinal of Baltimore was clearly illustrated by the debates on papal infallibility. After the public announcement of March 6 two more months were given to drafting the decrees, to private discussions thereon, and then to revision of the drafts. Finally on May 9 the revised text was presented to the council and four days later the great debate began and ran until June 3. During those three weeks sixty-five bishops — thirty-nine in favor and twenty-six opposed to defining the pope's infallibility — were heard from the ambo. But the heat was now becoming oppressive and there were growing signs of fatigue. A motion was circulated among the bishops, therefore, to apply a cloture to the general debate, and when the presidents asked the pleasure of the fathers a large minority were for cloture, although the following day a minority of eighty protested this action. The debate on the text of each of the four chapters of the proposed constitution was still to come, however, and during the course of it every conceivable aspect of the question was aired, culminating on July 11 in the exhaustive exposition by Vincenz Gasser, Prince-Bishop of Brixen, whose speech lasted a little under four hours.[41] After due consideration as well of the 144 amendments proposed to the chapter on infallibility, one of the council's high moments arrived with the vote scheduled for July 13.

By this time a good number of prelates had ceased to play any active role in the council as may be illustrated by reference to the bishops from the United States. As far back as March 15 the strong inopportunist opinions of certain Americans showed up when Peter Richard Kenrick of St. Louis, John B. Purcell of Cincinnati, and Edward Fitzgerald of Little Rock, joined in a protest against a report that the infallibility issue would be advanced out of its regular order on the agenda, and that at the next general congregation it would be carried without discussion. They could not believe that anyone but a madman would tolerate or approve such an action. "But we give notice . . ." they warned, "that if the impossible should happen, we would immediately leave the council, and make public the reason for our departure."[42] Although the sequel proved that their fears had been exaggerated, four months later a number of these same churchmen were still firmly opposed to the definition. On Wednesday, July 13, which one of the council's historians calls its "crucial day,"[43] there were 601 bishops present for the trial bal-

[41] Butler devoted a separate chapter to the Gasser speech (II, 134–148).
[42] Mansi, op. cit., LI, 714.
[43] Butler, op. cit., II, 149.

lot on the *Pastor aeternus* constitution as a whole. Of these 451 voted *placet*, eighty-eight *non-placet*, and sixty-two *placet juxta modum*, or acceptance of papal infallibility with reservations. And it is significant to recall that there were then about seventy-six bishops still in Rome who absented themselves from this session. On July 13 only the Hungarian delegation of fifteen bishops maintained a solid bloc against the definition, while the other hierarchies divided more or less along the lines of the Americans where fifteen voted *placet*, four *non-placet*, and five *placet juxta modum*, with twenty-one absent. On July 17 the minority party made its final and vain effort to win a compromise solution from Pius IX, whereupon fifty-five bishops sent a formal protest to the pope against holding the fourth public session scheduled for the following day. They would not be present in the council chamber since, they said:

filial piety and reverence, which not long ago drew our spokesmen to the feet of Your Holiness, will not suffer us, in a cause so closely touching the person of Your Holiness, publicly and before a Father to say: *non-placet*. . . . We will return, therefore, without delay to our flocks. . . .[44]

Again using the Americans as illustrative of the action of most of the national hierarchies, this document bore the signatures of the Archbishop of St. Louis and the Bishops of Pittsburgh and St. Augustine. Of the forty-five Americans who had come to Rome the previous autumn, therefore, twenty had by now either departed for home or had absented themselves from the session of July 18 when the final vote was taken. On this occasion 533 bishops pronounced their *placet* to the definition of papal infallibility of whom twenty-four were Americans, while the two *non-placets* were registered by Luigi Riccio, Bishop of Cajazzo in southern Italy, and Edward Fitzgerald, Bishop of Little Rock, Arkansas. Students of church history are familiar with the dramatic character of the closing scene when a furious electric storm broke over Rome and so darkened the skies that large candles had to be held close to Pio Nono so that he might see to read the text of the *Pastor aeternus*. Some of the minority interpreted the storm as a sign of divine displeasure at the definition of the pope's infallibility; but Archbishop Manning, the majority whip, was in no way disconcerted by talk of this kind. "They forgot," he said, "Sinai and the ten Commandments."[45]

[44] Mansi, *op. cit.*, LII, 1325.
[45] Henry Edward Manning, *The True Story of the Vatican Council*, 2d ed. (London, 1877), p. 147.

In conclusion what were the general results of the Church's twentieth ecumenical council? Perhaps, they can best be summarized from the three-fold viewpoint of the papacy, the bishops, and the secular governments. First, insofar as the newly defined doctrine on the primacy and infallibility of the sovereign pontiff was concerned, there could be little doubt that, generally speaking, the position of the pope had been enhanced in the eyes of the Catholic world. In a sense it was a culminating point in the centralizing tendencies that had been discernible within the Church since the early years of the century. In fact, some men of our own generation, whose fundamental loyalty to the Holy See is beyond question, feel that this tendency is still a living force and that it does not always necessarily operate to the Church's advantage. As for the vast majority of Catholics in 1870, they had never seriously questioned the fact that the pope was infallible in his judgments on faith and morals, even if they did not have the theological acumen to explain what that meant. With the exception, therefore, of the old Catholic group who followed the teaching of Döllinger and Friedrich and lapsed into schism in Germany, Switzerland, and the Netherlands — the estimates of whose numbers vary so greatly as almost to defy accurate calculation — once the doctrine had been defined neither priests nor laity felt much change in their traditional religious commitment. For example, Newman who all along had believed the doctrine himself but had opposed its definition, remarked to a friend after he had read the text, "I saw the new definition yesterday and am pleased at its moderation . . ."[46] What made matters easier, and at least to some degree disarmed the critics, was the sparing use made of the prerogative by Pius IX and his successors, it having been employed in solemn manner only once in the last ninety years when in 1950 Pope Pius XII defined the assumption of our Lady. Thus the wild prophecies and anticipation of frequent definitions of extreme neo-ultramontanists like Louis Veuillot and William George Ward, which had repelled so many both within and outside the Church, were proven entirely false.

As for the bishops, the struggle of conscience in the case of some was clearly a severe one. We have already mentioned the delay of a year and a half before Bishop Domenec of Pittsburgh sent in his adhesion to the constitution *Pastor aeternus*, and that of the fiery bishop from Bosnia, Joseph Strossmayer, did not come through until December, 1872. But unlike earlier councils, in 1870 there were no episcopal defections such,

[46] Ward, *Newman*, II, 307.

for example, as Nicaea when in June, 325, two bishops refused to sign the Nicene Creed and about eighty ultimately passed over to the Arians, or at Ephesus in 431 where thirty or more bishops refused to accept the hypostatic union of the two natures of Christ in the single person of the Word and to accord to our Lady the title of Mother of God. Obviously, the minority would have preferred that papal infallibility had not been defined at all, but with it a *fait accompli* even the bitterest foes ultimately gave way. Part of their chagrin and disappointment stemmed, incidentally, from the council's failure to explore, let alone to reach any conclusion, about the bishops' place in the magisterium of the Church, a subject which ninety years later some of their successors still feel should be clarified and which may thus be aired in the Second Vatican Council.

Finally, in regard to the secular governments, the immediate effects of the definition of papal infallibility were almost uniformly unhappy. As an indication of Austria's profound displeasure Vienna repudiated its concordat of 1855 with the Holy See. In Germany the making of a quarrel between Church and State was already at hand and the definition heaped fuel upon the fire. The more that Bismarck, the iron chancellor of the new German Empire, thought about what had happened the more alarmed and indignant he became, fancying, as he did, the pope's infallibility would lessen the State's assurance of allegiance of the German Catholics. That was the spirit in which he supported the *Kulturkampf* that broke over the German Church early in 1872 as it was the intent which in the course of the Reichstag debates on the religious question informed his famous boast of May 14 of that year, "Do not fear, we will not go to Canossa either in body or in spirit."[47] As a consequence the German Catholics were to experience a decade of acute suffering before the State's persecution of the Church would finally be abandoned in the face of the dangerous peril of Socialism.

As for France, once the restraining hand of Marshall Marie Edmé de McMahon was removed in January, 1879, and the Third Republic was firmly launched under Jules Grévy, the French Church was to feel the full force of the most virulent anti-clericalism, although it would be a mistake to attribute the ordeal of the French Catholics primarily to the definition of papal infallibility, for in all likelihood it would have befallen them in any case. Finally, the defeat of Gladstone and the Liberal Party in the elections of February, 1874, left him time to ruminate about

[47] C. Grant Robertson, *Bismarck* (London, 1918), p. 316.

189

the evils of the Vatican Council, to visit Döllinger in Munich in September of that year, and to come home to publish two months later the pamphlet that revived all the old English fears of papal aggression, even though it did call forth the notable replies concerning the *Syllabus of Errors* and papal infallibility of Archbishop Manning to the London *Times* and of John Henry Newman in the well-known *Letter Addressed to His Grace the Duke of Norfolk*. Although the controversy had, indeed, stirred up anew bitter debate, it had not provoked any crippling legislation such as occurred in Germany and France, and by the end of the decade at least a surface tranquillity had returned to English public life.

But let the last word be said by the Archbishop of Westminster whose conduct during the assembly at Rome had been consistently vigilant, vigorous, and sharp, and not always answering to the rules of fairness to one's opponents. But even his most unrelenting enemies could not challenge Manning's sincerity in so forcefully urging the definition, and with the hindsight afforded by the ninety years that separate us from those exciting days of 1870 it is apparent that the words which he used in retrospect to describe the council could hardly be gainsaid. He stated:

. . . in due time it will be perceived that never was any council so numerous, nor were ever the dissentient voices relatively so few; that never was any council so truly ecumenical both in its representation and in its acceptance; that never were the separations after it fewer, feebler, or more transient; and that never did the Church come out from a great conflict more confirmed in its solidity, or more tranquil in its internal peace.[48]

CHURCH HISTORY AND
THE SEMINARIAN

In reflecting on the subject of what the history of the Church can mean in the life of a seminarian, one thinks of the tremendously high evaluation that educated men have placed on a knowledge of that subject, and that whether or not they believed in the Church's doctrines

[48] Manning, *op. cit.*, pp. 207–208.

and whether or not they felt attracted to it as one of the chief civilizing forces in human history. In other words, throughout nearly twenty centuries the Catholic Church has been loved and hated, praised and reviled, but it has rarely been ignored. And if one considers the reasons for that well-nigh universal interest, the most compelling reason may well be its quality of endurance. The Church's ability to ride out storms, to outlive the most formidable foes, has constituted for countless men a fascinating study, and no man has expressed the sense of wonderment created by this survival more majestically than Lord Macaulay. In a review article of Leopold von Ranke's *History of the Popes,* the noted Englishman paid the Church a tribute the like of which will probably never again be matched. If you will bear with me I should like to quote it in full. Macaulay said:

There is not, and there never was, on this earth, a work of human policy so well deserving of examination as the Roman Catholic Church. The history of that Church joins together the two great ages of human civilisation. No other institution is left standing which carries the mind back to the times when the smoke of sacrifice rose from the Pantheon, and when camelopards and tigers bounded in the Flavian amphitheatre. The proudest royal houses are but of yesterday, when compared with the line of Supreme Pontiffs. That line we trace back in an unbroken series, from the Pope who crowned Napoleon in the nineteenth century, to the Pope who crowned Pepin in the eighth; and far beyond the time of Pepin the august dynasty extends, till it is lost in the twilight of fable. The republic of Venice came next in antiquity. But the republic of Venice was modern when compared with the Papacy; and the republic of Venice is gone and the Papacy remains. The Papacy remains, not in decay, not a mere antique; but full of life and youthful vigour. The Catholic Church is still sending forth to the furthest ends of the world, missionaries as zealous as those who landed in Kent with Augustine; and still confronting hostile kings with the same spirit with which she confronted Attila. The number of her children is greater than in any former age. Her acquisitions in the New World have more than compensated her for what she has lost in the Old. Her spiritual ascendency extends over the vast countries which lie between the plains of the Missouri and Cape Horn — countries which, a century hence, may not improbably contain a population as large as that which now inhabits Europe. The members of her communion are certainly not fewer than a hundred and fifty millions; and it will be difficult to show that all the other Christian sects united, amount to a hundred and twenty millions. Nor do we see any sign which indicates that the term of her long dominion is approaching. She saw the commencement of all the governments, and of all the ecclesiastical establishments, that now exist in the world; and we feel no assurance that she is not destined to see the end of them all. She was great and respected before the Saxon had set foot on Britain — before the Frank had passed the Rhine — when Grecian eloquence still flourished at Antioch — when idols were still worshipped in the temple of Mecca. And she may still exist in undiminished vigour when some traveller from New Zealand shall, in the midst of a vast solitude, take his stand on a broken arch of London Bridge to sketch the ruins of St. Paul's.[1]

If the Church's history could produce that kind of an impression on the mind of a man who in no way subscribed to its doctrine, how much more might one expect it to attract those who are of the household of the faith. For as Father de Lubac remarked in describing the 'man of the Church,' as he called him, "Being a man of the Church, he will love the Church's past. He will meditate over her history, holding her tradition in reverence and exploring deep into it."[2] The historical traditions of purely secular events often take a lasting grip on men's minds as, for example, the extraordinary attachment that so many Americans manifest for the history of their Civil War, or the touching loyalty of most Englishmen to their royal family and all that is associated with the crown. So much the more, then, might one anticipate that Catholics — and especially seminarians — as privileged citizens of the City of God on earth would be moved by the story of the triumphs and tragedies of the world's oldest living institution, an institution which to their eyes of faith is the Mystical Body of Christ.

So much for the reason why the Church's history should hold an honored place in our reading habits, and, too, for the attraction it might

[1] Thomas Babington Macaulay, "Revolutions of Papacy," *Edinburgh Review*, LXXII (October, 1840), 119–120. Recalling the Macaulay statement over a century later a reviewer of Edward E. Y. Hales' book, *The Catholic Church in the Modern World* (New York, 1958), expressed the same idea when he said: "The century that has passed since Macaulay wrote has seen onslaughts even more grievous than those he had in mind, but, after reading Mr. Hales' absorbing account of revolutions and calamities of every sort, from without and within, one is left with the impression of a resilience in face of disaster, which simply as an historical fact, must be without parallel." *Times Literary Supplement*, No. 2,966 (January 2, 1959), 10.

[2] Henri de Lubac, S.J., *The Splendour of the Church* (New York ,1956), p. 179. Alluding to the profound loyalty that Australians show toward the British crown, Robert Speaight touched on this point in a felicitous phrase when he said that this loyalty "in itself breeds a respect for tradition and for the graces which are the gift of time." "Australian Impressions," *The Tablet*, CCI (May 16, 1953), 415.

be expected to hold for us. Were one to think in terms of encouragement for the study of ecclesiastical history, it has not been lacking, for a number of the supreme pontiffs have urged it, notably Pope Leo XIII in his letter on historical studies of August 18, 1883, and sixteen years later in his encyclical letter, *Depuis le jour*, to the bishops and priests of France, where he likened the Church's history to a mirror that reflected its life through the ages. Emphasizing that there was a body of dogmatic facts that none might call in question, the pope went on to speak of the Church's divine and human character, the latter of which he maintained should be described with genuine probity since, as he said in making his own the words of Job, "God has no need for our lies."[3] In the judgment of Leo XIII the ecclesiastical historian was all the better equipped to bring out the Church's divine origins the more loyally he refrained from extenuation of "the trials which the faults of her children, and at times even of her ministers, have brought upon the Spouse of Christ during the course of centuries."[4]

Nor has the subject been ignored by more recent popes. Less than a decade ago Pope Pius XII addressed himself to the same theme on the occasion of the 400th anniversary of the Gregorian University. He paid tribute to the Jesuits' service to all the sacred sciences, and in speaking of their work in church history he mentioned the research and publications of the Bollandists whom he characterized as "the honor and ornament of the Society of Jesus." The pontiff had special praise for the Gregorian's School of Church History, which has its own dean and faculty distinct from the other divisions of the University — the only school of its kind in the world, incidentally, under Catholic auspices — and he stated that, providing the church historian gave a balanced treatment to what he wrote, "We are sure that there is scarcely anything which is more effective than the study of Church history in nourishing, sharpening and bringing to maturity the power and capacity of thinking with the church. . . ."[5]

[3] "Leo XIII on Ecclesiastical Studies," *Catholic University Bulletin*, V (October, 1899), 494. The full text of the pope's letter is printed here (pp. 487–502). For the text of Leo XIII's letter on historical studies cf. *The Tablet*, LXII (September 1, 1883), 321–323.

[4] Leo XIII, *Depuis le jour*, p. 494.

[5] "The Pontifical Gregorian University, October 17, 1953," *Irish Ecclesiastical Record*, LXXXIV (August, 1953), 129. Cf. also Pius XII's address to the Tenth International Congress of Historical Sciences on September, 7, 1955, published in

More is owed, however, to Pope Leo XIII than to any single person of authority for inaugurating and sustaining in Catholic circles a new era in the scientific approach to ecclesiastical history. Not only did he furnish Catholic historians with their *magna carta* in his famous letter of 1883, but four years before he had already provided the means by which the principles enunciated in 1883 might be implemented in opening the Vatican Archives to scholars. What that meant for Catholic history was again made clear when the memories of Ludwig von Pastor, historian of the popes, appeared in 1950. Pastor explained that at the time that he first undertook his task Monsignor Francesco Rosi-Bernardini, then in charge of the secret archives, found it almost impossible to believe that anyone — let alone a layman — should have been granted access to the archival deposits, and as a consequence for a time Pastor was badly frustrated by the custodian's obstructive tactics.[6] Then in June, 1879, Rosi-Bernardini died and the successor — recently created a cardinal — Joseph Hergenrother, a distinguished historian in his own right, came to occupy the post newly established by Leo XIII as first Prefect of the Vatican Archives where he launched an enlightened program for research and publication.

The change in policy, needless to say, speeded Pastor's labors, and when he presented the first volume of his *History of the Popes* to Leo XIII and remarked that it was based on a generous use of the original documents, the pontiff replied, "We have no fear of the publication of documents" (Non abbiamo paura della publicità dei documenti.)[7] Yet opposition was by no means at an end, for as Pastor stated when Volume III, covering the pontificate of Alexander VI, came out one of those who was thoroughly shocked by his portrait of the Borgia pope was Monsignor Gaetano De Lai, the future cardinal and Secretary of the Consistorial Congregation. "First charity and then truth in history"

The Tablet under the title of "The Catholic Church and History," CCVI (September 24, 1955), 292–294. In an audience of April 6, 1961, granted to a group of Italian seminarians, Pope John XXIII, while not speaking directly of history, urged his hearers to take the kind of realistic view of life that would be helpful to a better understanding of the Church's history. The pope said that the true priest did not live by nourishing dreams of unattainable earthly rewards. "Nor does he waste time," he continued, "lamenting past happy ages, which never were in reality. It is the same today as it was yesterday and always will be: we shall have to fight and to remain solid in faith and charity." *The Tablet*, (April 15, 1961), 369.

[6] Wilhelm Wühr (Ed.), *Ludwig Freiherr von Pastor, 1854–1928. Tagebücher-Briefe-Erinnerungen* (Heidelberg, 1950), p. 128.

[7] *Ibid.*, p. 179.

(Prima la carità c poi la verità nella storia),[8] exclaimed De Lai. To that Pastor rejoined that if De Lai's principle were followed, all historical work would become impossible. Fortunately, it was Leo XIII and not De Lai who prevailed, and as a result the historian of the popes was able to pursue his great undertaking to completion with the same freedom and amplitude with which it had been begun.

True, it would be an exaggeration to say that the effort in behalf of candor and freedom of expression in the writing of church history has even now fully achieved its goal. Yet matters are much improved over what they were when Pastor began his work in 1879. It is the kind of contest, however, that is never finally won, for by temperament too many people suffer from what Newman referred to as a "perennial fidget" about the scandal that arises from candid history. The problem has harassed numerous historians — both ecclesiastical and secular — and among the former are to be found some of the foremost names in Catholic historiography. For example, it was a question that bothered Dom Jean Mabillon in the seventeenth century, and in writing about it the famous French Benedictine compared the historian to a judge who must give to everyone his due. In other words, the historian must act as the judge for the reading public of what they are to know of the past. Mabillon then stated:

he is therefore guilty of deception unless he has a candour of mind which prompts him to say frankly and openly what he knows to be true . . . he must not seek to hide facts that tell for or against either party to an issue. Piety and truth must never be considered as separable, for honest and genuine piety will never come into conflict with truth.[9]

Such has been the attitude of the most progressive churchmen whether or not they were professional historians. Thus Jean-Baptiste Lacordaire, probably the most famous Catholic preacher of the last century and the man who refounded the Dominican Order in France, put it well when he asked Henri Perreyve, Cong. Orat., professor of church history in the Sorbonne, if history should hide the faults of men. He answered his own question as follows:

[8] *Ibid.*, pp. 695–696.

[9] Quoted by M. D. Knowles, "Jean Mabillon," *Journal of Ecclesiastical History*, X (October, 1959), 169. A striking example of the damage that is done to honest history is seen in a number of entries in Herbert Thurston, S.J., and Donald Attwater's critical edition of *Butler's Lives of the Saints* (New York, 1956). Cf. especially the first entry under February 8 (I, 276–278).

It was not in this sense that Baronius understood his duty as an historian of the Church. It was not thus that the Saints laid open the scandals of their times. Truth, when discreetly told, is an inestimable boon to mankind, and to suppress it, especially in history, is an act of cowardice unworthy of a Christian. Timidity is the fault of our age, and truth is concealed under pretense of respect for holy things. God, indeed, has conferred upon His Church the prerogative of infallibility, but to none of the members of His Church has He granted immunity from sin. Peter was a sinner and a renegade, and God has been at pains to have the fact recorded in the Gospels.[10]

Lacordaire's view would have been received more readily a generation later, for the effect of Leo XIII's letter on historical studies was real. Henry Edward Manning, Archbishop of Westminster, made that fact known to the pope in an audience early in November, 1883, on the occasion of the English cardinal's final visit to Rome. In a diary which he kept of his trip he noted:

In the first audience with the Holy Father we spoke long about his Letter to the three Cardinals on history. I told him it had made an impression in England; that our papers had written largely about it, that our histories were mistrusted as partial and dissembling; that his Canon about hiding nothing and writing sincere history would give much confidence in England. I said, *Se l'Evangelista non ha celato il peccato e la caduta del Guida, perchè dobbiamo noi celare il peccato di vescovi ed altri personnaggi?* The Holy Father took this up as a text and spoke long and fully in the same sense.[11]

Near the end of the last century the subject was discussed in this country by a distinguished priest of the Archdiocese of New York. Deploring the backward state of church history in American seminaries, John Talbot Smith wondered if it might be due in part to the conflict between what he termed the two most common opinions as to how the subject should be taught. On the one side, he said, there were those who maintained that the Church's history should be unfolded to seminarians "with all the reserve possible," since they were not yet sufficiently experienced to withstand "disagreeable impressions." The opposite group contended, however, that suppression of facts was not only unnecessary but actually harmful to young minds, and if care was taken to see that the seminarian distinguished between human frailty and the

<hr>

[10] Lacordaire to Perreyve, April 2, 1855, M. Foisset, *Vie du R. P. Lacordaire* (Paris, 1870), II, 532.

[11] Manning Diary, Nice, December 9, 1883, Edmund Sheridan Purcell, *Life of Cardinal Manning, Archbishop of Westminster* (New York, 1896), II, 580–581.

incorruptible Church, no danger need be feared, to which Smith added, "The writer heartily indorses the latter opinion. . . ."[12] And it has been that opinion that has steadily gained ground in the present century as numerous scholarly works in ecclesiastical history bear witness.

The title of this essay is a broad one and would admit of a wide variety of approach and treatment, but I shall confine myself in what follows to four main points: 1) the history of the Church as a source for the enrichment of the mind and the cultivation of one's reading tastes; 2) as a subject that will assist one in making a balanced judgment on events; 3) as a help to acquiring a just and proper attitude toward other men; and 4) as a source of edification and the renewal of hope in a time of personal trial.

In regard to the enrichment of mind and cultivation of reading tastes, it is doubtful if any other subject affords a broader perspective and a more generally enriching knowledge than history, and what is said of history in general is equally true of the history of the Catholic Church. For example, the man who has a good knowledge of the troubled sixteenth century will enjoy a ballad like Chesterton's *Lepanto* far more than one who does not understand the threat posed by the Mohammedan invasion of Europe, who sees no significance in the expediency and ambiguity of the religious views of Queen Elizabeth I of England and in the pitiful weakness of the sons of Catherine de Medici and Henri de Valois who followed one after another upon the throne of France only to die without issue. Amid all these swirling and conflicting currents there was the figure of Pope Pius V hoping, as it were, almost against hope that he might rouse the princes as once his predecessors had done to a crusade against the Turks. He who knows this background can fully appreciate lines like these:

> They have dared the white republics up the capes of Italy,
> They have dashed the Adriatic round the Lion of the Sea,
> And the Pope has cast his arms abroad for agony and loss,
> And called the kings of Christendom for swords about the
>   Cross,
> The cold queen of England is looking in the glass;
> The shadow of the Valois is yawning at the Mass.[13]

[12] John Talbot Smith, *Our Seminaries. An Essay on Clerical Training* (New York, 1896), p. 311.

[13] *The Collected Poems of G. K. Chesterton* (London, 1927), p. 100.

197

And for the sensitive reader whose sympathies have often been aroused in recent decades over the plight of those caught in the cruel grip of totalitarian regimes, Chesterton's evocation of the tragic fate that overtook the victims of the Mohammedans' advance through southeastern Europe and across the Mediterranean suggests the days of the twelfth Pius whose reign was darkened by so many events that more than paralleled the horrors of the age of Pius V. The parallel is clear in lines like these:

> The Pope was in his chapel before day or battle broke,
> (Don John of Austria is hidden in the smoke).
> The hidden room in man's house where God sits all the year,
> The secret windows whence the world looks small and very
>   dear.
> He sees as in a mirror on the monstrous twilight sea
> The crescent of his cruel ships whose name is mystery;
> They fling great shadows foe-wards, making Cross and
>   Castle dark,
> They veil the plumbed lions on the galleys of St. Mark;
> And above the ships are palaces of brown black-bearded
>   chiefs,
> And below the ships are prisons, where with multitudinous
>   griefs,
> Christian capitves sick and sunless, all a labouring race
>   repines
> Like a race in sunken cities, like a nation in the mines.[14]

And what is said in this regard of poetry is even more frequently applicable to works in prose. Thus for countless readers a knowledge of the Middle Ages made their reading of the famous novels of Sir Walter Scott more meaningful. The same is true for historical novelists of our day like Helen C. White whose *A Watch in the Night*, for instance, can be appreciated more by a reader who has some understanding of the reform movement within the Franciscan Order which made Jacopone da Todi so memorable a character in the early years of the Franciscans. Or another of Miss White's stories, *To the End of the World*, where one of the principal themes is the agony of the Church during the French Revolution, from which troubled time there emerges the figure of Jacques André Emery, Superior General of Saint Sulpice, who bore the

[14] *Ibid.*, p. 104.

198

major responsibility for the Church in France through the Terror and into the regime of Napoleon Bonaparte.

Needless to say, what applies to works with a European setting is likewise true of literature that finds its theme in the history of the United States. A brilliant example of that in the 1930's was Margaret Mitchell's *Gone With the Wind* which contained so vivid a picture of the Civil War. The reader who brought to Miss Mitchell's novel a familiarity with the history of Ireland in the last century, and some acquaintance with Irish immigration to this country, felt thoroughly at home with the family of Gerald O'Hara, clinging with some difficulty to their Catholic faith in a South that knew few priests, and showing the depth of the traditional Irish attachment to the land. For who can ever forget Gerald's attempt to soothe Scarlett's downcast feelings after she learned she could not have Ashley Wilkes by suggesting that she take Cade Calvert, and he would then leave them Tara, his beloved plantation. To the old Irishman it was well-nigh incredible that she should spurn both, especially Tara, and he cut loose at his daughter in a way that showed well how Margaret Mitchell had read her Irish history. He said:

"Do you stand there, Scarlett O'Hara, and tell me that Tara — that land — doesn't amount to anything?"

Scarlett nodded obstinately. Her heart was too sore to care whether or not she put her father in a temper.

"Land is the only thing in the world that amounts to anything," he shouted, his thick, short arms making wide gestures of indignation, "for 'tis the only thing in this world that lasts, and don't you be forgetting it! 'Tis the only thing worth working for, worth fighting for — worth dying for."

"Oh, Pa," she said disgustedly, "you talk like an Irishman."

"Have I ever been ashamed of it? No, 'tis proud I am. And don't be forgetting that you are half Irish, Miss! And to any one with a drop of Irish blood in them the land they live on is like their mother. 'Tis ashamed of you I am this minute. I offer you the most beautiful land in the world — saving County Meath in the Old Country — and what do you do? You sniff!"[15]

A passage such as that would draw the envy of most historians who could never hope to convey in so clear a way as it does the almost sacred love of the Irish for the land.

Another American novel where a reader's knowledge of the history

[15] Margaret Mitchell, *Gone With the Wind* [Permabook Edition] (New York, 1961), p. 35.

of the Irish immigrants and their descendants came alive was in Edwin O'Connor's *The Last Hurrah*. Thousands of readers must have felt the same strange fascination as Monsignor Killian, young secretary to the grumpy old cardinal, for Frank Skeffington, the city boss whose dubious political morals were mingled with a concern for the downtrodden in a roguish charm that was quite irresistible. When the priest encountered Skeffington at Knocko Minihan's wake, therefore, and the monsignor's ruminations about the boss began to unfold, there were probably few readers who would not confess to having shared his thoughts. The scene was described in these words:

The old politician captivated his imagination; he saw him a unique, a rich, extraordinary personality who contained within himself a part of local history which soon would be no more and which never again would reappear. It was a vein that called out to be tapped before it disappeared, first, from view, then even from memory . . . .

Monsignor Killian felt a momentary temptation to suggest to the old man that they might meet some day for lunch; but then the sudden thought of the cardinal quickly banished the temptation. Instead, "nodding towards the parlor, [he] merely said, 'I suppose we'd better go in now.' They went in, they knelt, and the Monsignor led them in the Rosary." [16]

The second point which I should like to make is more difficult. It has to do with that often trying experience by which conscientious men attempt to arrive at a proper judgment of the factors involved in a given situation. As Pius XII told the historians of the Gregorian University in his congratulatory letter of 1953, one must measure and weigh all elements in order

that the consideration of this or that event, or crisis, is not dwelt on too minutely or too long, but rather individual things related to the whole, the negative to the positive and great, lasting things are truly regarded as great and lasting, while lesser and fleeting things are treated as such.[17]

To accomplish this requires constant vigilance to make certain that one's judgment is not swayed or clouded by his emotion, pride, or prejudice which so often tip the scales and cause us to view events in a biased way. In this respect, it seems to me, the lives of those who have played

---

[16] Edwin O'Connor, *The Last Hurrah* (Boston, 1956), pp. 207–208.

[17] Pius XII, *op. cit.*, p. 128.

prominent roles in the history of the Church are often revealing and helpful. Let me illustrate by a few examples.

It is generally agreed that the best and most effective servants of the Church have been those men who were able to submerge their personal interests in favor of the cause which they were supposed to serve. The paramount importance of disinterestedness of this kind was shown in the life of Andrew Zamometic, O.P., Archbishop of Krania in Thessaly. As a young man, he had been a fellow student of Francesco della Rovere, O.F.M., the future Pope Sixtus IV, at the University of Padua. Years later on a visit to Rome in 1481, Zamometic openly criticized the worldly atmosphere of the papal court, whereupon his former schoolmate had him arrested and imprisoned in Castel Sant' Angelo from which he was freed only by the intervention of one of the cardinals. The Dominican friar left Rome filled with bitter hatred for Sixtus IV, and in March, 1482, he sought revenge by issuing a manifesto from Basle on the need for a general council to reform the Church, a move which, incidentally, won no hearing among his contemporaries. There was undoubtedly need for reform at the time, but as the historian of Trent has said, Zamometic failed

because he himself lacked that self-forgetting devotion to the cause of God, that indefinable mixture of courage and humility which alone achieves great things in the Church. The apostrophes to the Pope in the manuscript edition of his manifesto betray the fierce passion of a mortally offended man; they are not inspired by selfless zeal for God's house. Zamometic was not the man of destiny to renew the Church.[18]

In time the Church was, indeed, renewed and a century later the Roman Curia was more concerned with an internal theological problem than with a crusade for reform. The minds of churchmen were then absorbed in the intricate, complicated debates over divine grace which came to be called the Molinist-Thomist affair. Among the stoutest supporters of Luís de Molina, the Spanish Jesuit who gave his name to the controversy, was the famous Italian Jesuit cardinal, Robert Bellarmine. By 1600 Bellarmine ranked as, perhaps, the first mind in the Church, and when Pope Clement VIII acted in a way that Bellarmine felt was not altogether fair to the Molinists, he respectfully made this fact known to the pontiff. But Bellarmine's forthright counsel was apparently too

[18] Hubert Jedin, *A History of the Council of Trent* (London, 1957), I, 105. Zamometic was later imprisoned again and committed suicide in November, 1484.

vigorous for Clement's taste and in 1602 the latter found a way out of his uncomfortable position by appointing Bellarmine as Archbishop of Capua. As the saint's biographer expressed it:

The Pope, who appears to have been worried by the presence of such a highly qualified but too candid critic at his court, began, it would seem, to look about for some means of gracefully "rusticating" him.[19]

One of the aspects of this case that caused no little wonder — at a time when Trent's legislation had not yet eliminated absenteeism among bishops — was the promptness with which Robert departed for Capua, and the fidelity with which he spent the following three years giving to that neglected see the first active administration it had known in a generation. He stayed on in Capua, in fact, until Pope Paul V asked him after the conclave of May, 1605, to resume his former role as a cardinal in curia.

Here, then, was a man who knew how to weigh the factors in a situation, a churchman of immense learning who felt it his duty to enlighten the pope once his conscience directed him to do so. In this sense he was a good exemplification of what de Lubac meant when he spoke of the right of a subject to offer advice to a superior as being in certain circumstances, "something which is not merely a right but also a duty, the discharge of which will sometimes oblige him to heroism." But the principal point of the story is that in availing himself of that right Bellarmine likewise accepted without reservation its sequel, namely, that the subject should always realize that "the last word does not rest with him."[20] Cardinal Bellarmine's unhesitating obedience in undertaking the government of the See of Capua was the clearest evidence of his recognition that the last word rested with Clement VIII, not with him.

Let us now examine a case where, in contrast to Bellarmine, the princial actor failed to weigh properly the controlling elements in a

[19] James Broderick, S.J., *Robert Bellarmine, 1542-1621* (New York, 1950), II, 61. The depth of Bellarmine's humility may be measured by the fact that during the ceremonies of conferring the red hat he wept most of the time, and in answer to the congratulations of Pietro Cardinal Valier, he wrote: "I, certainly, dearest Father, can make this confession to your paternal heart that I have never set any value on the purple, and now, so far from valuing it, I rather marvel greatly at those who do. I pity them, too, for they seem not to care for the glory of the Eternal King if only they may gain some fleeting, counterfeit honours and the shadow of renown." Bellarmine to Valier, May 1, 1599, *ibid.*, I, 406.

[20] de Lubac, *op. cit.*, p. 195.

situation involving his relations with his religious superiors. Over two centuries after Saint Robert's defense of Molina and his residence in Capua, a young French priest showed signs of affording to the Church of his time something akin to the enlightened leadership that Bellarmine had given to an earlier age. In this instance, however, the unquestioned talents of the Abbé Félicité de Lammenais were marred by his inability to balance the commitment he had made to the liberal philosophy and the democratic way of life in the scale of the obedience that he owed to Pope Gregory XVI. Lammenais' personal brilliance had won him a large following, and the movement he headed had undoubted values for society if properly interpreted and employed. But they struck the rock of Gregory XVI's ultra-conservative nature, and when the encyclical, *Mirari vos*, of August, 1832, condemned the principles upon which Lammenais and his adherents had built their movement and made their organ, *l'Avenir*, sound out of tune with Catholic teaching, it brought the matter to an abrupt end.

At first Lammenais was apparently so stunned by the blow that he said nothing. But gradually he became deeply embittered and by 1836 when his book, *Affaires de Rome*, appeared it was evident that he had broken with the faith of his childhood. The personal tragedy of the man was laid bare when he wrote in this volume:

What one rejects is not authentic christianity, but a certain sterile and material system that has taken its name and disgraces it; what is dying is not the divine tree, but the withered bark that covers it.[21]

What Lammenais could not see was that it was his supernatural faith that was dying and not the caricature of Christ's Church which he fancied he saw in the Roman Curia and its head. Like Bellarmine before him, Lammenais had stood for principles which many of his coreligionists shared, and which are today a commonplace in much of the Catholic world. But unlike Bellarmine, he had never submitted his will to the test of choosing what was of first rather than secondary importance in the life of a priest, nor had he ever determined the prime place that obedience must always occupy in a priest's scale of values. In the end self-will and self-interest engulfed the accomplished abbé and carried him out of the Catholic communion, depriving him of the fame and

[21] Quoted in Alec R. Vidler, *Prophecy and Papacy. A Study of Lammenais, The Church and the Revolution* (New York, 1954), p. 262.

merit that his talents might otherwise have won within the fold had they been disciplined by subordination to the supreme authority of the Church.

Church history is so rich in examples illustrating the necessity for a balanced judgment of events in the part of all of us that one is tempted to cite more of them. But a brief summary of one further instance that was nearer to our own time will suffice. As is well known, the movement that arose among certain ultramontanists for the definition of the pope's infallibility had drawn opposition quite some time before the opening of Vatican Council I in December, 1869. Among the opponents no two names were better known than those of Johann Döllinger, professor of church history in the University of Munich, who at the time enjoyed the greatest renown for scholarship of any priest in German university circles, and John Henry Newman who by the time that the council convened had been a Catholic for nearly a quarter century. As early as March, 1869, Döllinger had begun writing against the infallibility question in a series of unsigned articles carried by the Augsburg *Allgemeine Zeitung* which came out in book form in July of that year under the signature of "Janus" and with the title of *The Pope and the Council*. These essays were so powerfully expressed and interwoven with so much seeming erudition that the Bishop of Birmingham, William B. Ullathorne, O.S.B., was not far off the mark when he predicted that they would be "a great storehouse for the adversaries of the Church." [22]

Meanwhile, Newman, who was equally opposed to the definition on the grounds of the difficulties it would make for outsiders interested in Catholicism, and because of what he considered the lack of necessity for such a definition, did not write for publication. But he did not hesitate to speak his mind plainly in his private correspondence. The most memorable episode in that regard was his letter of late January, 1870, to his superior, Bishop Ullathorne. The intensity of his feeling was evident when he wrote:

I look with anxiety at the prospect of having to defend decisions which may not be difficult to my private judgement, but may be most difficult to defend logically in the face of historical facts. What have we done to be treated as the Faithful never were treated before? When has definition of doctrine *de fide* been a luxury of devotion and not a stern painful necessity? Why should

[22] Quoted from a letter of October 22, 1869, Cuthbert Butler, O.S.B., *The Vatican Council* (New York, 1930), I, 111.

an aggressive and insolent faction be allowed to make the hearts of the just to mourn whom the Lord hath not made sorrowful?[23]

There could be no question, therefore, about how Newman felt concerning the efforts of the infallibilists. But the difference between these two distinguished priests was the manner in which they reacted when they learned that their cause had lost and that the definition of the dogma had been voted by the council in July, 1870. To say that Newman was pleased would be quite false, but there was never any question about his acceptance of what had been defined, for after he had seen the text of the decree he told a friend, "I saw the new definition yesterday and am pleased at its moderation — that is, if the doctrine in question is to be defined at all." [24]

It was quite otherwise with Dr. Döllinger. In the late summer of 1870 he joined with about a dozen other German savants in repudiating the Vatican Council and appealing to a future council to be held outside Italy which would, according to them, be properly ecumenical. Meanwhile Döllinger asked his superior, Gregor von Scherr, O.S.B., Archbishop of Munich, for time to study the matter anew and the archbishop allowed him until March 15, 1871. Having won an additional two weeks, on March 28 he despatched his final decision which was summarized in these words, "As Christian, as theologian, as historian, as citizen, I cannot accept this doctrine." [25] Thereby he put himself formally outside the Catholic Church, an action which brought deep pain to Newman who continued to work for his return to the fold. Eight years after Döllinger's formal break Newman was made a cardinal, and it was his intention to return from the consistory by way of Germany in the hope that he might persuade Döllinger to submit. As it turned out, the new cardinal's health was in so delicate a condition at the time that he had to hasten home, and in the end Döllinger died unreconciled on January 10, 1890, just seven months before Newman's own death. The two men had held much in common, but the one vital dissimilarity made for a vastly different ending to their earthly careers.

The third major point in our inquiry is closely related to the foregoing, for in endeavoring to employ one's knowledge of church history

[23] Newman to Ullathorne, January 28, 1870, Wilfrid Ward, *The Life of John Henry Cardinal Newman* (New York, 1912), II, 288.

[24] *Ibid.*, II, 307.

[25] Butler, *op. cit.*, II, 185.

to acquire a just attitude toward others one is compelled to seek a balance of qualities, good and bad, much as the man who wishes to arrive at a measured estimate concerning the varying factors involved in a chain of historical events. In this regard the evidence from history is clear that few men are altogether depraved and that fewer still, perhaps, approach perfection. In other words, when one seeks to pass judgment on another he must distinguish and weigh and balance the good and the bad in order to achieve the true measure of his character and worth. Here the history of the Church can again be helpful by way of demonstrating how men of even surpassing ability have lessened their own stature because of their prejudices.

One of the most interesting examples of this type in the English-speaking Catholic world was Henry Edward Manning. Those who are familiar with the life of the second Archbishop of Westminster would not question his greatness as an apologist and vigorous defender of the Catholic faith that he accepted in middle life. Nor would they challenge the assertion that the cardinal was among the leading social reformers of his time, as his crusade for temperance, his championship of land reform for the Irish, and his arbitration of the London dock strike of 1889 — to name only three of his manifold activities — testify. Moreover, Manning was a lasting inspiration to several generations of the clergy through his numerous spiritual conferences and writings such as *The Eternal Priesthood*. In fine, it is beyond dispute that for nearly thirty years he was the peerless primate, in fact if not *de jure*, of the Catholics of the British Isles.

Yet this splendid churchman had grave weaknesses that took their rise in the exceedingly strong prejudices that at times warped his judgment and caused him more than once to espouse a course of action that he lived to regret. While one can readily understand the cardinal's opposition to Catholic young men attending Oxford and Cambridge in the 1870's lest they should lose their faith, it is less easy to condone the stubborn insistence with which he pushed ahead in founding his University College at Kensington in 1874 as a substitute for secular university training, and that in the face of almost certain failure. Particularly was this true when one recalls his ignoring of Newman, his unfortunate choice of Monsignor Thomas J. Capel as first rector, and the all but unanimous opposition of England's leading Catholic families and of many of the clergy as well. That University College should have closed within eight years in about as dismal a failure as one will find in the history of Catholic higher education should occasion no surprise, especially in view of the close relationship of that failure to another of Manning's blind spots, namely, his dislike of religious orders.

It became an *idée fixe* in the mind of the Cardinal of Westminster that the members of religious congregations were an aggressive and disobedient lot who worked for their own interests and not for those of the Church. That attitude made doubly certain the failure of his Kensington college when he barred from its faculty the Jesuits and other religious who were the best trained Catholic educators in England. That the cardinal had on occasion reason for opposing the religious in matters of policy, was true. And it was natural, therefore, that his sympathies should be with his friend, Herbert Vaughan, Bishop of Salford, in 1874 when the quarrel broke between Vaughan and the Jesuits over the latter's persistence in trying to start a school in Manchester against the bishop's express wishes. What is less easy to undertand, however, in one in Manning's position, was the vehemence with which he pursued his opponents and the extreme language to which he gave expression. The battle was a lengthy one, but finally in May, 1881, Leo XIII's constitution, *Romanos pontifices*, gave the victory to the bishops. In acknowledging Vaughan's wire about the decision Manning coupled the names of the English Jesuit provincial of that time, Peter Gallwey, with the founder of the Jesuit English mission in 1580, Robert Parsons, when he told Vaughan:

I received your telegram on Sunday, but the *Observer* had been before you. . . . It has been a hand-to-hand fight, not with Peter Gallwey but with Robert Parsons, and I hope he will now lie still in his grave. . . . It is, as you say, a great victory over the most powerful conspiracy in the Church.[26]

[26] Manning to Vaughan, May 18, 1881, J. G. Snead-Cox, *The Life of Cardinal Vaughan* (London, 1910), I, 354. On the subject of how the historian should judge character, one could not do better than to read David Knowles' inaugural lecture as Regius professor of modern history in the University of Cambridge delivered on November 17, 1954, and published as *The Historian and Character* (Cambridge, 1955). Knowles summarized as follows the principal tests which the historian can apply to determine whether or not an historical personality had character: "whether a man, by and large during his life, shows any evidence of acting according to a divine or moral law outside himself, whether he ever sacrifices his own profit or pleasure for the sake of a person or principle; whether he shows evidence of loving other men, where by love we understand the classical definition of wishing them well and doing well to them; whether he puts justice before expediency; he is sincere and truthful." (pp. 19–20).

Yet a student of church history would be in serious error were he to make a final and single judgment about Manning on the strength of his fumbling efforts in higher education and his dislike for religious. Real defects the cardinal had, but balanced against them were qualities of true greatness which he implemented in a way that left a notable over-all heritage to his successors after his twenty-seven year rule at Westminster.

On our own side of the Atlantic an able contemporary of Manning's offered a similar case study. For over forty years Bernard J. McQuaid, first Bishop of Rochester, gave to his diocese an enlightened administration by his conspicuous energy, zeal, and general competence. Yet the same Bishop McQuaid was not free of deep prejudices which made him an unreliable witness insofar as certain persons and projects were concerned. Among these was a strong dislike of James Gibbons, Archbishop of Baltimore. When, therefore, in 1884 Gibbons appointed a committee of the hierarchy with himself as chairman to plan for a national university for the American Church, McQuaid set his teeth against it. Quite some time before the decision had been made to locate the university in Washington, the Bishop of Rochester got it into his head that the project was the doing of a group of 'southern bishops,' with Gibbons at their head, quite unaware that at the time the latter did not even want the institution in his archdiocese. In any case, in 1887 McQuaid complained to his friend, Richard Gilmour, Bishop of Cleveland:

There has been so much scheming in this whole affair that no rascally trap sprang [sic] on us will surprise me. . . . I for one do not propose to build a University in the South, to be governed by a Board of Southern bishops, priests and laymen in a large majority.[27]

And the fact that the prime movers for a university were John Lancaster Spalding, Bishop of Peoria, and John Ireland, Bishop of Saint Paul, did not seem to remove the 'southern' curse from the university in the bishop's mind.

Before the Archbishop of Baltimore was made a cardinal, Bishop McQuaid had more than once interpreted his action — or lack of action — in terms of Gibbons having his eye fixed on a red hat with everything done, or not done, with that in mind. After the hat came to Baltimore

[27] McQuaid to Gilmour, Rochester, January 26, 1887, John Tracy Ellis, *The Formative Years of the Catholic University of America* (Washington, 1946), p. 219.

in 1887 the Bishop of Rochester often pictured his *bête noir* as a man whose ambition prompted him to pose as the head of the Church in the United States, as well as to think of himself as a likely candidate for the papacy. For example, when Gibbons paid the first visit of any member of the College of Cardinals to the Far West in the fall of 1887 to confer the pallium on William H. Gross, Archbishop of Oregon City, the newspaper men naturally made much of the event, and frequently referred to the prelate in exaggerated and inaccurate terms. One would gain the impression that McQuaid thought these expressions had been inspired by the cardinal himself, for he told Michael A. Corrigan, Archbishop of New York, during the course of Gibbons' western tour:

This everlasting talk about the *head* of the *American church* annoys me. The good little man can't see that he is making himself ridiculous. He will go so far that somebody will have to call him to order.[28]

Some years later when within a brief time death took Cardinals Manning and Giovanni Simeoni, Prefect of Propaganda, rumors began to circulate about new cardinals and a possible successor to the aged Leo XIII. In this context there was some speculation that as the cardinals died off the chances were improved for Gibbons being elected to the papacy. Alluding to this in a letter to Monsignor Denis J. O'Connell, Rector of the North American College in Rome, McQuaid remarked:

The miracle of credulity is found in the fact that there are people, himself included, who believe that he has a ghost of a chance.[29]

Yet here, as in the case of Manning, it would be unjust to permit the evidence of McQuaid's dislike for Gibbons — and for Archbishop Ireland as well — to tip the scales against a worthy bishop in an assessment of what was on the whole a highly useful career. True, Bernard McQuaid illustrated how the prejudices of an able churchman can cause him to be guilty of injustice toward his fellow bishops and, too, to refuse assistance to a cause that might well be expected to merit his approval and support like that of a national Catholic university. But in the final analysis of weighing the good against the bad the Bishop of Rochester, like the Cardinal of Westminster, would be found to have more of the former than he did of the latter.

[28] McQuaid to Corrigan, Rochester, October 9, 1887, John Tracy Ellis, *The Life of James Cardinal Gibbons, Archbishop of Baltimore, 1834–1921* (Milwaukee, 1952), I, 327.

[29] McQuaid to O'Connell, Rochester, January 16, 1892, *ibid.*, I, 673–674.

That brings me to the fourth and final point, namely, the service that church history can render, at a time when one is feeling depressed and in need of something to lift his spirits. Every man has moments of this kind, to be sure, but they may occur more frequently in the lives of seminarians, priests, and religious than they do in the lives of those who are in the midst of their own families. In any case, whether one be a priest or seminarian or layman at one time or other he will have felt that he has been betrayed by his associates or misunderstood by his superiors, and at such a time the temptation to bitterness and cynicism is often very real. It is then that one can find genuine consolation in the experiences of those who have trod the winepress before him in the Church's history, and from their personal stories he can derive not only edification but, too, a renewal of hope that will enable him to shoulder his burden once more and face the future with confidence and serenity in spite of his awareness of its inevitable reverses.

An extraordinary example of how this value can accrue to one familiar with the history of the Church is found in the life of Saint Thomas More. There were many episodes in the career of this truly great soul where his conduct set a model for what a Christian worthy of the name should do in an encounter with misfortune and loss of every earthly honor. But to my mind the most striking instance has always been the scene in Westminster Hall in London on that July day of 1535 when Sir Thomas Audeley, the Lord Chancellor, had pronounced sentence of death upon More after a trial that was a travesty of justice, and had then instructed the commissioners, in accordance with the court practice of the time, to ask the prisoner if he had anything further to say in his own defense. At that point the fallen chancellor replied:

More have I not to say, my Lords, but that like as the blessed apostle St. Paul, as we read in the Acts of the Apostles, was present, and consented to the death of St. Stephen, and kept their clothes that stoned him to death, and yet be they now both twain holy saints in Heaven, and shall continue there friends for ever, so I verily trust, and shall therefore right heartily pray, that though your Lordships have now here in earth been judges to my condemnation, we may yet hereafter in Heaven merrily all meet together to our everlasting salvation.[30]

After these words there was nothing further to be said in Westminster

[30] R. W. Chambers, *Thomas More* (London, 1935), p. 342.

Hall, nor is there anything further to be said here. It was a situation that calls to mind Browning's lines:

> Then they left you for their pleasure: till in due time, one
> by one,
> Some with lives that came to nothing, some with deeds as
> well undone,
> Death came tacitly and took them where they never see
> the sun.[31]

Three hundred years removed from Saint Thomas More a Catholic layman of the nineteenth century likewise left upon his own and future generations a wonderfully deep impression by the splendid virtue which illumined the forty brief years that he was given in this world. That man was Frédéric Ozanam whose accomplishments, such as having inspired the famous conferences of Notre Dame in Paris and founded the Society of Saint Vincent de Paul, are too well known to need rehearsal here. The exquisite charity and sensitivity of the man for the feelings of others was well brought out in a letter that he wrote when he was being charged by Louis Veuillot with having deserted the Catholic cause because of his sympathy and friendliness for those outside the Church. About this accusation Ozanam wrote:

I am sometimes charged with excessive gentleness toward unbelievers. When one has passed, as I have, through the crucible of doubt, it would indeed be cruelty and ingratitude to be harsh to those to whom God has not yet vouchsafed to give the priceless gift of faith. [He insisted, therefore, that in apologetics] we must not compromise the holiness of the cause by the violence of the means. . . . Begin by pitying the unbeliever; he is already wretched enough. . . . It is never a question of mortifying but of convincing him.[32]

That the young Sorbonne professor exercised an uncommon influence of his contemporaries was manifested in many ways; but nowhere, perhaps, was it more touchingly revealed than in the letter that Charles Comte de Montalembert addressed to his widow shortly after Ozanam's untimely death. He wrote:

[31] *The Poems and Plays of Robert Browning* [Modern Library] (New York, 1934), p. 36.

[32] Ozanam to his brother Charles, Thomas P. Neill, *They Lived the Faith* (Milwaukee, 1951), p. 158.

He leaves to us, as to you, Madame, the almost complete certainty of his immediate and eternal happiness. It is not for one like me to speak of God and of Heaven to a soul still flooded with the light which radiated from the deathbed of such a Christian as he. . . . When you pray for him and with him, when you seek his soul in the serene regions in which it awaits yours, please, Madame, remember me at least once, offer him the pious grief of an old friend, of an old fellow-member of the Society of Saint Vincent de Paul, of an old soldier in the same cause, who will forget neither his instruction nor his example.[33]

The American Church, as is true of all branches of the Church Universal, has had its quota of great souls who have ennobled its history after the fashion of Thomas More and Frédéric Ozanam. One of these was Isaac T. Hecker, founder of the Paulist Fathers, who in good faith set out for Rome in 1857 as the delegate of a small group of American-born convert Redemptorists to lay before the rector major and his council their proposal for an English-speaking house of the congregation in this country. To his amazement Hecker was summarily dismissed from the Redemptorists for having come without the general's permission, and for some months he was cut adrift from his moorings and made to feel acute humiliation while he awaited a final decision in his case. At one point he wrote his associates in the United States in words that clearly portrayed the ordeal through which he was passing. He said:

I have lived a history in a few months. . . . I have been cut and slashed at in every direction and before everybody up to His Holiness; and have lost any idea of ever having had any character at all. If these fellows don't make me a saint it will not be because they have not done their utmost to present me with opportunities. But the grace of God has guided me through it all, and thus far I am happy in having nothing to regret.[34]

[33] Montalembert to Madame Ozanam, Roche-en-Breny, n.d., Louis Baunard, *Ozanam in His Correspondence* (New York, 1925), p. 406.

[34] Hecker to his associates, Rome, December 18, 1857, Joseph McSorley, C.S.P., *Father Hecker and His Friends* (St. Louis, 1952), p. 63. The literature of church history is replete with cases of this kind. For example, in a note dated July 23, 1846, Jean-Baptiste Henri Lacordaire, O.P., stated: "In proportion to my vocation in the Church, God has heaped upon me during almost twenty years an unbroken succession of painful trials. From my entrance to the seminary in 1824 up to my assignment to Paris in 1844, I have been the butt of a stubborn hostility on the part of a certain group of men capable of inflicting great harm, and who have neglected nothing in order to ruin my reputation and to drive me to extremes. Twenty years of patience, of kindness, and of perseverance have been needed to arrive at a little peace which will endure as long as it may please God." Le Comte de Montalembert, *Le Père Lacordaire* (Paris, 1862), p. 170.

When one thinks of Hecker's vindication in the spring of 1858 in the Holy See's permission for him to establish his own religious congregation according to his own ideas, it furnishes a good example of the happy sequel that sometimes follows a period of suffering for those who have had the stamina to bear their cross in a calm and forbearing way.

Suffering is not confined to individuals alone, for at times it overtakes entire nations. Surely few periods in the history of the Church have witnessed more widespread suffering on the part of its faithful people than our own, for one would have to return to the age of the early martyrs to parallel the bloodshed, the cruelty, and the daring attempts to erase the very concept of God and His Church from men's souls that have characterized the last forty years of Communist expansion. Whole nations have, indeed, fallen victim to atheistic regimes, and in that connection I am reminded of a memorable pastoral letter of the Polish hierarchy issued some years ago when they were feeling — as they are still feeling — the sharp edge of Communist tyranny. The Polish bishops uttered many wise and consoling thoughts in that letter, but there is one passage in which, it seems to me, they mirrored the depth of their understanding of the significance of the Church's suffering in past ages and suggested how much that knowledge has helped to sustain them in their present trial. The passage read as follows:

The eyes of the Church are filled with historical wisdom. Thanks to this, she sees her eternal mission more and more deeply, because she endures while the times, the conditions of life and of people, are changing. . . . We are taught by history that the Church has always stepped boldly from old to new centuries with the very Bethlehem freshness of the new-born Christ, carrying God's salvation to them. That is why we, the servants of God, together with His blessed people, can maintain complete freedom with regard to the new times, and a quiet courage regarding the new conditions of life in which it is given to the Church to lead people towards God.[35]

Is it too much, I wonder, to see in these words a wisdom that could have been born only of the possession of divine faith enriched by the knowledge of the history of God's Church that has given to the bishops, clergy, and laity of Poland a steadfastness and courage that have inspired men over all the world?

While episodes such as those I have described serve as a consolation to many when their own spirits are overcast, they can likewise be the

[35] "Church and State in Poland," *The Tablet*, CCI (April 18, 1953), 328.

source of edification to those who are strongly influenced by the actions of other men. It would be difficult, for example, to conceive the priest, seminarian, or religious who would not be moved by the mutual charity shown after the stern encounter of the two great priest historians, Jean Mabillon, O.S.B., and Daniel Papebroch, S.J. Father Papebroch had sought in 1675 in the April volume of the *Acta Sanctorum* to lay down a set of rules for authenticating charters and documents, and in so doing he had chosen as an illustration of forgery certain early charters of the Abbey of Saint Denis. Mabillon rose at once to a defense of his beloved Benedictines, and his reply was so crushing that for a year Papebroch was reduced to silence. The Jesuit then broke his silence by a truly noble admission when he told Mabillon:

I was indeed at first pained by your book, where I saw myself refuted beyond hope of reply, but in the end the value and the beauty of such a precious work overcame my weakness, and I was filled with delight at seeing the truth presented in its most attractive shape. . . . Count me as your friend, I beg of you. I am not a learned man, but I desire to be taught.[36]

A confession of that kind merited a warm and generous reply which, fortunately, it received when Mabillon replied: "Pray for me that God may grant that I, who seek to imitate you in the scientific excellence of the *Acta Sanctorum*, may imitate you also in the paths of Christian humility." [37] Nor did the Benedictine, it is pleasant to recall, content himself with mere words, for when Papebroch was under a cloud at Rome for his forthright attack on legend — and this at a time of tension between Mabillon's Maurists and Papebroch's Bollandists — Mabillon wrote repeatedly and in strong terms to the procurator of his congregation at Rome and to other friends in the Roman Curia in favor of his Bollandist adversary of an earlier day.

Another striking instance of charity and forgiveness of injury — at least on the part of one man — involved the two ranking personalities of Church and State of their time. All students of church history are acquainted with the abandon with which the Emperor Napoleon I heaped insults and injuries upon the Church and its supreme pontiff after having signed the concordat of 1801 which restored the Catholic religion in France. The most severe blow came in 1805 when at the emperor's command the gentle Benedictine monk who had ascended Peter's

[36] Knowles, *op. cit.*, p. 160.
[37] *Ibid.*

214

throne five years before as Pius VII was removed from his capital and started upon the long road of a nine-year exile, first at Savona and then at Fontainebleau. Only after Bonaparte's defeat by the allied armies was the pope freed and permitted to return to Rome which he reached in May, 1814, to live out his days in comparative peace.

In spite of all that he had suffered at Napoleon's hands, Pius VII was the perfect Christian when the mother and other relatives of the fallen emperor appealed to him in 1817 to intercede in behalf of the famous exile on the Island of Saint Helena that his sufferings might be mitigated. The pope told his Secretary of State, Ercole Cardinal Consalvi, that he had learned the news of Bonaparte's distress "with very great pain." Recalling that the restoration of religion to France in 1801 was owed principally to Napoleon's initiative, it was that event, he said, that caused him "to forgive and forget all subsequent wrongs." His own imprisonment at Savona and Fontainebleau were passed over as "errors of judgment, or chimeras of human ambition," whereas to Pius VII the concordat had "saved society by its heroic and Christian nature." When the appeal of the Bonapartes reached him, therefore, he wished to act at once, and he felt confident that Consalvi would share his sentiment and avail himself of his good relations with the allied sovereigns, especially the Prince Regent of Great Britain [the future George IV], to ask the latter if he would "soften the sufferings of so formidable an exile." The pope then concluded:

It would be an incomparable joy for Our heart to have contributed toward diminishing the anguish of Napoleon. He no longer possesses the means of wronging anybody: We wish him to cause remorse to no man.[38]

Less than a year before this letter was written, which the latest historian of the pope and the emperor has called "the last action undertaken by either of these two men in the strange drama of their relations with each other,"[39] there had appeared at Oxford in December, 1816, an English youth who in the course of the next thirty years was destined to electrify the university by his brilliant mind and then, to the consternation of many, to leave their world for the Church of Rome. During the years that followed John Henry Newman's conversion to Catholicism in 1845, there were few men who, owing to the peculiarly insensitive

[39] Pius VII to Consalvi, October 6, 1817, Mary H. Allies, *The Life of Pope Pius the Seventh* (London, 1875), pp. 351–352.
[38] E. E. Y. Hales, *The Emperor and the Pope* (New York, 1961).

treatment accorded him by persons highly placed both within and without the Catholic fold, and by reason, too, of his extraordinarily sensitive nature, would suffer more than he did. One thinks of the Achilli trial, the Irish university, the proposed translation of the Scriptures, the projected oratory at Oxford, the editorship of the *Rambler*, and the relations with Manning, to say nothing of a host of minor ills and disappointments. Opposed, frustrated, belittled, contradicted, and intrigued against, at times, it is true, Newman failed to conceal his hurt feelings and on occasion he gave way to a suggestion of bitterness and even to a certain pettiness. Yet in the end he rose majestically above the deep internal struggle in his sensitive soul and triumphed over his own nature, emerging as an obedient son not only of the Church, but likewise giving obedience to a number of churchmen who in the order of grace and of nature were in no sense his equals.

When, therefore, his fellow Catholics in England found themselves — to their bewilderment and dismay — berated by their government, scorned by their countrymen, and insulted by their neighbors because Pope Pius IX had dared in September, 1850, to restore a hierarchy to the Catholic Church in England after its three centuries without a normal ecclesiastical government, it was Newman who was called upon to restore the balance and to calm their troubled minds. Such was the background to the famous lectures at the Corn Exchange in Birmingham in the summer of 1851 which later appeared in book form as *Lectures on the Present Position of Catholics in England*. Therein was set forth, as only he could do it, a ringing defense of his coreligionists that contained as well some of Newman's sharpest and most telling comments on the spirit of bigotry with which so many Englishmen had assailed the Catholics ever since the break with Rome.

But even more helpful, perhaps, to those who had been chosen by the Holy See to bear the responsibility of leading the English Church was the sermon that Newman preached at the first plenary council of the restored hierarchy at Saint Mary's College, Oscott, in July, 1852. For good reason a certain pall of gloom overcast the meeting of the thirteen Catholic bishops with the Cardinal Archbishop of Westminster, Nicholas Wiseman, at their head. But on that unforgettable occasion, as their minds were borne aloft by the pathos with which Newman expounded his theme of Catholicism's 'second spring' in their native land with incomparable grace and beauty, they were first moved to tears at the preacher's marvelous evocation of the Church's glorious English past now gone forever, as they were sobered by his warning that their suffering might not even yet be at an end, for they should not be surprised if this second springtime should turn out to be "an English spring, an uncertain, anxious time of hope and fear, of joy and suffering. . . ."[40]

It was after these somber words that Newman changed the mood entirely and in a magnificent peroration reassured the anxious bishops by reminding them of the weapons of advantage they possessed for any struggle that might ensue with the enemies of the faith, declaring:

One thing alone I know, — that according to our need, so will be our strength. One thing I am sure of, that the more the enemy rages against us, so much the more will the Saints in Heaven plead for us; the more fearful are our trials from the world, the more present to us will be our Mother Mary, and our good Patrons and Angel Guardians; the more malicious are the devices of men against us, the louder cry of supplication will ascend from the bosom of the whole Church to God for us. We shall not be left orphans; we shall have within us the strength of the Paraclete, promised to the Church and to every member of it. My Fathers, my Brothers in the priesthood, I speak from my heart when I declare my conviction, that there is no one among you here present but, if God so willed, would readily become a martyr for His sake. I do not say you would wish it; I do not say that the natural will would not pray that the chalice might pass away; I do not speak of what you can do by any strength of yours; — but in the strength of God, in the grace of the Spirit, in the armour of justice, by the consolations and peace of the Church, by the blessing of the Apostles Peter and Paul, and in the name of Christ, you would do what nature cannot do. By the intercession of the Saints on high, by the penances and good works and the prayers of the people of God on earth, you would be forcibly borne up as upon the waves of the mighty deep, and carried on out of yourselves by the fulness of grace, whether nature wished it or no. I do not mean violently, or with unseemly struggle, but calmly, gracefully, sweetly, joyously, you would mount up and ride forth to the battle, as on the rush of Angels' wings, as your fathers did before you, and gained the prize. You, who day by day offer up the Immaculate Lamb of God, you who hold in your hands the Incarnate Word under the visible tokens which He has ordained, you who again and again drain the chalice of the Great Victim; who is to make you fear? what is to startle you? what to seduce you? who is to stop you, whether you are to

[40] Charles Frederick Harrold (Ed.), *A Newman Treasury. Selections from the Prose Works of John Henry Cardinal Newman* (New York, 1943), p. 220.

suffer or to do, whether to lay the foundations of the Church in tears, or to put the crown upon the work in jubilation? [41]

As Newman told the English bishops in 1852, it is not the natural way of man to invite sacrifice and suffering, for they are rare souls, indeed, who are brave enough to say with Saint Teresa of Avila, "what I deserve is trials; may God give me many more for love of Him." [42] Most of us poor beings feel that about all we can measure up to is prayer for the strength to bear the trials that come our way without asking God to burden us with more. Nonetheless, every believing Christian will appreciate the spiritual value of the sacrifices and sufferings that have been the lot of the saints and that have helped to make them ready for their deaths and eternal judgment. If, therefore, what we find in the lives of holy souls and outstanding personalities of church history is helpful for us to live by, so may one likewise find in the example of many of these men and women models by which to die.

In conclusion I should like to speak of one of these whose story has much to teach us for life, and not the least of whose salutary lessons is that he can teach us how to die. It has been given to few men of any age to have made a more profound impression on their contemporaries and to have had more lasting influence with succeeding generations than Saint Bede, the great Benedictine of the early Middle Ages, who was the only Englishman whom Dante admitted to the *Paradiso*, as he was the only Englishman whom Rome had made a doctor of the Church. In his own lifetime Bede enjoyed a widespread reputation for his virtue as well as for his learning, and not long after he was gone Saint Boniface,

---

[41] *Ibid.*, p. 221.

[42] Teresa to Jerónimo Gracián, Toledo, October 23, 1576, E. Allison Peers (Ed.), *The Letters of Saint Teresa of Jesus* (Westminster, 1950), I, 319. The reader will find a wide variety of characteristics in Teresa's letters. For example, her business acumen was frequently shown. Thus in writing to the prioress at Seville, Teresa counseled: "Do not take the daughter of the Portuguese gentleman — or whatever he is — unless he first leaves a deposit as security for what she will pay, for I have heard that we shan't get a farthing out of him, and this is no time for accepting nuns without dowries. Be sure not to act otherwise." (Teresa to M. Maria de San José, Toledo, September 26, 1576, *ibid.*, I, 292). There are, too, numerous flashes of wit and humor as when she remarked to a friend about Don Juan de Ovallo: "We have a great deal to put up with in him. And yet I would wager he has a real desire to please you and serve you. God has not greatly blessed him; but God gives other people nice dispositions precisely so that they may put up with such as he, and that is what you will have to do." (Teresa to Don Lorenzo de Cepeda, Toledo, July 24, 1576, *ibid.*, I, 258–259).

laboring in his difficult mission among the pagans, wrote to the Abbot of Wearmouth and Jarrow and he said:

> We, labouring to plant the seeds of the Gospel among the wild and ignorant Germans, beg you to send us something of the writings of Bede the monk, who of late was shining among you like a lantern, with knowledge of the Scriptures.[43]

And Boniface's associate, Lull, sent a similar request to the Archbishop of York, asking that he be furnished with what he described as "a comfort in our exile, any one of these works, which Bede the priest of blessed memory wrote." [44] Nor did Bede's memory fade with time, for he has gone on instructing men ever since, as a Benedictine of our own day made evident less than a decade ago when he testified that in his search for truth it was Bede's *Ecclesiastical History of the English People* that supplied a turning point in his religious quest and helped to lead him to the Catholic Church. His concept of medieval England had never included the Church except in a vague sort of way until, as he said, in Bede's pages, "my whole perspective was changed." It was there that Dom Griffiths discovered that the Church in England owed its real origin to Pope Gregory the Great and that it was he who had commissioned the monk who became the first Archbishop of Canterbury, the knowledge of which filled for him a blank space in history and caused his entire outlook on the Catholic Church to change.[45]

If, then, through twelve centuries men have found so much to repay them in Saint Bede, he must, indeed, be a man worth knowing well, and his acquaintance is never more inspiring, it seems to me, than in the description of the way he died. Bede had been engaged in translating the Gospel of Saint John into the English of his time when, in the spring of 735, he took seriously ill. He realized that his strength was ebbing rapidly and in his anxiety to finish his appointed task he exhorted his monastic assistant, "Learn quickly, for I do not know how long I shall last, nor if shortly my Maker shall take me." The following day one of his confrères reminded him that a chapter still remained undone, whereupon Bede again counseled the copyist to hurry. After a time the young monk said, "There is still, dear master, one sentence not yet fin-

---

[43] Quoted in R. W. Chambers, *Man's Unconquerable Mind. Studies of English Writers from Bede to A. E. Housman and W. P. Ker* (London, 1939), p. 44.
[44] *Ibid.*
[45] Bede Griffiths, O.S.B., *The Golden String* (New York, 1954), pp. 85–86.

ished," to which the dying saint again urged that he write quickly. At last the final sentence had been copied down and all was declared completed, and then Bede remarked:

Well hast thou spoken . . . it is finished. Hold my head in thy hands (for it pleases me to sit opposite my little shrine, where I have been wont to pray), so that I too seated may call upon my Father.

Thus lying on the floor of his cell while reciting the 'Glory be to the Father and to the Son, and to the Holy Spirit,' the great scholar breathed his last.[46]

Not only had Saint Bede insured his place in the memory of men through his famous history and other works, but he had also taught them by personal example how to continue in their life work to the last ounce of their strength, and then with that completed, to breathe one's last, so to speak, in God's sight. In that sense Saint Bede had fulfilled perfectly in his living and in his dying the petition which long before he had embodied in his lovely prayer that one finds at the end of his *Ecclesiastical History*, and which may fittingly serve as a closing thought for each of us:

I beseech thee, good Lord Jesus, that thou wouldst lovingly give unto us to drink in with delight the words of thy wisdom, and that thou wouldst also grant us to attain to thee, the fountainhead of all wisdom, and to stand for ever before thy face.[47]

THE SANCTITY OF MOTHER SETON

In the *Catholic Directory* for the year 1959, it is noted that there were nearly forty million Catholics in the United States who were under the spiritual care of more than 200 bishops and over 52,000 priests. This is not to mention the approximately 175,000 men and women who were enrolled as brothers or sisters in the numerous religious orders and congregations and the steadily mounting number of Catholic schools and charitable institutions. It is obvious, therefore, that in matters such

[46] *The Ecclesiastical History of the English People by the Venerable Bede.* Translated by Thomas Stapleton and edited by Philip Hereford (London, 1935), p. xxix.
[47] *Ibid.*, p. 336.

220

as numerical and physical growth, in organizational life such as the National Catholic Welfare Conference and its numerous subsidiaries, and in the worldwide Catholic charities the American Church has reached its maturity.

But what, one may ask, of the deeper signs of the faith of the Catholics of this country in the realm of the spirit? Here, too, there has been an impressive showing as, for example, the more than 140,000 converts who entered the Church during 1959. Equally remarkable is the intensification of the contemplative life and the spread of the liturgical movement among the American Catholics. In fact, the thriving state of contemplative religious orders like the Cistercians, the more recent establishment of the Carthusians, and the opening of the first American house of the Camaldolese monks in California — to say nothing of the increase among the cloistered Carmelite nuns, the Poor Clares, and other contemplative orders of women — has been the source of no little astonishment to our coreligionists in other lands. To many outside this country the United States is a place where a hopelessly hedonistic philosophy with its materialist values predominates so strongly that the contemplative life cannot flourish. The years since World War II have given a telling refutation to this widespread belief, to what Jacques Maritain in his book, *Reflections on America*, has called the "grand slander" of Americans in which so many foreigners have indulged in years gone by.[1]

The Church in the American Republic has, indeed, made giant strides in both spiritual and material development, but there still remains something unfulfilled in the Catholic life of this land. No native-born American has as yet been declared blessed or been canonized as a saint. We are now some years removed from the four hundredth anniversary of the establishment of the first parish in what was later to be the United States when the Spaniards founded St. Augustine, Florida, in 1565. During those four centuries countless holy souls have lived, toiled, and died on this soil; yet no one of these native sons or daughters has yet been raised to the honor of the altars of the Universal Church.*

[1] Jacques Maritain, *Reflections on America* (New York, 1958), pp. 121–127. In this regard Maritain remarks: "But the significant thing for me is that I have never met any real contemplative, any true soul of grace, any man genuinely aware of the ways of the spirit, who, knowing America in actual fact and through personal experience did not have for her a love in which his very love for mankind and a sort of reverence for the workings of divine Providence were involved" (p. 126).

* Since this was written Elizabeth Anne Seton was beatified on March 17, 1963, and John N. Neumann, fourth Bishop of Philadelphia, was likewise honored by the Church on June 23, 1963.

In our failure to achieve this additional sign of spiritual maturity we are unlike our neighbor to the north. Canada has her Blessed Marguerite Bourgeoys (1620–1700) who was beatified in 1950. True, this holy woman was born in France, but in addition to this, Pope John XXIII gave formal beatification on May 3, 1959, to a native-born Canadian woman when Marie-Marguerite d'Youville (1701–1771) was the subject of this signal honor. Likewise to the south of us for over two centuries Peru has had her canonized saint in Turibius, Archbishop of Lima (1538–1606), a Spanish-born prelate, and the Peruvian Catholics have long gloried in their native daughter, St. Rose of Lima (1586–1617), the Dominican tertiary, who was canonized in 1671, as well as the lowly Dominican lay brother of mixed blood, Martin de Porres (1579–1639), who was beatified in 1837 and canonized in 1962.

To be sure, within the last thirty years official action has been taken by the Holy See in regard to the cause of a number of men and women whose lives of outstanding virtue were led in part in this land. In 1930 the eight intrepid martyrs of North America, all of whom were French-born, were canonized by Pope Pius XI, and every American Catholic is both proud and grateful for the fact that two of their number, Isaac Jogues (1607–1646) and René Goupil (1607–1642), shed their blood on the soil of northern New York. Nor is there an American Catholic who knows anything about the careers of Philippine Duchesne (1769–1852) and Francesca Xavier Cabrini (1850–1917) who is insensible to the splendid pages which this French-born Religious of the Sacred Heart and this Italian-born foundress of the Missionary Sisters of the Sacred Heart have contributed to the history of American Catholicism. To Blessed Philippine, beatified in 1940, we owe one of the most striking examples of religious zeal in the new American West, an example that she gave through the more than thirty years that she worked and sacrificed for both the Indians and poor white settlers of the frontier before her death at St. Charles, Missouri, in 1852. And of St. Francesca Xavier, canonized in 1946, the Catholics of this country will always be mindful for the heroic efforts she put forth in behalf of the poor and friendless immigrants of her native land who had found their way to these shores in such tremendous numbers in the late nineteenth and early twentieth centuries. This naturalized citizen of the United States had more than earned a distinguished place in its Catholic history before she entered upon her eternal peace at Chicago in 1917.

We are fully conscious, therefore, of the splendid achievements of the Jesuit martyrs of the seventeenth century, of Blessed Philippine in the nineteenth century, and of St. Francesca Xavier in our own century, achievements that have immeasurably enhanced the religious history of our beloved country. Yet these holy souls were not in the strict sense American saints, but rather providential men and women of extraordinary holiness whose noble deeds illumined the life of the Church in the land of their temporary residence or adoption.

When we inquire, then, who among the Catholics of native birth might seem to be a fitting candidate for beatification and canonization there is almost universal agreement that no American-born Catholic is a more appropriate subject for the supreme honor of the altars of the Universal Church than the remarkable lady whose memory we honor here. In this holy ground lie her mortal remains in the lovely valley that she sanctified by her presence through twelve years before death claimed her in January, 1821, on the spot where now stands the replica of the house in which she died. I shall not trespass upon your patience by recounting in detail the biography of Elizabeth Seton, for most of you know its broad outlines very well, and for those who do not, there is ample material available in the books that have been written about her. Permit me rather to dwell upon certain aspects of the life of this noble woman which suggest her appropriateness as a candidate for canonization insofar, that is, as the limited vision of our human eyes can see and the record of history can tell.

On Sunday, June 21, 1959, we marked the 150th anniversary of the departure of Mother Seton and her little community from Baltimore for their long and trying journey over the primitive roads that led them to the hamlet of Emmitsburg. Four years before the cultivated widow of a prominent New York family — for the families of both her late husband and herself had stood high in the New York society of those days — had surrendered everything that such connections imply when she entered the Catholic Church in March, 1805. In taking this significant step Elizabeth Seton cut herself and her five little children adrift not only from the Protestant Episcopal Church into which they were born, but from her own and her late husband's families, from her friends, yes, even from her source of income. And when one recalls that during that first winter in Emmitsburg there were nights in the old Stone House which they then occupied when that dwelling did not even shelter them from the snow which they found about them upon waking, one can capture something of the depth of sacrifice which this new life entailed for the young widow, her children, and the pious women who had gathered about her. Such was the character of Mother Seton's original surrender of her own will to the will of God which, as it turned out, proved to be but the beginning of a lifetime of surrenders and sacrifices that left upon her the stamp of a holiness quite beyond the normal piety of men. In other words, Elizabeth Seton understood from the outset, and she practiced to the end, the fundamental principle of the spiritual life that if one is to live close to God he must give, and not receive.

In every saint there is found evidence of an heroic practice of the virtues; in fact, there may not be present a persistence in serious defects nor a grave moral deficiency of any kind. In Mother Seton there were, indeed, no major defects, and in her life there were mirrored many virtues which she exemplified to a very high degree. From among these I should like to choose three in which, it seems to me, she possessed a special quality of holiness. First, Elizabeth Seton was a humble woman in the sense meant by Thomas Merton when he says, "Humility consists in being precisely the person you actually are before God . . ."[2] For to this pious widow her own worth was always measured according to what she believed was the norm applied to her by God, and in that she attained the very difficult but essential quality of humility. Our Blessed Lord was, of course, the perfect exemplar of all the virtues. But it is significant, I think, that in only one regard did He ever call attention to Himself as a model to be followed, and that was in humility. This Christ did on two occasions. In the early period of His public life He told His disciples on one occasion, "Learn from me, for I am meek and humble of heart."[3] And again at the last supper He — the Son of God — rose from the table and stooped to wash the feet of the lowly and ignorant fishermen who had been His followers. And when He had finished Christ said to them, "I have given you an example, that as I have done to you, so you also should do."[4]

In this regard Elizabeth Seton patterned herself after the Master as the record of her life bears witness. For example, the hardship and deprivation of her first days here in Emmitsburg were rendered more

[2] Thomas Merton, *Seeds of Contemplation* (Norfolk, Connecticut, 1949), p. 66.
[3] *Matthew*, 11:29.
[4] *John*, 13:15.

acute when the Sulpician superior in Baltimore saw fit to transfer Father Pierre Babade, a spiritual director who had understood Mother Seton and brought her much spiritual consolation, and to appoint in his place another who did not understand her and whose rather arbitrary ways at times proved a severe cross to the holy foundress. She humbly accepted the decision of the superior, but what it had cost her was revealed when she told Archbishop Carroll in a letter late in 1809:

I have had a great many very hard trials, my Father, since you were here, but you will of course congratulate me on them as this fire of tribulation is no doubt meant to consume the many imperfections and bad dispositions our Lord finds in me. Indeed it has at times burnt so deep that the anguish could not be concealed, but by degrees custom reconciles pain itself, and I determine, dry and hard as my daily bread is, to take it with as good grace as possible. . .[5]

Proud and haughty men do not bend their wills to the will of another in this fashion; it is only the humble who are able to bow beneath the cross of disappointment and contradiction in the spirit of Mother Seton.

A second indispensable quality of sanctity is sacrifice, that is, the giving up of what we hold dear out of love for God, for the gain of our own soul, and for the welfare of others. Do you recall the occasion in our Lord's life when a rich young man approached Him as He was preaching near the Jordan River? He had been listening to Christ for a time and now the young man drew near to inquire what he must do in order to gain eternal life. In answer the Master told him that he must keep the commandments. But these, he said, he had kept from his youth, and he then added the question, "What is yet wanting of me?" At that point the Son of God replied, "If thou wilt be perfect, go, sell what thou hast, and give to the poor, and thou shalt have treasure in heaven; and come, follow me." And to this St. Matthew added the revealing comment, "But when the young man heard the saying, he went away sad, for he had great possessions."[6]

It would be an exaggeration to call Elizabeth Seton a woman of great wealth, although she came of a family that we would describe as well to do. Yet she did not hesitate to abandon that comfort and security when she heard the call of the Master, and unlike the man in the gospel,

[5] Elizabeth Seton to John Carroll, Emmitsburg, December 14, 1809, in Annabelle M. Melville, *Elizabeth Bayley Seton, 1774–1821* (New York, 1951), p. 171.
[6] *Matthew*, 19:20–21.

225

it was without sadness that she turned her back upon all worldly connections to follow Christ. Thus she took the counsel of perfection that was declined that day by the rich man at the banks of the Jordan, and she was faithful to it from the hour of her conversion in 1805 to her death sixteen years later. In so doing she sacrificed to the point where her friend, Archbishop Carroll, a man wise in the things of God, could truthfully say to her, "It seems to be the order of divine providence to lead you to perfection thro' the road of sufferings . . ."[7]

The sacrifice practiced by Mother Seton entailed, as we have said, the loss of family, and economic security before ever she had left New York. In turn the starkness of her single year in the little house on Paca Street in Baltimore was deepened in her early months in Emmitsburg. Added to the surrender of physical comfort and ease, and to the loss of cherished loved ones through estrangement over differing religious faiths, there were the anxieties which filled her days as leader of a new and poverty-stricken foundation and the keen personal sorrow as she watched her two devoted convert sisters-in-law go down to death at her side. But even these crosses were overshadowed in the anguish she experienced in parting with her two lovely daughters, Anna Maria and Rebecca, whom death carried off while they were still in the gaiety of their childhood. Thus within the brief span of seven years Mother Seton came four times to yonder cemetery with the mortal remains of a loved one who was laid away near the spot that she would one day occupy. She knew, moreover, the heartache which only a mother feels and understands in the waywardness of one of her sons and in the prolonged absences of the other son as he pursued his dangerous occupation as a man of the sea. If you and I would relive something of the poverty, discomfort, and hardship endured by Mother Seton here in a remote frontier community of the early nineteenth century let us follow her footsteps across this broad valley and up the side of the mountain above Mount Saint Mary's College. There we may appreciate, perhaps, the trial of this holy widow and her companions each Sunday as they walked the full way to hear the Mass of Father John Dubois in the little chapel on the mountainside and to remain throughout the day in the open forest so that they might assist at vespers in the afternoon.

No soul steeped in humility and seared in sacrifice, however, can

[7] John Carroll to Elizabeth Seton, Baltimore, December 28, 1809, in Melville, *op. cit.*, p. 173.

achieve any degree of perfection in those virtues without love, that is, love of God, and because of that love of God, love of one's fellowmen On the night before He died Christ told the apostles, "A new commandment I give you, that you love one another: that as I have loved you, you also love one another. By this will all men know that you are my disciples, if you have love for one another."[8] And when we remember that the classical definition of love, in the sense in which our Lord used it, is wishing other men well and doing well to them, we come upon another of Elizabeth Seton's predominant virtues. For like the woman described in the book of *Proverbs*, Mother Seton "reached out her hands to the poor and extended her arms to the needy."[9] From the time she opened her arms to receive her sisters-in-law after they had lost so much for their faith in Catholicism to the last day of her life here in Emmitsburg, surrounded by her religious sisters and the little ones who composed her school for poor children, no one was refused her charity and love. The meager amount of this world's goods that she had, she shared; the talents with which God had endowed her, she gladly expended and passed on to the women and the children who had gathered about her and who knew her as their mother.

And beneath all this love for others, this constant concern for their welfare, comfort, and spiritual advancement, was the depth of this holy lady's love for God Himself. Her letters abound in expressions of affection for God and His goodness, of complete submission to His will, and of anticipation of His visible presence in the beatific vision. In fact, one of the most notable features of the spiritual life of Elizabeth Seton was her unceasing preoccupation with the presence of God and her longing for the day when she might see Him face to face. Just six months before the end, when she had already been stricken with her fatal but lingering illness, she told her friend, Father John Hickey, in a letter of July, 1820:

Oh my father [and] friend, could I hear my last stage of cough and feel my last stage of pain in the tearing away my prison walls, how would I bear my joy — The thought of *going home*, called out by *his* will, what a transport.[10]

Thus when the end came on that early January day of 1821 it not only found Mother Seton ready but anxious to be joined to the One Whom

[8] *John*, 13:35.
[9] *Proverbs*, 31:20.
[10] Elizabeth Seton to John Hickey, Emmitsburg, July 2, 1820, in Melville, *op. cit.*, p. 294.

she had loved so intensely through all her life, both as a Protestant and as a Catholic. Death, indeed, held no terrors for Mother Seton; she had even sought it as the final act of life's drama that would unite her forever to the Source of strength that had sustained her through the years of hardship, suffering, and sorrow.

Faced as we are, then, with the testimony of the inspiring life of this wonderful lady who lived out her final years so close to the homes of each of us, what should it mean to us who wish to honor her memory? First, the cause of her beatification and canonization should evoke our prayers and sacrifices that, if it be God's will, her cause will move forward without further delay, and that the cardinals and other officials of the Congregation of Rites may be prompted by the Holy Spirit to hasten the process of that cause. Secondly, this life should offer to each of us a source of deep edification and an impetus to renewed zeal in our personal lives. And especially to American Catholic womanhood, to mothers and wives, to widows, yes, and to the more than 170,000 religious women of the American Church of whom Mother Seton was, in a sense, their prototype, here is a model for conduct as well as an object for prayers and heavenly petitions.

In many ways we have won the admiration of the world's Catholics for our unrivaled educational system, our stupendous charities, and our practical and effective parish life. But we are still lacking in that which will give the final stamp of completeness to the Church of the United States, a native-born saint. If France venerates her Joan of Arc and Bernadette, if Spain is proud of her Teresa of Avila, if Scotland has her St. Margaret the Queen and England her Blessed Margaret Clitherow, if Poland cherishes her St. Hedwig, and if Portugal and Hungary have each their St. Elizabeth, is it a matter for wonder that American Catholics should seek to have their Elizabeth Seton added to this noble company of holy women who have inspired the Christian centuries by the record of their virtues? Is it strange that we Catholics of the United States should yearn for the day when we may appeal directly to the intercession of one of our own whose presence at the eternal throne has been verified by the infallible word of our common mother, the Church? Thanks to the grace of God, we are not wanting in men and women of virtue and piety both in our national history and in this, our own generation. But what we seek in this cause, and what our presence here today is meant to testify, is the further grace that will enrich the American branch of the Universal Church when one of our very own is declared among the blessed by the voice of the Vicar of Christ, our common spiritual father.

To that end do we unite our prayers today, and for that intention we shall pray in the days to come. For through the happy sequel of this beatification we American Catholics may, in God's Providence, be brought a little closer toward intimate union with the Head of the Mystical Body by means of Mother Seton's love for God and her fellowmen overflowing, as it were, to embrace us, her fellow countrymen, and acting as the channel of divine grace to lift the spiritual tone of our common fatherland. We who know and love America realize full well the need in which she stands for constant spiritual renewal, for in her might and her riches she has, in the words of St. Paul in the Epistle to the Romans, been "subject to vanity." Yet as the great apostle told the Romans twenty centuries ago, it is not a vanity that is without hope. For when humility, sacrifice, and divine love rule the souls of men, as they ruled the soul of Elizabeth Seton, the sins and weaknesses of our created flesh can be overcome. Then we, too, after the fashion of the great lady whose memory we honor, can look forward to eternity with the same serenity that she watched the approach of death. In other words, as St. Paul expressed, we can anticipate the hour when "creation itself also will be delivered from its slavery to corruption into the freedom of the glory of the sons of God." [11]

[11] *Romans,* 8:20–22.

3 CATHOLICS AND EDUCATION

THE AMERICAN CATHOLIC COLLEGE (1939–1959): CONTRASTS AND PROSPECTS

To survey the changes that have transpired in Catholic higher education in the United States over the past twenty years is, I think you will agree, a formidable undertaking, and I do not flatter myself that I can accomplish that task here with anything like the thoroughness that it deserves. But I can, perhaps, suggest a few of the main lines of development of the years since 1939 and indicate where, in my judgment, there is likely to occur some of the more significant changes in the foreseeable future.

One of the first things that comes to mind in a review of this nature are the numbers involved in the vast commitment of the American Church to higher education. We Americans, I am afraid, are often more beguiled by numbers than we should be, and in this we of the Catholic faith are no exception. Yet numbers cannot be entirely ignored. In any case, the Catholic college world of this country (and I use the term to cover the universities as well, since practically all of them have a college as one of their most important units) has seen a tremendous upsurge since 1939. In 1938, the nearest point to our *terminus a quo* for which reliable figures are available, there were 187 such institutions that responded to the inquiries of the Department of Education of the National Catholic Welfare Conference for its biennial survey, and in these institutions there were then enrolled 143,617 students.[1] Unfor-

[1] *Universities and Colleges — Normal Schools* (Washington, 1940).

231

tunately, the figures for the 1958 report of this agency had not yet been published so I have had to fall back upon those for the year 1956 when 229 Catholic universities and colleges reported a total of 326,534 students.[2] In the eighteen years between 1938 and 1956, therefore, the student population of the Church's institutions of higher learning increased by 182,917 or over fifty percent.

I shall not try your patience with a further set of statistics by way of demonstrating the predictions of reputable educational authorities on the increases in student enrollment which all American colleges must anticipate during the coming twenty years. Many of you in this audience are more familiar than I am with that prospect. Suffice it to say that predictions of a student population by 1980 that will double the present number are not regarded as an exaggeration. In passing I might mention that one of the more diverting indications of change that turned up in this investigation was the fact that as recently as 1938 the *Official Catholic Directory* had not apparently as yet come to view the Catholic women's colleges as sufficiently numerous and important to warrant separate listing since for that year they were classified with the girls' academies. One need not tax his imagination to sense the outcry that would ascend from every section of the land if P. J. Kenedy & Sons were today to list the women's colleges in the same column as the academies for girls!

A further indication of change, and one that may, indeed, in its ultimate effects overshadow all the rest, has to do with the spirit in which the educational problems of the Catholic college are now being faced. In 1939, the year in which Delta Epsilon Sigma was born, the indefatigable Father John A. O'Brien, to whom we owe many good things, sponsored and edited a symposium which was published in book form under the title *Catholics and Scholarship*.[3] In that volume seventeen writers endeavored to analyze and assess the reasons for the failure of Catholics to make a greater contribution to scholarship and to attain distinction in the learned professions. The book caused a mild ripple in the placid academic waters of the period, but in the daily round of the Catholic educators' many preoccupations it was soon forgotten. For one reason, it suffered from the disadvantage of having appeared at a time when the combined forces of complacency, indifference, and hy-

[2] *Summary of Catholic Education, 1955–1956* (Washington, 1958).
[3] Huntington, Indiana, 1939.

232

persensitivity about our educational institutions still held the American Catholic community firmly in their grip.

In contrast to the slight stir caused two decades ago by Father O'Brien's book, we have been treated for the past several years to the most exciting debate that the Catholic academic family has experienced since the infant Georgetown Academy opened its doors more than 168 years ago to launch the Church's educational system in the newly born Republic. In itself this is a meaningful and immensely heartening contrast with the atmosphere that obtained twenty years before. There are among us, to be sure, those who feel that the frank and open character of this recent discussion of the weaknesses of Catholic higher education has done a disservice to the cause we all have at heart. Needless to say, in the free society that we inhabit they are at perfect liberty to maintain and to propagate their point of view. But those of us who do not entirely share their sentiments would, in turn, beg the right to invoke the same freedom in criticizing the shortcomings of our institutions and in searching out the possibilities for remedy and improvement without, we trust, being thought subversive of the sacred trust that we assumed when we elected the vocation of educators in the colleges and universities of the American Church.

Surely any system of higher education that embraces over 260 colleges and universities that enroll close to 350,000 young men and women – to say nothing of the 516 seminaries of the country with their nearly 40,000 students – may be said to have attained at least the outward signs of maturity, even if its inner spirit at times reveals that in some respects it is not as yet fully aware of its new status. Yet the searching and constructive scrutiny to which the Catholics have subjected their institutions during the past four years – allowing for the inevitable voices that have been raised by those whose thinking would still seem to be conditioned by the siege mentality of what was once a despised minority in this country – this scrutiny, I repeat, is evidence of the fact that we have advanced in more than mere numbers. Beyond the growth in size the American Catholic college community has also proved of late that it has come of age in the art of adult criticism, in mature self-analysis, and in what one may characterize as the sense of security that enables men calmly and openly to review institutional defects without fear that their exposure may imperil the entire structure. And all of this, it should be remembered, has happened in a way that has enlisted a widespread and sustained interest that would have been unthinkable two decades ago. In a word, the majority of American Catholics would now seem to have arrived at a point where they can confront the serious problems that beset their colleges and universities with the realism that is merited by their dignity and intrinsic worth as centers of the intellectual virtues. And in doing this, incidentally, the Catholics of this country have in this instance anticipated rather than followed, as has so often been our wont, our coreligionists of other lands, as those of you know who have read the summer 1958 issue of the *Dublin Review* with its stimulating series of articles devoted to higher education among the Catholics of England.

Before taking leave of this point I should state that in an effort to view the scene as it appeared twenty years ago I checked the spring education numbers of *America* and *The Commonweal* for April, 1939, to see what they were saying about the problems of higher education at that time. *The Commonweal* (April 14, 1939), interestingly enough, carried an article by Mortimer J. Adler entitled "Can Catholic Education Be Criticized?" The numerous appearances of this friendly Jewish scholar on Catholic campuses, as you will recall, had made his name a household word among us two decades ago. In this instance he approached the subject with his customary straightforwardness, and in alluding to the constructive criticism which he had at times endeavored to present to Catholic college and university groups, he made a statement that in good measure answered the question posed in his title. He said:

My experience has uniformly been to have the faculty agree with the main points, only to discover that they were enjoying my remarks as reflections on the poverty and perversity of other institutions, but not their own.[4]

Allowing for the improvement that has been noted of late, I suppose there are few of us who would have the hardihood to maintain that the type of reaction experienced by Dr. Adler has even now entirely disappeared from our ranks.

In the corresponding issue of *America* (April 15, 1939) Daniel M. O'Connell, S.J., writing in anticipation of the thirty-sixth annual meeting of the N.C.E.A. then about to open, called his contribution, "Educators Convene for Their Annual Advance." Father O'Connell recalled the

[4] Mortimer J. Adler, "Can Catholic Education Be Criticized?" *The Commonweal* (April 14, 1939), p. 682.

fight waged by *America* to defeat the Smith-Towner Bill some years before, a measure which, in his words, "would have put Catholic education under the control of a Federal bureau with all its lamentable consequences."[5] The appointment of a committee three years previous by the N.C.E.A.'s College and University Department to compile "a bibliography of books by Catholic authors of collegiate standing," was characterized as a practical program for the development of scholarship. By the time that Father O'Connell wrote the fears that had haunted Catholic educators for a generation concerning what were termed "the obnoxious features" of the secular accrediting agencies had been largely laid to rest so that they could now give their support, as Father O'Connell said, to the "sane technique" that had been evolved by these accrediting bodies. Finally, in regard to graduate work under Catholic auspices, the Jesuit author found "one of the cheering signs of solid intellectual development in our Catholic life,"[6] in the fact that whereas in 1922 the Catholic graduate schools had conferred only thirty-five Ph. D. degrees, by 1937 the number had risen to ninety-five. So much for the educational picture as seen in the pages of our two leading Catholic weekly journals of opinion twenty years ago.

There is still another change that has taken place since 1939, and it is on this as a final point that I should now like to dwell. I refer to the increasingly essential role of the lay professors in the Catholic institutions of the United States. Beginning with the pontificate of Pius XI and its emphasis upon the layman's place in the specialized works of Catholic Action, and continuing through the reign of Piux XII, there has emanated from the Holy See a mounting tone of urgency as the supreme pontiffs have sought to set in focus for the present century the share that the layman should take in the varied aspects of the Church's divine mission. Safeguarding always the prerogatives of the bishops in the sacred magisterium, which is their unique possession as the *Ecclesia docens*, the papal directives have insistently pleaded for a more active participation of the laity in the universal apostolate. I shall not trespass upon your time in an attempt to trace the course of that development here since there is scarcely an issue of a weekly Catholic newspaper or

[5] Daniel M. O'Connell, S.J., "Educators Convene for Their Annual Advance," *America* (April 15, 1939), p. 6.
[6] *Ibid.*, p. 8.

monthly journal that does not bring fresh evidence of the manner in which this distinctive note of the twentieth-century Church as sounded by the popes is being echoed by the bishops in their respective dioceses. Let me simply recall the unprecedented World Congress of the Lay Apostolate that convened at Rome in October, 1951, in support of which the Holy Father employed every device at his command. In his address to the delegates the pontiff termed the assistance of the laity "an indispensable necessity," and he went on to say that the varying circumstances of our age had, as he phrased it, "opened wider the gates for the collaboration of layfolk in the Church's apostolate."[7] Moreover, in his allocution on that occasion in enumerating the possible avenues of lay effort, Pius XII specifically mentioned education and what he called "the apostolate in the intellectual and cultural field." In view of the late pontiff's words, and of more recent pronouncements of a similar character, one is prompted to ask how this emphasis of the Holy See relates to the lay faculties of our Catholic colleges and universities.

First, a word about the altered numerical status of lay professors since 1939. In 1938 the laymen and laywomen in the institutions reporting to the Department of Education of the N.C.W.C. constituted 49.3% of the Catholic faculties. By 1956 that figure had risen to 61.1%. While that was a considerable gain for eighteen years, the true nature of the increase since 1939, I believe, is not fully realized until one studies at closer range the large and predominantly male institutions, since the smaller women's colleges have not as yet shown so marked a trend in the rise of their lay faculties. In order to arrive at some kind of an estimate of the situation within the larger universities I chose six from that category on the basis of their representative character as to size, location in different geographical areas, and their variety in types of administrative control. These six universities are: Fordham, Notre Dame, St. Louis, San Francisco, Seton Hall in New Jersey, and Xavier in New Orleans. The pertinent data are as follows[8]:

[7] "Pius XII to the First World Congress of the Lay Apostolate, October 14, 1951," *Catholic Documents*, VII (1952), 3. If Pope John XXIII was correctly quoted in a recent article it would seem evident that the present pontiff shares the ideas of his predecessor on this subject. While Patriarch of Venice he is said to have cautioned the clergy in an important speech against an "authoritarianism which robs the layman of proper incentives in running his affairs." Robert Neville, "The Pope and the Vatican," *Look* (March 31, 1959), p. 72.

[8] *Official Catholic Directory* for 1938 and 1958.

	1938			1958		
	Religious	Lay	% of Lay	Religious	Lay	% of Lay
Fordham	74	258	77.7	119	383	76.2
Notre Dame	52	340	86.7	106	379	79.7
St. Louis	196	581	74.7	135	1026	88.3
San Francisco	31	59	65.5	48	153	76.1
Seton Hall	35	56	61.5	37	180	87.5
Xavier	28	57	60.0	44	192	81.0
(New Orleans)						
	426	1351	76.0	489	2314	82.5

These figures speak for themselves. It is evident that during the last two decades Catholic higher education in this country has become steadily more dependent upon the lay professors. In fact, without their assistance the majority of our larger universities and colleges would either have to close entirely or drastically curtail their educational programs. Parenthetically, I might mention that this situation is not unique to the Catholics of the United States since in 1958 the Catholic University of Louvain had 460 laymen and 116 priests and religious on its total teaching staff of 576 professors.

In comparison to other countries the proportion of priests, brothers, and sisters in the American Church is still relatively high. But it is a sobering thought that their ratio is losing ground every year when set beside the far faster growing Catholic laity, more and more of whom are clamoring for a higher education within the institutions of their own Church. By concerted efforts vocations to the priesthood and the religious life have been stepped up in the last few years, but they are not gaining at a speed to overtake proportionately the great army of high school graduates who are seeking college instruction in our institutions. As Pius XII told the First World Congress of the Lay Apostolate, to man adequately the ramparts of the world-wide apostolate there simply are not enough clergy. "It is a noble task," he said, "but it is rendered all the more difficult for the Church by the fact that, though, on the whole, the numbers of the faithful have increased enormously, the ranks of the clergy have not filled up in the same proportion."[9] Nor is there any

[9] *Catholic Documents*, VII, (1952), 3.

indication that the years immediately ahead will see a reversal in these trends. On the contrary, it is now a generally accepted fact that the Church's educational system at all levels will lean even more heavily on the lay teacher as we move farther into the second half of the present century.

What, in brief, has been the position of the laity as revealed in the history of American Catholic higher education? In 1958 there was published a volume on that subject by Edward J. Power of the University of Detroit. It is not a book that will make pleasant reading for the layman, for historically speaking, his place has been that of a subordinate and his return, both in money and in influence, has been exceedingly meager. Yet the lay professor of 1959 will find some comfort when he reads the following description of his counterpart of a century ago in these words:

A lay teacher could not leave the grounds without special permission and his candle was to be extinguished by nine in the evening. He was forbidden the use of alcoholic beverages and tobacco; if he violated any of the many regulations to which he was expected to conform, part of his meager salary was withheld.[10]

We Catholics can thank God that on the whole relations between the clergy and laity of the United States have been of a cordial and constructive character, and we are grateful, too, that we have escaped the corroding influences of an anticlericalism that has poisoned Catholic life in many lands. True, these relationships in our country suffered a rude and dangerous break in the late eighteenth and early nineteenth centuries in the movement known as lay trusteeism. Fortunately, however, its ugly manifestations did not linger — except in isolated spots — beyond the Civil War. But the heritage of that unhappy experience helps to explain in part the fact that until quite recently in practically all that pertained to the policy-forming functions of the Catholic community the clergy have taken the lead and the laity have simply fallen in line. And in purely spiritual matters, we will all agree, that was precisely as it should have been.

[10] Edward J. Power, *A History of Catholic Higher Education in the United States* (Milwaukee, 1958), pp. 95–96. One could scarcely imagine today the problem that worried Charles Warren Stoddard in 1884 when the thought of a teaching post in English at Notre Dame prompted him to inquire of Father Daniel Hudson, "Could I write freely to my friends and receive letters which would not necessarily be opened to the inspection of the Rev. Provincial or the Rev. General, or anyone but myself?" *Ibid.*, p. 96, Stoddard to Hudson, September 12, 1884.

But a community that still felt close to the evils of lay trusteeism, and that counted a total of twenty-six laymen teaching in all of the twenty-five colleges for men in 1850, was one that bore little or no resemblance to the American Catholics as we know them today. The pattern of clerical leadership that has perpetuated itself in this country has, I believe, borne within it the seeds of a certain danger in what might be termed the tendency to carry over into areas of activity where often the layman, by reason of his special training, is just as competent to lead — and at times more so — than the priest. And aside from the realm of the sacred sciences, this holds true in higher education. Over a century ago one of the greatest minds ever to apply itself to the theory and philosophy of education recognized this fact. When John Henry Newman was maturing his plans for the Catholic University of Ireland he was intent that the layman should occupy a prominent role in the new university. In the postscript to a letter dealing with the appointment of a vice rector, he said:

I forgot say, in reference to our University appointments, that it is sovereignly unwise to confine our selections of either Officers or Professors to priests. The public does not give us priests credit for ability to fit young men for the world; and certain I am that the word and example of a pious layman will always be less suspected and more efficacious with boys than those of an equally pious priest. They have a prejudice that piety is an obliged profession with us, in fact, our trade. I desire, therefore, if I may speak of myself without arrogance, to see eminent laymen in numbers in the Chairs of the University.[11]

Precisely how the majority of the lay professors of the present day view their position, it is not easy to say. Most of us, I presume, are acquainted with the scolding administered by one of their number in the article of Oscar W. Perlmutter in *The Commonweal* of April 11, 1958, and with the lively correspondence which it set off in the pages of that journal for a month or six weeks thereafter. Again most of us have read the account in *America* for January 17 of 1959 by Seymour L. Gross, Jewish professor of English in the University of Notre Dame. From my own experience of nearly thirty years in college teaching, four of which were spent as a layman, and from what I have heard and read by way of reactions among lay colleagues to ideas such as those expressed by Mr. Perlmutter and Mr. Gross, I should be inclined to say

[11] Fergal McGrath, S.J., *Newman's University: Idea and Reality* (London, 1951), p. 197.

that the situation is not quite as dark as the Vice President of Saint Xavier College saw it in the spring of 1958, nor is it as bright as Professor Gross viewed the matter some eight months later.

The present — or, should one say, dawning — actuality of the layman's position in our Catholic institutions, and the improvement it implies, were, it seems to me, highlighted by the refreshing little book of Thomas F. O'Dea of Fordham University.[12] Here, surely, is a volume which it would be difficult to conceive coming from a lay professor in the year that your fraternity was born when the layman's standing in our colleges was still largely that of necessary, and often merely temporary, adjuncts in a few departments. Today, however, not only does a lay professor feel free in at least one university to write critically of Catholic higher education, but he does not scruple to assign one of the fundamental weaknesses of the system to clericalism. And what is even more remarkable, he tells us that the first person to suggest that his manuscript should be put into print was the Jesuit president of his university. This, indeed, is progress such as Professor O'Dea's opposite number of twenty years ago would not so much as have dreamed in his wildest imagined flights of emancipation from the clerical yoke.

If the mind of the majority of the lay faculty members is not a subject that admits of facile generalization, the facts that pertain to their numbers, indispensability, and mounting influence are beyond dispute. In view of these facts, and, too in view of the desire that is cherished by every sincere Catholic for an increase of intellectual eminence and national prestige on the part of our institutions of higher learning, one is warranted in drawing certain conclusions by way of what the present situation would seem to suggest and, perhaps, even to demand. First, the material rewards in salary and fixity of tenure of the laymen and laywomen on Catholic faculties need to be further strengthened if our colleges and universities are to enable these devoted men and women to approach equality of status with their colleagues in the best secular universities and, too, if the finest brains among them are to be dissuaded from yielding to the lure of higher remuneration offered by schools outside the Catholic system. Secondly, in the less tangible realm of influence and authority, a more open and wholehearted confidence in the layman's ability to fill top administrative posts and to share

[12] Thomas F. O'Dea, *The American Catholic Dilemma: An Inquiry into the Intellectual Life* (New York, 1958).

240

directly in the making of educational policy, is something that cannot long be deferred if, once more, we are to retain the tremendous reservoir of talent embodied in those who now carry the major portion of the routine burden of instruction.

The Catholic college and university community of the United States represents an incalculable investment in brains, dedicated lives, physical plants, and money, and its noble purpose deserves the best that we of the clergy, and you of the laity, can give in its service. And since the number of the clergy and religious no longer permits them to staff our institutions as they once did, the reason that originally brought them into being would seem to dictate that a generous sharing of the burden of instruction should now be more fully matched by an equitable sharing of influence and authority. Beyond these general remarks, however, it would be both presumptuous and in doubtful taste were I to particularize in more detail. For it would be unfair to those clerical administrators who are fully aware of the problem and who have already made earnest efforts, often against heavy odds, to cope with it, as it would be unjust to a growing number of priests and religious educators who in recent years have entrusted to the laity high administrative offices in some of our Catholic institutions.

The situation that I have endeavored to describe has about it certain features that remind one of a condition that arose in the history of the infant Church. Not long after Pentecost the apostles found themselves overwhelmed by the obligations to which the enlarging flock of Christian converts had given rise. The twelve, therefore, called together the general body of the Lord's disciples and told them frankly of their difficulty in trying to preach God's word amid the harassment of so many other tasks. The solution that Peter and the eleven offered is described in the *Acts of the Apostles* in these words: "Come then, brethren, you must find among you seven men who are well spoken of, full of the Holy Spirit and of wisdom, for us to put in charge of this business, while we devote ourselves to prayer, and to the ministry of preaching."[13]

In this manner were the Church's first deacons chosen to assist the apostolic college. There is here, of course, no exact parallel with the situation to which we have just addressed ourselves. Yet, *mutatis mutandis*, like the apostles of old the clergy and religious of our day find the burden too great for them to bear alone. They need the assistance

[13] *Acts*, 6:3–4.

of the trained and learned laity who will march at their side and who, like Stephen, Philip, and the other deacons will not only bear their share of the daily burden but who will enjoy a place of honor in breaking the bread of intellectual life in the Catholic colleges and universities of the land. In so doing the Catholic layman and laywoman will be assured both of the support of the same Holy Spirit who accompanied Stephen and his companions as they will be encouraged by the legitimate hope of attaining the same honored role as these chosen disciples who walked the world at the side of the original twelve as they jointly advanced the apostolate of the kingdom of God on earth.

HEIRS OF AN AMERICAN CATHOLIC TRADITION

Almost a century ago there arrived in St. Paul four Sisters of St. Joseph of Carondelet to inaugurate in the Northwest a splendid chapter in the history of Catholic education for American womanhood. These valiant and devoted women began their labor a few days thereafter in the vestry of an old log church. Such, in a few words, were the humble and impoverished beginnings of an experiment in Christian education which has earned through the passing years notable blessings from Almighty God. God has, indeed, given to this effort increase in numbers and resources until today the graduates of the College of St. Catherine step forth into the world with a degree from an institution which enjoys the esteem of educators of all faiths in all sections of the land. In the perfecting of this center of Christian culture in the Northwest the most powerful source of strength of the Sisters of St. Joseph has been their faith in God and their certainty that a life led in dedication to the ideal of enlightening and fashioning the minds of the coming generations in the truths of eternal wisdom was the richest reward which they could win and the most enduring joy which this world could impart to them. It would be superfluous for me to speak of their achievement. This College — to say nothing of the numerous elementary and secondary schools of the Archdiocese of St. Paul — gives eloquent testimony to the eminent success which has attended their efforts in behalf of so high and so noble a cause. The Sisters of St. Joseph and the large number of priests, laymen, and laywomen who have been associated with them on the faculty of this College would be the first to acknowledge that the principal source for their impressive accomplishment in higher education has been the unfailing strength given to them by the light and counsel of the Holy Spirit Whose octave of prayer and song the Church concludes with the week of Pentecost.

While the deposit of divine wisdom willed to the Church nineteen centuries ago by the Son of God and transmitted to the bewildered apostles in the Cenacle on the morn of Pentecost has been the touchstone of the progress of the College of St. Catherine, the attainments of this institution are due, too, to the fidelity with which the administration and professors have cherished and preserved the tradition which was established at Le Puy nearly three centuries ago. It was almost exactly two centuries from the time of the origin in France of the congregation which conducts this College to the day when its American daughters first saw St. Paul. Now nearly a third century has passed, and yet if Father Jean-Paul Médaille and Bishop Henri de Maupas were to come forth from their tombs today and to walk through the halls of St. Catherine's they would witness the same zeal, the same high spiritual ideals, the same devotion to the Church which distinguished their first spiritual daughters at Le Puy three hundred years ago.

I can readily understand the thought passing through the minds of many of you: What has this to do with our commencement? What relation has all this recalling of the dead past to the purpose of this gathering and to the life which lies before us? I submit that it has everything to do with the original aim of coming to the College of St. Catherine and that it bears, and will continue to bear, a direct relation to the life you lead when you depart today from the institution that has trained and molded your mind through the years that have just come to a close. You are the heirs of a great tradition; you are the inheritors of something precious and rich in American Catholic life; you are to be the representatives before the world of what Christian education can mean in the life of a Catholic woman; you are to be the spokesmen of the Sisters of St. Joseph and the traditions of this College in the communities where you will live. You are, in fine, to be the embodiment of the inheritance willed to you through three centuries of time. This is your precious privilege and this is your high responsibility.

Over nineteen centuries ago when the Son of God was about to take leave of His apostles He imparted to them a final mandate. He said to them: ". . . you shall receive power when the Holy Spirit comes upon you, and you shall be witnesses for me in Jerusalem and in all Judea and Samaria and even to the very ends of the earth."[1] As you stand today on the threshold of a new chapter in your lives the faculty of the College of St. Catherine say to you that you, too, shall be witnesses for this College in St. Paul, and in all Minnesota and Wisconsin and even to the very ends of the United States. Like the apostles before you, you too have received the Holy Spirit and His seven-fold gifts have brought to you an inner illumination and a depth of understanding of the problems of life which are not vouchsafed to thousands of American young women who this month will receive degrees across the vast expanse of the United States. To the spiritual resources which are yours by reason of your faith and the sacraments which channel grace to your souls, you have added the finished instruction of your mind which your collegiate training has supplied for you. You have thus been raised far above the masses of American womanhood, and by that very token you have added weight to your responsibilities.

No graduate of a Catholic college in this country can escape the responsibility which her training and her superior intellectual discipline have brought to her. You are going forth into an America which teems with thousands who have little more than a slightly veiled contempt for the eternal truths of religion and the values which you were here taught to regard as having transcendent importance to all earthly gains. It will be your duty to bear witness to these truths wherever you are and in whatever profession or vocation you elect. Yours is a post-war generation wherein the already severe losses in the realm of the materialistic philosophy of life threaten to dominate every segment of society. Speaking to such a generation as yours nearly thirty days ago when the United States was emerging from World War I, A. Lawrence Lowell, President of Harvard University, wrote:

After a great war . . . and not least, perhaps, after a war that has awakened so great an enthusiasm and devotion, it is wise to beware of a materialistic reaction. Among the strong agencies to prevent such a relapse ought to be our

[1] *Acts,* 1:7–8.

244

colleges and universities, which should feel more than ever their duty to keep before the minds of young men the eternal values and the spiritual truths that endure when material things pass away.[2]

The wisdom of President Lowell's prophecy was more than borne out in the days after 1918, and every thoughtful mind in this present hour which follows an even greater world disaster can bear witness to the progress which this materialistic philosophy made in the generation between two wars. If we needed a reminder of the apparent victory of the purely natural and material in the regions of the highest thought control of our time, we received it in the recently published brochure of the United Nations Educational, Scientific, and Cultural Organization entitled, *UNESCO. Its Purpose and Its Philosophy*. Therein Julian Huxley, the Director General of UNESCO, sets forth the philosophy which is to guide this interesting and hopeful experiment in international educational effort. You and I, trained in the tradition of the Christian West, look in vain for the slightest acknowledgment of man as a creature of God in this blueprint for international education. Rather are our misgivings for UNESCO aroused when we read, in the words of its director general, that: "Throughout evolution, progress has consisted in the raising of the upper level of certain properties of the 'world stuff' of which we, as well as the stars, are made."[3] There do you have the educational philosophy of one who has been placed in what may become the most influential single post in the world for shaping the course of educational thought and procedure. By the decisions taken in UNESCO and by the workings of that organization your own children may very well be affected and their minds molded and patterned. This is but one example of the current philosophy of naturalism and materialism which pervades our generation and which offers a fierce resistance to the educational traditions of which you are the recipients and the heirs. Here, then, is one area of life which presents a challenge to your leadership, namely, that you summon the best of what you have mastered and made your own during your days in the College of St. Catherine to combat the force which would erase from the memory of man his spiritual character and his ultimate destiny as a child of God.

You are accustomed to hear from commencement speakers the charge

[2] *At War with Academic Traditions in America* (Cambridge, 1934), p. 276.

[3] Julian Huxley, *UNESCO. Its Purpose and Its Philosophy* (Washington, 1947), p. 14.

245

of responsibility to graduates. I offer you today no variation from that theme. If the Catholic Church of the United States cannot look to you — and the thousands like you who go forth this month from the ninety-eight Catholic senior colleges for women in this land — then in whom can it rest its hope for a strengthened family life, an improved moral tone in American society, and a defense of ethics in the professions and avocations where you young women will find employment and service? Is the Church of America expecting too much of you to anticipate that the years ahead will never record a divorce and remarriage among the graduates of the College of St. Catherine? Is the Church of this Republic asking too much of each of you to demand that God's eternal law on the procreation of human life will never find infringement at your hands? Does your Church and your College ask too much in hoping that you will stand out as a model in your own community for keeping high the standards of the Legion of Decency in what relates to the moral law as reflected in the films? Are we too optimistic when we say today that in your presence we believe the Church of the United States will find strong and faithful daughters who in the professions of law, medicine, nursing, and teaching will carry into the practice of their chosen vocations the exalted concepts of conduct learned in the classes of Christian ethics and religion which you followed here? I think not. Yet, I cannot too much insist that our generation is one which has all but lost its appreciation of these eternal values, and you will be, therefore, in the unenviable company of a minority doing battle against the hosts of worldly and materialistic forces.

Nonetheless it is precisely there that you will vindicate your training. You will be asked — and please God you will respond — to give leadership to the failing fortunes of morality in American society in a hundred different ways. You have been equipped for that task. The apostles nineteen centuries ago could not escape the responsibility of the mandate of Christ once they were enforced by the mighty and divine surge of the Holy Spirit in their souls; no more can you escape the responsibility which is yours. True, you will not, we hope and pray, be called to suffer active persecution and martyrdom, but you will most positively be summoned to defend morality in public and private life, modesty in conduct, and Christian ethical principles in the course of your daily living. There is nothing strange in the fact that to you, graduates of a Catholic college, the Church of America should look for leadership in the myriad causes in which it is called to struggle. This thought was well expressed fifty-two years ago this month by the greatest single figure which the Catholic Church of the Northwest has given to the Church of the United States and one of the most striking personalities of all American Catholic history. Speaking on the subject of "The Catholic Church and Liberal Education," John Ireland, Archbishop of St. Paul, said:

Whence will come Catholics fit to be models and leaders? I answer, from Catholic colleges and universities. If they do not produce such Catholics, and in large numbers, our Catholic colleges and universities will have failed in their work.[4]

The question is as pertinent to this hour as the day Archbishop Ireland asked it, and his answer is as compelling and insistent as it was in 1895.

You have found your weapons for the battle of life on this campus; you have sharpened their points and their edges in these classrooms; you have drunk deep of the source of divine life and wisdom in yonder Chapel of Our Lady of Victory. You are ready, therefore, for the fray. These are your weapons and your tools, and over them all is the mantle of the Church's incomparable fund of knowledge and wisdom of which you have been made the participants. The traditions of western Christendom are yours through your study of history, philosophy, and literature, and the traditions of American Catholicism are your possession through your investigation of the religious, social, and economic forces that have gone into the creation of this glorious Republic. The Sisters of St. Joseph have preserved these traditions in their congregation that they might share them with you; your priestly and lay professors have not denied to you their own measure of the knowledge and enlightenment which are theirs from the Christian and American past. You have a solemn duty before God to keep these traditions fresh in your minds and to live the Catholic life boldly before all men wherever you may be. In this way you will be the bearer of the richness and the goodness of the past to a future generation which will stand in such dire need of their healing qualities. Our age is one which sets slight store by tradition and the achievements of a by-gone age. But you, daughters of St. Catherine, unlike thousands of other American college graduates, have been taught to respect and to revere the accomplishments of past ages. Be loyal to tradition in its true and best sense, taking from the rich heritage of

[4] *The Church and Modern Society* (St. Paul, 1905), I, 252–253.

Christian knowledge as willed to you from the Church of western Europe the countless and priceless beauties to which it gave birth. Be loyal, too, to the increasingly rich tradition of your own American Church. Know the great names of the American Catholic past and the splendid thought and philosophy which they have bequeathed to you. Our age is, sad to relate, one of the most confused and frightened amidst all its amazing advances in science and technology. All glory to science and to its accomplishments! But too many of the leaders of this generation have found their shrines in the laboratories and counting offices of the land. You have been saved from this distorted vision by an education which balanced a just and right respect for the findings of science with the greater regard for Him from Whom all science takes its rise.

The character of the education given in the College of St. Catherine should assure the American Republic that in you it will find no purveyors of subversive doctrines which would corrode the foundations of the state. Neither will your presence in society give rise to uneasiness of mind that in you is to be feared a fellow traveler of clubs and committees more intent upon spreading the insidious poison of Communism than defending American freedom and liberty. The social ills from which our country suffers today have a right to expect to find in you — with minds enlightened by true doctrine and spirits alert to social justice — remedial healers of the inequities practiced, for example, against our Negro brethren and fellow citizens, strong supporters of the demands of the toiling masses in the labor unions when those demands are just, keen and critical citizens who will use the privilege of the ballot with discrimination and an informed conscience lest the public offices of state and nation be dishonored by those who would employ them for their selfish purposes. In these, and in a hundred other ways, do the Church and the Republic look to you, our Catholic college women, for leadership in the public and private causes which may spell triumph or defeat for both Church and State in the years ahead.

Your highest privilege — next to that of giving yourselves in consecration to one of the Church's religious orders — is to be the guardians and the defenders of the integrity of family life. It is not too much to say that if family life is permitted to disintegrate in this land then ruin will certainly follow for the Church, the nation, and for all society. You can exercise this function of guardian of the highest Christian traditions of the family both within and without the married state. You can shield its interests at the ballot box, in the hospital, in the classroom, in the court-room, and in the office. In any one of these areas of public and private endeavor you can — and, indeed, you must — demonstrate that your lives show forth the complete Catholic integration which the Church of this generation has a right to expect of you. In this way will you be fulfilling your duties as witnesses to Christ, in this manner you will be vindicating the education which you received in this College, in this way, too, will you be honoring your Church and ennobling your country, and, finally, in this service will you be fulfilling the mandate given to your Roman sisters by the supreme pontiff when on October 21, 1945, Pope Pius XII said to the Catholic women of the Eternal City:

The fate of the family, the fate of human relations are at stake. They are in your hands. Every woman has then, mark it well, the obligation, the strict obligation in conscience, not to absent herself but to go into action in a man-ner and way suitable to the condition of each so as to hold back those cur-rents which threaten the home, so as to oppose those doctrines which under-mine its foundations, so as to prepare, organize and achieve its restoration.[5]

NO COMPLACENCY

As the old Cardinal turned with disgust from the television after having watched and listened to a campaign speech of Kevin McCluskey, the young candidate for mayor, he asked his secretary: "Is he representa-tive of what we have to offer? I have spent my life in establishing a system of diocesan schools, in encouraging our people to send their children to them, to our Catholic colleges and universities. Is this the result? A McCluskey? . . . What is our contribution?"

In an effort to arrive at as honest an answer as possible to the question that troubled the aged churchman in *The Last Hurrah*, the present writer prepared a paper with the title "American Catholics and the In-tellectual Life" for the annual meeting of the Catholic Commission on Intellectual and Cultural Affairs in St. Louis on May 14, 1955. The paper

[5] Pope Pius XII, *Your Destiny Is At Stake. Woman's Duties in Social and Political Life* (Washington, 1946), p. 9.

was published on the following September 19 in the autumn number of *Thought*, and is now available in pamphlet form. It was the belief of the editor-in-chief of *America* that his readers might find it of interest to learn something about the reactions to the article.

With that in mind the data was assembled and correlated, though it should be made clear at the outset that the present essay is a reportorial summary of the opinions of others and is not intended as a discussion of the views of those who are quoted. It is hoped, however, that this report may convince others, as it has convinced the writer, that whatever defects there are in the intellectual life of American Catholics — and there are many — it may be said for a numerous group of those engaged in the things of the mind that a stubborn complacency is not one of them.

To date well over 4,000 reprints of the article have been distributed. Of this total *Thought* accounted for 1,065, while the *Catholic Messenger*, the weekly newspaper of the Diocese of Davenport, which reprinted the entire article minus the footnotes, disposed of 2,515 copies. In addition, it was published in the spring of 1956, along with several related papers, in book form in a minimum edition of at least 5,000 copies. A lengthy news release was circulated by the NCWC News Service on October 3 to the Catholic newspapers; *Newsweek* printed a similar column in its issue of October 10; and on November 11 the *Commonweal* did the same.

As a sequel to these summaries, in so far as the writer is aware, nine newspapers and one Catholic magazine carried editorials, and a dozen or more letters to editors were counted in various publications. The essay was made the subject of a luncheon talk by Bishop John J. Wright in Worcester on October 8, and the bishop devoted a considerable part of his founder's day sermon at St. Louis University on November 16 to the same theme. Likewise, Donald McDonald, a news editor of the *Catholic Messenger*, was prompted to write a series of four articles in his "Essays in Our Day," between October 27 and November 17.

A friend wrote that the Northwest Regional Unit of the National Catholic Educational Association at its meeting in Spokane in mid-November employed the article as the basis for discussion in one of the sessions. A month later the Catholic papers reported that the December meeting of the deans of the Catholic graduate schools at Boston College had done the same. On December 30 the essay was the subject of a ses-

sion at the mid-winter meeting of the chaplain directors of the National
Newman Club Federation at Coral Gables.

Members of the faculties of ten universities, colleges and seminaries
have written that the essay was read publicly in the refectories of their
religious communities, and a symposium on the topic, which included
representatives of Georgetown University and the Catholic University
of America, was held at the latter on January 19. Finally, the College and
University Department of the NCEA and the deans of the Catholic
graduate schools each scheduled a session on some of the problems
raised in *Thought* for their meetings during the NCEA's annual convention in St. Louis, April 3–6.

Over and above the notice taken by various groups and by the press,
the writer received between September 23, 1955 and the date of writing
(March 13) a total of 196 letters, which may be classified as follows:

Bishops	5
Business executives	4
College and university administrators	5
College and university professors	70
Deans and directors of medical education	2
Editors	25
Graduate students and seminarians	16
Lawyers	7
Laymen	7
Laywomen	4
Newman Club chaplains	5
Parish clergy	6
Priests in special work	15
Publishers	5
Scholars in government service	3
Seminary professors	17
	196

A rereading of the correspondence and the newspaper coverage in preparation for the present report revealed twenty or more separate cate-
gories into which the reactions might legitimately be divided. Obviously,
it is impossible in the space allotted to give more than a partial summary
of the many thoughtful views expressed. It has seemed best therefore, to

classify the reactions under a few main headings and to supplement these with a sampling from the remainder.

There may, indeed, be some who will question the wisdom and propriety of an essay of this kind. With that in mind, the identity of the persons quoted has been concealed in order that they may suffer no embarrassment. The sole motive of the writer has been the improvement of the situation described in the essay. It is to be hoped, therefore, that the service rendered to the common good will outweigh in the eyes of readers any harm that they might otherwise feel would derive from its publication.

DUPLICATION OF EFFORT

One of the most pronounced points of view to emerge from the correspondence dealt with the grave mistake which Catholics are making in duplicating programs of graduate study in so many institutions, that none of them possesses the facilities for work of a truly high quality. Stating that he was singling out merely one item, the editor of a learned journal lamented "the fatal duplication of intellectual activity in our higher institutions." The same point struck a seminary professor who remarked: "Catholic graduate schools have too few resources in men, money and equipment to allow any to be wasted by widespread dispersal. Unified action poses many problems, but I certainly agree with you it is now a necessity."

An internationally known scholar was particularly emphatic about "the unnecessary multiplication of Catholic graduate schools." One of the most widely known Catholic scholars in the country commented: "For a goodly number of years I have been shocked by the multiplication of Catholic colleges and so-called 'universities' without any increase of scholarly-minded graduates, and have been sorely tempted to write a series of articles on the subject." (Parenthetically, it should be said that he was strongly urged to do so.)

A graduate student named his own religious order as one that, in his judgment, had been guilty of two of the mistakes mentioned in the *Thought* essay, viz., what he termed "the trend toward 'big business' universities and a lack of cooperation, and even competition with other Catholic colleges." He believed that the latter defect was being slowly remedied, but the former, he thought, was being accentuated.

In this connection Catholic institutions in certain areas might profitably investigate the joint programs for collegiate and graduate studies

252

inaugurated in 1953 by seven colleges in southern California. The project was outlined by a committee of fifteen scholars who received a grant from the Fund for the Advancement of Education and whose report was published in December under the title, "The Graduate School Today and Tomorrow. Reflections for the Professions' Consideration (New York, 1955)."

RESPONSIBILITY OF CHURCH LEADERS

It was the opinion of a number of the correspondents that there was little hope for effective remedy until the bishops and major religious superiors could be persuaded to take the situation in hand. On this point some of the seminary professors were among the most outspoken. One who believed that intellectual life in the seminaries had deteriorated as much as in the colleges and universities illustrated what he had in mind by citing a bishop now dead — himself a former professor — who used to ask the seminary professors "to pass the boys along." Another bishop had suggested that they "take it easy" on one of his poorer students since the diocese was badly in need of priests. Another seminary professor found that the effort to raise the intellectual level in the classroom brought only a puzzled inquiry from the superior: "Why all this scholarship? All the professors are supposed to do is to train young men for the priesthood." It elicited a comment from the correspondent: "In other words, there is a complete lack of awareness of the necessity of clerical scholarship beyond and above the comfortable minimum necessary for licit ordinations." A third seminary professor hoped that the reverberations would multiply until they had produced "some true understanding of the situation in religious superiors and some effective action."

Among the college and university professors some were no less insistent in looking to the hierarchy and religious superiors to lead the way. One member of a religious order felt that a certain amount of blame must be laid at the door of ecclesiastical and religious superiors "who didn't dig deeply enough while they were building broadly." If the faculties of seminaries and religious houses of formation put no premium upon scholarship, there was little hope, he thought, that the clergy of the next generation would be much interested in intellectual matters.

A priest professor summed up his views thus: "Malum est in capite" (the evil is in the head), and he wondered if he was not too optimistic in believing that the essay would afford material for meditation on the part of bishops and religious superiors. A lay professor hoped that the essay would be read by "many, many Catholics, and especially by members of the hierarchy," while another observed: "If the bishops would only see that so much of our effort is only sound and fury and little else, I doubt that many of them understand what the problem really is." Lastly, a priest graduate student, noting the emphasis in *Thought* on the necessity for high-level planning in Catholic higher education on a national scale, inquired: "Has anyone directly suggested to the hierarchy that something ought to be done?"

In fairness to those at the top, it should be stated that it is not, perhaps, altogether realistic to think exclusively in terms of an over-all step on their part that would embrace the Church of the entire nation. The very diversity in character of the Catholic institutions in different sections of the country might, indeed, militate against the effectiveness of too broad an approach. Here, it would seem, is where the bishops and major religious superiors might rightly expect informed guidance from the educational administrators and experts whom they have trained and appointed to the responsible offices of higher education. If the latter are sensitive to the superior values to be derived from allotting additional funds for higher faculty salaries, for scholarships and for publication of high-grade research, they will have an enduring effect for the better on the intellectual tone of American Catholic Life. They would be more profitably employed thus than in spending effort, time and money in seeking publicity for their institutions, expanding their facilities beyond what they can legitimately undertake, and pursuing the specter of a fame that for the most part eludes them.

RELATIONS OF CLERGY AND LAITY

Allied to the foregoing were comments on the relations of the clergy and laity in the American Church. It should be clearly stated that none of the letters touching this aspect of the problem displayed anything that could rightly be interpreted as anticlericalism. Yet in a number it would not be difficult to detect faint signs of a cloud on the horizon, to which John Courtney Murray, S.J., referred as "presently no bigger than a man's hand," in the Christmas 1955 issue of *Life*.

A business executive, for example, wondered if Catholics' failure to develop outstanding leadership might not be attributed to the fact "that laymen are not allowed to assist significantly." The laity show too much of a tendency to yield to the clergy in fields where the former possess competence, and if the layman does not yield at times "ecclesiastical position is invoked and one is made to appear, perhaps, rude." This situation often renders objective discussion between the two groups virtually impossible, and for that reason this man wondered if it did not in part account for the "underlying conformity, almost subservience, lack of intellectual curiosity and possible resultant lack of leadership."

A university lay dean held that certain evils in Catholic higher education could not be overcome "until the clergy becomes more willing to take into its policy-making activities the educated laity." A lay professor would make only one addition to the conclusions expressed in *Thought*, viz., that young Catholic scholars must have it proved to them that they will be allowed "all the room in the world to move around without fear of sanctions." The Holy See he thought, had in recent years shown the way, but it was his belief that "a good many college administrators have not."

OPINIONS OF FOREIGN SCHOLARS

Several Catholic scholars outside the United States expressed opinions on the article. A distinguished French Jesuit tactfully observed that while it was not for a foreigner to pass judgment, he was in complete agreement with the conclusions of the essay. He had had occasion, he said, "to know from the other side what is the opinion on Catholic intellectuals and scholarly activities." An English Catholic editor was both surprised and saddened by what he read. Having met one or two first-class American Catholic scholars in London and corresponded with several others, he remarked, "I was not prepared for the grim story you tell."

A professor in one of England's leading universities wondered if English Catholics would show up any better in a similar investigation. In his opinion his co-religionists in England were weak in what he called "the type of solid upper-middle-class people who have formed so large a proportion of English dons, intellectuals and people in public positions in the last hundred years, and so many of whom are related to each other in great blocks of families. . . ." After a residence of four years in China a priest professor declared: "The same attitude against intellectual work is the cause of our small amount of influence there; the same in Japan."

Speaking of Catholic intellectual circles abroad, a seminary professor in the United States believed that the benefits to some Americans trained in Europe were rather marked. He recalled that all his philosophy teachers had studied at Louvain, and he was of the view that their students had derived from them a sense of "the importance of absolute and rigorous devotion to the spirit of truth, as well as the realization that real intellectual achievement demands a complete dedication." An American lay professor paid tribute to the European Catholic intellectuals in another way. He conceded that the *Catholic Encyclopedia* was the American Catholics' greatest monument to scholarship, but to his mind its achievements were due to what he termed "the cosmopolitan (especially European educational) background of Pace." (He was referring to Monsignor Edward A. Pace, Vice-Rector of the Catholic University of America.) And to this he added: "There is a dramatic difference in quality between the contributions of the Americans and the Europeans. With the Europeans there is front-line scholarship. And it is this scholarship which accounts for the 'monumental' character of the work."

REACTIONS OF AMERICAN SECULAR SCHOLARS

Something should likewise be said about the reactions of certain non-Catholic American scholars. One nationally known historian commented:

While it [the essay] was written for Catholic intellectuals, I hope others can be again and again reminded of the great intellectual tradition of the Church, of its significant role in sustaining and promoting knowledge and of the specific factors in American history which have in some ways militated against that role.

A former president of the American Historical Association confessed to a "very spotty knowledge" of the subject, but from what he knew he was inclined to the same conclusions as reached by the article. Another professor who had written critically of the intellectuals felt that the article was indicative of anything but a "desertion." As he said, "the test of desertion is not . . . a critical attitude toward particular aspects of American culture, but rather a certain neurotic or acid flavor of complaining."

An instructor in a large secular university, at present working on a research project with a view to putting to rest "some of the myths concerning American Catholicism," gave his students a series of lectures on the Catholic Church. They elicited an impressive response since, as he observed, "the unknown excited their interest." It was his judgment that the most revealing reaction came from his Catholic students, "who seemed almost pathetically eager to find out something of their past."

The most surprising attitude of any, perhaps, was that of a non-Catholic professor in a large secular university who is also on the editorial board of two scholarly journals. As a result of his editorial experience he was prepared to say that Catholic scholars "have proved themselves to be on the whole far superior to the average run of American secular scholars," in part because they seem able to read Greek and Latin. This reader of excerpts from my essay used in a *Commonweal* editorial (November 4) closed his letter with the annoyed comment: "In other words, you need not feel it necessary to express publicly such an inferiority complex!" A check of the gentleman's two journals over the past three years turned up only three Catholic contributors, all foreign-born scholars, about whom the original article was not talking in the first place.

CATHOLIC AND SECULAR UNIVERSITIES

The need for close and friendly contacts between Catholics and their opposite numbers in secular universities, as well as for a more informed and sympathetic attitude on the part of some Catholic newspapers toward these institutions, likewise provided the basis for comment. A professor in a state university, well known for his devout faith, summarized his view by saying:

While I have doubts about American secular universities, real winds do blow there from time to time. I have discarded many an outer garment that I wore ten or even five years ago, yet feel I am a better Catholic and student because of this change.

A Catholic scholar now in government service was reminded of his student days at Chicago and California and of "how provoked I used to be with Catholic friends . . . who regarded these schools as hotbeds of atheism, communism, etc." Mentioning by name two distinguished Catholic professors at Chicago and California, he maintained that he had never known greater influence in "developing respect for Catholic intellectuals" than that exercised by these two men.

A young religious trained in a leading secular university deplored "so many hasty articles in the Catholic press these days" about the evils of non-Catholic colleges and universities. It occasioned the observation that if the intellectual excellence urged in *Thought* were to obtain in the Church's schools of higher education, "Catholics could hardly afford not to attend them." To a priest graduate student it would be much better if Catholics were to attend secular graduate schools in greater numbers. They should be, he warned, Catholics who "understand their faith and the relevant philosophy in more than a catechetical way." He had done graduate work at one of the ranking universities in this country and was pleasantly surprised "at the gracious way in which I was received and at the general atmosphere of objective inquiry I found."

THE PRESS

Of the ten editorials seen by the writer, nine were friendly in tone and for the most part were in agreement with the evidence presented in *Thought*. The Saginaw *Catholic* (October 9) and the San Francisco *Monitor* (November 11) sought to balance the unfavorable picture by calling attention to the achievement of the parochial school system on which the Church had been compelled to concentrate.

The Boston *Pilot* (November 12) maintained that those who might wish to dispute the article's thesis could win a hearing for their case only "when they give us names and numbers." Nor was the *Pilot* disposed to permit any hedging on the score of demands for the exact meaning to be attached to the term intellectual since, it said, "this is a ruse which we must not allow ourselves."

The principal concern of the Hartford *Catholic Transcript* (October 27) was with the lack of reading habits among Catholics. The *Transcript* writer warned against basing one's opinion of the essay on "snippets," for, as he said, "out of context, they can easily be misunderstood and engender resentment." The *Priest* (December) acknowledged that it was difficult to apportion the blame for the situation, but felt that "a large share of responsibility must be assumed by all of us who are guilty of a siege mentality." The writer foresaw no harm resulting to anyone from a frank recognition of the lack of industry on the part of some Catholics and their failure to achieve good habits of work. "Above all," he stated, "the ideal seems to be lacking or to have grown dim; there is basically a failure of motivation." The editor of the *American Ecclesiastical Review*, in an article entitled "Appraisal in Sacred Theology," in the issue of January 1956, first castigated two lay writers who ventured into the realm of theology; he then lamented the "naive depreciation of theology" in the United States which, he thought, was only another manifestation of a phenomenon to which the Catholics of our country have long been accustomed. There is, and there has long been, an element among American Catholics which seems to enjoy making corporate and public acts of contrition for what are supposed to be deficiencies in the scientific or cultural achievements of our schools and the value of our literary productions. There would seem to be no particular reason why the work of our theologians should be exempted from the adverse criticism accorded by such individuals to the efforts of American Catholic educators and writers in general.[1]

The Philadelphia *Catholic Standard and Times* (November 4) commented in an editorial called "Intellectualism at Low Tide?" To them all the talk about Catholic defects and failure was exaggerated, and they contended that a "realistic evaluation" would portray a much more favorable picture. Until, therefore, "more objective standards of judgment" have been arrived at, they saw no reason to underestimate the achievement of American Catholics.

It is interesting to note that in this case the writer did not advance a single fact to prove his point, nor did he specify wherein he felt the evaluation in *Thought* was unrealistic. The editorial prompted a priest to remark, "I have never seen a more definite proof that intellectualism *is* at low tide. . . ."

MISCELLANEOUS

It would be easy to gain the impression from the foregoing paragraphs that the present writer had escaped from the "brickbats and dead cats" about which one sympathetic correspondent warned him. He is quite aware, however, from indirect sources that there has been a considerable amount of adverse criticism. For example, certain scholastic philosophers have felt that their contribution was underrated, and others have criticized the essay's lack of a definition of an intellectual.

But judging solely by what was contained in the mail and in the press, the punishment meted out has been, all things considered, very mild. Out of nearly 200 letters only five were in clear dissent, and of these three were based on excerpts rather than on the article itself. Among these a priest stated that the column in *Newsweek* had left him "with a bad taste in my mouth." A month later the same man wrote to say that a reading of the entire text "righted my rash judgment," and on the

[1] Joseph C. Fenton, *American Ecclesiastical Review*, CXXXIV (January, 1956), 125.

whole he found the article "a searching examination of conscience that should be helpful and healthy for us all."

Space forbids more than a mere listing of a few other comments. For example, there was the bishop who "agreed entirely" with the conclusions. There was the college president who, perhaps unwittingly, sounded a rather despairing note by wishing that all the students in the college would read the article; since that would not be the case, would the present writer come and give them a lecture on the subject?

There was the scholar at a secular university who wondered if the influence of the Irish clergy might not be accountable in part, for the attitude of American Catholics on intellectual matters. He recalled his belated effort of some years ago to share in the annual collection for the Catholic University of America, when he had been absent from town on the previous Sunday and took the pains to deliver his check to the rectory in person. "Oh, that's all right," said the pastor, "I never have that collection counted separately; I just send $50." To which the professor appended the comment: "He was the graduate of a well-known Catholic college."

A secular priest teaching in a rather remote minor seminary was determined after reading the essay to bring his institution more in touch with the best in education. He made sure that every member of his faculty read it the week it came out, and at the next faculty meeting he urged that they should at least inaugurate a program for visiting lecturers to help them keep abreast of developments. From more than one correspondent came perceptive observations on a point made by the St. Louis *Register* (October 14) concerning the defects in American education in general and the pervading philosophy of materialism. It is an old complaint. One is reminded, for example, of the words of Giovanni Grassi, S.J., who in the years 1812–1817 served as President of Georgetown College. In his *Notizie varie*, a volume of American impressions published at Milan in 1819, Grassi said: "In the United States, where the spirit of trade and avidity for profits distinguishes all classes, it is not surprising that the flowers of poetic genius fail to flourish."

WHAT NOW?

On the whole, therefore, the reactions summarized in the present report reveal a substantial agreement with the principal conclusions reached in *Thought*. That so large a segment of Catholic opinion should have been roused to express its ideas on this theme is in itself immensely encouraging. It does, however, logically suggest a further question: what is going to be done about the situation?

There is, of course, no pat answer to that question. That the matter cries for a remedy would seem to be the consensus of most of those whose opinions have been canvassed. Yet any effective remedy will require plain speaking and courageous action. Individual Catholics engaged in intellectual pursuits might here make an adaptation of the words of Cardinal Suhard, addressed directly to them in another connection in his famous pastoral *Growth or Decline?*: "In this effort you must not involve any consideration of interest be it even apologetical: you must seek only what is."

The "what is" in the present instance constitutes a remarkably low state of intellectual attainment among Catholics in this country in proportion to their numbers and resources. Have we, then, the fortitude to apply the axe where the accumulated undergrowth in Catholic higher education threatens to choke and smother every prospect for the achievement of high quality? If we have not, then mediocrity will continue to be our portion. If we have, the collective talents, resources and facilities of the Catholic Church in the United States offer the brightest promise of enduring accomplishment. While those whose office it is to initiate the reform ponder what, if anything, is to be done, it may be helpful for all of us to recall the axiom of Edmund Burke: "It is better to run the risk of falling into faults in a course which leads us to act with effect and energy, than to loiter out our days without blame and without use."

THE PAULIST FATHERS:
A CENTURY IN THE APOSTOLATE TO AMERICANS

One hundred years ago there came aboard the trans-Atlantic ship *Vanderbilt* in the harbor of Le Havre in France a young American priest who, after a stay of eight months in Europe, was now taking passage for his native land. With his arrival in New York on that May 10 a century ago preparations were begun for the launching of what proved to be a new and exciting chapter in the history of the Catholic Church of the United States. That chapter was formally opened when on July 11, 1858, an agreement was signed between John Hughes, Archbishop of New York, and the four convert priests whose leader was Isaac Thomas Hecker. In company with Augustine Hewit, Francis Baker, and George Deshon, Father Hecker — then only thirty-eight years of age — had evolved a plan for a society of missionary priests, the principal objective of which was the conversion of the American nation to the Catholic faith. Thus in simple and humble circumstances, dictated by poverty of both numbers and resources, did there come into being the Missionary Society of Saint Paul the Apostle, the first religious community for men of native American establishment, the centennial of whose founding we honor today.

This is not the place to retell the stirring personal story of the founder of the Paulist Fathers, nor is it the occasion to sketch the history of his religious family, for these larger tasks have now reached completion and have appeared in the volumes written by two of Hecker's sons of our own day.[1] Rather today's celebration offers to those of us who are not members of the Paulist community, but who know something of their contribution to the spiritual welfare of this country during their first century, an opportunity to present to them our sincere congratulations on this notable anniversary and to attempt to appraise, be it in ever so inadequate a way, the significance of their founder's religious ideals for Catholicism in this country, as well as the place that his congregation has come to occupy in the religious life of the American Republic.

What, in brief, were the conditions in the United States to which Isaac Hecker returned in that spring day of 1858? A nation of over thirty millions of people numbered scarcely more than three million Catholics in its midst. And the fact that in that very decade of the 1850's nearly one million foreign-born Catholics had reached these shores as immigrants, accounted in no small measure for the suspicion and hostility shown toward those whose spiritual allegiance was centered in the Church of Rome. Just six years before there had emerged out of a secret society a formidable campaign against the Catholic Church and the foreign-born, a campaign that in the interval had mounted to dangerous

---

[1] Joseph McSorley, C.S.P., *Father Hecker and His Friends* (St. Louis, 1952); Vincent F. Holden, C.S.P., *Yankee Paul: Isaac Thomas Hecker* (Milwaukee, 1959). Only the first volume has so far appeared.

proportions in some states, and had deprived the Catholic bishops of Father Hecker's own State of New York of the right to hold church property in their name. Parallel with this ugly menace to Catholic rights and liberties a deeper and more fatal division in the American community was then rapidly overshadowing all other national concerns, for these were the days when the shrill cry of "bleeding Kansas," and the opening in the summer of 1858 of the Lincoln-Douglas debates in Illinois, heralded the advent of civil war over the issues of human slavery.

In an atmosphere such as this it required courage based upon something beyond mere human strength and natural means to embark upon so original and untried a course as that taken by Hecker and his three companion priests. It demanded steadfast determination in holding to an ideal born of divine faith and a supernatural vision, and these qualities Isaac Hecker had to a superlative degree. The sixty-nine years of life given to this extraordinary man were as rich in virtues as they were beneficent in achievements informed by the spirit of high ideals. Obviously, it is not possible to do justice to them all. I should like, therefore, to dwell upon what, it seems to me, was one of the most fruitful and enduring of the many lofty sentiments that occupied the minds of the Paulist founder and his associates for the spiritual progress of themselves and those for whom they conceived their mission, that is, their prime objective to bring the light of the Catholic faith to their fellow countrymen.

In a land steeped in prejudice against Catholicism an undertaking such as that conceived by the first Paulists was fraught with an unpleasant prospect and even a certain danger. Yet, who more than these men would have made their meditation and drawn inspiration from the life of him whom they had chosen as their heavenly patron, tho record of whose missionary career was filled with the perils that beset one who would carry Christ's message concerning His Church to those who knew it not? How many times must the Paulist founders have read and reread the epistles of Saint Paul, and how many times must they have asked themselves the same questions that the great apostle addressed to his converts at Rome concerning those whose minds were darkened by unbelief: ". . . how are they to hear," Saint Paul had asked, "if no one preaches? And how are men to preach unless they be sent? . . . [for] Faith . . . depends on hearing, and hearing on the word of Christ." [2]

[2] *Romans*, 10:14–15, 17.

Hecker and his associates realized that the price they would have to pay would be high, even if they did not always foresee the sharp edge of personal sacrifice which that payment would often entail. But they were heartened by the knowledge that Saint Paul's sacrifice and suffering had wrought incalculable good to innumerable souls of the ancient world who had been touched by the influence of his preaching. What, then, was to prevent them, after the fashion of their patron, from working a similar good for the Americans of their day? Difficulties there would be aplenty, but it was not for nought that Hecker had cherished and cultivated a special worship of the Third Person of the Blessed Trinity, and among the seven gifts that recompense a devotion to that source of divine wisdom is one called fortitude, a gift which has been defined as "a permanent power which the Holy Spirit communicates to our will to assist us in overcoming the difficulties which might deter us in the practice of what is right." [3]

Amid all the reverses of his early years Hecker had shown to a marked degree a fortitude of this kind, and through the thirty years that he served as first superior general of the Paulists this supernatural courage of their leader was one of the principal sources of support and inspiration upon which the young community leaned as it moved out upon its high adventure.

To a deep and thorough knowledge of the essentials of the spiritual life these first Paulists brought a unique qualification as missionaries to their non-Catholic fellow countrymen. Each had himself been a Protestant into his adult life, and in this they possessed an insight and appreciation of the American mind and religious temper that only an experience of this kind can give. Keenly aware that their fellow Catholics occupied the status of a small and often scorned minority, they sought, as it were, to build a bridge of understanding and brotherly love between the children of the Church and those not of their religious faith. That Father Hecker appreciated what the Catholics' isolation meant was made evident in a memorable essay that he had written while at Rome in the early winter of 1857. Seeking to portray the most attractive features of his native country for the critical audience of a learned Roman journal, he noted that the history of the Church revealed how

[3] Moritz Meschler, S.J., *The Gift of Pentecost. Meditations on the Holy Ghost* (St. Louis, 1903), p. 260.

264

many converts had for years sought the light before it broke upon them. He then said:

And this is particularly true of the United States, where the Catholic community, being for the most part composed of Europeans, are not so commingled with those born in America as to exert that intimate and established social influence which is so powerful to dissipate prejudice and to insinuate truth.[4]

Thus it was this advantage of their native American birth, of numerous close ties with prominent Americans of other religious beliefs, that the first Paulists realized could be turned to profit for the Church of their adoption. It was that same advantage, for example, that enabled Isaac Hecker to win as a close personal friend one of the greatest publicists of his time, Orestes A. Brownson, and six years after Brownson had entered the Church he told Father Hecker:

I am more indebted to you for having become a Catholic than to any other man under heaven. . . . I owe you a debt of gratitude I can never repay.[5]

And Brownson's testimony concerning what the friendship of Hecker had meant to him could be multiplied a hundredfold by uncounted Americans who had been either brought within the Catholic fold by this man of singular grace and his convert associates, or who had had dissipated from their minds the distorted image of the Church which had been their inheritance from childhood.

It is a strong temptation to follow the course of these valiant men as they worked out from their New York motherhouse at Ninth Avenue and Fifty-ninth Street, preaching parochial missions that spanned the continent, instructing and explaining in long and wearying consultation everything that touched the Church to the individual inquirer as well as to the large and attentive audiences that heard or read them in the pulpit, the public platform, or in the press. For from the very outset the Paulists put the highest premium upon the value of the written word in bearing witness for Christ. And from their informed pens there flowed a constant stream of books, articles, and religious tracts that reached

[4] New York *Freeman's Journal*, December 12, 1857, reprinted in translation from *La Civiltà Cattolica* of November 6, 1857.

[5] Brownson to Hecker, March 28, 1851, Vincent F. Holden, C.S.P., *The Early Years of Isaac Thomas Hecker, 1819–1844* (Washington, 1939), p. 89.

far and wide into the lives of those whom they could not reach in person. In the month that Appomattox brought to a close the long and bloody civil conflict there appeared the first issue of the *Catholic World*, the familiar monthly magazine that has endeared itself to so many readers, and which since that April of 1865 has gone on uninterruptedly spreading its message of enlightenment in the doctrines, practices, and cultural values of the Catholic faith.

One would wish to expand upon the bonds of close affection that were forged with the passing years between the Paulist Fathers and the bishops of the American Church, on significant events such as the bishops' choice of Hecker as one of only three priests honored to preach before the hierarchy's Second Plenary Council at Baltimore. Sensing as he did, the strain of the ordeal of the Civil War and the havoc that had followed in its wake for many of these bishops and their flocks, he sought in a vein that was characteristic of his buoyant spirit to lift their hearts to a new wisdom. Nowhere, said the preacher on that October day in 1866,

is there a promise of a brighter future for the Church than in our own country. Here, thanks to our American Constitution, the Church is free to do her divine work. Here, she finds a civilization in harmony with her divine teachings. Here, Christianity is promised a reception from an intelligent and free people, that will give forth a development of unprecedented glory.[6]

One thinks, too, of Father Hecker's trip to Rome in 1869 where he served at the Vatican Council, in the distinguished post of consulting theologian to the leader of the American hierarchy, Martin J. Spalding, Archbishop of Baltimore, and of the spiritual riches of the books that he wrote to advance the faith. And what is said of Hecker in this regard may be said as well of those who for a generation walked at his side and were proud to follow him as their religious leader.

But there is opportunity only to record the impression left by the life of this man and his associates upon two princes of the Church of the English-speaking world. In many ways Hecker's apostolate had paralleled that of a distinguished Englishman who had followed him into the Catholic fold a year and three months after Hecker's own conversion. They had much in common, these two, and such was the note struck by John Henry Cardinal Newman when, in learning of the

---

[6] *Sermons Delivered during the Second Plenary Council of Baltimore, October, 1866* . . . (Baltimore, 1866), p. 84.

Paulist founder's death, he sent his sympathy to Father Hewit. "I was very sorrowful at hearing of Father Hecker's death," said the great English cardinal,

I have ever felt that there was this sort of unity in our lives — that we had both begun a work of the same kind, he in America and I in England, and I know how zealous he was in promoting it. It is not many months since I received a vigorous and striking proof of it in the book he sent me [*The Church and the Age*]. Now I am left with one friend less, and it remains with me to convey through you my best condolement to all the members of your society.[7]

And if Cardinal Newman at so great a distance appreciated what Hecker had meant to the cause of religion in this country, how much more was that true of the only American cardinal of that day, James Gibbons of Baltimore? A decade after Hecker had gone to God a threatening shadow enveloped for a time his beloved community by reason of a false imputation relating to the founder's doctrine and good name. In that moment of anxiety and sorrow Cardinal Gibbons promptly threw the mantle of his powerful protection about the sons of Hecker in a letter meant for publication in which he said:

He was undoubtedly a providential agent for the spread of the Catholic faith in our country, and did immense good in drawing non-Catholics nearer to us, allaying prejudice, obtaining a fair hearing for our holy religion, besides directly making a multitude of converts. . . . Divine Providence associated with him a body of men animated by the same noble spirit.[8]

Few men knew better than the Cardinal of Baltimore how well the Paulist Fathers had imbibed the high and noble spirit of their founder, and how after his death they had carried on the work he had inaugurated thirty years before. When the Paulists' heavenly patron was a prisoner at Rome for the last time and the shadow of death had already gathered above him, in a final letter written to his disciple, Saint Timothy, he said:

my child, be strengthened in the grace which is in Christ Jesus; and the things that thou hast heard from me through many witnesses, commend to trustworthy men who shall be competent in turn to teach others.[9]

[7] Newman to Hewit, Birmingham, February 28, 1889, Walter Elliott, *The Life of Father Hecker* (New York, 1809), p. 422.

[8] Gibbons to Elliott, Baltimore, April 14, 1898, *Catholic World*, LXII (June, 1898), 428.

[9] *2 Timothy*, 2:1–2.

As Isaac Hecker lay dying at the New York motherhouse in that Christmas week of 1888 he could with the utmost sincerity have uttered these very words of Saint Paul to the grieving confrères who stood about his bedside. And it is the highest compliment that we can pay to the Paulist Fathers on their centennial to state that they have been true to the things that they have heard from Isaac Hecker through the many witnesses who have intervened during the seventy years that have passed since he departed their ranks. They have done more; they have commended these same eternal truths to trustworthy men, and today there come forward as witnesses to the fruit of their apostolate not only you, their friends of old Saint Mary's here on Wabash Avenue, where for fifty-five years they have ministered to your spiritual needs. But at Saint Paul's on New York's Fifty-ninth Street, on the fringes of Chinatown in San Francisco where at another old Saint Mary's they have been these sixty-odd years, and at the twelve other American parishes in their charge; from their trailer chapels in the Southland; at the forty-two Newman foundations where they witness to Christ on the campuses of secular colleges and universities; in the eight information centers in the heart of crowded and busy cities; in foreign stations at Toronto and in far off Johannesburg, as well as at the hospitable Church of Santa Susanna in the capital of Christendom. And marching close behind the more than 220 priests of this Congregation of St. Paul — a number that will be soon increased by fifteen newly ordained — come 150 or more other young Americans in the Paulist seminaries to swell the ranks of this apostolic body and to uphold and cherish the traditions of Isaac Hecker and his first three convert priests of a century ago.

In conclusion I confess to a certain uneasiness lest other good works of this noble company should have gone unmentioned. And yet the Paulist apostolate is too rich and varied a thing to assess in its entirety in so brief a time. May I, then, make bold to be your spokesman in extending to the Paulist Fathers our heartfelt felicitations and prayerful gratitude? In doing so I could scarcely do better than to wish for them in the years that lie ahead an ever-mounting success in bringing into the Catholic fold as many of our separated brethren as God shall will their ministry to reach. And if in the case of some that happy sequel should elude their efforts, then at least we pray that they may be strengthened and enlightened by the Holy Spirit to pursue their admirable Paulist ideal of making better known and understood to our non-Catholic fellow citizens what is this Church and what it says of itself, as Father Hecker envisioned a hundred years ago. In that respect you Paulists of the twentieth century will bring all Americans — Catholic and non-Catholic alike — a step nearer to the blessed reality of a day — distant though it may be — when in the language of Saint Paul it can be said of the great army who have felt the benign influence of your apostolate:

You are now no longer strangers and foreigners, but you are citizens with the saints and members of God's household; you are built upon the foundation of the apostles and prophets with Christ Jesus Himself as the chief cornerstone.[10]

[10] *Ephesians*, 2:19–20.

4 BENEDICTINA

SAINT JOHN'S: A LIVING TRADITION

In reflecting upon the honor that Saint John's University has called us to receive I am reminded of Dante's words in one of the opening cantos of the *Divine Comedy* after he had been offered the guidance of Virgil and the greetings of Homer, Horace, Ovid, and Lucan. Of these greatest of the poets of antiquity he said:

> They all with signs of welcome turned my way, . . .
> And greater honour yet they did me — yea,
> Into their fellowship they deigned invite
> And make me sixth among such minds as they.[1]

If I may presume to speak for my colleagues, as well as for myself, I would say to the Benedictines of Saint John's that, like Dante, we are deeply moved by the warmth of your welcome, but we are even more sensible of the greater honor you have done us in inviting us, as it were, into the fellowship of your noble company.

Over a half century ago a famous English Benedictine made a pilgrimage to a hallowed spot in the mountains some forty miles from Rome, and of that experience he later wrote:

One morning, in the early spring of the first year of the century, I was standing at a cave, looking out into the darkness that still enshrouded the scene. And as I looked the first streaks of dawn began gradually to lift the shroud of night and to reveal . . . the wild grandeur of the scene in its simplicity and solitude. And as the features of the landscape gradually took shape, my

[1] *The Comedy of Dante Alighieri the Florentine.* Translated by Dorothy L. Sayers [Penguin Books] (Harmondsworth, Middlesex, 1949), p. 94.

271

thoughts went back to a youth who just fourteen centuries before had passed the years of opening manhood in that cave. . . . And the thought of that youth, that boy, arose in my mind — what he could have been like, who had the courage and the strength to live for three years in that cave, feeding his young heart on God alone . . .[2]

The scene that meets our eyes on this spring morning fifty-seven years after the visit of Dom Cuthbert Butler to Subiaco is strikingly different in its physical contours, but the two share in that which is of incomparably more value than the stark beauty of the Apennine Mountains or the verdant prairies of the upper Mississippi Valley. They share the tradition of the youth in the cave, for both are the heirs of Saint Benedict of Nursia.

During the course of the centennial year of this great monastic foundation of the new world, eminent churchmen, distinguished educators, and prominent men of the world of business and the professions have been drawn to Saint John's where, in their several capacities, they have paid tribute to the remarkable record of achievement of this institution's first one hundred years. Virtually all of these men have alluded to the antiquity and richness of the Benedictine tradition as it has expanded and flourished since the father of western monasticism laid its foundations at Subiaco and Monte Cassino more than fourteen centuries ago. That this emphasis should have been a recurring theme in what they had to say, will come as no surprise to those who know something of the history of the monks of Saint Benedict. To such a one merely to speak the name "Benedict" is to summon the vision of an ancient heritage, an undying tradition, and a priceless history. And to know history is to appreciate what high and noble ideals have meant in terms of enduring value for Christian civilization, for an historic ideal, in the felicitous phrase of Robert Speaight, "breeds a respect for tradition and for the graces which are the gift of time."[3]

This is not the place to review the majestic sweep of the Benedictine centuries. Nor is it the occasion to retell the history of this particular abbey whose entrancing story has already been related with scholarly integrity and amplitude of detail by one of its own sons. In December, 1955, the gracious gentleman who presides over this abbey and university stated in a letter to the members of his community: "The purpose

[2] Cuthbert Butler, O.S.B., *Benedictine Monachism* (London, 1919), p. 1.
[3] "Australian Impressions," *The Tablet* (London), CCI (May 16, 1953), 415.

272

of the centennial celebration is to *rededicate ourselves* to our ideals as Benedictines, rather than to invite recognition."[4] Conscious as I am of the stern command of the blessed Benedict that "the first degree of humility is obedience without delay,"[5] I would beg the indulgence of Father Abbot on what is to follow since it is a recognition spontaneously offered rather than invited. To withhold such recognition on this occasion would be to deprive those of us who are not of the Benedictine family of the inspiration to be derived from even so inadequate a recounting of the graces and good works that have accompanied Saint John's first century.

Writing to the Romans about the year 57 of the salvation that awaited all men through a knowledge of the Son of God, Saint Paul asked:

How then are they to call upon him in whom they have not believed? But how are they to believe him whom they have not heard? And how are they to hear, if no one preaches? And how are men to preach unless they be sent?[6]

How, indeed, in any age are men to be saved unless those who possess the truths of divine revelation be sent to make them known? That was the question that filled the mind of Pope Gregory the Great when he sent Augustine and his monks to England a half century after Saint Benedict had gone to God; that was the question that pressed for an answer when Saint Benedict Biscop returned from Rome to Northumbria in the late seventh century to found the Abbeys of Wearmouth and Jarrow which, if they had done nothing else, would have earned their fame in Christian history by nourishing the lofty spirit of Saint Bede, the father of Britain's history and England's only doctor of the Church. That was the question that would permit no denial in the restless mind of Saint Boniface when he thought of the pagan Germans and finally won his commission to be sent to their aid and there to found the Abbey of Fulda in 741. And before the end of the same century the ever-recurring questions of Saint Paul inspired other monks to settle at Metten where they sowed so deeply in the soil of southern Germany the seed of Catholic belief that for over a thousand years it flourished,

[4] Abbot Baldwin Dworschak to his community, Collegeville, December 30, 1955, quoted in Colman J. Barry, O.S.B., *Worship and Work. Saint John's Abbey and University, 1856–1956* (Collegeville, 1956), p. 341.

[5] *St. Benedict's Rule for Monasteries.* Translated by Leonard J. Doyle (Collegeville, 1949), p. 18.

[6] *Romans*, X, 12–15.

withstanding even a cruel suppression only to be born anew and to play an active role in Bavaria's Catholic revival in the days of King Ludwig I.

And it was at Metten in the midst of that revival that there was conceived in the dreams of a young monk the idea that Benedictines should again be sent, this time to the young Republic of the West. As Saint Paul long before had heard in a vision the appealing cry of a man who said, "Come over into Macedonia and help us,"[7] so Father Boniface Wimmer could not still his anxiety at the disturbing news that reached him concerning his fellow Germans who had crossed the Atlantic to settle in the United States. "To us it cannot be a matter of indifference how our countrymen are situated in America," he wrote, and "I, for my part, have not been able to read the various and generally sad reports on the desolate conditions of Germans beyond the ocean without deep compassion and a desire to do something to alleviate their pitiable condition."[8] In less than a year that desire had been realized and the American Benedictine movement had been born in the little settlement in Westmoreland County, Pennsylvania. But once arrived in the new world, Wimmer's great and generous heart reached out to all who were in need wherever they might be. It was this expansive charity that moved him when he learned of the spiritual plight of immigrant communities here in Minnesota, and it was his courageous resolve to send monks to their relief — even before his own religious family was as yet solidly upon its feet — that brought the Benedictines to this upper Mississippi Valley slightly over a century ago.

It was, indeed, a bold thing to do in that year 1856 when the angry debate over "bleeding Kansas" had already foreshadowed the approach of civil conflict, and when the Know-Nothing Party, intent upon turning back every Catholic purpose, had only a few months before held its national convention and was in high hope of implementing its dark designs. And yet there were also promising omens upon the horizon of this new West to which Father Demetrius di Marogna and his four companions came on that May day of 1856. Less than two weeks before their arrival in Saint Paul the first railroad bridge to span the mighty Mississippi had opened between Davenport, Iowa, and Rock Island in Illi-

[7] *Acts*, XVI, 9.

[8] John Tracy Ellis (Ed.), *Documents of American Catholic History* (Milwaukee, 1956), p. 287.

nois, and four months after they reached Saint Cloud the Illinois Central Railroad completed its long and difficult route through the State of Illinois. Here were the outward symbols of a new era that was breaking for the American West, and the monks — to be followed in a year by their Benedictine sisters — were now at hand to mingle the civilizing influences of their ancient traditions amid the exciting prospects opening before the rough inhabitants of this rich heartland of the continent. If, as many have long believed, the expanding frontier is the key by which one may best interpret the realization of the American dream, it should be obvious that the frontier cannot be fully understood in terms solely of the farmer, the miner, the rancher, and the trapper. For if one omits the bishop, the priest, the monk, and the nun he has missed one of the most important sources out of which the civilization of western America evolved, and in this respect the Minnesota sons and daughters of Benedict and Scholastica hold a high and honored place.

In recent years salutary correctives have been given to this rather narrow American interpretation of the frontier, and nowhere with more cogency than in the presidential address of Carlton J. H. Hayes before the American Historical Association in December, 1945. Professor Hayes well said that this favorite theory of explaining America's past has been one of the most fruitful sources of intellectual isolationism in this country. Regardless of how successive generations of frontiersmen may have fancied themselves as exclusively American, they remained largely European in their thinking and their social customs. The frontier in the United States was never more than a transitory phenomenon, constantly changing from a primitive culture to the more mature and cultivated way of life that lay behind it. As Hayes remarked:

The abiding heritage of traditional civilization out-weighed, in a relatively brief period, the novelties acquired from Indians and wilderness. Continuity proved stronger than change. The transit of culture was not so much *from* as *to* the frontier.[9]

And in all of this movement and change from primitiveness to cultural maturity who, one may rightly ask, had more to offer than the Benedictines? Whose cultural background was a stronger dissolvent of intellectual isolationism than theirs? And who among all the varied groups on the frontier made a more lasting contribution to this western country

[9] Carlton J. H. Hayes, "The American Frontier — Frontier of What?" *American Historical Review*, LI (January, 1946), 206.

as we know it today than they, the conscientious heirs and transmitters of one of Christendom's oldest living traditions?

Even to those of us who have not had the advantage of being nurtured in the Benedictine tradition the familiar motto of the order, *Orare et laborare*, carries a wealth of meaning. Everything for which the Benedictines stand is summarized in those three simple Latin words. And to what manifold expressions these words have given life in the course of time! Thinking solely of the institution whose centennial we honor today, one is, in fact, almost baffled when called upon to summarize the ramifications of its spirit and the extent of its beneficent influence. I trust that you will pardon me, therefore, if I dwell upon only three of the major aspects of the good works that have emanated from this center of prayer and labor, a choice which, I regretfully confess, must leave untouched other worthy activities into which these Benedictines and their lay associates have channeled their energies over the years. To speak of all that they have done for the advancement of Church and State would be to trespass upon your patience and, perhaps, to submit the modesty of these men, which is one of their most endearing characteristics, to too great a strain.

The first of the three ways in which, in my judgment, Saint John's Abbey and University have made a notable contribution to the United States of their time is the high-born sense of obligation and service which they have shown from the outset toward the general community of which they form a part. To say that the pioneer monks found here a wilderness, is to state the obvious. Yet in the painful process of converting the crude forest and naked prairie into an attractive habitation for themselves, they never lost to view the welfare of the neighbors among whom they had come to live. Spiritual ministration to these rural settlers and their large families was, of course, their prime concern. But beyond the special service which they rendered through the consolations of religion — the just estimate of which is recorded only in eternity — they were alert to assist the frontiersman in his daily toil in order that these prairies might yield a richer harvest through the application of both the age-old art of farming which the Benedictines knew so well and the modern techniques in which American scientific genius was soon to lead the world. To speak, for example, of making bricks in the abbey kiln, of charting from the old observatory the uncertainties of the weather, of cultivating new types of fruit trees in the monastic garden, of maintaining a hatchery for fish, of instructing immigrant farm lads and Indian boys in the skills of carpentry — all these sound quite prosaic and, perhaps, a trifle quaint to modern urban ears. Yet it was in these wholesome pursuits that the monk — often a humble lay brother whose identity is probably lost to history — helped to raise from this wilderness a civilized settlement, and in so doing rendered an inestimable service for which hundreds of pioneer families through generations called his name blessed. In recollecting what they did, one is reminded of the description in which Cardinal Newman spoke of their predecessors of the early Middle Ages. To these monks of Minnesota, *mutatis mutandis*, there may fittingly be applied the words of Newman when he wrote:

Silent men were observed about the country, or discovered in the forest, digging, clearing, and building. . . . There was no one that 'contended, or cried out,' or drew attention to what was going on; but by degrees the woody swamp became a hermitage, a religious house, a farm, an abbey, a village, a seminary, a school of learning, and a city. Roads and bridges connected it with other abbeys and cities, which had similarly grown up; and what the haughty Alaric or fierce Attila had broken to pieces, these patient meditative men had brought together and made to live again.[10]

Moreover, in the carrying out of these tasks the monks bestowed — and are still bestowing — moral value upon American life of which it now stands in greater need than it did in an earlier age when work was more in honor. That is the concept of human labor as a sacred thing. A decade ago Pope Pius XII emphasized in his encyclical, *Fulgens radiatur*, how Saint Benedict had taught that lesson which, as the pontiff remarked, is today widely proclaimed but too often not properly reduced to practice. It is the lesson that labor, in the words of the Holy Father, "is not a distasteful and burdensome thing, but rather something to be esteemed, an honor and a joy." Reminding workers of all kinds that in earning their daily bread they are performing a noble task, Pius XII added that they are "not only providing for themselves and their best interests but (they) can be of service to the entire community." [11] Personally, I know of no group in the history of the American Church who has with more consistency and success held aloft the sacred dignity of labor, and through

[10] John Henry Newman, "The Mission of St. Benedict," *Historical Sketches* (New York, 1912), II, 410.

[11] *Encyclical Letter of Pope Pius XII on St. Benedict of Nursia* [N.C.W.C. edition] (Washington, 1947), p. 16.

the practical execution of that ideal bestowed upon their fellow citizens a greater service, than the monks of Saint John's Abbey. In this respect the revered command of their ancient founder has been linked with what was one of the most salient features of life on the American frontier in a combination that has produced the happiest results.

That Saint Benedict should have had much to say in his famous rule concerning labor and prayer, but little of study, has puzzled many men who are conscious of what is owed to his great order by the world of learning. I shall say no more about the matter than to remark that to know Benedict's own era and the transformation that came over the subsequent ages is to understand what might otherwise seem a curious departure from the *magna carta* of the monks. That the Benedictines were the principal preservers of ancient learning during the turbulent centuries that followed Benedict's death, and that their monasteries became the very citadels of scholarship down to modern times, is too well known to bear repetition. The single name of Jean Mabillon may stand here for what is meant. I wish merely to indicate that as heirs of this glorious tradition the monks of Saint John's have been faithful to their heritage, and that the creditable record of their first century has not only been continued but surpassed by the progress they have made within the memory of living men.

It was scarcely more than six months after their advent to Minnesota in 1856 that the Benedictines opened in a small frame building the first school in the city of Saint Cloud. And once they had received the state's authorization in March, 1857, for an institution of higher learning they lost no time in getting underway what was to become the oldest college in continuous existence in the Northwest. In the ensuing years the educational efforts of these men took a variety of forms. But it is not their variety of which I should like to speak. It is rather the spirit that informed this effort and the manner in which the pursuit of the things of the mind were made to blend, and at times to challenge, the rapidly changing pattern of American educational thought.

Every friend of Saint John's knows and rejoices in the fact that for some years now it has had far more applicants for admission than it could accommodate. This is, surely, a gratifying situation which bespeaks the confidence of a growing number of Catholic parents and their sons in the kind of education that is imparted here. Yet in spite of this increasing pressure one can detect in Collegeville no frantic efforts, as is true of too many American colleges and universities today, to enlarge facilities in order to absorb this surplus. That serious thought has been given at Saint John's to future expansion is altogether true, but it has progressed in the measured pace of men who look out upon the educational world of our day from the vantage point of fourteen hundred years of service in this cause and who are not, therefore, to be hurried. In other words, this university has not been put in a state of panic by what Dr. Harold W. Dodds, President of Princeton University, has called "the awesome challenge of numbers." [12] Loyal to the majestic cultural tradition of the Benedictine centuries, Saint John's realizes that to sacrifice quality of intellect to quantity of numbers would be to jeopardize the ultimate objective upon which it has always fixed its vision. For this generation is only slowly, and with great difficulty, learning what of late some of the most distinguished scientists have been at pains to tell us, that it is the man who is at once a sterling character, a cultivated mind, and a person whose background has been enriched by a broad and deep contact with the classic learning of western Christendom who is best equipped to cope with the vexing problems of an atomic age. No one who has any knowledge of the manner in which a Benedictine abbey conducts its business would say that democracy is foreign to its affairs. The abbot, it is true, is master and rules for life, but he is also the father of a family that has a voice in shaping its own destinies. Yet the Benedictines of Saint John's, alive to the cherished values of democracy in the government of a religious community, a state, or a nation, have never been so rash as to confuse an ideal of government in these realms with the standards that should obtain in higher education. It is no disparagement of American youth, nor is it a yielding to the lure of snobbery, to say that the Creator never intended that every youngster coming forth from the high schools of this land should be either capable of or entitled to a college education. As Benjamin F. Wright, President of Smith College, told his trustees a little over a year ago:

To talk of a liberal college education for all, or for half, of those from 17 to 22 is sentimental and dangerous nonsense. To advocate an education for all in accordance with their capacities and the country's needs is sober sense. [13]

[12] New York *Times,* September 24, 1956.
[13] *Newsweek,* February 6, 1956.

And that, as far as I have been able to observe, has been the enlightened policy to which this university has subscribed in this, the most vibrant and productive generation of its life.

A second characteristic of the intellectual life of this institution which is worthy of note is the steady manner in which it has withstood the temptation to pervert the true purpose of a university by a capitulation to the menacing shadow of vocationalism and professionalism. No one of sound mind would for a moment question that vocational and professional training are in themselves legitimate and even necessary parts of the general educational processes of our time. But they are not the primary responsibility of universities, and even less so of the college of liberal arts. Whenever a university or a liberal arts college enters upon the expensive and dissipating effort called for in these fields it inevitably lessens its chance to fulfill with distinction the function for which it was created. That this has been the conscious practice of Saint John's University was made clear more than twenty years ago. In response to a question from the United States Commissioner of Education concerning the provision made here in the teacher training program for a course in radio and movie appreciation, the late Abbot Alcuin Deutsch replied:

I beg to state that I think such special courses an unwarranted waste of time and money. If the general education that the future teacher gets does not fit him to give his pupils sufficient education and instruction to appreciate the radio and motion picture, then it is not likely that a special course in appreciation of radio and motion pictures will equip him.[14]

That, I submit, was the language of a university president who understood what true education means.

A third point that I should like to make regarding the educational ideals that have motivated this instituion is what I might call the atmosphere of respect for learning that has been inculcated on this campus. There has been constant encouragement of athletics, as there should be, but they have never been permitted to become a paramount interest. Secondly, a premium has been placed upon the specialized training necessary for the proper conduct of a university, a fact which is evidenced by the variety and high quality of graduate degrees represented on this faculty, and by the increasing number of the students of these men who have caught their spirit and in rigorous competition

[14] Abbot Alcuin Deutsch to John W. Studebaker, Collegeville, May 4, 1936, quoted in Barry, *op. cit.*, p. 285.

earned scholarships and fellowships for graduate study in universities both here and abroad.

In another way this atmosphere of respect for learning has made itself felt, even if it has not, perhaps, been so well known nor manifested in so tangible a form. It is the spirit of self-criticism and healthy inquiry that has characterized many of the professors of Saint John's. It is my deep conviction that in this particular our American Catholic institutions have been sadly deficient in comparison to the secular universities and colleges of the land. Yet almost twenty years ago the voice of a professor of this university was raised in recognition of this basic requirement of true learning, that is, of the need for application of the critical faculty to whatever one does. Recently, it is true, there have been encouraging signs in Catholic circles of a growth in this wholesome kind of self-scrutiny. It should not be forgotten, however, that it was the lamented Father Virgil Michel who called for this essential to sound scholarship long before much was heard of it elsewhere.[15] It would be idle to pretend that Dom Michel's mature and enlightened approach met with universal response, even within his own community. But it would be equally false to say that this extraordinary man did not leave the strong imprint of the ideal he so courageously expressed upon this university. And if there should be any need to adduce proof that the Benedictines of Saint John's have never allowed their ancient and sublime tradition to dominate their thinking to the degree that they have remained out of touch with the realities of modern life, that the dead weight of the past has prevented them from fulfilling their role as men of the twentieth century, it is to be found in this divine discontent, this remarkable alertness that they have displayed to look at themselves critically so that they might keep their university abreast of every worthwhile development that contemporary life has to offer.

On this campus likewise, insofar as I am aware, even the more subtle forms of anti-intellectualism have found no welcome. The monks and their lay associates have too keen an appreciation of what scholarship means and they have entertained too deep a respect for the things of the mind to indulge in a betrayal of this kind. For these men have known, and they have taught their students, the value of an idea ex-

[15] Cf. Virgil Michel, O.S.B., "Let's Examine Ourselves," *Catholic Educational Review*, XXXVI (February, 1938), 65–77; and "Catholic Leadership and the College," *Orate Fratres*, X (November, 1935), 22–27.

pressed by the Cardinal Archbishop of Chicago:

A mere reflection shows how important and even imperative are profound scholars. They have a duty and responsibility in giving to society a recognition of its highest needs. To belittle the scholar is to belittle man. To fail in a society to cultivate profound scholarship is failing to make its civilization worthy of a 'homo sapiens.'[16]

In a word, Saint John's University has conducted the grave and sacred mission upon which it was launched a century ago in a spirit of reverence for the intellect, of respect for the past, of responsibility to the present, and above all, of profound love of God and consciousness of the ultimate meaning of life. This is a university with a definite religious faith, and it has been the goal of religion on this campus to fashion in its students a philosophy which, as its published statement of aims informs us, "is sensitive to the sacramental nature of Christianity and to the personal and social obligations arising from membership in the Mystical Body of Christ."[17] Nor has that purpose remained a hidden and empty phrase in Saint John's *Bulletin*; rather it has been the vital and informing principle upon which it has operated from the beginning. I know no better way to convey something of the manner in which it has achieved its aim than to say that, in my judgment, it has realized to a remarkable degree the ideal of which Christopher Dawson wrote in these words:

The greater is our knowledge of nature and man and history, the greater is the obligation to use these increased resources for God, not merely in the way of moral action, but intellectually also, by the re-interpretation of the tradition of Christian culture in terms of the new knowledge, and by relating the instruments of culture to their true spiritual end.[18]

If in what has already been said of this Benedictine century in terms of labor and study it has seemed necessary to offer apology for certain omissions, how much more relevant is such an expression of regret when one turns to the third and final aspect of life at Saint John's, namely, that of worship and prayer! We do not need to be told that through-

[16] Address of His Eminence, Samuel Cardinal Stritch, before the annual meeting of the Catholic Commission for Intellectual and Cultural Affairs, Chicago, April 27, 1957. N.C.W.C. News Release.

[17] *The Saint John's University Bulletin*, LXXXVIII (1956–1958), 7.

[18] Christopher Dawson, *Understanding Europe* (New York, 1952), p. 253.

out the history of the abbey and university this has been the inspiration of the other two, for without the spiritual motivation that has given energy and direction to the good works of willing hands and devoted minds the fire that was lighted here a hundred years ago might, indeed, have long since flickered and gone out amid the reverses and vicissitudes of time. From the first catechism lesson taught in the primitive school of 1856 down to the impressive manifestation of a mature and enlightened national movement witnessed here in the Liturgical Week of 1957, the cultivation in men's souls of the heavenly graces has been a major aim of Benedictine endeavor. Formed as they have been in the ancient rule of Saint Benedict that has endowed them with intimate knowledge and joy in the things of God, these monks have sought in every way that lay open to them to spread the glad tidings and thus to uplift the souls of other men and to share with them the divine wisdom which is theirs. As Saint Paul once told the Corinthians, so they have told all Americans and others who would listen to them, "God, who commanded light to shine out of darkness, has shone in our hearts, to give enlightenment concerning the knowledge of the glory of God, shining on the face of Christ Jesus." [19]

In the imparting of that knowledge, solidified by their personal participation in the holy sacrifice of the Mass, in the singing of God's praises in the divine office, and in the meditation and mortification that are their daily practice, they have recognized no barrier of frontier, of race, or of creed. When, for example, in 1891 a call reached them from the distant Bahama Islands they did not hesitate to sacrifice the services of valued confreres to be sent upon that arduous mission, any more than a decade ago did they falter when asked to share their growing manpower and resources in behalf of the pagan Japanese, the Puerto Ricans, and, too, the Catholics of Mexico weakened by the evil inheritance of years of civil proscription. Fidelity to Christ's mandate, and to their order's splendid record in its execution — the mandate, that men must be sent to preach His name — has therefore, carried the Minnesota Benedictines beyond the frontiers of the United States into Asia, Latin America, the British possessions in the Caribbean, as well as over the border into Canada. Likewise the dictate of Christian charity that we should have a special love for our own, has been the compelling motive for the relief afforded by this abbey through the years to beleagured

[19] II Corinthians, IV, 6.

Benedictines encompassed by debts and administrative difficulties as far away as Manila in the Philippines, in Oklahoma, in Colorado, and in neighboring North Dakota.

Another of the varied religious works that has characterized Saint John's first century calls, it seems to me, for special comment. For in this there have been achieved at once a sacred task of singular difficulty and a notable contribution toward the ultimate solution of what is probably the gravest social problem haunting the American people in this hour. I refer to the monks' accomplishment in what is commonly termed the field of race relations. To the Benedictines of Minnesota, men of a race different from their own have been no novelty, for since that November day in 1878 when Father Aloysius Hermanutz departed for the White Earth Reservation to launch a career of over half a century among the Indians they have expended generously of their spiritual and material substance in behalf of the red man, a fact of which we were again reminded six months ago when the veteran Indian missionary and patriarch of this religious family, Father Thomas Borgerding, departed this life in his ninety-sixth year, of which sixty had been spent with the red men.

Yet trying as the Indian missions have often been, they have never presented problems of quite the same delicacy and acuteness that confront the man of God who endeavors to offer the charity of Christ as a true dissolvent of the rancor that has stained so many unhappy chapters in the white man's relations with his colored brother. In his encyclical, *Sertum laetitiae*, to the American hierarchy in November, 1939, Pope Pius XII confessed that he felt "a special paternal affection" for the Negroes of this country since, as he said, "in the field of religion and education We know they need special care and comfort and are very deserving of it."[20] That special care and comfort have been afforded for many years in this mother abbey where white and black Benedictines have gone about their round of prayer and study and labor in fraternal harmony. But what is more remarkable is the foundation that Saint John's made in 1948 in the form of an interracial monastery — the first in the United States — at Saint Maur's Priory at South Union, Kentucky. There on the border of the southland Americans of every creed and class have witnessed the success that has attended an

[20] Ellis, *op. cit.*, p. 654.

enterprise suffused with the kind of love that Christ bade us to have for one for another.

True, these are but a few of the more striking manifestations of the zeal of this religious family. One thinks as well of the ten archbishops and bishops, and of the nearly 1,700 priests, of the American Church who proudly call Saint John's their *alma mater*, of the lay retreats in which hundreds of souls have been brought closer to God in this hallowed spot, of the thriving parishes in Saint Paul, New York, and other cities where the sons of Saint John's minister to a busy urban world far removed from the quiet of their monastery, of the thousands of guests — among whom have been a conspicuous number of our separated brethren — who through the years have made their way to this holy house and have found during their brief sojourn here not only the peace which is inscribed above its portal, but the literal fulfillment of the blessed Benedict's command, "Let all guests who arrive be received like Christ, for He is going to say, 'I came as a guest, and you received Me.'"[21] Here, too, countless devout souls have benefited from the instruction of the liturgical summer schools, an experience that has sent them away with an understanding of the depth of meaning and the richness of inspiration of the Mass and the other acts of worship that they had never known before. Through this medium, but even more through the monthly journal, *Orate Fratres* now called *Worship*, and the other numerous publications of the abbey's Liturgical Press, millions of American Catholics have by now been touched by the liturgical movement inaugurated here a generation ago by Abbot Alcuin and Father Virgil. And if they have received the recent liturgical changes commanded by the Holy See with enthusiasm and understanding it is owed in no small measure to the intelligent guidance in these matters which for a genera tion has emanated from this center. It has been said, and I think rightly, that the American Church has now come of age, and in this respect one of the surest signs of this dawning maturity is the expanding influence of this movement. A hundred years from now some historian of the Church in the United States will probably write afresh its inspiring story, and when that time comes he may well assign the promotion of true liturgical worship as Saint John's most significant contribution to American Catholicism in the twentieth century.

[21] *St. Benedict's Rule* . . . . p. 72.

When in retrospect one looks back upon the record of this venerable abbey — for in young America a century bestows that title — of its varied and beneficent works, of its solid contributions to scholarship and to the deeper meaning and enhanced dignity of religious worship, of its manifold services to the general community, one senses what Cardinal Newman felt as he surveyed its sister abbeys of the distant centuries. "Ancient houses such as these," he said

subdue the mind by the mingled grandeur and sweetness of their presence. They stand in history with an accumulated interest upon them, which belongs to no other monuments of the past.[22]

Saint John's has, to be sure, compiled a record of which its sons, and all American Catholics, may well be proud. Yet it has not been an utterly spotless record, for these monks and their associates have now and then been prey to the human faults and errors that at times mar the lives of every one of us. If we know that to have been at times the case with them, it is but further evidence of the basic integrity and devotion to truth that govern all they do, for they have not in a squeamish spirit hidden from the world the few untoward events and episodes which here and there have left upon their history the mark of human frailty. The candid publication of these frailties in their midst has only earned them a stronger title to our confidence and affection.

As Saint John's Abbey and University approach the close of their centennial year the ancient Benedictine tradition is here, as we have said, still a living reality. But the men who conduct their destinies are also tremendously alive to the challenge of the present age. It would be difficult, I think, to demonstrate that point with more effect, to show, in other words, how beautifully there has been blended in this institution the sacred traditions of which it is the heir with the daring of contemporary thought than to cite an action of four years ago. It was as a consequence of the determination to embark upon the ambitious undertaking of a new abbey church that Abbot Baldwin and his community revealed how thoroughly up to date they really are. Addressing himself to twelve famous architects whose artistic talents he invited to participate in designing the proposed church, the abbot said: "The Benedictine tradition at its best challenges us to think boldly and to cast our ideas in forms which will be valid for centuries to come."[23] As a result we have

[22] Newman, *op. cit.*, pp. 389–390.
[23] Abbot Dworschak to architects, Collegeville, March 7, 1953, quoted in Barry, *op. cit.*, p. 337.

today the startling and original design of Marcel Breuer which, I think, symbolizes as nothing else I know the modern spirit of Saint John's and offers a guarantee that here no slavish adherence to the past will obstruct the path of progress. In summary, it symbolizes the fact that on this campus the past and the present meet in friendly converse, and that by the mingled contributions of these two streams of thought Saint John's teaches to all Americans the lesson of the reconciliation of what is of priceless merit in its ancient heritage with the fresh and imaginative approach that our age brings to all it does.

Before we bid farewell, then, to you, this immense Benedictine family of nearly 400 men, we extend our heartfelt congratulations on the century that is closing, and we can hardly do more than to wish for you and your successors in the century that lies ahead an equally rich return from your prayerful labors. Long before the next hundred years will have run their course you Benedictines of today and we, your friends and guests, will have passed away. May each of you meanwhile have been given the grace of perseverance to the end after the manner of Saint Bede, who with almost his last breath dictated the closing words of his translation of the Gospel of Saint John, knowing that this final earthly effort would be pleasing in God's sight. And as you approach that inevitable hour may each of you experience the fulfillment of the great English doctor's lovely prayer that, having in life drunk in with delight the words of heavenly knowledge, you may be granted, as Bede asked of Christ, "to attain to thee, the fountain-head of all wisdom, and to stand for ever before thy face." [24] And may we, your friends and admirers, beg the saving grace of your prayers in our behalf so that at the end our feet, too, may be set upon the royal road seen in the luminous vision of the two monks on the day that Saint Benedict died. Thus with your help, secure and confident of the goal of that brilliant highway that reached upward toward the sky, we may be vouchsafed a share in the promise of that vision and see the majestic figure who will ask of each of us, "Do you know who passed this way?" And when we answer 'no,' that we may hear him say, "This is the road taken by blessed Benedict, the Lord's beloved, when he went to heaven." [25]

[24] Venerable Bede, *The Ecclesiastical History of the English People*. Translated by Thomas Stapleton; edited by Philip Herford (London, 1935), p. 336.

[25] *Life and Miracles of St. Benedict. (Book Two of the Dialogues) by Pope St. Gregory the Great*. Translated by Odo J. Zimmermann, O.S.B., and Benedict R. Avery, O.S.B. (Collegeville, 1949), p. 75.

YOU ARE THE LIGHT OF THE WORLD

You are the light of the world. A city set on a mountain cannot be hidden.
. . . Even so let your light shine before men, in order that they may see
your good works and give glory to your Father in heaven. (*Matthew*, V, 14–
16).

He comes with more than fourteen hundred years of history behind
him. No tradition of the western world — except the sacred heritage
which is the special possession of the Universal Church — is more richly
laden with the wisdom of the centuries than is that of Saint Benedict
and his descendants. So extraordinary was the contribution of the black
monks to the Christian civilization of the West that what historians
have at times called the "dark ages" was with more appropriateness,
perhaps, termed by Cardinal Newman the "Benedictine centuries." Of
no other religious order in the Church can this be said, for the Benedictines were present at the birth of western civilization, if they did not,
indeed, give to it its first breath of life.

The blessing of a Benedictine abbot is no ordinary event in the religious life of an ecclesiastical jurisdiction. It is understandable, therefore, if the Archdiocese of Washington takes pride in this ceremony as
the formal inauguration in its see city of the regime of the first abbot of
the national capital. He has been set to rule over the Abbey of Saint
Anselm which, we prayerfully hope, may for ages to come shed increasing luster upon the religious and intellectual life of this community.
That this abbey may flourish with the brightness that once shone
from Monte Cassino and Bec and Canterbury and numerous other noted
predecessors, of which it is the most recent offspring and of which it is
the heir to the treasures of the fourteen centuries that have passed since
Benedict went to God, is our sincere and heartfelt prayer for its monks
on this day that will ever remain one of the most memorable in their
history.

If the Abbey of Saint Anselm brings to Washington, and to the unique
assembly of houses of religious and intellectual formation which constitute its immediate neighbors, an ancient tradition which every enlightened Catholic values highly, so does Washington offer to the new
abbot and his monastic family an environment that, in terms of the relatively young United States, is not without its own historic significance.

288

Here in this archdiocese was born John Carroll, the first American bishop; here as a cherished part of his diocese is the spot where he lived as a priest with his mother upon his return from Europe in 1774, and here is the hallowed ground where she lies buried. Thus two traditions — the ancient Benedictine and the young American — meet in this place, and since 1924 when Saint Anselm's community had its beginning, these traditions have blended in the religious formation of the young men who have presented themselves as candidates to be fashioned according to Benedict's holy rule by masters of the spiritual life of whom many have been English-born.

In truth, the Benedictine and American traditions had met at a much earlier time when John Carroll chose to receive episcopal consecration in August, 1790, at the hands of the English Benedictine, Charles Walmesley, at Lulworth Castle in Dorsetshire not many miles from where the Douai community of Saint Gregory's would in less than a quarter century lay the foundations of Downside Abbey. From contacts made while in England at this time Bishop Carroll had been led to anticipate that he might have the black monks in his diocese, for in a letter to Father Michael Pembridge at Dorking in Surrey four years later the Bishop of Baltimore remarked:

nothing can be more pleasing to me than the prospect of having in my diocese a settlement of English Benedictines. I will not enter now into the reasons of my attachment and veneration for them: suffice to say, that I trust in God they will honour and extend religion; and that I never can forget that they were the apostles of England, Germany & many other countries. . . . I have now only to pray earnestly and sincerely to God, that He may not suffer this prospect to be delusive, but that it may be realized, to the great advantage of my diocese.[1]

In the sequel the first American bishop's hope remained unfulfilled, although by a curious coincidence Carroll's suggestion to the English monk of the neighborhood of Pittsburgh as the most proper place for a foundation and a school was realized in the location of the first permanent house of Benedictines in the United States when Father Boniface Wimmer and his companions from the Abbey of Metten in Bavaria settled there in 1846.

That the nation's capital should have profited for the past thirty-seven

[1] Carroll to Pembridge, Baltimore, September 19, 1794, photostat, Manuscript Collections, University of Notre Dame.

years from the presence of the Benedictines, was at the outset due in no
small measure to the prayer, the imagination, and the initiative of one
of the most noted professors ever to teach in the Catholic University
of America. In the person of Father Thomas Verner Moore there was
combined to a remarkable degree the twin ideal aptly expressed in the
title of a recent Benedictine book as "the love of learning and the desire
for God." [2] Dom Moore's training as a psychologist was not intended
to make him a specialist in ecclesiastical history; yet as a man of cultivated mind he was no stranger to the magnificent tradition of learning
that had once flourished in the Order of Saint Benedict among groups
like the Maurists of the Abbey of Saint Germain des Près in Paris, as
well as in the more recent scholarly endeavors of the monks of San Ger-
onimo in Scripture, of Beuron in art, of Solesmes in sacred music, to say
nothing of the splendid impression made by the English-speaking Benedictines in their native university world in the record of Ampleforth's
monks at Oxford, of the sons of Downside at Cambridge, and those of
Fort Augustus at the University of Edinburgh of whom Abbot Alban
is himself a conspicuous example.

It was to the same Abbey of Fort Augustus in Scotland, where Saint
Anselm's new abbot received his monastic training, that Father Moore
and his associates went for their initiation into Benedictine life, returning to Washington in September, 1924, where in temporary quarters
they opened the second foundation in this country of the monks of the
English Congregation. For nearly twenty years their numbers and resources permitted them to do no more than to hold several professor-
ships and lectureships in the university, to lend assistance now and then
in the city's parishes, and to give spiritual direction to individual souls
who sought their counsel. But by 1942 Saint Anselm's community had
grown to the point where it felt warranted in embarking upon the activity that has ever since been one of its principal concerns, namely, the
conducting of a select preparatory school for boys. The Priory School
has steadily gained in strength and prestige until today it is recognized
by all discerning judges as one of the leading private secondary schools
of the American Church, and though still hardly more than an infant in
age with only sixteen graduating classes behind it, a total of 303 boys

[2] Jean Leclercq, O.S.B., *The Love of Learning and the Desire for God* (New
York, 1961; paperback, 1962).

have met its exacting standards, of whom a number have already distinguished themselves in colleges of their choice.

That the Priory School has achieved an honored place among American secondary schools received striking proof last year when of five National Merit Scholarships bestowed on students in the District of Columbia, three were won by its graduates. Perceptive parents have long since sensed that in the balanced moral and intellectual training imparted by the Benedictines and their lay masters there is to be found both a wholesome respect for traditional values in education as well as an open-mindedness concerning every modern pedagogical advance that gives promise of improving the mind. In this respect the monks of the Priory School have practiced the moderation and good sense that marked the educational career of their heavenly patron, and which was illustrated on one occasion when a neighboring abbot complained to Saint Anselm of his inability to make a success of his school. "Tell me, my lord Abbot, I pray you," said Saint Anselm,

were you to plant a young tree in your garden, and so hem it in betimes on every side as to prevent its stretching forth its branches . . . what sort of tree would it then grow into? Useless timber, of course, with gnarled and crooked branches. And . . . no one would be to blame but you, who had gone to such extremes with your restraints upon it. Surely this is what you are doing with your boys . . . and the consequence of all this indiscriminating repression is that they contract such a base — what shall I say? — such a crooked moral habit as reminds one of the tangled branches of a thorn tree. . . .[3]

Priory School students have in general shown that they know how to respond properly to the kind of freedom of which Saint Anselm spoke, as their later careers have likewise demonstrated the wisdom of their Benedictine masters in refusing to be swept along with the current of mass education by lowering academic requirements in order to admit larger numbers. Nor have they beguiled themselves with the false belief that in the quantity of their patrons there was mirrored the progress of their school. From its inception this has been an institution intended for a limited number, since the monks have held the conviction that the highest quality of intellectual training cannot be imparted by teachers whose time and energy are exhausted in a daily struggle with more students than they can properly instruct.

[3] Martin Rule, *The Life and Times of St. Anselm* (London, 1883), I, 148.

Behind the success that has attended the Priory School, as behind the achievements in higher education of the five monks of Saint Anselm who at present are members of the faculty of the Catholic University of America, and of their predecessors at the same university, there lies, to be sure, something beyond mere intellectual prowess. It is the solid spiritual doctrine of Saint Benedict that for centuries has nourished the uncounted thousands who have dwelt within the Order's worldwide network of abbeys, priories, and convents. For if any single characteristic of Benedictine spirituality recommends itself to our sophisticated twentieth-century it is the patriarch's eminent sanity and moderation in all things. So sane, in fact, was he that though his Order has undergone numerous reforms and been the parent to many and varying offspring, it has never been Saint Benedict's own holy rule that has had to change so much as it has been man's interpretation and observance of it. That is why these monks of the Abbey of Saint Anselm, like their Benedictine brothers and sisters everywhere, have a sturdy staff upon which to lean in the trials and troubled circumstances that are a part of the life of every man. That is what makes them so modern and up-to-date while at the same time they cling to what is so very old. For as a well-known Benedictine has recently said:

it is the future which a monk has in mind when he searches the past. He is rooted in tradition, not to copy it, but to live by it. He cannot live by it as long as he does not understand it. This is what makes him a historian. A man of the present, he searches the past that he may better witness to the truth of the life he has embraced forever.[4]

In that spirit Abbot Alban and his monastic family of Saint Anselm will have their eyes trained upon the past, that the priceless heritage that Benedict and Augustine of Canterbury and Bede and Anselm and all the others have passed on to them may never be tarnished while in their keeping. But as they scan the past they will improve the future, both for themselves and for those who are committed to their care. The new Abbey of Saint Anselm does not, it is true, rise to the height of a city set on a mountain such as was described by our blessed Lord in the Sermon on the Mount. Yet, on its little hillside there to the east of us it does rise above the common level of men in the light that has shone from the good works of its five priors — one of whom, we are happy to say, is with us today in the person of Abbot Wulstan Knowles — and

[4] Damasus Winzen, O.S.B., in foreword to Leclercq, *op. cit.*, p. x.

of their devoted subjects over the last thirty-seven years. These sons of Saint Benedict have, indeed, let their light shine before men, whether that be in the classrooms of the Priory School or in the lecture halls of the university, in their books and learned articles, and above all, in the example of their priestly lives. Thus there has been a steady procession of good works that have come forth from the Benedictines of Washington, works that have been motivated and performed in no spirit of personal vainglory, but, rather, in the monks' dedication of all that they have done to the glory of their Father in heaven.

In conclusion we could not do better, I believe, than to wish for the gracious gentleman upon whom there is being placed the formal blessing of his exalted office here this morning, that the light that has shone into the lives of each of us who have been fortunate enough to have been touched by his exemplary priestly bearing during the fifteen years that he has dwelt among us — that this light may grow brighter as the years go on. For if the light of an inner spiritual and intellectual fire shines from the abbot it will reflect itself in the lives of his monks and of all who come within the sway of his influence until, as Saint Paul told the Corinthians in the Mass of the last Sunday of Advent, "the Lord comes, who will both bring to light the things hidden in darkness, and make manifest the counsels of hearts."[5] May we, therefore, express our wishes for you, Father Abbot, on this day of your solemn blessing in a paraphrase of the words addressed nearly 900 years ago by your abbey's patron on the occasion of the consecration of his beloved friend and master, Lanfranc, as Archbishop of Canterbury. In that letter of 1070 Saint Anselm quoted the passage from Saint Matthew concerning the light shining from the lampstand with which we began this sermon, and he then said to Lanfranc — as we say to you:

And so we pray to Almighty God that it may so burn as not to be consumed; may it so give light to others that it may itself never be extinguished. That after the long sharing of your light with the Americans, it may be carried to an eternal participation in the divine light with the angels.[6]

[5] I Corinthians, IV, 5.
[6] Saint Anselm to Lanfranc, Anselm R. Pedrizetti, O.S.B. (Ed.), "Letters of Saint Anselm and Archbishop Lanfranc," American Benedictine Review, XII (December, 1961), 440.

LIVE AS FREEMEN

Such is the will of God, that by doing good you should put to silence the ignorance of foolish men. Live as freemen, yet not using your freedom as a cloak for malice but as servants of God (1 Peter 2:15–16).

If today mankind may be said to have a besetting passion, it would not be far wrong to say that it is the desire for freedom. The profound stirrings that have shaken the continent of Africa during the past decade are, perhaps, the most striking and large scale example of this characteristic of contemporary society. It was the same impulse that provided the driving force behind the brief and tragic uprising that broke over Budapest in the last days of October, 1956, and that for one short week focused the world's admiration on the courageous struggle of the Hungarian people to be free from the Communist despotism that had crushed their authentic national life. For many in our own country the crusade for freedom has taken the form of a preoccupation with the extension and enlargement of civil rights. The desire for freedom is, of course, a phenomenon that in one form or another is as old as man's time on this earth, and until the end of time it will continue to leave its mark on human history, for its roots lie deeply imbedded in the very nature of man, and its impulse cannot and will not be denied.

Freedom has been interpreted in a great variety of ways, but one of the simplest and most direct statements of how it can be acquired and retained at the highest level, was that given by the Son of God when He told the apostles at the last supper that if they abided in His word (that is, in the way of life that He had taught them) they would know the truth — to which Christ added, "and the truth shall make you free." [1] In other words, our Lord did not conceive freedom primarily in negative terms, that is, as a condition that would set men at liberty *from* something. Rather it was a state wherein, if properly lived, man would be enabled to gain a positive objective, in this case, the greatest of all objectives, eternal life.

I do not wish, however, to devote the time allotted to me during this baccalaureate Mass to a discourse on the nature of human freedom. I should prefer to propose for the consideration of you graduates a single

[1] *John*, 8:32.

aspect of your status as freemen, and the responsibilities which that status implies. For although it is unquestionably true that freedom presupposes rights, it is likewise true that it imposes upon the disciplined and civilized mind certain responsibilities. Most of us Americans enjoy freedom to so marked a degree that it has made us the object of envy on the part of our fellowmen in every corner of the world. But of late there have appeared in the land such signs of flagrant violation of the duties that are owed to a society of freemen as to suggest the presence among us of an inner corruption that may, indeed, rob the United States of its blessed heritage of freedom unless these trends should be reversed. The manifestations of this spirit are too many and too varied to admit of thorough treatment on this occasion. May I, then, concentrate on only one major cause that lies at the heart of this open contempt for the Christian ideals that inspired America's national greatness, namely, the flaunting of the natural virtues.

Alert young Americans that you are, you need no one to elaborate in detail on the sins that have stained the record of this generation as few other periods in our nation's history. From the courts and the committees of Congress and state legislatures there has poured a steady stream of incontrovertible evidence of the gravest thievery from the public treasury. Corruption continues almost without challenge in the sordid realm of gangsterdom. Decent men have watched with a kind of fascinated horror at the revelations of the deceit and dishonesty practiced by operators and participants in national television programs. And they have read with dismay the disclosures of connivery and theft among the policemen of Chicago and Richmond — among, that is, a class of men engaged specifically to guard the public's property and welfare. The nation has felt a mounting alarm as well at the constant lies of juvenile delinquents, when they have not be shocked at the description of their more heinous deeds.

Just a short time ago Professor Jerome Ellison of Indiana University, writing in one of the most widely read national weeklies, revealed the extent to which dishonesty had penetrated the faculties and student bodies of our colleges and universities in the form of cheating in examinations.[2] And more recently the exposé of fraudulent institutions offering academic degrees for a price has given still another jolt to the public

[2] "American Disgrace: College Cheating," *Saturday Evening Post* (January 9, 1960), pp. 13, 58–60.

conscience. Thus one might go on, adding to the litany of sins and crimes that has prompted thoughtful men to wonder if the foundations of the social order are not in danger of corrosion to a point where the Republic itself may before long be in jeopardy. To you graduates, educated as you are, one does not have to recall the ominous parallels that are found in the history of once mighty empires that fell because of their inner moral decay, nor does one need to remind you of the pertinence of all of this for the present hour when we face the frightening power wielded by a government that has set its heart upon America's destruction.

In the search for a norm by which to weigh the value of truth and honesty, both for society and for the individual, the Christian mind turns instinctively to the sources of divine revelation as its safest guide. In doing so one thinks at once of God imparting the ten commandments to Moses on Mount Sinai, among which were these two: "You shall not steal," and "You shall not bear false witness against your neighbor."[3] I sometimes wonder if we are not prone to place so much stress on certain of the other commandments that we slight those that relate to honesty and truthfulness. If so, it is a woeful error, for it should never be lost to mind that on Mount Sinai no distinction was made between idolatry and adultery on the one hand and theft and falsehood on the other. Here, then, are two of the fundamental roots of individual character and of national stability which, if neglected, will not only destroy the possibility of an individual's moral freedom and integrity, but will likewise forfeit the hope of a nation's enduring greatness.

The compelling reason for the existence of a college such as this from which you will be graduated today is the principle that informs its educational system, namely, the living presence of the Son of God as the supreme model upon which this system counsels you to fashion your lives. And in the New Testament, the primary source of His teaching, it is significant, I think, that you will find not a single instance in which Christ manifested the trace of divine anger save in those moral infractions that involved truth and honesty. Disapprove He certainly did of sins of every kind, yet there is a marked difference between our Lord's serene reprobation of the numerous faults and crimes He met among those with whom He associated and the divine fury with which He lashed the money changers in the temple or castigated the insincerity of the Scribes and Pharisees. The main sin of the money changers was one

[3] *Exodus*, 20:15–16.

against religion in desecrating God's house, but they were also guilty of deceit in pretending to employ the holy precincts of the temple to serve the devout Jews who came to seek articles demanded for divine sacrifice, whereas in reality they were using this favorable location to profit from their commercial traffic.

As for the Scribes and Pharisees, never in His earthly life did Christ employ language such as He used in warning others of their insincerity and in denouncing these supposed paragons to their face. In exposing the true motivation that lay behind the deference they demanded, He told His disciples: "They love the first places at suppers and the front seats in the synagogues, and greetings in the market place."[4] And when He confronted them directly He uttered eight terrifying maledictions, the very words of which twenty centuries later almost make one shudder. "Woe to you, Scribes and Pharisees, hypocrites!" said Christ, "because you are like whited sepulchres, which outwardly appear to men beautiful, but within are full of dead men's bones and of all uncleanness. So you also outwardly just to men, but within you are full of hypocrisy and iniquity."[5] For one who recognizes the Author of those words for what He is, there is further sobering thought that He never said anything that He did not mean. The weakness of the woman taken in adultery, he would and did pardon; the panic and cowardice of Peter in denying that he ever knew Him, He lovingly forgave; the foolish ambition of James and John, He gently rebuked in fixing their eyes upon the true nature of their eternal destiny. But when face to face with dishonesty of purpose, with pretense and sham, Christ's divine wrath erupted in a manner evoked by no other human frailty or sin.

Christian history is replete with striking examples of steadfast adherence to principle and of costly fidelity to honesty and truth among that glorious company whose personal integrity entitles them to be named among the saints. This audience does not have to have retold the inspiring life story of Saint Thomas More, the great English chancellor, whom Pius XI raised to the honors of the altar in 1935. After an imprisonment of many months, More was brought to trial and condemned to death for his attachment to God's law in the sanctity of the marriage bond and in the spiritual supremacy of Christ's vicar on earth. But there still lingered a hope on the part of the court that tried him that this mar-

---

[4] *Matthew*, 23:5–8.
[5] *Ibid.*, 23:27–28.

velously gifted man might yet be saved for the royal service. In that hope Lord Audeley made a last effort by reminding More that though he had offended His Majesty, if he would but repent his obstinacy he might yet taste the king's gracious pardon. To this tempting offer the condemned chancellor, standing before the bench of Westminster Hall that July day of 1535, calmly replied, " 'My Lords, I humbly thank you for your great good will. Nevertheless, I make my petition unto God Almighty that it may please him to maintain me in this my honest mind, to the last hour that I shall live.' "[6] Thus did Thomas More forfeit the final chance to save his life, but thus did he also display an honesty of mind anchored in high moral conviction that all the blandishments of Henry VIII and his minions could not shake, and in so doing he won for himself a place among the world's immortals. This, I submit, is the hallmark of character.

During your years at Belmont you have been trained, in the incomparable Benedictine tradition, to recognize the true meaning of freedom. Almost a century has passed since that March day of 1876 when Bishop James Gibbons welcomed to this western region of North Carolina the first monks from St. Vincent's in Pennsylvania. Thirteen years later the same prelate, by that time the Cardinal Archbishop of Baltimore, looked back upon the Benedictine's time here, and he remarked, "I regarded this Abbey with unbounded satisfaction. . . . My intimate knowledge of the poverty of the past made me keenly relish the richness of this spiritual Foundation. In my judgment it is most intimately related to the best interests of Catholicity in the Southland."[7] In the intervening seventy years since those lines were written the monks of St. Benedict have fully justified the cardinal's confidence in the spiritual wealth with which they would enrich the lives of men here in North Carolina. And were Cardinal Gibbons present today his heart would rejoice in the realization that the foundation that he had seen laid in poverty and sacrifice by Father Herman Wolfe and his pioneer band had flourished, and he would not, I believe, ask of it any finer service to the Southland than that that it is now rendering, evidence of which is before our eyes as these young Americans depart with their degrees from the institution of higher learning that has grown out of the modest foundation of 1876.

[6] R. W. Chambers, *Thomas More* (London, 1935), p. 335.

[7] John Tracy Ellis, *The Life of James Cardinal Gibbons, Archbishop of Baltimore, 1834–1921* (Milwaukee, 1952), I, 132.

By virtue, then, of the advantage that is yours in having been trained in this Benedictine college, you incur as you step today into adult life the obligation to set an example for others in the proper use of the talents that have received their cultivation here. That obligation might be expressed in a paraphrase of the words that St. Paul wrote to the Corinthians centuries ago when he told them, "God, who commanded light to shine out of darkness, has shone in your hearts, to give enlightenment concerning the knowledge of the glory of God, shining on the face of Christ Jesus."[8] If, therefore, each of you pledges himself this morning to maintain in his individual life the highest standards of truthfulness and honesty in his dealing with other men, not only will you be fulfilling the hope that Belmont Abbey College reposes in you, but you will be vindicating your status as freemen worthy of the name. You will demonstrate to your contemporaries, in other words, that you have been delivered from that slavery to corruption Saint Paul spoke of when he held up before his converts of the first century the ideal of walking before all men in what he called "the freedom of the glory of the sons of God."[9]

In this way you will at the same time yield a rich return upon the investment of sacrifice and labor that have been expended in your behalf by your parents and benefactors, and you will offer the most rewarding recompense which these sons of Saint Benedict and the lay professors of this college would ask for the instruction and guidance which they have endeavored to impart to you. In the achievement of this lofty goal each of you will frequently need to remind himself of his duty to show forth in his own person the sublime qualities of the Christian freeman, and here you will find your surest guarantee in prayer to God that He may enable you through His divine grace to influence for good those whom you encounter on life's way. And in your turning to God you may find inspiration in the beautiful petition of John Henry Newman in which he sought for the divine illumination with which to light the pathway of his fellowmen. In conclusion, then, may I extend to each of you my sincere congratulations, and in so doing express the prayerful wish that at the end of the journey that lies before you, you may have the gratification of knowing that at least in some measure you have fulfilled what was in the heart of Cardinal Newman when he said:

[8] 2 *Corinthians*, 4:6.
[9] *Romans*, 8:21.

Stay with me, and then I shall begin to shine as Thou shinest: so to shine as to be a light to others. The light, O Jesus, will be all from Thee. None of it will be mine. No merit to me, It will be Thou who shinest through me upon others. O let me thus praise Thee, in the way which Thou dost love best, by shining on all those around me. Give light to them as well as to me; light them with me, through me. Teach me to show forth Thy praise, Thy truth, Thy will. Make me preach Thee without preaching — not by words, but by my example and by the catching force, the sympathetic influence, of what I do — by my visible resemblance to Thy saints, and the evident fulness of the love which my heart bears to Thee.[10]

[10] John Henry Newman, *Meditations and Devotions*, edited by Henry Tristram (New York, 1953), p. 279.

ARTICLES, ADDRESSES AND SERMONS*

ARTICLES

1. "Can We Have a History of the Church in the United States?" *Bulletin of the Catholic University of America*, XII (March, 1945), 2–3; 11.

2. "Peter Guilday: March 25, 1884–July 31, 1947," *Catholic Historical Review*, XXXIII (October, 1947), 257–268.

3. "The Sixtieth Birthday of the *American Ecclesiastical Review*," *American Ecclesiastical Review*, CXXI (October, 1949), 261–280.

4. "The Centennial of the First Plenary Council of Baltimore," *American Ecclesiastical Review*, CXXVI (May, 1952), 321–350.

5. "Teaching American Catholic History in Our Schools," *Bulletin of the National Catholic Educational Association*, XLVIII (May, 1952), 7–16.

6. "Church and State in the United States: A Critical Appraisal," *Catholic Historical Review*, XXXVIII (October, 1952), 285–316.

7. "Archbishop Carroll and the Liturgy in the Vernacular," *Worship*, XXVI (November, 1952), 545–552.

8. "Church and State: An American Catholic Tradition," *Harper's Magazine*, CCVII (November, 1953), 63–67.

9. "American Catholics and the Intellectual Life," *Thought*, XXX (Autumn, 1955), 351–388.

10. "No Complacency," *America*, LXXXXV (April 7, 1956), 14–25.

11. "Catholics in Colonial America," *American Ecclesiastical Review*, CXXXVI (January through May, 1957), 11–27; 100–119; 184–196; 265–274; 304–321.

* As noted in each case, not every item in this listing is available in print.

12. "A Letter from Washington," *Dublin Review*, CCXXXII (Winter, 1958), 363–371.

ADDRESSES AND LECTURES

1. "The Catholic Tradition in the Northwest," Commencement address at the College of Saint Catherine, Saint Paul, Minnesota, June 2, 1947. (Published in a brochure.)

2. "Patriot Churchmen," five addresses delivered on the Catholic Hour of the National Council of Catholic Men, November 2, 9, 16, 23, and 30, 1952, and treating:
   John Carroll, Archbishop of Baltimore
   John Hughes, Archbishop of New York
   John Lancaster Spalding, Bishop of Peoria
   John Ireland, Archbishop of Saint Paul
   James Cardinal Gibbons, Archbishop of Baltimore
   (Published by N.C.C.M., February, 1953, in a brochure of thirty-four pages.)

3. "Saint John's: A Living Tradition," address at the centennial honors convocation of Saint John's Abbey and University, Collegeville, Minnesota, May 17, 1957. (Published in a nineteen-page brochure of half-page size each.)

4. "The Cult of Quality," Commencement address at the College of Saint Teresa, Winona, Minnesota, June 2, 1958.

5. "The American Catholic College, 1939–1959: Contrasts and Prospects," address at the annual luncheon of Delta Epsilon Sigma, Atlantic City, New Jersey, April 2, 1959. (Published in *Delta Epsilon Sigma Bulletin*, Series 1959, No. 2 [June, 1959], 3–12.)

6. "Character and the Catholic College Graduate," Commencement address at Trinity College, Washington, D.C., June 1, 1959. (Published in the *Alumnae Journal of Trinity College*, XXXII [Summer, 1959], 191–196.)

7. "A Half Century of Dedication," address at the golden jubilee commencement of Saint Mary's Dominican College, New Orleans, Louisiana, May 29, 1960.

8. "American Catholicism in 1960: An Historical Perspective," address at the symposium on "The Present Position of Catholicism in America," Rosary College, River Forest, Illinois, June 11, 1960. (Published in the *American Benedictine Review*, XI [March–June, 1960], 1–20.)

9. "Honors and Work," address at the honors convocation, Loyola College, Baltimore, Maryland, September 16, 1960. (Published in the *Evergreen Quarterly*, XV [Autumn, 1960], 8–16.)

10. "The Vatican Council of 1869–1870," a lecture in the series on ecumenical councils sponsored by the Catholic University of America, Washington, D.C., March 13, 1961.

11. "Saint Patrick in North America," lecture at the Patrician Congress commemorating Fifteenth Centennial of Saint Patrick's Death, Dublin, Ireland, June 22, 1961. (Published in *The American Benedictine Review*, XII [December, 1961], 415–430.)

12. "Church History and the Seminarian," The Father Cyril Gaul Memorial Lecture, Saint Meinrad's Archabbey, Saint Meinrad, Indiana, September 24, 1961. (Published by *Saint Meinrad's Essays*, XIII [May, 1962], 1–37.)

13. "The Catholic Tradition in the Far West," Commencement address, Carroll College, Helena, Montana, May 27, 1962.

14. "The American Catholic Laity—1962," Commencement address, Saint Mary's College, Moraga, California, June 9, 1962.

15. "The Catholic Press: Reflections on Past and Present," address at the eastern regional unit meeting of the Catholic Press Association, Baltimore, November 8, 1962. (Published in *American Benedictine Review*, XIV [March, 1963], 45–61.)

SERMONS

1. "Submission of the Anglicans to the Holy See," preached during the Church Unity Octave, National Shrine of the Immaculate Conception, January 20, 1939.

2. "The Priesthood — The Light of the World," preached at the first solemn Mass of the Reverend Roland E. Murhpy, O. Carm., Saint Cyril Church, Chicago, May 31, 1942.

3. "The American Centennial of the Immaculate Conception," preached in the National Shrine of the Immaculate Conception, May 12, 1946.

4. "The Centennial of St. Thomas Church, Wilmington, North Carolina," Saint Thomas Church, Wilmington, North Carolina, May 11, 1947.

5. "Saint Matthew, Patron of the Cathedral of the Archdiocese of Washington," preached at St. Matthew's Cathedral, Washington, September 21, 1947.

6. "The Holy Name Man's Loyalty to Church and to State," preached at the Holy Name Rally, Monument Grounds, Washington, D.C., October 26, 1947.

7. "A Venerable Church of Maryland," preached at the sesquicentennial Mass of St. Ignatius Church, Bel Alton, Maryland, September 26, 1948. (Published in the *Bulletin of the Catholic University of America*, XVI [November, 1948], 8–10.)

8. "Armistice Day — Thirty Years Later," preached at Memorial Mass, Ritchie Stadium, University of Maryland, College Park, Maryland, November 14, 1948. (Published in *Knight Cap*, IX [November, 1948], 3–4.)

9. "Devotion to the Mother of God," preached at the World Sodality Day commemoration, Catholic University of America, Washington, May 20, 1951.

10. "Saint Francis in the New World," preached at the Mass opening the annual meeting of the Academy of American Franciscan History, Mount Saint Sepulchre, Washington, D.C., December 9, 1951.

11. "The Paulist Fathers: A Century in the Apostolate to Americans," preached at Saint Mary's Church, Chicago, April 27, 1958.

12. "The Spirit of Achievement," preached at the solemn pontifical diamond jubilee Mass for the Sisters of Saint Joseph of Concordia, Marymount College, Salina, Kansas, June 24, 1958. (Issued in mimeographed copies.)

13. "The Sesquicentennial of an Historic Chapel," preached at Saint Mary's Seminary Chapel, Paca Street, Baltimore, November 19, 1958. (Published in the *Voice*, XXXVI [December, 1958], 14–16; 25–26.)

14. "Eulogy of Monsignor Charles A. Hart: Priest, Philosopher, and University Professor," preached at Saint Patrick's Church, Ottawa, Illinois, February 2, 1959. (Printed in a brochure by the Hart family.)

15. "The Sanctity of Mother Seton," preached at the open air service for the pilgrimage of the Archdiocese of Washington, Saint Joseph's Central House, Emmitsburg, Maryland, June 14, 1959. (Published in a brochure by the Daughters of Charity of Saint Vincent de Paul, Emmitsburg, Maryland, Pp. 19.)

16. "Mother Seton in Emmitsburg," preached at the solemn pontifical Mass marking the sesquicentennial of Elizabeth Seton's arrival in Emmitsburg Central House, Emmitsburg, Maryland, July 31, 1959. (Published in a brochure by the Daughters of Charity of Saint Vincent de Paul, Emmitsburg, Maryland, Pp. 17.)

17. "The Quality of Mercy," preached at the dedication of the generalate of the Sisters of Mercy of the Union, Bethesda, Maryland, November 1, 1959. (Distributed in a mimeographed copy by the Sisters of Mercy. Pp. 6.)

18. "Integrity in the Life of the Catholic Graduate," preached as the baccalaureate sermon at Belmont Abbey College, Belmont, North Carolina, June 7, 1960.

19. "John Lancaster Spalding, First Bishop of Peoria, American Educator, 1840–1916," preached at the solemn pontifical Mass of the annual meeting of the Catholic Superintendents of Schools, Saint Mary's Cathedral, Peoria, Illinois, October 25, 1960.

20. "Saint Patrick's Fifteenth Centennial," preached at the annual celebration Mass commemorating the patronal feast, Saint Patrick's Church, Washington, D.C., March 17, 1961.

21. "The Blessing of an Abbot," preached at the blessing of the Right Reverend Alban Boultwood, O.S.B., of the Abbey of Saint Anselm, Washington, D.C., the National Shrine of the Immaculate Conception, December 30, 1961.